Meissen

Otto Walcha

Porcelain

PHOTOGRAPHS BY ULRICH FREWEL

AND KLAUS G. BEYER

EDITED BY HELMUT REIBIG

ENGLISH TRANSLATION

BY DR. EDMUND LAUNERT

STUDIO VISTA/CHRISTIE'S LONDON

A Studio Vista / Christie's book
published by Cassell Ltd.,
35 Red Lion Square, London WC1R 4SG
and at Sydney, Auckland, Johannesburg,
an affiliate of
Macmillan Publishing Co., Inc.,
New York

This edition copyright © 1981 VEB Verlag der Kunst Dresden
Originally published as *Meissener Porzellan*
copyright 1973
VEB Verlag der Kunst Dresden

ISBN 0 289 70852 4

Printed in the German Democratic Republic

PREFACE

Otto Walcha was born in Riesa on August 6, 1901, the son of the local health officer. He attended the Meissen Realgymnasium and subsequently studied at the Kunstgewerbeakademie and the Technische Hochschule in Dresden. In 1924, he began to teach art appreciation at the Franziskaneum (a Realgymnasium and Oberrealschule), and later taught at the Fürsten- und Landesschule St. Afra in Meissen. He started to paint and write during those early years, and also to study ceramics. He completed a course of training under Feuerriegel, a well-known ceramicist. After World War II, during which he was for some time a prisoner of war, he devoted himself entirely to painting and writing. In his literary and art history works he often dealt with themes taken from the field of ceramics, as in his novels *Rivalen* (1963) and *Feuer, Wasser, Luft und Erde* (1966) or in the books *Bunte Erden aus aller Welt* (1951) and *Porzellan* (1963). In 1957, Walcha was appointed curator of the archives at the VEB Staatliche Porzellan-Manufaktur Meissen. A result of his archival studies were many papers on the history of Meissen porcelain, and it was not long before experts hailed him as a leading authority. In 1960, he began to write a complete and detailed history of Meissen porcelain. After producing a carefully researched manuscript in 1968, he fell ill and was unable to undertake the final revision, for he died on May 25 of that year. The manuscript lay dormant for four years, but an editorial revision was begun in 1972. An introduction has been added to give a brief outline of the historical circumstances under which Meissen porcelain was first created. Brief outlines of historical events have been inserted here and there into certain chapters (8, 10, 11, 12, 14, 15, 16). The last three chapters are new but based on Walcha's manuscript and the notes of Herbert Neuhaus, the first postwar Meissen director. Thanks for helpful suggestions in revising the text are owed to Professor Rudolf Forberger (Akademie der Wissenschaften der DDR) and Professor Gerhard Schilfert (Humboldt-Universität, Berlin).

H. R.

CONTENTS

INTRODUCTION

European porcelain was first developed in the late Baroque period, and to the present day it is by the unique characteristics of pieces in the Baroque style that artifacts in porcelain have been judged. In Meissen porcelain, the oldest and noblest of Europe, we have the strongest and most enduring manifestation of the Baroque spirit. Meissen gave European porcelain the vocabulary and style in which it was to speak to us for more than two hundred years. Certainly, in the public imagination Meissen porcelain and Baroque have become synonymous.

The spirit of porcelain best matches the period during which it was first made. The suitability of material for the creations intended was so complete that Meissen Baroque seemed to be the definitive form craftsmanship in porcelain would take. These works are the art form of an aristocratic society that felt no need to emphasize the spiritual or intellectual in its creations, but that used art for self-glorification, as a source of luxury, and as a method of impressing upon the world—especially its inferiors—its autocratic power. Not until the twentieth century was porcelain used to express deeper artistic impulses, and even then artists had to beware of any treatment of the material that exceeded its possibilities and was foreign to it.

Since the character of Meissen porcelain was determined in the eighteenth century, and a considerable proportion of it continued to be manufactured along the same lines, the detailed discussion of the Baroque period of Meissen to be found in this book is justified, and it becomes equally necessary to consider the social background during its innovation and development.

Baroque did not grow naturally from the Renaissance. It was a reaction. In Germany the Renaissance had been embraced by the prosperous urban classes as the rejection of the mystical Gothic and the adoption of reality, humanity, and the visible world. The decline of the Renaissance came with the decline of the urban classes and the reemergence of feudal power, a process that began in the sixteenth century and was completed by the end of the Thirty Years' War. In the towns, trade and manufacturing began to stagnate. Discovery of new sea routes, which replaced the routes via Germany, aggravated this unhappy situation. By the end of the Thirty Years' War the feudal elements had regained the upper hand. The war largely destroyed the foundations of middle-class prosperity, and revival could only come slowly. The peasants were living in the direst poverty but still clung to the land. This made them even more dependent, as more and more of their produce was appropriated by the landlords. The overlords consolidated their position by perfecting their system of oppression which may be defined in one word: absolutism. As Professor Gerhard Schilfert has written, "The nobleman no longer ruled jointly with the monarch, the State's chief nobleman—the monarch now ruled as sole potentate with unlimited power in matters concerning the nobility. In other words the dictatorship of the nobility emanated from one person, who in turn had the nobility's interests at heart."[1]

Feudalism's pattern of manufacture and trade, already out of date at the end of the fifteenth century, could only continue to survive through the use of coercion and indoctrination. And so in certain parts of Germany at the time of the establishment of absolutism, a medieval ideology resided in the phenomenon of the Counter-Reformation.

In the Counter-Reformation and in absolutism we find the social foundations of Baroque. Counter-Reformation churches and the palaces of absolute monarchs constitute the greatest achievements of this style. The aim was to overwhelm ordinary people with lavish ostentation. Characteristics such as exaggerated dimensions and spectacular display of the power of those who commissioned it suggest that Baroque architecture's impressive façades disguise the brute coercion of the social order. No longer do the statues of saints show ascetic men and women of the people such as those that grace the Gothic churches. Here elegantly robed lords and ladies dominate—sculpted portraits of the ruling classes in theatrical, worldly poses. Their movements do not spring from the spiritual inner energy of the Gothic being, but are exuberantly superficial, calculatedly beautiful. As absolutism gains in confidence, however, these bombastic forms begin to lose favor. Art grows more intimate, serves exclusively to enhance the life-style of the ruling classes and, as a result, the most decorative elements are mainly reserved for interiors rather than for external show. Life seemed secure and its delights could therefore be concentrated upon and enjoyed to the full. Instead of a deliberate show of power, elegance prevailed. Delicate pavilions were preferred to heavy Baroque palaces, and powerful forms and colors were replaced by subtlety and the mutual interplay of elegant surfaces. Everything—painting, sculpture, poems, music, and architecture—became lighter, gayer, more playful. With the aristocracy at the zenith of its power and surrounded by every indulgence, a gorged feeling—satiation with the styles of its own applied arts—set in, with the result that foreign cultures became the new rage. France and China came into fashion, the former the epitome of absolutism, the latter also an example of an anachronistic society and an overrefined culture.

Such was the *mise en scène* for the introduction of porcelain making in Europe. Johann Friedrich Böttger's experiments with porcelain came at the right moment. It may seem accidental that the breakthrough came in Dresden at the court of Augustus the Strong and under his patronage; but in fact no other place in eighteenth-century Germany offered better economic, social, political, or artistic conditions: conditions not good in a general sense but favorable for the discovery of porcelain and for the setting up of the first European porcelain factory. It is doubtful whether European porcelain would have conquered the world from any place other than Dresden.

Of the German-speaking nations in the sixteenth and seventeenth centuries, Saxony was one of the most advanced economically. It was densely populated. Trades and crafts were thriving in its towns. It possessed a strong mining industry and fertile agricultural land worked by peasants who enjoyed more freedom than those in other German territories. The Reformation, originating in Saxony, had brought the country to the attention of other lands and increased the self-respect of both its rural population and its urban middle classes. Then, unfortunately, the evils of the Thirty Years' War were visited upon Saxony. A result of this war was an important social upheaval. The social classes in Saxony's devastated and impoverished towns showed a polarization even greater than before. The importance of the crafts and craftsmen waned and a powerful new class emerged, made up of merchants and lawyers. This class was detached from the people. Corruption and self-advancement at the expense of the community became commonplace. In the countryside the picture was as gloomy as in other German lands. The aristocracy continued to deprive the peasants of their traditional rights and made them "almost bondsmen," as Sturmhoefel wrote.[2] The peasants of Saxony who sought legal redress invariably saw their efforts wasted and their hopes denied.

In Saxony conditions were therefore ripe for absolutism, but it nevertheless failed to establish itself in its ultimate form on account of the resistance it encountered from various organized classes, the Estates. These Estates—the clerical, the noble, and the burgher (which had originated as a form of parliament in the Middle Ages)—had as their main privilege the right of granting taxes to the ruler. The nobility dominated this parliament. In Saxony the nobility was made up of a homogeneous group of landowners of middling wealth and it knew how to defend its privileges from attack by the ruling monarch. It was only toward the end of the reign of Augustus I, known as the Strong (1694–1733), that the power of the Estates was reduced.

Augustus had visited the widely admired court of Louis XIV at Versailles at the age of seventeen. He tried to translate all he saw into Saxon terms, but failed to establish an absolute monarchy. His accession to the Polish throne had raised his position among the other rulers in the German Empire and it represented a triumph over the French king, but the wars it brought in its train, the enormous bribes paid to the Polish nobility to secure his election, and his religious conversion, abhorrent to both the common people and to the Protestant Estates, heightened the tension already existing between the monarch and the Estates. Since he could not eradicate the latter he tried to make them more malleable and to decrease his dependence on them. The corruption in many of his domain's townships provided an excuse for thorough revisions of their charters, so as to bring the various town councils better under control. A decree of 1700 expelled the lesser nobility from the Estates. In 1704, the king elector founded a secret cabinet to provide himself with an instrument to attack the nobility, and in 1709, the permanent deputation of the Estates was dissolved. A change in the constitution of the Estates in 1728 increased the power of the supreme ruler to the disadvantage of the Estates, carefully evading the issue of the right to raise taxes. The hostility of the Estates was turned away from the ruler and directed against those whom they were originally ordained to protect. The power of the local bourgeois-aristocratic councils was legalized, and all remnants of the democratic relationship between council and citizens destroyed. In the countryside the peasants were ruthlessly exploited by their feudal lords, and at the same time a gulf widened between the old and new nobility.

We owe to Augustus, however, our inheritance of much that is great and worthwhile from that period. Under his rule art and science, manufacturing and trade, were encouraged. He was without doubt more talented than most rulers of his day, but his foreign policy, for which he must bear responsibility, was that of a dilettante and brought nothing but misfortune to Saxony. An illustration of this is the war he waged against Charles XII of Sweden, a senseless and mismanaged undertaking if ever there was one, which brought Saxony to the verge of ruin. All his enterprises, including those of his dissolute personal life, consumed vast amounts of money, which was largely raised by selling or mortgaging estates, granting privileges, hiring out Saxon troops, and ruthlessly exploiting both peasants and townsfolk. Saxony was able to survive this drain on her finances—and, indeed, prosper—only because her manufacturing capacity developed rapidly and many new production and organizational techniques were adopted.

Saxony already had a diversified economy in the sixteenth and seventeenth centuries, but its real history as a manufacturing nation began during the reign of Augustus the Strong. Although most manufactories were capitalist enterprises in a feudal society and were for the most part run by the bourgeoisie, they were sponsored by the monarch. His motive was not primarily the possibility of new sources of revenue; concern for profit was not so fully developed at that time. The product itself was the prime interest, and firms were created which met the needs of the State: to furnish the army with supplies, including the *Leonische Waren* (paraphernalia for uniforms), and the court with showpieces. The Germanic countries still could not rival France in either the quantity or the quality of finished products. At the time of Louis XIV and his minister, Colbert, more precisely between 1662 and 1672, for instance, at least one new factory was founded annually. One founded by Colbert in 1662 on the property of the Gobelin family, dyers by trade, initially concerned with the production of furniture for the court and later famous for its tapestries, employed more than 800 people. It numbered among its employees, as did the Meissen manufactory later, many a celebrated craftsman-artist.[3]

The growth of manufacturing firms was a natural consequence of the increase in the work force available to them, a work force not created, but intensified and exploited by the feudal state, and which was also destined to be a cause of the downfall of the feudal system.[4] Yet the Saxon monarch failed to make full use of his industrial patronage to establish his absolute rule once and for all. Neither was the Meissen manufactory built to make money: it was erected to satisfy the king's desire for a much admired luxury product.[5] It cannot be said that Augustus the Strong greatly encouraged the development of Saxon factories; he took a personal interest in the fate only of the Meissen Porcelain works. The development of Saxony's economy was supervised by other men, among them Ehrenfried Walther von Tschirnhaus.[6] His scientific and practical work and his inventions were essential to the invention of European porcelain and to the foundation of the Meissen manufactory, although he did not live to witness these events.

Although Meissen bore from the very beginning the character of a capitalist enterprise, employing independent wage earners, in the early years one could still observe vestiges of feudal ties. One example of this was the restriction of movement imposed on the employees in order to safeguard manufacturing secrets. Even when he was factory administrator, Böttger was also subjected to such restrictions.[7] There are other characteristics to show Meissen was no purely capitalist venture: it was not merely a production line but an institution with a cultural and political role to play. These facts, and not economic development, make Meissen exemplary. It has maintained its special position through the changing tides of fortune, even down to the present day.

THE INVENTION OF EUROPEAN PORCELAIN

The glorious inventory of any Baroque court would have been scandalously incomplete without its porcelain. The largest collection of oriental porcelain was owned by the elector of Saxony and king of Poland, Augustus the Strong. The East India Company was instrumental in the supplying of this costly product, revered as much as gold, and it cannot have been long before Augustus was toying with the idea of extending his collection by home manufacture. If a Saxon porcelain could be established, not only could he enlarge his collection still further, but he could also collect enormous revenues from sales. Hence his interest in experiments conducted by Ehrenfried Walther von Tschirnhaus, an expert in the science of optics and already respected for his supervision of the establishment of various glassworks. Ehrenfried Walther von Tschirnhaus (1651–1708),[8] mathematician, physicist, Lord of Kieslingswalde, royal and electoral adviser, had studied at the ancient University of Leyden, famed for its faculties of natural history, physics, and mathematics. A number of visits to France had given him an insight into that country's scientific and industrial innovations and enabled him to envisage ways and means of improving Saxony's economic position. He realized that the natural resources of the Electorate first had to be established and then exploited in the manufacture of a superb and unrivaled product. Only through such a unique achievement would Saxony obtain prosperity of any note or duration.

Before his fourth visit to France he had succeeded in locating some mineral deposits in the Electorate and now he hoped to observe methods in Holland, especially in Delft, and the work of Pierre Chicaneau in France at the St. Cloud factory, in order to ascertain how best to set up similar profitable enterprises in Saxony. His observations were evidently useful in his later research aimed at the hoped-for reinvention of porcelain. In Delft he learned how to construct a kiln, and in St. Cloud he mastered the method of making soft-paste porcelain.[9]

The most important contribution Tschirnhaus made to the exploitation of mineral deposits in Saxony was the construction of gigantic concave mirrors and burning glasses to obtain the utmost concentration of solar heat. He was successful not only in fusing some minerals but also in discovering by these empirical methods an essential factor in the compounding of the porcelain mixture. He discovered that quartz and chalk, on their own considered infusible, could be made fusible if mixed in a certain ratio. It must be noted that Tschirnhaus never rose above the conviction that porcelain was a product of vitrification, that is, fusion into a glasslike state.

Augustus the Strong offered surprisingly little financial aid to this eminent man, since he was basically not entirely convinced that this complicated experimentation would offer a quick solution to his own precarious financial situation. He preferred to lend an ear to courtiers like Egon von Fürstenberg, who persuaded him that help could be obtained through the magic arts. In spite of Rationalism and the Enlightenment, there was still in 1700 a widespread belief in alchemy and hopes that it would lead to ever-flowing sources of wealth. Alchemy flourished especially in the courts of bankrupt princes, and was resorted to as a cure for every ailment and for the transformation of base into precious metals. Charlatans intent on fraud journeyed from palace to palace and claimed to be on the track of the mystery, the "arcanum" (the great secret of making gold). Such people did not always have to advertise themselves; they were sought out as great alchemists. In 1701, when the king of Prussia demanded the extradition of an apothecary's apprentice who had fled from Berlin to Wittenberg, Augustus the Strong not only refused to cooperate but had the youth immediately transferred to the Fürstenberg Palace near the Royal Palace in Dresden. His motive for doing this was that the nineteen-year-old Johann Friedrich Böttger had acquired, in Berlin, the reputation of being able to make gold by transmutation.

Böttger, baptized, according to the church register in Schleiz, on February 5, 1682, grew up at Magdeburg in the house of his stepfather, Tieman, the town official, engineer, and mint administrator. He soon showed himself a bright youth, eager to learn, so his parents placed him with an apothecary named Zorn in Berlin. There he became involved with men preoccupied by the search for the philosophers' stone. It was seriously believed that by the addition of this mysterious elixir, molten base metals could be turned into pure gold, on condition that the person conducting the process had the necessary mystic power and could direct an extraordinarily strong concentration of mind into it. Escape from this circle was made more difficult for the young Böttger, with his penchant for the fanciful, by his association with an out-and-out charlatan, the mysterious monk Lascaris. Soon Böttger was reputed to be in possession of the elixir.

A public experiment by Böttger, who was a known show-off, had probably increased this doubtful prestige. When the king of Prussia began to make inquiries about the alleged gold-maker, Böttger made a speedy departure to Wittenberg, a Saxon town with an old university. As a Saxon subject he had no difficulty, with the help of a relative, in enrolling at the faculty of medicine. "Medicine" at that time embraced the study of all the natural sciences. Augustus the Strong put an end to these intentions. Böttger was imprisoned, but was treated so well that his living standards resembled those of a gentleman of quality. Over the years, it was only with the greatest difficulty that he was able to conceal from the king, the Prince von Fürstenberg, and the Count von Lesgewang his inability to make gold.

Eventually he was forced to flee, but he was recaptured in Bohemia, imprisoned for a time on the Königstein, then sent back to Dresden and from there to the Albrechtsburg in Meissen. This time he was not required to discover the philosophers' stone, but given the task of organizing the development of new industries.

The industries in question were those proposed by Tschirnhaus and other experts, such as the mining superintendent Pabst von Ohain. One of them was to be concerned with the production of porcelain, the term "porcelain" being used loosely to include such products as *"Delffter Guth."*

It is clear, from a report made by one of the six experts in mineralogy who were assigned to aid Böttger in 1705 in work on the Albrechtsburg in Meissen on the development of a high-temperature-fired ware, that the aim was to dis-

Johann Friedrich Böttger

cover how to make porcelain.[10] Mention is made, for example, of the use of twenty-four kilns and of the production of specially hard-fired clay slabs. As both a check on and an encouragement to Böttger, visits were paid by Dr. Nehmitz and Dr. Jacob Bartholmäi, experts in medicine and natural history, a certain Monsieur Burchardt, intendant of Prince Egon von Fürstenberg and, most frequently, by von Tschirnhaus. Tschirnhaus instructed him in the use of mathematical equations and kept him supplied with scientific literature.

Notes made by Böttger during this period on the Albrechtsburg have survived, and in them we find a rather approximate description of porcelain. He had now realized that certain clays could be made fusible only with the admixture of a calcareous flux.

Discovering the correct formula was to prove an arduous process. No real results had been obtained when political factors brought his experiments to an end. Augustus the Strong believed that the Treaty of Altranstädt between Saxony and Sweden in 1706 would force him to protect his alleged gold-maker from the clutches of Charles XII and therefore had him precipitously removed to the fortress on the Königstein. Three of his workers accompanied him, not to assist him in further work but to prevent his making contact with prisoners of noble birth housed in the fortress's Georgenbau. At first Böttger was bitterly disappointed to be dragged away from his work when on the way to success, but he resigned himself to his lot. His resignation, however, was not complete enough to prevent him from falling under the suspicion, not quite without foundation, of planning an escape with the Counts von Beichlingen.

In the autumn of 1707, Böttger was suddenly taken to Dresden. A laboratory had been installed in the dungeons of the Jungfernbastei, the eastern part of the fortifications facing the river Elbe. Böttger had much larger kilns here than in Meissen. The firing experiments involved great health risks for the

Ehrenfried Walther
von Tschirnhaus

men, however, since the ventilation was insufficient and the damp vaulting was continually full of smoke. But genuine dedication drove Böttger on and he spared neither himself nor those who worked with him. Now that it was clearly a search for the "true porcelain," all ingredients were a closely guarded secret and were usually compounded only in small quantities. Early in 1708 the king, informed that the experiments were nearing their climax, paid a visit to the "secret" laboratory with the electoral governor, the Prince von Fürstenberg, to witness a trial firing. One of the few records of experiments kept by Böttger states that on January 15, 1708, three out of seven firings showed a result which was white and transparent, so this date may be taken to mark the birth of European hard-paste porcelain.[11]

Unlike Tschirnhaus, who had apparently only achieved a vitrified product, Böttger made the first true porcelain, a ceramic material that could not be deformed by high temperatures and became impervious after the final firing. Nevertheless, a year passed before Böttger, on March 28, 1709, dared to proclaim his discovery.[12]

Böttger submitted his findings for examination by an official commission. He was summoned to various sittings covering economic questions. Information was required as to whether sufficient raw materials were to be had and whether the available transport was adequate to guarantee continued production in the future. Since Böttger employed various specialists, craftsmen, and artists, it was possible that his product would prove more expensive than that imported from the Far East. Further information was required about the quality of his porcelain, particularly as to whether the glazing was of the necessary perfection, and whether it could boast a range of color equal to the imported ware. Also, the question as to the use to which Böttger's vessels could be put had to be answered before they could become a viable commercial proposition. Böttger was optimistic. When dubious aspects were discussed, he tried to divert attention to the more positive sides of the matter.

Although speedy development was impossible for economic and bureaucratic reasons, Böttger had already established a modest output. He had a larger kiln built on the Jungfernbastei; the court potter, Fischer, was enlisted; and he produced many attractive objects of all kinds. It is possible that statuettes were already being made.

Dr. Bartholmäi, Böttger's personal physician, made several rooms of his property in the Moritzstrasse available for storage purposes.

Fischer demanded a fixed daily sum of one taler for his assistance in Böttger's laboratory. This high price had to be paid, for although notices offering high wages for potters and throwers had been posted at the Dresden town hall, no one had applied for work. Later, a Delft-trained master potter from Berlin, Peter Eggebrecht, was found. Eggebrecht was prepared to work harder than Fischer for a lower wage. His aim, however, was to work as an independent craftsman, so Dr. Bartholmäi, who appears to have been in charge of hiring,

The Jungfer, eastern bastion of the Dresden fortress

looked among the potters of the town of Pirna where he found one Peter Geithner whom he hired as a thrower at the newly established factory. Geithner
proved himself a useful and reliable worker.

That craftsmen were reluctant to sacrifice their independence for a very
remunerative but insecure engagement is shown by their suspicion of any attempts to reorganize their craft. Dr. Bartholmäi had great difficulty finding
craftsmen for Böttger's steadily growing output. He had to pay the first two modelers employed on piecework out of his own pocket immediately on delivery of
each finished article or they would leave the works. It was not simply the
shortage of native craftsmen but also local distrust that caused Böttger to bring
in *"Holländische Meister und Steinbäcker"* from Amsterdam when he opened
his faience manufactory, on June 4, 1708.

In charge of this first manufactory founded by Tschirnhaus was Master
Christoph Rühle, who received a monthly sum of twenty-four talers, while his
son-in-law, Gerhard van Malcem, earned sixteen as a *Schilderer*, or decorator. It
is not known how many workers were at the disposal of these two craftsmen in
the early days. In 1711, there were thirteen under Peter Eggebrecht, to whom
Böttger leased the faience manufactory. These were employed as compounders,
molders, throwers, glaziers, kiln masters, or general hands. Böttger's reason for
founding this faience manufactory was the lack of space in his laboratory on the
Dresden Jungfernbastei. His plans were not realized exactly as he intended, for
the only purpose the new premises served was to staff the main porcelain manufactory with workers. Two of the first from these Dresden-Neustadt works,

Johann Ehrenfried Stadler and Christoph Horn, later worked under Höroldt on the Albrechtsburg in Meissen as craftsmen of no mean distinction.

It was natural, considering Böttger's incredible foresight, that he visualized the royal enterprise as the ideal in economic cooperation: the supply of raw materials, a transport system, and the use of men and facilities all coordinated under a central administration. In this way periods of crisis in individual factories could be averted and growth encouraged by a ready supply of funds. There were limitations to this plan, however, as occurred in the 1730s when considerable sums from the net profit of the Meissen works were set aside to counter the losses of the Dresden Mirror Factory but still failed to offset them.

Augustus the Strong delayed formal announcement of the discovery that had been the dream of every European court for at least a decade until Böttger had perfected the so-called red porcelain, had obtained the "very finest glaze" on the white, and a full-scale factory could be constructed. The forthcoming foundation of the Meissen manufactory was announced to the world at large on January 23, 1710, in four languages: German, Latin, French, and Dutch. This announcement emphasized the mercantile nature of the manufactory. Everything was to

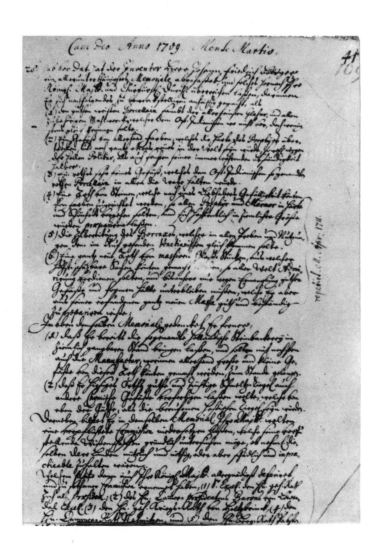

The announcement
of the invention
of porcelain,
March 28, 1709

be done through the encouragement of industry and commerce to set the country on its feet again after the Northern War. The inventor of the process was not named but referred to as "persons well acquainted with the sciences" to whom the discovery, extraction, and commercial exploitation of "the subterranean treasures with which our land is richly endowed" had been entrusted.

The pride, satisfaction, and superiority expressed by the only Western country to possess the secret of porcelain was intentional, to ensure that no one in Europe should be under the false impression that Saxony and Poland, the domains of Augustus the Strong, were still suffering from the effects of the Northern War. This "white gold" was already, *in statu nascendi*, being used as a political instrument.

THE ALBRECHTSBURG MANUFACTORY AND PORCELAIN IN THE BÖTTGER PERIOD

On June 6, 1710, control of the Meissen Albrechtsburg passed from chief civil borough officer Carl Gotthelf von Bose and his assistant, Ernst Friedrich von Döring, to the first director of the new porcelain manufactory, the royal electoral chamberlain Michael Nehmitz. Bose gave exact details of the area which could be allotted to the manufactory, taking into account that the regional authorities and the Cathedral Chapter still required rooms for administration, archives and, above all, living quarters for officials in the castle precincts. In other words, from the outset there was a conflict of interests regarding use of the buildings, a problem to recur in the following decades with battles between the factory management and the Cathedral Chapter, which had from the beginning opposed the idea of having a factory so near the cathedral. The Protestant clergy interpreted establishment of the factory as an attack by the Catholic court on their centuries-old right to the fortress site, but Augustus the Strong was not to be deterred. He tried to bring about a settlement by mediation and, as far as possible, took a diplomatic approach to the matter, but he pursued his aim rigorously, ordering strict supervision of those attending the church and forbidding entry to the factory premises.

The conflict had still deeper roots—in the struggle between the various classes and their absolutist overlord. The townspeople, believing that their privileges were seriously endangered, supported the clerics. Indeed, the people of Meissen were by no means enthusiastic over the establishment of a "genuine porcelain" factory, in spite of the ruler's claims that it would improve the town's depressed living standards. The citizens remained suspicious of the venture for a long time, even though it meant a dramatic improvement in Meissen's trading position. Members of the Meissen craft guilds had vested interests in seeing that new businesses did not proliferate nor established ones expand, and thus intermittent shortages and high prices resulted. The different social levels of the independent but largely poor craftsmen in the town on the one hand and the wage earners of the manufactory on the other were the source of constant friction.[13] Even Böttger's workers were skeptical about their transfer to Meissen. One of the reasons for their reluctance was the fact that the "inventor" of porcelain was to remain in his laboratory on the Jungfernbastei in Dresden. The king was adamant on this point. Periodic inspections by Böttger were few, for they were rendered difficult by a host of formalities. It is recorded that, apart from his compulsory residence in 1705, only five such visits took place, obviously inadequate for a man in charge of the smooth flow of production, and of matters pertaining to personnel and to the commercial aspects of the business.

In July, 1710, Böttger came for the first time as administrator to the Albrechtsburg. No record has survived of the results of his inspection and his subsequent recommendations. An indication of what Böttger, who occupied a comfortable suite in Dresden with a small orangery and a few exotic animals, must have thought is evident from the fact that on his next visit, on September 17, 1711, he brought along an interior decorator by the name of Johann Heinrich Blumenthal. A report gives an idea of the layout of the manufactory premises.[14] The *"grosse Saal"* (large hall) on the first floor was to be divided into north and south workrooms with a gangway between partitions made of canvas stretched over a wooden framework. One room was a packing room and another smaller one, with gilded tiles, an office for the administrator. It appears that after a full year of existence the manufactory had a representative exhibition of porcelain in its storage rooms. One detects, however, a certain departure from the original aims. Few of Böttger's promises to the king had been realized in one and a half years. In November, 1711, neither the production of white porcelain nor operation of the kiln had been achieved. It may be deduced from this that the administrator had grossly miscalculated and was too divided in his activities. The fact that the manufactory survived the birth pangs of the early years is really owing to the interest and dedication of Böttger's first team of workers.

An early list of November 11, 1711, supplies us with names, duties and modelers' marks of the first thirty-three employees in Meissen and Dresden.[15] Most of these could be sent by the administrator to one or another of his factories according to his wishes at the time, so that Böttger's laboratory on the Jungfernbastei, the polishing works on the Weisseritz, a tributary which joins the Elbe near Dresden, and the "red and white porcelain factory" in Meissen were in certain respects interdependent. But this attempt at cooperation took place ac-

The Albrechtsburg 1726, engraving by Alexander Thiele

cording to immediate need and showed a lack of farsighted planning. The fact that people of the most varied levels of education and social status were employed together gave rise to entirely new problems, which remained and sometimes occasioned tensions and disagreements. It aroused displeasure and even opposition, and sometimes led to setbacks such as the return to South Germany of the very gifted thrower Kratzenberg, who could turn out high-quality vases of hitherto unknown dimensions at an incredible rate.

But the majority of the craftsmen remained loyal to the manufactory for the rest of their working days. One wonders what nourished their loyalty. Certainly there were still traces of fidelity to their feudal lords in the workers' minds, but above all it was the wages, which, compared with those of other craftsmen, servants, or agricultural workers, were very high. The weekly wage of a factory worker was about two talers, and there were opportunities to earn as much as three. The price of wheat, incidentally, in Saxony at that time was 2 talers and 20 groschen for a *scheffel* (about 105 liters); a *kanne* (about one kilogram) of butter cost 7 to 8 groschen (24 groschen per taler). So, relatively good remuneration, the prospect of certain promotion, and the satisfaction of belonging to a State factory kept the employees at their jobs.

Resentment arose among the workers when wages could not be paid at the end of the week. If it were a question of merely two weeks, as happened in August, 1711, the employees remained patient, but when, as was not infrequently the case, more than two months' wages were owed, some courageous ones, in spite of the risk of imprisonment, would complain to Inspector Steinbrück. More than once they marched to Dresden and barred the king on his way to the riding square. They usually received immediate payment, but Böttger made sure that deductions were made for loss of work time. Absenteeism was punished in the following manner: for every hour lost, a day's wages were deducted; and for every day, a week's. Maintenance of a full working day was the responsibility of the inspector, who was under pressure from both below and above.

Johann Melchior Steinbrück, a scholar who had been a reliable tutor to the two sons of von Tschirnhaus in Kieslingswalde for fifteen years and who, on the death of his patron, had found a niche working mainly as a secretary, was chosen as local inspector of the factory in 1710. His duties concerned the interests, wishes, demands, and complaints of both management and workers. It is amazing that a theologian and philologist could handle such difficult matters as the supply of raw materials, the direction of production and personnel, and administrative business.

Steinbrück's desire to act objectively and uncompromisingly was frequently evident, and was in no way affected by his marriage to Böttger's sister. Steinbrück's weekly reports came to Böttger for approval, received the latter's pencilled comments in the margin, then were returned to Meissen. Later, after Böttger's death, they were submitted to the manufactory commission. The inspector made known in the report that followed which decisions had been enacted. From 1719, the commission held regular sessions on the Albrechtsburg. In the two to three days set aside for this purpose, the success of the steps taken could be measured then and there and the inspector's activities reexamined. Personal contact with the workers, which was made in the course of inspections without too much formality, was beneficial to factory discipline. Misunderstandings and petty jealousies among the employees were quickly and informally ironed out.

Before this happy stability was achieved, however, the young manufactory faced several crises. The instability of the management arose mainly from the fact that the responsibilities of Böttger and the director, Michael Nehmitz, were not properly defined. So that the frequent discords could be smoothed out by a higher body, the king appointed a special commission. It was set up on April 2, 1711, and consisted of Count Wackerbarth (minister in the cabinet), Privy Councillor Ludwig von Seebach, Count von Lesgewang, Privy Councillor von Döring, and the mining official Pabst von Ohain, from Freiberg. It was almost never consulted, however, for everyone knew that it would have no positive influence. At a sitting on October 22, 1712, at which Böttger, Holtzbrinck, Michael Nehmitz, Steinbrück, and Dr. Bartholmäi were present, it was recommended that every attempt be made to solve the manufactory's financial problems. It was concluded that the manufactory was suffering from a deficit; Stein-

brück had calculated that expenses exceeded earnings by approximately 50 percent. In the search for the sources of this deficit "there was unanimity about the correctness of the administration," but the sitting left those present as unenlightened as before. Even a small subsidy from the royal purse could not improve this stagnant state of affairs. It was not until 1719, when Steinbrück submitted his analysis and the commission undertook a thorough investigation into the conditions required for expansion, that the foundation for continued progress was laid.

There were, however, further problems: one of the main reasons for transferring the manufactory to the Albrechtsburg had been to protect the arcanum (the costly recipe for the mixture), kiln construction, and the secrets of the firing processes. These secrets were entered in the notebooks of the arcanists but could easily be absorbed by the paste compounder and kilnmasters during the course of their work. To counteract this, paste compounding, modeling, and firing had been located in different places in Dresden, so that for many years no one except Böttger was familiar with the entire sequence of processes.[16]

Dr. Bartholmäi and the mining official Dr. Heinrich Wilhelm Nehmitz were the first officially recognized arcanists. Even then each knew only his particular half of the business. Dr. Bartholmäi was instructed in paste compounding, and Dr. Nehmitz in the preparation of the glaze. They received this instruction at the king's command because of the constant fear that one day Böttger might carry his secrets to the grave. Another reason for the king's order was the fear that the unreliable Böttger might keep back information. If this were suspected, Dr. Bartholmäi was to report the matter to Dr. Nehmitz or to the king himself.[17] The Dresden and Meissen factories owed much to Dr. Bartholmäi. The coordination of work in the initial months was entirely the result of his circumspection and infectious enthusiasm. He resigned, however, when he lost all heart for the work because of Dr. Nehmitz's intrigues and when he saw that he was powerless against the director's brother. From 1712, he was seldom, if at all, seen in Meissen.

Dr. Bartholmäi's instructions emphasized that he was to obtain information on new sources of china clay and to estimate their value and quantity. No financial support was forthcoming for this project, however, although the court was spendthrift in many other directions. Indeed, it was stated without concern that there were no funds for such exploratory trips and that any such undertaking was to be discussed in advance with the administrator. Contact had already been made before this with a certain Veit Schnorr, the owner of the Weisse Erde Zeche St. Andreas, a clay mine opened in 1701 between Schneeberg and Aue. This white clay first came to Böttger's laboratory in 1705. Already in October, 1709, a laissez-passer was issued by royal command for the delivery of this material from Schnorr's mine to Meissen. Regular consignments began in 1711. Veit Schnorr's son, Hans Enoch, was a farsighted and cunning businessman. It was clear to him from the beginning that the manufactory was entirely dependent upon his goodwill, and he made the most of this. By occasionally delaying a consignment, by delivering clay that was too wet, by alleging transport difficulties, by refusing to send further consignments until the previous load had been paid for, he and his heirs after him determined the terms of contract and commanded their own price.

Only in the nineteenth century were the business ties dissolved. The price of a ton of china clay, initially 16 groschen, soon rose to a taler (24 groschen) and had reached 27 groschen in 1720 with an additional 13 groschen transport fee. Before the time of the consignments from Schneeberg, however, deliveries of a different sort had taken place regularly. For the red porcelain (Böttger's stoneware) a red clay from the Zwickau region was used, and later clay was brought from the environs of a village near Meissen called Ockrilla. The first white material, Colditz clay, had already been used in the faience factory at Dresden-Neustadt. The so-called kapsel clay (sagger clay), which proved to be a suitable material, was found near the village of Mehren, not far from Meissen. The construction of kilns presented another considerable problem insofar as building materials were concerned. The necessary "white" tiles, which had been developed by Böttger for their heat-resistant quality, had to be brought upriver from Schmiedeberg, not far from Pretzsch on the Elbe. Later, Stöltzel invented a recipe in which clay was mixed with fragments from a previous firing, and the bricks thus formed were fired in available spaces in the high-temperature kiln during the final hard firing.

The earliest kilns were vault-shaped; the interior was about 2.8 meters long, 0.8 meters wide, and 1 to 1.25 meters high. With certain modifications, this type was used until 1815.[18] It was, however, many years before the Meissen works found a fuel supply of dependable quality, the best being dried split pine wood. Böttger had to rely on the various kinds of firewood from the royal forests surrounding Moritzburg and Tharandt. Not until Bohemian wood from the estate forests of Count Thun, around Tetschen, was regularly imported did a wood of consistent quality become available. Charcoal for the muffle kiln came mainly from the charcoal kilns east of Grossenhain.

References to the early technical equipment in the manufactory are few and imprecise. It is certain that there had been some time- and labor-saving mechanization before the move to the Albrechtsburg; that there were, for example, grinding machines in the *Stein- und Rundbäckerei*. Surface polishing, which was of greater importance to Böttger's stoneware than later to the making of white porcelain, had to be carried out for many years in the *Schleifmühle* in the Weisseritz valley near Dresden. Steinbrück, who as a philologist underestimated or totally discounted the importance of mentioning technicalities, gives us almost no information about sources of power for the machines. Since vast quantities of porcelain could not have been produced without machinery, there must have been a horse-driven transmission in the Kornhaus. This was later moved to the north basement rooms of the Albrechtsburg.

Long before the "Porcellain-Fabrique" was working at full production, sales propaganda had been launched and modest quantities of the new ware were being purchased.[19] A large amount of porcelain appeared at the Easter Trade Fair in Leipzig in 1710. This display was essential to advertise the opening of the manufactory, since Saxon porcelain had to compete with a wide range of rival products, particularly in the ceramic field. The greatest obstacle to be overcome was the belief that the Oriental was superior to the young European product. In addition it was necessary to outdo the faience manufacturers of Europe both in quality and quantity. The public showed some reservation toward Böttger's stoneware, and the small amount of white porcelain available aroused very little interest for it was only exhibited and not for sale. The first exhibition ended in depressing financial loss. Expenses incurred through the employment of factory representatives and salesmen were openly in excess of earnings through orders.

The Leipzig Fair was by no means, however, the only place where the first Meissen porcelain could be sold. The manufactory very cleverly found a market in those places to which the rich seasonally migrated. On June 11, 1710, *Kaufdiener* Johann Wilhelm Stürtzel, the first traveling salesman for the royal manufactory, was sent to Karlsbad with a selection of ware worth 1,328 talers. Meissen porcelain was also on show at the Peter and Paul Fair in Naumburg on June 26, 1710. In the summer of that year Stürtzel set off for Berlin with a *"Parthie Porcellain Waare,"* requisitioned a portion of the ware on commission

Report on the manufactory's consignment for the Fair of 1710

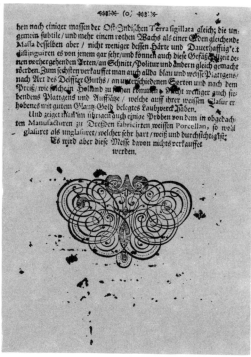

to Hamburg, and was successful: at the end of the year Steinbrück had netted a profit of 6,150 talers through these procedures.[20]

But this success had its limits and could not dispel the belief that Böttger's factory would never pay its way. Böttger himself had always been aware of the ground to be covered before his discovery would prove commercially viable. He himself states in a memorandum how difficult it will be to sell the public an unknown ware continually and profitably in competition with already established articles of a different sort.[21]

Böttger also realized that decoration on the monotonous red porcelain would have to be more varied in order to obtain the necessary commercial breakthrough. If we study the announcement that appeared in the *Leipziger Zeitung* of May 4, 1710, drawing attention to the attractiveness of the wide range of ware from the Königliche Porcellain-Fabrique, as yet not fully established, and compare pieces of the Böttger period existent in museums, we are able to identify them from their descriptions.

Böttger's courage and imagination were amazing: his experiments had by no means come to an end—he wanted to create a white porcelain with all the appropriate decoration—but he still worked on developing his earlier discovery, the red porcelain, artistically. The extraordinary hardness of the material, which undoubtedly excelled the Far Eastern product and which Böttger always stressed in his pronouncements was, in spite of and perhaps even because of its unsuitability for any form of tooling, an excellent vehicle for decoration. Apart from the variety of relief decoration, Böttger enhanced his porcelain by cutting, polishing, etching, by adding a graffito-like adornment, or by setting it with precious stones. Bohemian craftsmen and lapidaries from the Unsruce had been employed in the former mirror factory "an der Hertzogin Garthen" and later at the cutting and polishing works in the Weisseritz valley to put the final touches—the *rechten Schliff*—to table jugs, tea and coffee pots, mugs and cups, thrown and fired by the court potters Fischer and Eggebrecht. Nearly every kind of artistic activity was tried as a form of decoration.

Even within individual grades of clay, variations in the compounding and differences in the firing produced a range of effects varying from light brick-red to a dark iron color with an unusual luster. A newly revived ceramic decoration of the walls, graffito, was achieved by an overlay technique of different-colored mixtures. The ornament cut into the surface revealed the lighter layer charmingly. A further dimension was obtained by polishing certain parts, especially the raised ornament, which now stood out most effectively against the dull background. Böttger's preoccupation with producing an extraordinarily rich-looking article lay in the taste of the times and resulted in astounding diversity. These early years of European porcelain produced a quantity of objets d'art of a character and quality never again equaled. Until his death in 1733 the king himself sought above all to obtain pieces of the brown or red porcelain made in the manufactory. The small statues of him in his coronation robes were produced in only small quantities of white hard-paste, but continued into the thirties in Böttger's stoneware and showed a much more monumental style accentuated in its details. The brown examples appeared in catalogues until 1735 and fetched extremely good prices, a fact indicative of the increasing public interest.

Böttger never tired of looking for new ways of embellishing his red porcelain. Perhaps in order to distract attention from his failure to produce a white glaze on white material, as may be assumed from a testimonial of Böttger's to Steinbrück,[22] he offered special items such as finger bowls, pastry boxes, salt cellars, large and small flowerpots, and even crucifixes with decorated pedestals. A few days later the list bore certain addenda: he promised entire stoves and chimneys, paneling for walls, tiles for floors, urns and coffins, sets of bells and other things, convinced that he could deliver the same, all in his red stoneware.[23]

Böttger's boldness in making such advertisements shows how clearly he was aware of the possibilities of the new material, but ignores the reject quota for 1712, which was high enough to give rise to concern. In this instance too, however, a virtue was made of necessity and a system of grading was established. This grading of *"Brack"* (rejects) begins with "useless fragments" at the bottom of the scale; continues with "broken vessels, impossible to use"; "damaged vessels, which could be used if necessary"; and goods that were "fairly usable but

not salable." Rejection for sales purposes was based on one of three grounds: the vessel was misshapen, "full of bubbles," or cracked or mottled.

Early Meissen ware may be divided into three groups: imitations of the Eastern article, vessels inspired by silverware, and a small group of statuettes and medallions made after various models. The fact that the Chinese had a thousand years' experience in the making of porcelain almost guaranteed that Meissen vessels and statuettes modeled on Far Eastern examples would in every respect reflect the ideal form porcelain could take, yet Böttger was hardly aware of this. He and his employers were only aiming at imitation. Chinese vessels, corruptions of the original, were turned out mechanically. Shrinkage during firing was acceptable. A simple satisfaction was derived from producing Chinese-looking objects cheaply.

In many museums we can still see the beakers, cups, jugs, boxes, tea caddies and mugs, usually showing the popular relief decoration of twigs or blossoms and strongly resembling the original. Characteristic of these pieces are the quiet silhouette, the generous curves, and the plain surfaces that cry out for decoration. This decoration, usually raised, sometimes in intaglio, was rarely subservient to the shape of the piece of porcelain but existed in its own right, developing its own exuberant life, at times lavish in its application, at times sparse, but always creating a certain tension in relation to the piece on which it was execut-

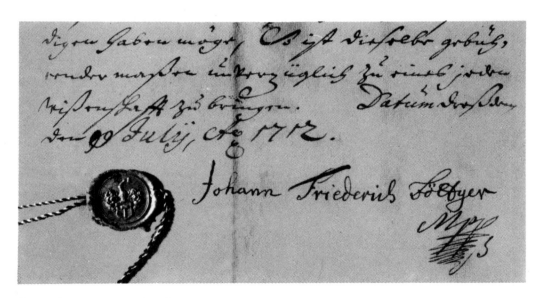

Böttger's signature and seal

ed. Architectural design was avoided since distortion through shrinkage, which occurs in ceramic work during firing, is more obvious in a geometric than in an organic shape, such as a more or less stylized fruit. Figurines, statuettes of goddesses, seated Buddhas, and domestic animals were modeled. The Buddha seems to have been the most popular of all, usually referred to as *Bajode* in the catalogues and appearing in great variety. This figure later was adopted for the white porcelain and had various pedestals. There are only a few indications that free interpretation of Chinese themes was attempted at Meissen during Böttger's time. A certain artistic liberty is evident in the decoration where, for example, there is a European flavor in the Asian flora. For reasons of profitability Böttger aimed at using not only native materials, but native talent too. He stressed at a meeting of the commission that on no account were Chinese artists or craftsmen to be brought in. Neither did he require a new range of models for his porcelain, since his potters, silversmiths, and pewterers had a certain repertoire which could be adapted for porcelain without difficulty. This policy gave his work the character of a craft rather than of an art. Böttger's failure to appreciate the particular nature of his material is explained by the rapidity with which the technical processes were developed. The new material was placed on the same level as precious metal, and silver vessels were taken as models for Böttger's stoneware. To make such vessels in porcelain, however, presented greater difficulty, for where the molding takes place before a firing process requiring exceptionally high temperatures, the rate of failure is higher than where the heating process takes place before the material is given shape. The creation of objects in the Baroque style made great demands on the skill and abilities of the modeler. The work of molder and thrower had to be carefully prepared and continually supervised by him. The *"Bossierer"* (embosser), had to assemble the piece, adding the separately molded parts and smoothing the surface. The decorative elements such as masks, flower garlands, and applied foliage required the aid of independent modelers. There have only been tentative suggestions as to which of the Dresden sculptors was employed during the first years of the eighteenth century. Suitable employees of the faience factory would naturally participate in the work of modeling as far as their talents allowed. They were assisted by the court sculptor and carver of altarpieces, Benjamin Thomä, who joined them on August 14, 1711, in order to design and make statuettes. In the same year, however, he was redirected to cooperate in work on the Zwinger, and only reappeared in the Meissen manufactory when the designing of the Sulkowsky Service began in 1734. The discovery of thirty original bills presented to Dr. Bartholmäi by a Dresden artist, Bernhardt Miller, for sculptural work carried out between October 9, 1708, and April, 1709, shows that independent artists were also being employed. Apart from the fact that the work consisted of figures of minute dimensions, we learn nothing of its nature; the same applies to the occasional employment of sculptor Paul Hermann.[24] Another sculptor by the name of Stange is mentioned from time to time, but we do not know what kind of pieces he worked on.

The artistic quality of this early Meissen work, achieved in spite of a certain lack of assurance, must be attributed to the Saxon court silversmith Johann Jacob Irminger. Böttger must have met Irminger in the autumn of 1711, for on October 29 the court silversmith made a tour of the works in the Albrechtsburg and was extraordinarily favored by the administrator in being allowed to take back to his Dresden workshop three tons of the *"allerfeinsten rothen Massa"* (finest red clay) for modeling. On November 16, Böttger made impatient inquiries about the sample items Irminger had promised him, the cane handles and hunting knives, and in June, 1712, as acting head of the manufactory (Augustus the Strong was in Warsaw), sent him certain instructions. These reveal that Irminger was now artistic director in charge of the design of all porcelain vessels and figures, that he was to avoid damage to the items, make any suggestions he might have for improvement and, above all, to submit completely new designs. To attract the widest possible market, the designs were to suit the means of the "smaller" man. That is, they were not to be too costly. He was also to devise architectural items in Böttger's stoneware for the "enhancement and beautifying of the Lustgebäude" under the direction of the central authority for building and construction.[25] Since he was not only to design the tableware but also to undertake its manufacture, the craftsmen had to be placed under his command. Even foreign craftsmen, the lacquer workers, enamelers, gold and filigree craftsmen, had to conform to Irminger's wishes. In this carefully thought out set of instructions it was also recommended that a system of numbering designs be employed, but fifty years were to pass before this was put into practice.

In order to maintain production in its increased quantity and range and to retain quality of the same, it follows that Irminger must have been responsible

for the further training of the craftsmen. He was also constantly occupied with technical problems, including the form of decoration and the manner of obtaining the blue underglaze painting. He was the first artistic director to grasp correctly the extent and totality of his task. That patience was necessary on his part is evident from his inclusion in the list, published at the time of the 1719 reform, of those to whom wages were owed, the figure at this time standing at 1,261 talers.

His duties only occasionally required his presence in Meissen. He designed the decorative elements in his Dresden studio, hammered the models carefully in copper, and sent them to the Albrechtsburg. Their rendering in Böttger's stoneware was personally supervised by him in the manufactory. He used these week- or month-long visits to guide and train throwers and molders.

Comparisons between the work produced in Meissen and the costly silver court vessels of this time show that Irminger knew the red clay presented a completely different form than precious metal or stone. Even though he could not free himself entirely from the influence of classical antiquity, at least he tried to translate its austerity into simpler and warmer terms. The tasteful decoration, floral or figurative, is in all his creations in Böttger's stoneware both harmonious and distinguished. The conventional character is hardly eliminated, but nothing is required of the material that it cannot provide.

If we look at the many showpieces adorned with acanthus motifs, beadings, masks and female heads, we cannot fail to be aware of his efforts to give this new valuable material its noblest expression. In Irminger's work the interchange of polished and mat surface played a great part. He would, for example, leave the vine branches mat and polish the ground to a high finish. Sometimes, however, the polished lion or human heads would stand out effectively from the body of the vessel. A particularly attractive group of beaker-shaped vases, amphorae, craters, covered goblets, shallow bowls, jugs, and beakers is devoid of any applied ornament and simply offers the nobility of its classical form. The only decorative element is supplied by the delicate handles adopted from the forms of metal vessels. The vessels are polished and with their timeless appeal belong to the finest achievements of the artist-craftsman.

Some of the craftsmen who cooperated with Irminger, although doing independent work, deserve mention. A successful molder and embosser was Johann Georg Kittel, a potter of long experience (born 1669 in Rosenthal, on the border between Saxony and Bohemia) who according to records was entrusted with special work by Bartholmäi in Dresden. From a work report of 1713 it is clear that he was to make the statuette of Augustus the Strong from a wooden model. The statuette was impatiently awaited at the court, and since it found complete approval, Kittel was required to mold it again and again. All other models which had to be executed with special care were entrusted to Kittel. Independent work was also done by the modeler Krumbholtz. Ambitious, he applied for a year's study in Benjamin Thomä's studio in order to graduate to the status of sculptor. Since he was nevertheless obliged to commit himself to returning to his old position after his study, he gave up this idea. He remained in Meissen and later became one of the most reliable embossers in Kaendler's studio. Paul Wildenstein from Freiberg was one of the first of Böttger's craftsmen to witness the earliest decisive experiments in the Albrechtsburg, the inventor's imprisonment on the Königstein and the feverish excitement of the Jungfernbastei experiments. He was especially skilled in the difficult process called cutting out, that is, the making of double-walled openwork pieces after Chinese examples. As he had a knowledge of carpentry, he was often employed in the making of alabaster molds. Along with Christoph Rühle, first leaseholder of the faience factory, Johann David Kratzenberg, a skilled thrower, joined the work team, arriving in Dresden from Brunswick in 1711. After a few months the administrator transferred him to the Meissen works so that he could make "fifty large grotto vases according to the design supplied" (monumental vases with relief decoration). There his privileges were extraordinary: a separate shed where he could work undisturbed, his own kiln and a large quantity of alder wood, and first one, then two, and eventually three hands so that the production of his monstrous vases could be made possible. He produced good quality work in an extraordinarily short time. Yet his employers were not prepared to meet his demands ad infinitum. His notice, dated July 19, 1713, was accepted.

The small group of statuettes and medallions completes the range of early Meissen work. It must be noted that these, with their varied motifs and styles, were not designed especially for porcelain. They derive from Baroque sculpture and in some cases are obviously in the tradition stemming from Bernini and continued by Permoser. Böttger believed that the new material, with its plasticity and resilience, was ideally suited for the mass production of popular minor works of art. Nevertheless, difficulties often arose. Although the small Eastern figures could be easily reproduced in Böttger's stoneware, European statues were often impossible models for this ware owing to their complicated undercutting. Even if a small figure, a clay model, a wax figure, a carved figurine suitable for interpretation in the new material were found, the skill of the craftsmen would occasionally fail to rise to the task of producing an article of equal artistry. It was not merely a question of molding. The seams had to be smoothed out (and this was often carried out in a rather haphazard manner, as museum pieces testify) and individual pieces such as curls, mouths, eyes, hands, and fingers had to be formed with a wooden tool. Although such additions often show little skill, the large number of such surviving items indicates that the public was satisfied enough with the work to create a demand for it. A particularly happy result of this period is the figure of a putto bearing a seashell, a charming statuette of harmonious proportions in a delightful and truly Baroque conception.

A crucifix included in Böttger's catalogue was certainly based on one in silver. It is superior to all the other smaller sculptural items of the Böttger epoch in its very expressive molding, and one can detect the influence of Baltha-sar Permoser. The same quality is evident in the statuette of the king. Augustus is shown in the pose of absolute monarch, in the flowing coronation robes of an emperor. Although it is small, in it the sculptor has understood how to give the face the character of a portrait. Hundreds of these were made in three different sizes and in two or three versions.

When they succeeded in the firing of enamel paints, work was turned out which was considerably poorer than that of the earlier period, but which aimed at putting Böttger's in the shade as far as colors, sheen, and gilding were con-cerned. Some copies of reliefs, such as that of the head of a martyr complete with curls, and a representation of Judith, show the continued efforts to pro-duce the widest possible range of items. Yet the imitative and eclectic character of the pieces cannot be denied, even though in certain figures one detects a unique and personal note. As early examples of the birth of the series of collection pieces mention must be made of the six figures from the Commedia dell' Arte. Here we see the first figure of Pantaloon with pointed beard and raised index finger, a Capitano Spavento in armor, the bloated Doctor, drunken Scaramouche, the exuberant Harlequin, and the coy Lucinda. The Callot figures are distinct-ly superior in their freedom of line and spontaneity to their stiffer imitations.

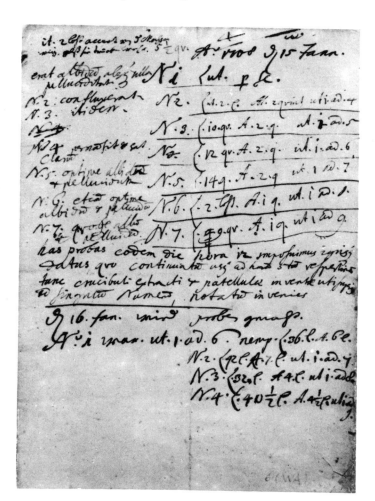

Böttger's memorandum,
January 15, 1708

They were made repeatedly and, because of their popularity, made in white porcelain and in different versions. That Böttger's stoneware was equal to metal in hardness and suitability for fine modeling is proved by the few commemorative coins and medallions of this period. These were directly molded from silver coins which showed the skill of South German and local craftsmen in portrait relief at its best.

A staff and wages list dating from 1712 shows that the court lacquerer Martin Schnell was engaged as a top-ranking artist at the new royal factory with a salary of one hundred talers per month. This included, however, the cost of the gold which he needed for the painting of carvings, chimney pieces, a variety of turned items, objects worked in leather and metal and, lastly, decoration of the new black-glazed porcelain. Although the work of many independent artists is described in the factory archives, there is no such information about the porcelain decorated by Schnell. We must not attribute to him the many examples of antique beadings and acanthus sprays somewhat dully applied in gold lacquer to Böttger's stoneware. These are undoubtedly the work of the "gold worker" employed immediately after him, Johann Carl Bähr. One group of pieces stands out: these are vases with a black glaze and some examples of the so-called *Pilgerflaschen* (pilgrims' flasks) which are decorated with free compositions of Chinese landscapes, of blossom or flower sprays in delicate col-

ors outlined in gold. These come from the hand of a master and must inevitably be associated with the extremely wide range of work done by Schnell. They comprise a very small quantity of porcelain but are the first evidence of an accomplished use of color in decoration. The Baroque style still dominated, however, and it was not until ten years later with the beginning of Höroldt's influence that new tendencies began to appear.

The individual piece of porcelain did not then command the attention it did later in the Rococo period, but was displayed as one of a group forming some architectural arrangement, and white porcelain was the most ideally suited for this purpose. Its cold whiteness enhanced the air of spaciousness and was therefore by no means considered artistically poor and unfinished. In fact the warm yellow tone of Böttger's porcelain was considered a distinct disadvantage and the inventor tried hard, but without real success, to change the composition of the paste in order to obtain a cold white effect. On the other hand, the king insisted, in view of the fact that white porcelain could now be reliably produced, that painted decoration, the *zugehörige Mahlwerck*, as promised by Böttger, should be applied. The so-called red porcelain, Böttger's stoneware, still continued to provide the shapes for models in white, but they made the mistake of simply using the old shapes without realizing that the raised decoration showed up much better on Böttger's stoneware than on the glazed white porcelain. When they began to feel that it did not stand out enough from the surface it was enhanced with lacquer colors.

In the long run this compromise was unlikely to prove satisfactory either to employer or craftsmen, so Böttger concentrated more on the colors that could be fired. For many years he had met with disappointment in his search for a quick and easy solution to the problem of enamel-painting on porcelain. Little help was gained from a study of recipes for colored glass given by Kunckel in his *Ars Vitraria*. Neither could the suggestions of the numerous gilders experienced in the art of enameling on metal be applied to porcelain. Occasionally he incautiously confided in the dishonest alchemists who constantly surrounded him, drawn by his reputation of being able to make gold. He often gave away his secrets under the influence of alcohol, and such indiscretions no doubt led to the early founding of the Vienna manufactory in 1718. Whether it was the metallurgist Gottfried Meerheim or the enameler C. C. Hunger who was in touch with him, there certainly was an exchange of knowledge on the subject of the arcanum, and Böttger contributed much more than he derived. Nevertheless he began, regardless of technical difficulties, to look for one or more painters. As early as 1711, Stechmann and Schäffler were taken on as "painters of the good porcelain," although what they actually did is not known. On October 11, 1712, Johann David Strohmann and Anselm Bader were engaged, but disappeared on November 29, never to return. It is not known whether they were not paid punctually or whether David Köhler was simply unable to prepare the colors necessary for their work.[26] There is also no record of any work done by them. From the summer of 1715, large quantities of porcelain were sent for decoration to Johann Georg Funcke, an independent Dresden gilder and enameler whom Böttger reports he had often encouraged to experiment with enamel colors. In the meantime Böttger himself tried, unsuccessfully, to invent satisfactory recipes. At first Funcke too was unable to achieve the desired results with the far from satisfactory muffle kilns in his workshop. Only when he worked in the castle laboratory did he succeed in firing the first colors. He avoided the label of "inventor" and laid the blame for the holdups in development on the manufactory's financial distress. According to his report, however, and the bills dating from May 13, 1713, to April 5, 1719, he had spent no less than 318 talers on the making of his own colors (deep red, green, blue, yellow, black— from 1718— and dark red) including the fuel for the muffle kilns. From the quantities listed it becomes apparent that from 1717 he and his son, and later also his co-worker Johann Jacob Gäbel, must have decorated about two and a half times more white porcelain than in the first year of their employment.[27] In the same year Böttger had finally achieved results with enamel colors, and especially with the gilding and silvering and also with red colors, namely crimson and purple, and also green.

It is not known whether Köhler assisted Böttger in his experiments or whether, experienced as he was with metal oxides, he conducted his own. The question as to who takes the credit for the first enamel color at the Meissen works, whether it was Böttger, Funcke, or Köhler, cannot be answered categorically. Only one thing is clear: without the discovery of the perfect glaze for white porcelain, in which it was essential to find a suitable flux for each metal oxide, the development of enamel colors would have been ineffective.

The following groups of enamel color decoration were used during the 1717 to 1720 period. Gilded decoration presumably came first. This appears in delicate ornament in the style of the South German interlaced strapwork and foliage where the monotony was soon relieved by the addition of silhouette-like chinoiserie scenes. This was followed by a completely different group of paintings in red monochrome richly carried out in the style of Dutch genre paintings. Similar work was executed in black monochrome. In an attempt to offer variety, combinations of gold and silver were tried. The silver oxidized, however, and the desired effect was lost. Böttger was particularly proud of the discovery of a pinkish-violet luster color, the subtle shade of which, in combination with the gilded interior of the vessel, gave a delightful appearance and seemed entirely natural to porcelain. The grotesque figures in white porcelain were decorated with colors that had already proved successful.

To conclude remarks on the development of enamel colors, mention must be made of an aspect of the work which is represented in several trial pieces but which did not come to fulfillment: blue underglaze painting. It is stressed in Steinbrück's report on the results of Böttger's color experiments in the summer of 1717 that the latter had not succeeded in developing and making use of the recipe for blue underglaze painting. Since the king had offered a prize of 1,000 talers for the discovery of the same, the compounders in Meissen, that is David Köhler, Samuel Stöltzel, and Johann Georg Schuberth, directed their efforts to this end. They were evidently successful, for on August 28, 1717, Michael Nehmitz was able to submit to the king a small dish with blue underglaze decoration. The prize was not, however, presented, for the following reason: although it was established in a later sitting of the commission on March 13, 1722, that David Köhler had discovered the blue color in 1719, they nevertheless decided to recommend that His Majesty not pay out this gracious offer in one sum but in successive installments (*"tractamenta successiva"*) together with certain other concessions. Samuel Stöltzel, Köhler's colleague and rival, as had been proven, had contributed to it to a varying degree. The first successful results were, as the contradictory dates indicate, largely fortuitous. The technique of blue underglaze painting was not mastered for many years to come. The reason for this was that Köhler and Stöltzel went their separate ways in their experiments, Köhler carefully trying out all the various cobalt ores and Stöltzel mainly concentrating on the improvement of the paste and glazing, but each jealously keeping his secrets from the other. The king therefore decided that the sum should be paid out in the form of an occasional bonus, if Köhler and Stöltzel would communicate their own arcana truly and without any reservation. The two rivals were not, however, prepared to do so. For many years the quality of blue underglaze painting varied considerably, as is indicated by Köhler's references to results of different experiments.[28] After this unhealthy secrecy came to a head, Köhler's recipe led in dramatic circumstances to a broader application. The main beneficiary was Johann Gregorius Höroldt. This story belongs, however, to the second phase of the factory's history.

THE FIRST MANUFACTORY REFORMS: 1719

The nature of Böttger's administration of the Meissen manufactory, sporadic and temperamental as it was owing to his commitments to his other enterprises, was less of a threat to production than the ever-present and disturbing lack of capital. The lack of sufficient reserves meant that special wage demands and expenses could not be covered. As early as the summer of 1711, the new manufactory hovered between life and death. Böttger was almost in despair and he begged the king, who was in Warsaw at the time, for immediate help. Augustus the Strong had other preoccupations at that moment, however. In accordance with the treaty with Sweden he had been forced to cede Poland, but after the Swedish king's defeat near Poltawa in 1709 Augustus reneged on the agreement, seized the Polish crown, and renewed his alliance with Russia and Prussia against Sweden. The war was resumed. Following the death of the Holy Roman Emperor in 1711, Augustus assumed responsibility for the office until the October election of the new emperor. The war and Augustus' need to reestablish his credibility in Poland made enormous demands on his treasury. The brilliant show required of him to this end daily swallowed a fortune a fraction of which would easily have brought about a healthy state of affairs in the manufactory's finances.

Böttger's letters often failed to reach their destination—evidence of the rivalry between him, the administrator, and the commission represented by Michael Nehmitz. The web of intrigue stretched as far as Warsaw. Finally a commission was set up in the autumn of 1711 to investigate the profitability of the enterprise, based on a works inspection and stock-taking. Böttger was bombarded with questions to which he replied with a mixture of apologetic explanation and hard bargaining: the kiln house, which had been planned from the start, should be built as soon as possible; the material and timber transport costs should be lowered; and the royal treasury should be requested to guarantee capital in exchange for the constant delivery of porcelain ordered by the king himself. Instead of an effective remedy they came to a curious arrangement whereby assets were pawned to a fictitious, dummy firm called Schwarz and Co. This "firm" had the sole selling rights for the manufactory's products. Michael Nehmitz, the privy councillor, was also involved in this with a considerable investment. Yet, contrary to all expectations, even Böttger seems to have derived quite considerable advantages from this situation for himself. He was even able to persuade the king that a repetition of such crises could only be prevented if the administrator had control of all manufacturing and commercial dealings. Thus the power of the commission was broken.

One year later all obligations were fulfilled. The fact that at last, at the Easter Fair of 1713, the "true porcelain" had been on show and sold well could have led to a new and uninterrupted growth, but the king again let everybody down. Since production would have to rise after the 1713 Trade Fair, more kilns would have to be built, the supplies renewed, and wages paid punctually. The demanded credit was released by the treasury only on the oddest terms: the king wanted to repay the money, borrowed from private finance houses, in kind—namely in porcelain. As long as the king resided in Dresden, this unusual transaction seems to have worked well, but then the bankers underwent the usual bitter experiences with Starke, the royal chamberlain and secretary of the treasury, who became increasingly reserved, and Böttger watched his money sources dry up as a result.

Böttger then fell seriously ill. His sight was failing, and this compelled him to shift Steinbrück from his important work in Meissen to supervision of the Jungfernbastei in Dresden. His condition worsened considerably. The degree of his decay can be deduced from the bills of his personal physician, Dr. Jacob Bartholmäi, and the long list of prescriptions.

On April 19, 1714, the king granted him his freedom, an act of mercy that was now of little consequence to the sick man. Neither did the manufactory benefit when Böttger was given complete authority in policy and organization. All these steps were taken too late, and even then they were not accompanied by the financial aid desperately necessary for the survival of the Meissen manufactory. Böttger arranged for Vollhardt, a Dresden lawyer, to attend the court in Warsaw. Although he remained there for more than twenty months, he never gained an audience with the king. Since Böttger had financed this plan from his own pocket, the burden of debts became very heavy. He was compelled to borrow at a high rate of interest in order to cover them, but this was only a short-term solution and did not prevent his being cast into a debtors' prison. When the king learned of this he was shocked into ordering his immediate release, but again this resulted in no essential changes in Böttger's personal financial difficulties or in those of the manufactory. Meanwhile Steinbrück could only stand by helplessly when confronted by enraged workers, led by the throwers Geithner and Lohse, who had invaded the counting house in the autumn of 1715 to make more energetic demands for the immediate payment of the more than four months' salary still outstanding.

The first rival factory had in the meantime been established. In 1713 in Plaue on the Havel, the Prussian minister of state, Friedrich von Görne, had founded a factory for the making of a red stoneware, incredibly like that invented by Böttger. The recipe had been supplied by Samuel Kempe, formerly a compounder and kilnmaster in the faience factory at Dresden-Neustadt leased by Peter Eggebrecht beginning in 1712. Johann Gottlieb Mehlhorn, who later pledged to set up a porcelain factory at the court at Zerbst, presumably worked on the decoration of this ware. Plaue ware was already being offered at the Leipzig Fair in 1715. It did not attain the quality of the "red porcelain," but Meissen was extremely perturbed by the evident betrayal of the arcanum. Above all, other European courts realized that industrial espionage in Meissen and Dresden could bring great rewards. This was made easier by dissatisfaction among the workers and petty jealousies among those who had access to the secrets of the compounding of the paste and the firing processes. Johann Melchior Steinbrück had already warned of the possibility of sudden competition. He had also made efforts to prepare the ground for eventual reform by keeping a journal in the form of a work analysis.

The manufactory's first visitors' book, 1714

The most comprehensive report on all the ills besetting the Meissen manufactory is the eighty-page memorandum of 1717 which, by order of the cabinet, commanded the setting up of another commission of the privy councillors von Löwendahl, von Watzdorf, von Alemann, and von Holtzbrink. In his report Steinbrück had, for the first time, made a bitter attack on Böttger's unreliability, moodiness, and increasing unfairness; consequently the administrator underwent a rather stiff interrogation by the commission into the causes of his failures and mistaken decisions. His excuse was that he had been hindered in his work by internal wranglings and that the Nehmitz brothers in particular had always undermined his orders and actions. To draw attention to the more positive aspects of his work, he pointed out the progress made in the production of white painted porcelain and listed the number of enamel colors for which he claimed to have successfully invented the recipes. After thorough investigations, the remedies came slowly and proved insufficient. Even Böttger began to concern himself less with production and renewed his experiments in blue underglaze painting.

A daily visitor to the Jungfernbastei was Gottfried Meerheim, a deceitful speculator and alleged metallurgist, who later, on the basis of secrets wheedled out of Böttger, was able to blackmail the commission for years.

Toward the end of his turbulent life, roughly from the autumn of 1718, Böttger's sense of responsibility declined considerably. His scientific interests turned once more to alchemy. We have evidence that the king and his governor in the Electorate of Saxony, Egon von Fürstenberg, never abandoned the crazy dream that one day Böttger would find a way of making gold. Early in 1719, Böttger's physical and mental condition deteriorated. During the first days of March, Steinbrück entered a daily report of Böttger's agony in the annals. Johann Friedrich Böttger died on March 13, about six o'clock in the evening. His possessions were sealed up, too late, as it turned out. The inventor of European porcelain was buried ten days after his decease without much ceremony in the Johannstädter cemetery.

It is unlikely that Böttger had really appreciated the damaging consequences of the flight of one of his colleagues, Samuel Stöltzel from Scharfenberg, who had been fairly well acquainted with the arcanum, to the Vienna factory established in 1718. Böttger himself was partly to blame for this, for by loquacity and incredible indiscretion he had imparted more information than he should have regarding porcelain manufacture to C. C. Hunger, an enameler from Weissensee. Hunger went to Vienna in 1717 and together with the imperial *Hofkriegsagent* Innozentius Claudius du Paquier, and the help of Viennese merchants, he had founded a porcelain manufactory in nearby Rossau. At first, however, they were unsuccessful in their attempts to make porcelain. Only when Böttger's stepbrother, Tieman, brought a papier-mâché model of an early Böttger kiln, made by the older Mehlborn, and when through Mehlborn's influence Schnorr's white earth was finally obtained, did they manage to produce perfect porcelain. This occurred in April, 1719.

Rivalry with David Köhler and discontent with his salary caused Stöltzel's departure. The Meissen manufactory was again threatened. Fortunately the supply of Schnorr's clay to Vienna was cut off after a year had passed and Samuel Stöltzel was lured back to Meissen.

As a result of the betrayal of the arcanum, Dresden had become extremely circumspect, so that even before Böttger's death a study of his written work had been embarked upon. It was assumed that among his papers would be found notes on scientific and economic matters which would later prove useful for the management of the factories he had founded, yet nothing of any use was found among the disarray of books and papers. The suspicion seemed to be confirmed that while he was still clear in thought Böttger must have informed his friends, especially Meerheim and Mehlhorn, of certain recipes, proposals for new manufacturing ventures, and a list of mineral resources.

To prevent any further misuse of manufacturing secrets, however, a new commission was set up by Privy Councillor von Seebach, Baron Alemann, and Count Lesgewang, known for his dabblings in alchemy. They met at Meissen after Böttger's death to reestablish the smooth running of the manufactory.

First the employees came under immediate and strict screening. Stöltzel's flight and the administrator's death demoralized the workers. Their listing of the deficiencies that had crept in brought in fact no more results than the three previous investigations of the years 1711, 1715, and 1717. Only one point in the commission's lengthy report comes as a surprise: the conclusion that the factory's near ruin is quoted as being its organization on "much too large and costly" a scale.

In fact, the lack of investment and capital were the main causes of this turn of events. On the basis of the profitability report, the position of *Oberdirektor* was judged useless and abolished. Directives were to be based on a careful report from the local inspector, Steinbrück, and issued by the commission. Nehmitz became redundant, and Meerheim, who had been chosen by Böttger as his successor, was also relieved of his post. Holtzbrinck, who by order of the cabinet was given access to the arcanum during Böttger's lifetime and who had therefore counted on a profitable income as *Oberdirektor*, was also dismissed. Mehlhorn and two of Böttger's servants, Schurmann and Pyrner, suffered the same fate. Finally, the dishonest marketing assistant Krügelstein, who had cleverly enriched himself by pandering trade samples, was discharged. His duties were passed on to the Leipzig accountant Chladni, who soon rose to be director of the Dresden branch and played a decisive part in the successful running of the factory for many decades. He worked in Dresden, where the members of the commission usually met for their deliberations. The gilder Funcke, his son, and his colleague Gäbel also worked in Dresden. Irminger's connection with Meissen was reauthorized and given wider scope by the new commission.

Steinbrück was made departmental director of the Albrechtsburg, authorized to engage and dismiss workers. To prevent further desertions by the craftsmen, the commission had very farsightedly increased wages, by as much as 51 percent in the cases of those involved in secret processes. In 1719 Böttger's kiln house was built at last on the unfinished foundations laid by him, and two further kilns followed within the next two years. A glazing works brought from Eggebrecht's faience factory was improved and rebuilt in the northwest wing of the Albrechtsburg.

At last decisions were being made not only based on careful study but also acted upon. Sales rose considerably in Leipzig, Dresden, Naumburg, Karlsbad, and Teplitz. Not the least contribution to Meissen porcelain's good name was the careful sorting into *"gut, mittel und brac." Brac*—articles that were only barely usable—were of course not offered to a very discerning public. After the Spring Trade Fair of 1720 there was a satisfactory balance of payments, so the firm no longer needed the help of the royal treasury. It was self-supporting without, however, yet being greatly profitable. The commission, which now included the deputy mining director von Ponigkau in place of the deceased Baron Alemann, wisely saw to it that the manufactory was made independent of all others. Even when the king saw the opportunity to recoup Böttger's debts from this gradually thriving enterprise, the commission made sure that its growth was not retarded by any such action. Böttger's debts stood at 22,563 talers. The outstanding wages for which he was, in accordance with his contract, personally responsible were not included in this sum. Only 700 talers had been found in cash, all valuable items were in pawn, a large part of his luxurious furnishings had not been paid for, and the rest of the contents of his Dresden apartment in the Jungfernbastei were only hired. Augustus the Strong's edict of 1712, in which he had agreed to answer for all Böttger's bad debts, paying them not in cash but in porcelain, was still valid. It presented the commission, which was trying to avoid any watering down of its recommendations for the good of the enterprise, with no mean problem, if it were to avoid the recurrence of decline. How the debtors were repaid in the end is described only in individual cases in the archives. Some method of long-term repayment was probably resorted to, as in the case of Böttger's personal physician, Dr. Bartholmäi: his claims were met only in 1741 with a large consignment of porcelain which, however, included a considerable measure of faulty ware or unsalable remnants.

The rebirth of the works was fairly free from hindrance. This perceptive and active commission succeeded in protecting it from harmful influences, even against the king's excessive demands, and thus paved the way for lasting prosperity. Although the time was ripe for it, new vitality stemming from fresh artistic inspiration did not appear for a few years yet, but perhaps this was an advantage, for a stormy development of the sort initiated by Johann Gregorius Höroldt needed to be preceded by a period of reorganization and reflection.

JOHANN GREGORIUS HÖROLDT—THE EARLY DAYS

The most glaring defects had been corrected after the first reform, and production had achieved a certain stability; prestige rose visibly and demand continually increased. There were still delays in wage payment, but crises were now averted more quickly. If the porcelain sometimes failed to satisfy the commission and, more importantly, Steinbrück, the manufactory inspector, it was because the desired technical improvements had not been realized. Above all, there was a lack of artists to give new life to both the decoration and the basic form of the material. In spite of Funcke's and Köhler's development of enamel colors, a satisfactory standard in decoration was by no means consistently achieved. David Köhler did provide the Meissen artists with a wider palette, but he often jealously guarded the secrets of his discoveries, locking them in a cupboard in his apartment. It was frequently necessary to remind him that his instructions obliged him to grind colors for the casually employed *Schilderer*. He did this very reluctantly, perhaps because he was afraid that his arcana would be stolen or because he was displeased with the quality of the work produced by these men who appeared so sporadically. Probably, he wanted one good artist. He did not realize that the first steps toward the fulfillment of his wishes were already being taken many miles away. The Saxon ambassador in Vienna, Christian Anacker, had, in fact, succeeded in persuading Samuel Stöltzel, who a year earlier had fled to the porcelain factory in Rossau, to return to Saxony. To make this decision easier for Stöltzel, who had hesitated at first, fearing punishment, Anacker offered him the money for his journey, amounting to fifty reichstalers. In mid-April the former compounder and kilnmaster arrived at the house of the *Oberbergrat* Pabst von Ohain in Freiberg. On his own initiative and at his own expense he had brought with him a *"wohl ein- und abgerichteten Kunst Mahler, nahmens"* (a well-trained painter named) Johann Gregorius Höroldt.

How was Stöltzel able to adapt knowledge gained from the enameler Hunger to the field of porcelain color recipes and to pass his discoveries on to Höroldt for practical application? Hunger later protested in a memorandum on the subject to the manufactory commission that Stöltzel and Höroldt, since they had been employees in Vienna, had stolen his colors. Stöltzel recommended the painter he had brought back as well trained and instructed, since he wanted to draw attention to his own value as instructor from the very beginning. He hoped thereby to gain favor with the people who would decide the issue of his employment in Meissen and possibly also consider disciplinary action, for the register of his sins was by no means short: absence from work without permission, desertion to foreign parts, betrayal of important secrets, founding of a rival factory, illegal importation of Schnorr's white clay—these were crimes that could have cost him his head.

The manufactory commission took several weeks to settle the question as to how Stöltzel could be reemployed without a loss of prestige for the administration, without causing unrest among the loyal workers. It was decided that a policy of complete generosity would be best, and so it was. Stöltzel was a valuable man. He had gained wide experience in Vienna, having undertaken many kinds of tasks and learned how to overcome various problems. Every effort was made to ensure that Köhler's and Stöltzel's work did not overlap. All forms of rivalry, damaging to production, had to be eliminated. Had these steps been taken before 1719, Stöltzel would never have fled. Then, of course, Höroldt would never have come to Meissen. Höroldt made great use of the time that Stöltzel, seriously ill and afraid, spent in Freiberg awaiting the commission's decision. He became acquainted with the members of the commission, the director of the Meissen porcelain store, and probably some of the people close to the royal chancellory. He presented his sample pieces and on May 14, 1720, was called for an interview at the house of Herr von Bose in Wilsdruffer Strasse, which was used as business premises by the commission. The samples had made a lasting impression in court circles. Conversation with Höroldt also left a favorable impression. He appeared polite and modest, yet thoroughly self-confident. The commission agreed that Höroldt was to be engaged as an independent artist. Köhler and Stöltzel were to prepare for him all necessary colors. He was not held responsible for pieces spoiled during firing. To calculate his salary, his work on individual pieces was to be placed in three grades according to difficulty.

Augustus the Strong was in Warsaw at this time. To acquaint him with the competence of this new artist, he received, according to a list of May 22, 1720, a consignment of the following pieces: "Three blue smooth bowls, a matching cup and two chocolate cups, four red enameled bowls, a matching cup and three chocolate cups."[29]

Meanwhile Höroldt received 6 talers for his subsistence in Dresden during the month of May. In June, he was paid 11 talers 21 groschen; in July, 30 talers 15 groschen; in September, 49 talers 9 groschen 6 pfennig, and in December as much as 63 talers 20 groschen for the pieces he was busily turning out. Höroldt had done well to obtain a contract which allowed him to judge for himself the grade of difficulty to which a piece belonged. His monthly earnings in April, 1721, amounted to 82 talers 8 groschen, but this included money for his work materials, such as the ingredients for his colors, which varied considerably in price. The cost of materials for underglaze painting was much lower, as we see from an entry dated March, 1721, amounting to only 27 talers. These *"monath-liche Cassen Extracten"* reveal nothing of the nature and content of his work. A vague impression may be obtained from the information that on September 9, 1720, 147 copper engravings arrived at the manufactory, and that *"der Wiener Mahler die meisten zu sich genommen hat"* (the Viennese painter took most of them). These genre representations by Dutch, Flemish, and French engravers were the inspiration for his inclusion of European themes in his work, which until then had been in keeping with the vogue for chinoiserie. Höroldt chose to work out of the factory in the *"Nohrsche Haus"* on the cathedral square in

Meissen. In January, 1721, he engaged his first apprentice, Johann Georg Heintze, the son of a Dresden storage hand. As demand for his work increased, one apprentice was not enough, so for the less lucrative blue underglaze painting he employed apprentices who had been trained at the Delft faience works. His relations with them were not particularly good, as is shown in the case of the blue underglaze painter Johann Caspar Ripp from Hanau. Ripp soon saw through his master's selfish approach to the work and tried, under the protection of Count Ludwig Alexander von Seebach, to oppose it. He offered to carry out underglaze work for two-thirds of the current price. But he soon lost his case and had to leave Meissen. With the help of his friends, Fleuter, a member of the commission, and Chladni, a court administrator, Höroldt persecuted and eventually managed to expel this colleague who had become a danger to his position. Making an example of him guaranteed that there would be no future trouble. No single employee in the whole factory could prevail against him, but he had become wiser as a result of this episode. Henceforth he avoided professional help and engaged only those with natural talent whom he could train for the work.

One year after Höroldt arrived, the state of affairs was as follows: in Dresden, Funcke and Gäbel continued to decorate Meissen porcelain with gold lacelike decoration and straightforward gilding. Employed in the factory on a regularly paid basis, Johann August Richter and Johann Gottfried Mehlhorn produced work of lesser quality, mainly underglaze painting. Mehlhorn, in fact, was soon put back on to molding, apparently because of incompetence. Neither was Richter heard of thereafter, so the manufactory was soon entirely dependent on craftsmen working away from the premises. Steinbrück admits in a report dating from May 17, 1720, that the sample pieces Höroldt had presented were proof of how much Vienna had already achieved, and that work there was equal, if not superior, to their own. This judgment pinpoints exactly the situation in April, 1720. This was Höroldt's best opportunity to prepare the way for the unique monopoly he was later to hold. In Vienna he had presumably managed to adapt his talent well enough to painting in enamel, but he lacked both the knowledge and the experience to prepare colors himself. The following years were consequently devoted to filling in the gaps in his knowledge.

We know almost nothing of Höroldt's early training. He was born in Jena on August 6, 1696, the youngest son of the master tailor Johann Wilhelm Höroldt. He is mentioned in the Jena municipal accounts on November 28, 1718, as being a painter living in Strasbourg, and at the beginning of 1719 as a wallpaper painter in Vienna. As little is known of the circumstances of his meeting Hunger in Vienna as of the work he did under du Paquier. But he must already have made a name for himself as a creator of delightful chinoiserie scenes and possibly as a miniature painter and copper engraver, at the time when he was occasionally asked to do work in the Rossau. When Stöltzel asked Höroldt to accompany him to Meissen, Höroldt probably did not have to think the proposal over for very long. What was expected of Höroldt in Meissen was not so much a new style of decoration as a perfection of the technique of painting with enamel colors. Smoothness, glaze, and the fastness of brush painting during firing in the muffle kiln were by no means guaranteed in 1720. Although Höroldt had at his disposal a limited number of colors (only blue and red are mentioned with regard to his sample pieces, and only iron red in his first regular pieces) his work left nothing to be desired as far as the fineness of execution was concerned. Indeed, it was the subject of great admiration and augured well for his future success. Above all, people were impressed by Höroldt's industriousness. Unfortunately we will never know exactly what he painted. Nevertheless we definitely know from the fact that Samuel Chladni requested as many *"indianische Stücke zu imitieren"* (to imitate Indian pieces) as possible, that Höroldt's creative imagination, fired by the copper engravings that had arrived in September, was at the height of its powers. Yet he was still very dependent upon Stöltzel, who had returned to his old post in June, 1720, and was, in contrast to earlier days, intensively occupied with the task of inventing new ground colors. On January 18, 1721, it is reported that Höroldt had again been very busy, for he had worked for three hours on a yellow lid passed on to him by Stöltzel.[30] This is proof that yellow ground color already existed in 1721. Presumably this met with great approbation at the highest level, for six months earlier Stöltzel had invented a brown, and shortly afterward a black glaze, which, however, had to be abandoned since it did not find favor. Höroldt had been busy on a new service design, for on March 3 he presented the molder Paul Wildenstein with a selection of new designs for tableware, which proved of no use to the latter, however, as he needed clay or wooden models and not mere drawings.

This scrap of information is of extreme importance, for it indicates when Höroldt began to be involved in all aspects of the manufactory's production. He was rightfully concerned that his painting be applied to pieces most suited to it in shape. At the beginning of his employment he was required to paint many a piece that still bore Jacob Irminger's relief ornament. Although he usually succeeded in achieving a happy synthesis of acanthus relief, gold lace decoration, and chinoiserie, he undoubtedly preferred to decorate plain pieces. When the French fashion for tableware with plastic ornament arrived in Saxony he showed his antagonism toward the sculptor and his work. His cooperation with Johann Joachim Kaendler, who arrived ten years after him, was made difficult owing to this prejudice. His approach to his work was opposed by the court chancellery, however, and he was frequently requested, via Chladni, not to obscure the porcelain entirely with his painted decoration. Augustus the Strong one day expressed his wish that as much as possible of the beautiful white glaze of which Meissen was so proud be seen. Despite this wish, however, he made increasingly energetic demands for a richness of color equal to that he had admired in the decoration of the Japanese Kakiemon porcelain, desiring most of all a red underglaze that appeared smoother than the blue one. Höroldt tried very hard to fulfill all these wishes, which were often quickly superseded by new ones. He worked feverishly, "day and night" according to his records. Precisely when he began his own experiments on the color range is not known. In June, 1721, he went to Freiberg with Stöltzel, presumably to investigate new mineral finds and to arrange for a steady supply to Meissen.

In 1720, "*Flemmingscher Stein*" containing feldspar was talked of. Seven hundred and fifty pounds were delivered to the manufactory before they even knew how to use it. The way in which the arcanists busied themselves individually was undoubtedly a great hindrance to the solving of urgent problems, for none of those concerned with the search for new color recipes would entertain the idea of sharing newfound knowledge as set out in their instructions. Höroldt would have been only too pleased to watch Köhler or Stöltzel at work or to have had an occasional glimpse into their journals. The fact that he had his home and workshop outside the manufactory prevented him from thus increasing his knowledge. To satisfy his scientific inquisitiveness he managed at last, on October 7, 1722, to obtain the use of a room in the castle. He had it renovated and, at the manufactory's cost, of course, supplied with a good stove. His personal move was a preliminary to the transfer of his whole studio to the Albrechtsburg, which took place on October 22. The transportation of ware awaiting decoration and firing proved a delicate and difficult operation. The policy of protecting the arcanum during the move created further difficulties, disturbed the smooth running of the manufactory, and also contributed to a high incidence of breakage.

The new kiln house, which was first in use from 1725, linked the west face of the Albrechtsburg with the so-called Kornhaus. In the "Albrechtsschloss," as it was then known, built by Arnold von Westfalen, the basement rooms served for storage, the first floor housed the mold makers; on the second floor were the molders and throwers and, in October, 1722, Höroldt's painters were finally allotted places, since in their previous quarters at Nohr the clerk's they had not had enough room. Their transfer to the castle is significant, for they were not counted as the manufactory's employees but as Höroldt's, engaged and dismissed by him. In February, 1722, he had three craftsmen and one apprentice under him. The blue underglaze painter Mehlhorn was outside his jurisdiction.

The manufactory commission had agreed with Höroldt on further training for all the apprentices, including those dealing with the molding of porcelain. Whether at this juncture Höroldt felt that the additional sum of one taler a month for an hour's work each week was inadequate payment or whether he did not care to instruct molders and throwers as well, at any rate the plan was quietly dropped; and the commission advised the inspector not to remind Höroldt, busy as he was, of the agreement if he appeared to have forgotten about it. Later, however, when Höroldt's section had grown and he was engaging people from other crafts rather than painting, he was forced to recognize that these assistants would require some kind of regular instruction. He limited this at first to teaching them how to execute the simplest blue painting; later they were brought into the routine painting of the most popular and frequent motifs.

Steinbrück was able to announce for the first time at the Spring Fair of 1722 that the *"Mahler Arbeit"* (painting) had so progressed that now ware painted in red monochrome as well as color could be sent to Leipzig.

The year 1722 saw the introduction of the famous crossed-swords mark. The suggestion that Meissen porcelain needed a factory mark to protect it from the competition of independent painters, the *Hausmaler*, and that which would undoubtedly come from Vienna was made by the farsighted Steinbrück. Various reports on this matter show uncertainty as to the form and extent of the marking. At the beginning of October, 1722, marking was being carried out.[31] After other abbreviations had been put forward, for example, K.P.M. (Königliche/Royal/Porcellain Manufaktur) and K.P.F. (Königliche Porcellain Fabrique), Steinbrück proposed on November 8 that part of the coat of arms of the Saxon Electorate, the crossed swords, be used, providing an unmistakable sign for Meissen products, in blue underglaze paint on the bottoms of the vessels. We do not know why they delayed for two years before adopting the mark. It is possible that they were careless in this matter for a long time, for in June, 1751, the "*Manufakturisten,*" as the employees of the Meissen manufactory were often called, were expressly required to use the official mark. Only after this date can we assume that wares were definitely marked with the crossed swords. Painting of the crossed swords was usually done by the youngest apprentice, whose brush control was still somewhat unsure. It is, however, not advisable to base one's dating of a piece on careless execution of the mark.

THE DEVELOPMENT OF PAINTING UNDER HÖROLDT
AND HIS FELLOW CRAFTSMEN

After Stöltzel's flight David Köhler was promoted. By taking this step the commission wanted to reward Köhler for his loyalty and his previous successes in the development of the invention and at the same time make sure that he would remain with the manufactory. Köhler was obsessed with his work; he applied himself to it with fanaticism, and had an almost crazed fear that someone would spy on him in his laboratory. The following incident illustrates how intent he was on being the only person to bring about innovations. In 1718 the manufactory commission was puzzled by the sudden rise in waste. An investigation showed that the paste had not been properly compounded. When the commission interrogated Köhler, he truculently admitted that he had deliberately organized the situation so that he would have the opportunity of saving it. One wonders less at Köhler's perverted pursuit of his aims than at the cynicism with which he admitted his strange behavior. Yet he achieved what he had set out to do: his admittedly important work was taken even more seriously. It was clear that without Köhler's recipes for the paste, without his successful experiments in the search for a reliable method of underglaze painting, and without his new enamel colors, the manufactory would progress no further. But on one point Köhler remained uncooperative: he refused to put down his latest discoveries on paper or to communicate them to Stöltzel, Schuberth, or Hoppe. He would not hear of it; he would not even enter into a discussion on the subject and quarreled with anyone whose conversation touched on it. He was little concerned with the instructions or *"Interims Verordnungen,"* which were drafted as loosely as possible so as not to challenge him. In February, 1720, according to his own statement, he had—at the same time as Mehlhorn—progressed so far in the development of an underglaze color recipe that it could, unlike earlier recipes, be introduced into the manufactory's production. Köhler, however, complained of the lack of suitable fuel, the lack of painters, and of other unsatisfactory aspects

Köhler's recipe for color

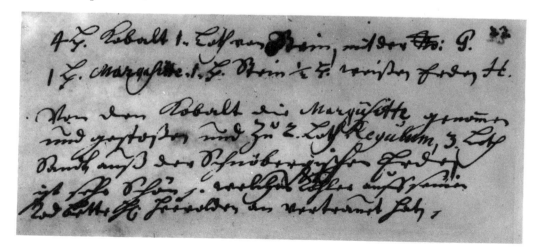

of the manufactory, but did nothing to enable further development of the blue painting after its promising introduction. He stubbornly refused to reveal his secrets and was not prepared to have them set down and sealed away for reference after his death. Höroldt's arrival hardly affected this situation. The *"Wienerische Mahler"* relied for help in technical matters on the man he regarded as com-

Drawing of a muffle kiln by Höroldt

petent, and that was Stöltzel. But Stöltzel too was so uncooperative that when the commission issued an order that he was to keep the painters at all times supplied with colors he only complied to a limited degree. There is no record of any particular tension between Höroldt and Köhler, so we may assume that they somehow managed to get along. Indeed, we may conclude from Höroldt's behavior during the first two years that he acted very courteously toward the *Obermeister*.

On March 1, 1723, Köhler reported the death of inspector Steinbrück to the commission, not expecting that his own death would occur shortly afterward. Köhler probably died of the complaint which affected all arcanists, a chronic illness caused by the poisonous fumes from the kiln. His agony lasted for three days. Stöltzel and Höroldt took turns watching over the deathbed: each was eager to be the first to have access to his book of formulae. He died while Höroldt was present, on April 30. Höroldt informed Fleuter, a member of the commission who had hastened over, that the dying Köhler had spoken of him as his "only friend" and desired him to open a small wall-cupboard and take out the secret writings. That very night Höroldt had studied the contents of the book and taken down the most important information. Fleuter was disgusted by Höroldt's ambition but said nothing, returned the book to its place, and sealed the cupboard. The manufactory commission was to decide what would become of the precious book, which contained details of experiments and Köhler's recipe for blue underglaze color. Many years later it was entrusted to Stöltzel so that he could use it. In 1738, it was recorded that nine pages of Köhler's eighty-two-page book had been cut out. It is now a precious relic in the Meissen Manufactory Archives.

It is necessary to know Fleuter's account of Köhler's death in order to understand the rapid success of Höroldt's further attempts to enrich the Meissen color palette. As early as May, 1723, the report reads: "What pleasant colors smoothly embedded in the glazing had been invented to suit the taste of the buyers." The new pieces were sold in Vienna, Augsburg, and England. In July, 1723, Höroldt promised to produce in eight days a green and yellow bowl to be made after a given model for His Royal Majesty in white porcelain. This was again an imitation of a Chinese bowl, which could not be carried out until 1723 because Köhler stubbornly refused to reveal the recipes for green and yellow. In this and the years that followed, the number of imitations mentioned in the delivery records increased. The interest of the court shifted visibly from tableware (coffee, tea, and chocolate services) to elaborate showpieces such as the four-sided, shell-shaped bowls, pedestaled flasks, and the difficult-to-make plates. At first these pieces were intended for the furnishing of the Dutch Palace in Dresden, but they were exhibited at the fair and found many admirers, especially from England. The *"neue Inventionen"* of this year were the new, more brilliant colors, the skilled application of which meant a richer variety of decoration. Höroldt's pieces attracted more and more attention until he was made court painter in June, 1724. It must be said, however, that he most cleverly engineered this appointment. When it was suggested to him that he ought to marry, he put forward his inadequate accommodation and his lack of a title as his reasons for not doing so. He said that only on the level of a court painter could he dare approach the daughter of a noble Meissen councillor. At this the manufactory commission made haste to obtain this desirable title for him without delay. Not long afterward the Jena Marriage Register records that the court painter Johann Gregor Höroldt married the spinster Rahel Eleonore Keil on October 6, 1725, in Meissen.[32]

Thus Höroldt strengthened his position in the Meissen works as no other artist had managed to do. He continued to carry out his work, not as a factory employee but as an independent artist with his own studio. Moreover, he employed at his own discretion whomsoever he regarded as suitable. Höroldt's monthly salary included not only payment for his work, but also expenses for the making of his colors, and other incidental expenditures. He received generous travel allowances when he had to go to Dresden on business or occasionally inspect localities for cobalt and china clay, and no rent was demanded for the rooms he had obtained in the castle for himself and his painters. As in the case of other privileged members of the manufactory, a good supply of fuel and candles had to be delivered punctually to his house. It was taken for granted that a good stove should be constructed for his living room; even so, he demanded a small stove upon which he could prepare his meal in wintertime. All this was done for him without objection. These apparently minor details of Höroldt's daily life may seem superfluous, but they complete the picture we form of his character. Only with them can we truly evaluate his success.

In 1724 his workshop employed twelve men, some of whom turned out to be thoroughly competent and others indeed quite original craftsmen. They were:

Augustin Dietze, born 1696 in Rochlitz
Hanns Christoph Hamann, born 1705 in Dresden
Johann George Heintze, born 1706 in Dresden
Peter Hohorst, born 1696 in Frankfurt-am-Main
Johann Christoph Horn, born 1698 in Berlin
Bonaventura Gottlieb Hoyer, born 1710 in Freiberg
Philipp Daniel Lippert, born 1702 in Dresden
Noa Ernst Petzoldt, born 1702 in Vierzehnheiligen, near Jena
Philipp Ernst Schindler, born 1695 in Dresden
Johann Ehrenfried Stadler, born 1702 in Dresden
Johann Carl Tüntzel, born 1710 in Meissen
Johann Heinrich Wolff, born 1687

Self-portrait by Johann Gregorius Höroldt, 1726

Only four of them, Hamann, Hohorst, Horn, and Stadler were experienced before entering Höroldt's employ, having been faience painters somewhere in Holland or the Main region. The rest had previously pursued other trades, and Höroldt had to teach, or rather drill, them in one particular routine task.

From 1725 onward, Höroldt was able to spend more time on his experiments to develop further enamel colors and, moreover, return to designing and painting some pieces himself. In fact, his output was amazing considering that most of the work from his own hand, sometimes signed, is of the short period 1725–1731. These pieces demonstrate his inventiveness, his artistic originality, and reflect his character. The satisfaction of having achieved success for the first and always most difficult time, the knowledge that he was supported by a loyal and industrious team of workers, the pride in being the first artist of note at the already famous manufactory probably drove him on in his efforts. We can only attempt an approximate reconstruction of the pieces Höroldt must have laid before the manufactory commission; but even if we had them at our disposal we would not be able to relate them to his later artistic achievements. They were imitations of Chinese pieces and had reached the desired degree of perfection in the brilliance of colors, the clear lines of drawing, and the *Glätte*, that is the fusing of the enamel colors into the glaze. They proved that Höroldt, with the help of Stöltzel, the experienced craftsman, could at last fulfill Böttger's promise of a *"dazu behörigen Mahl Werck"* (painting belonging to the porcelain). It was exactly what the manufactory had been waiting for. Originality of content was not required, for the royal collection contained a rich store of the most beautiful Chinese painting that could be copied. And when a whole parcel of copper engravings arrived at Meissen in September, 1720, the question of artistic inspiration appeared to have been satisfactorily solved. There is no mention of the new painter ever having been asked for *"Inventionen,"* but the word *"Imitationen"* crops up again and again and must be interpreted as meaning the exact and complete reproduction of another man's work.

Höroldt had his own artistic style before he came to Meissen, but it was by no means suited to such a difficult medium. Hence his preoccupation with the solving of all technical problems so that he would be free to give full vent to his artistic impulse in a material that he had already recognized when he was in Vienna as precious and offering great scope.

After two or three years in Meissen, Höroldt's reputation as the owner of a productive workshop was established. In the manufactory inspector's monthly report there is repeated mention of the new painter's incredible industry, but we learn little of the actual artistic nature of these first Höroldt pieces.

The character of his own pieces is first evident in the work dating from the period around 1724, and is already quite mature, for he was from the beginning keen to give his own handiwork a feeling of rich completeness and exuberant gaiety. For his paintings on the front and reverse of the porcelain, with its very clear and simple lines, he devised the following composition: the scene, one of his well-known Westernized chinoiseries, is enclosed in a stagelike frame with a very low-placed horizon that draws the eye into it.

In the early period of his Meissen work he limited himself, partly because of the poor range of colors available, to silhouette or monochrome representations of gay scenes. The gestures of his jesters and fan bearers, of the Chinese ladies, gentlemen, and high potentates are so free, spontaneous, and expressive that the connoisseur can already detect the hand of a master. No face is duplicated. The features are rendered so convincingly individual with a few brush strokes that his "laughing Chinamen" could not be imitated and may be identified without difficulty through their very uniqueness. In many cases the facing stage setting is defined by a quatrefoil frame and encloses a tiny landscape while the overall decoration of lively lace and strapwork seems to stand away from the white surface of the porcelain. In certain cases Höroldt may have entrusted skilled employees with the execution of this complicated frame and miniature landscape. On smaller items, such as cups, small boxes, and so on, the scene was painted all the way around. Here, too, in the beginning the silhouette-like effect with the low horizon prevailed. The ornamental work, which he could not bring himself to leave out in his desire to produce an effect of richness, consisted of borders around the base and rim of the vessel. With the increase in the range of colors and finally the almost unlimited choice of shades, Höroldt abandoned the silhouette-like technique and set his scene in a landscape which gave a definite impression of depth. The foreground is occupied by a stagelike scene with a wealth of figures who detach themselves from the peace-

ful atmosphere of the immediate background. The horizon, now placed higher in the composition, consists of blue mountains or cliffs crowned with fortresses, against a cloudy sky in which all kinds of birds hover. In the Chinese scenes fabulous creatures flutter on high.

In this period Höroldt's work rises to the heights of real art. Areas of color are juxtaposed without much definition by line. Only an artist completely at home with his material could have employed such a technique. Later it became clear that select pupils, perhaps only Heintze and Hoyer, were capable of following him in this method. The pictorial aspect of porcelain decoration, which had gained favor in preference to mere ornamental pattern, gradually extended at the expense of any surrounding decoration. In place of this came the colored ground with window-like free places (Reserven) on the front and the reverse for painting, often framed with a gold lace border in the finer examples. The colors for the background area were most carefully prepared to meet the higher technical demands and satisfy contemporary taste; in some cases they equaled the quality of the Chinese examples. They included Naples yellow, pea green, celadon green, cobalt blue, Bordeaux red, apple green, English red, dark purple, and even black grounds, the yellow and delicate greens being the most popular at court. On the front of a set of vases a cycle of some ceremonial act, or temple scenes and scenes of homage to pagan gods, or scenes of court pastimes would be represented; on the reverse, rich arrangements of stylized indianische (Indian) flowers. This contrast between ornamental and representational painting presumably did not jar, although two entirely different approaches would be found on one object. It is hard to say how far Höroldt's imaginative powers were fired by other artists' work, because he was able to transpose so skillfully and quickly. Every object, no matter how concrete and characteristic it was, could be transformed by his hands into a new artistic experience. Whatever the inspiration or model for the decoration's content, the result was never pedantically realistic but always in the playful, fanciful spirit of the incipient Rococo, embodying the richness of the art of this period.

Höroldt brought countless artistic ideas of an international nature from Frankfurt, Strasbourg, and Vienna back to Meissen. Inquisitive, he studied folios of copper engravings wherever he went. The manufactory had at its disposal a collection of several hundred graphic works, for the development of new decorative motifs and as reference material for the sea and harbor views which were then becoming fashionable. Now that these examples were being adapted in his style by his craftsmen, Höroldt himself did a considerable number of copper engravings. At his request a press was set up so that any number of prints of the motifs required were at the disposal of the increasing force of painters. If we compare the copper engraving Höroldt executed in 1726 (signed with the added abbreviation "inv. et fecit") with his porcelain painting, we are immediately aware that Höroldt's former work has captured the theme, the composition, the details, and the movements, but lacks expression. His lines are soft and influenced by brush technique, and he too obviously aims at a light and shade effect. Höroldt's prints, however, allowed the artist who was to work from them, in spite of their finality of execution, a certain freedom of interpretation. He could loosen the figure groups, rearrange the movements, put more expression into the faces, or eliminate various details. Höroldt may have wanted to provide himself with a visual record too, for there is no doubt that the manufactory's extremely busy artistic director had less and less time as the years went by to execute his own pieces from beginning to end.

Identification of Höroldt's work is a difficult task which continues to occupy historians and, for obvious reasons, even more urgently, the collectors of old Meissen porcelain. Today there are only three positively identified works. There is the splendid blue vase with a Chinese scene on the face and *indianische Blumen* painting on the reverse, the signature of which was discovered by Richard Seiffahrt at the Meissen Town Museum and which is now in the Zwinger collection at Dresden. Second, a box that was signed "J G Ht" was discovered by Ingelore Menzhausen in the Dresden collection. Finally, there is the frequently mentioned yellow vase, from the turret room of the destroyed Dresden Palace, which has been missing since the Second World War. Since this vase is merely signed *"inv."* by Höroldt, it probably was carried out by his employees according to his own design. In addition to these signed pieces there are the ones with dedications, such as the tankard for his brother-in-law Georg Ernst Keil, dating from July 9, 1724, the beaker for the forester Christian Friedrich Glasewaldt of August 24, 1724, the table jug for Johann Gottlieb Schlimpert of July 10, 1725, and the one for the master forester to the Count of Thun, Johann Friedrich

Hüttel, of September 27, 1727. Since they were gifts, these items would have been carefully executed by his own hands. They are invaluable to us, with their exact dating and the excellent script of the dedications, in our study of the master's artistic progress. The lovingly painted jug for Master Forester Hüttel shows that the supremacy of Chinese-inspired motifs was waning by the middle of the third decade. From an artistic point of view the manufactory's stock was rising. Its artists were throwing off the bonds of Oriental decorative traditions and becoming more independent and self-confident, seeking new motifs for their talent. Hunting scenes, park scenes, and battles, inspired by French engravings after Watteau and Lancret, were becoming popular. Dutch-style landscapes had already been added to the repertoire. This widening of the choice of motifs, which was partly a result of the increased exports of Meissen porcelain to Paris, led to an enriching and new lease on life for Meissen, but demanded a narrower allocation of tasks to the force of painters. As a result certain painters emerged with very specialized knowledge and skills. Höroldt watched these new developments with mixed feelings, half jealous, half proud of his artists' achievements, and he tried to suppress originality on their part so that his own fame would in no way be challenged. In this way a number of outstanding efforts were not allowed to come to fruition and at times the artistic director's policy was indeed damaging. The consequences of all this were to appear somewhat later on.

It was not pleasant to be in Höroldt's employ. Contemporary reports made by his workers contain no mention of satisfaction with their work but indeed constantly express their worries about how a family could be supported when the breadwinner was ill. Höroldt, however, was always able to avoid facing up to their criticisms. From 1728, the painters were subjected to the arbitrary behavior of Höroldt's brother-in-law, Carl Heinrich Keil, who had been a hunter by profession. Since he was of no use as a painter or color chemist he was tried out on the spraying of the ground colors. He was such a failure at this that Höroldt made him overseer in the painting shop. This mere youth of twenty-three vexed the apprentices and older craftsmen with his moods, yet he had the authority to keep a record of work done and to hand out new work. Höroldt, who because of his frequent absences was unaware of the deterioration in the running of the section, assumed that everything was in good order. Keil consequently grew more arrogant, kept making new demands for an increase in salary and even asked to be admitted to the arcanum and to be granted the title of co-inspector. This went on for many years during which Keil earned the loathing of all the painters and completely destroyed any confidence existing between master and pupils.

The life and work of Höroldt's oldest colleague, Johann George Heintze, is an example of how a competent and eager worker could, through a lack of foresight on the part of others, be frustrated, driven to unlawful dealings, and eventually to flight. Engaged by Höroldt as a young boy in the early days of the studio, he proved himself capable of learning and patient at his tasks. He soon became Höroldt's best figure and landscape painter, and proved an independent but self-critical worker. Continued failure to reward adequately the quality of his achievements compelled him to do other work in his spare time, and he experimented with his own enamel colors and constructed his own muffle kiln. He was repeatedly warned against this, although the master showed unusual patience with his activities, and indeed gave him the responsible post of overseer in the lower workshop. But Höroldt was not interested in Heintze's undoubted talent. The latter's income rose only insignificantly over the years and so he continued his private work, now to the apparent neglect of his other duties, experimenting with the forbidden process of enameling, not only on copper plate, but on porcelain too.

When this came out after an unexpected search of his premises he was arrested and taken to the Königstein fortress. Here he had to paint porcelain to pay for his keep. He managed to escape and although he was recaptured for a brief period in Prague he fled again and journeyed to Hollitsch and later to Breslau. From there he tried to contact Meissen, but eventually decided to travel to Berlin where his trail fades. It is difficult to recognize Heintze's work or estimate its extent. The only signature we have, for a long time doubted but now generally accepted, is on an enameled plate in the Württemberg Landesgewerbemuseum in Stuttgart. It shows a view of the Albrechtsburg in the style of Dutch harbor scenes with rich surrounding ornament. By comparing this technique with that of other paintings on porcelain we are able to attribute to him certain other views with richly executed foregrounds. A detail which Heintze

delighted in including took the form of an obelisk, a posting pillar, or a memorial which stands near a tree in a lonely landscape. He was such a master of figure painting that he used it freely and with ease, but his love for landscape was obvious. He mastered the illusion of depth and recognized the atmosphere that a vast area of sky could evoke in a composition. He should have been given more such work, but this was not Höroldt's intention. There were additional reasons for opposing Heintze's promotion. He had gained considerable knowledge of ceramic color manufacture. His friendship with the otherwise unapproachable Stöltzel provided a basis for his own experiments in this field. Stöltzel had intended to use him as supervisor of painting in his projected subsidiary factory to be established in the former Falkenhof near Dresden. In 1740, when no one dared take on the task of decorating a chimneypiece destined for the Hubertusburg Palace, Heintze offered his services to the king in a letter to Count Brühl. The latter succeeded in having Heintze removed from his piecework and employed with a regular salary. Heintze's career shows how difficult it was for a talented craftsman to give the manufactory the benefit of his acquired knowledge, for he reports resignedly his subsequent subjection to the hostility, persecution, and hatred of the superiors.

The painters' specialization resulted from the wider taste the public was beginning to show in the middle of the third decade. Höroldt tried to give preference to the chinoiseries, which he personally found most congenial, but the greater part of the engravings which were sent from time to time from Dresden were of European inspiration. The original division of painters into "blue" and "color" was no longer adequate. From the mid-twenties there had been on the wage list specialists for Indian flowers and figures, for fine Japanese figures and flowers, for foliage and flowers, and for delicate figures and flowers. Apart from these there were the following salaried employees: the gold lace painters, the sword painter (the Meissen mark), and the group colorer. Apprentices were soon introduced to actual work on the production line and had to practice underglaze painting, which demanded a free but sure hand, until they were promoted by Höroldt "to the color." So that their work could be constantly inspected they had to sign it. Otherwise the signing of work, no matter how complicated and excellent, was strictly forbidden, a fact which makes the attribution of a piece to one or another of Höroldt's employees extremely difficult.

There are, however, certain indicators: in spite of instructions to reproduce the original design, those artists who carried out their work with devotion, enthusiasm, and success naturally developed a personal style, as we have seen in the cases of Heintze and Höroldt himself. Thus we are able to compare a mainly graphic interpretation with a freer rendering according to artistic convictions, and thereby draw our own conclusions. Certain preferences as to subject are another indication. Attribution is very difficult, however, when an object has passed through various hands. The artist who painted the picture on a large vase or on the pieces of an elaborately decorated dinner service never also undertook the arduous task of executing the gold lace ornament. The records of 1731 tell us that Johann Leonhard Koch, born 1702 in Finsterwalde, had been working as gilder and painter of flowers and grotesques since 1726. Nevertheless, he would hardly have been able to carry out the major jobs in this special field completely on his own. The accounts bear proof that the gilders Funcke and Gäbel in Dresden were well supplied with work from the manufactory until the end of the thirties. Nevertheless, Höroldt was eager to replace all these outside workers with his own craftsmen. His reason was not lack of artistic influence over them, but rather that gilding brought good profit, which he did not want to slip through his fingers.

Christian Friedrich Herold, whose name was similar to that of Höroldt's, was born in Berlin in 1700 and had been working for him since 1724. He was one of the few employees who brought professional qualifications, for he was not without experience, probably having learned the art of enameling in the workshop of the steel engraver and gunsmith Fromery in Berlin. In Meissen he continued to do enamel work on copper boxes in his spare time with great enthusiasm. He tried to adapt his techniques to the new material, and experimented in the application of relief enamel work and especially relief gilding with the glaze. In one report he quotes himself as the inventor, later as the master, of this technique.[33] But Johann Gregorius Höroldt would hear of none of this and made sure that Christian Friedrich Herold was not only refused a guaranteed wage and the means and free time for his experiments, but was also forbidden to carry out any kind of further research. When he nevertheless did so, he was surprised by a house search, and a box containing costly enamel colors that he had himself prepared was confiscated. Indeed, when at the age of sixty-three, after thirty-nine years' faithful service with the manufactory, he petitioned for a raise in salary he was thrown into prison as an offender against all common law and justice for four months. His life was spent in hard work for unfair rewards and in the carrying out of successful experiments in the technique of gilding which were never acknowledged and which he did in secrecy, in constant fear of discovery. It is amazing that he continued to work indefatigably for the manufactory, that he stayed in Meissen in spite of many a tempting offer elsewhere, and that in this atmosphere of repression he lived to be seventy-nine. He must be given a prominent place among Höroldt's painters. Since he painted his signed enameled copper panels with the same motifs as the porcelain, we can identify some of his work by its inimitable style and superb brushwork. He had a rare mastery of figure drawing. Yet there is as a rule little action in his scenes, which usually show people engaged in quiet conversation. It is therefore a great surprise when we come across one of his turbulent, brilliantly painted battle scenes. Toward the end of his artistic career he turned—or perhaps was ordered to turn—to flower painting; in this we see that his delicacy of touch remained to the last, despite the fact that at the age of fifty he had complained that he found the climb from the Meissen Market up to the Burgberg very taxing.

The lives of Heintze and Herold provide an insight into the conditions under which the manufactory's employees worked together to produce Meissen ware. They destroy all illusions of a harmonious patriarchal system and reveal intrigue and ruthless exploitation.

In the same way Johann Gottlieb Erbsmehl, born in Dresden in 1708, spent his spare time painting enamel on copper. The quality of his work was often praised and brought its reward in 1739 when he was made supervisor of painting. In the same circle of friends was a gifted painter of Dutch genre scenes, Augustin Dietze, born in Rochlitz in 1696. He was evidently an excitable character, and his constant burden of debts often led him to ill-considered actions. He probably deteriorated still further under the conditions imposed by Höroldt. Once, Höroldt paid him three groschen for a piece of work which had taken him three days to execute; but this amount was at once increased to eight groschen when a certain Hage, a clerk responsible for tableware, protested about it. In a report from the inspector dated September 9, 1736, it is emphasized: "so arbitrary are the assessments of painters' pay by the court commissioner Höroldt."

When Höroldt had been reminded by the court chancellory of his obligation to produce imitations of imported Chinese and Japanese wares, not in single pieces but in series, he had not delayed in engaging faience painters from Eggebrecht's factory in Dresden-Neustadt. While he had unfortunate dealings with Johann Caspar Ripp, he must have had much better luck with the painters Horn, Hamann and, above all, Johann Ehrenfried Stadler. This last artist had developed such originality while still at Eggebrecht's that his work stands out remarkably in the artistic unity of its personal interpretation from the slavish imitations of his colleagues. Höroldt was aware of this and, contrary to his usual policy, called Stadler to Meissen. Since there exist two first-rate signed examples of his work, a tureen with cover and stand and a lantern, both in the Dresden Porcelain Collection, other pieces such as beakers, large vases, vases with covers (or lidded vases), parts of services, which similarly show Chinese decoration translated into a graphic style, may be associated with his name. We are immediately aware of Stadler's bold touch in the art of faience painting when we see it repeated in the brushwork—extremely fine parallel lines like the threads of silk embroidery. He undoubtedly belongs to the highest level of artists employed by Höroldt, who naturally looked upon him with distrust. Such distrust on the manufactory's part was not entirely unjustified, for Stadler, like Heintze, had a muffle kiln in his home so that he could carry out firing in his spare time. The commission made an unexpected search, but could find no illegal wares or proof that Stadler had sold such wares contrary to the regulations.

Two painters, Noa Ernst Petzoldt and Johann David Schultze, became, according to repeated entries in the list of painters, skilled specialists of foliage and other ornaments. Petzoldt particularly, who is named as an industrious member of Höroldt's workshop in 1721, was employed for difficult tasks on special commission. His work was consistently good and he produced it in such steady quantity that in 1731, unlike the other painters, he was already being paid a guaranteed wage. Undoubtedly the most attractive branch of Meissen painting, *"Feine Figuren und Landschaften"* (fine figures and landscapes), included a field which offered great scope and promise: French and Dutch genre painting. This had skillful exponents in the painters Dietrich (or Dittrich), Hoyer, Lehmann, and Wentzel.

Gottlieb Bonaventura Hoyer (or Häuer), born in 1710, is considered the most talented painter. He mastered the execution of peopled scenes and especially battle scenes with such sovereign skill that after serving loyally for several decades he was finally promoted to the post of overseer of the painting shop in 1757.

One special case which shows how arbitrarily the painters were employed and which elucidates the strange conditions in the manufactory before 1730 is the employment of the three brothers Löwenfinck. The mother of these three brothers had come as a war widow to Saxony from Biela near Kalisch. She had evidently found a place on the Naundorf estate near Grossenhain. When she was looking for suitable careers for her three fatherless children, she was advised by the owner of a neighboring estate, Johann Georg von Wichmannshausen, a chairman of the commission, to approach the Meissen manufactory, and in this way her sons were brought up by the manufactory and trained to be painters.

The eldest, and from the very beginning most talented of these, Adam Friedrich von Löwenfinck, was apprenticed to Höroldt in 1727 at the age of thirteen and progressed rapidly and promisingly in blue underglaze work. In 1734, as a fully fledged craftsman, he could be entrusted with more ambitious work and even with model designs. Along with his skill his self-confidence and a certain arrogance grew. Debts and quarrels within the studio made his position difficult and on October 6, 1736, he made his escape to Bayreuth on a borrowed horse. Then, in danger of being extradited, he went to Ansbach, and thence to Fulda in 1741. In 1746, on the strength of his assurance that he knew about the great arcanum, he became co-founder of the porcelain factory in Höchst. However, he had violent disagreements with his financial backers, left Höchst, and became director of Hannong's faience factory at Hagenau in Alsace. There, in 1754, he died, only forty years old, and his widow, Maria Seraphia, daughter of a Fulda painter and herself a ceramic painter of no mean talent, carried on the management of the factory.

The second Löwenfinck, Karl Heinrich, commenced employment in Meissen in 1730, but joined the army as a volunteer in 1735. He soon turned his back upon that career for the more lucrative business of faience painting, first at Fulda, then in Strasbourg. Christian Wilhelm, the youngest son of the Löwenfincks and a Meissen apprentice from 1734, is seldom mentioned, and then usually negatively, in the archives. Adam Friedrich had him come to Höchst in 1747. One year later he was working with the middle brother in Strasbourg.

The defection of the two younger Löwenfincks was not greatly regretted, although both had attained a fair degree of skill in their craft, but the commission spared itself no effort to recapture or at least keep its eye on Adam Friedrich von Löwenfinck. Twelve years after his flight they still wanted information from the manufactory's Frankfurt representative giving the actual extent of his knowledge in ceramics, proof that they must have been well aware of his value as a craftsman. We are not sure of what his total production was, or even what his relatively short but constructive period at Meissen involved, since the records supply little information. We know more about the characteristics of

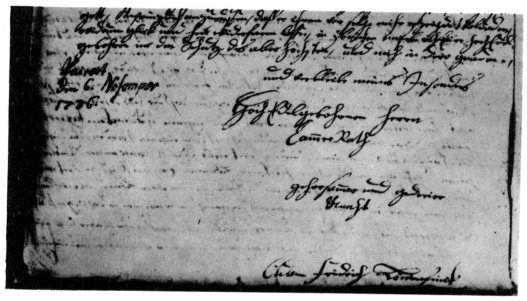

Letter written by Adam Friedrich von Löwenfinck, 1736

his art than of the actual number of his oeuvres. No one could deny that he is the most original, most varied, and most imaginative of all the painters Höroldt's studio produced. The elegance and freshness of his work, its entire suitability for the material on which it was executed, in the first instance porcelain and later faience, can only be described as inimitable. Strength of line dominates his imaginative compositions. His lively designs are rich in contrasts.

As far as themes go, he was attracted by the strange, the abstruse, the fabulous, and the grotesque. His depiction of hunting scenes, equestrian skills, burlesque events, trees hung with lichens, remarkable shaggy creatures, and birds of paradise enjoyed great success. But he also knew how to create a restrained scene in an original manner. The representational aspect is secondary in his desire for lively rhythm in his painting and to his highly developed feeling for the ornamental value of a design. He is aware of the unique conditions imposed by the form and material of an object, and he heightens the general aesthetic effect by ensuring that his decoration is in harmony with these. His technique of painting is based on an untrammeled and free-flowing line which, as has been established without doubt, he executed in an unceramic *Schwarzlot* (black enamel color), a material made fireable by a colorless flux. Thus all the elements of compositions, with their air of looseness and freedom, have silhouette-like clarity. They are not forced and appear scattered as if by chance over the white surface. Apart from the chinoiseries, creatures from fables play a great part in his wide repertoire, but we must beware of attributing all porcelain and faience showing these animals to Adam Friedrich von Löwenfinck or his influence. Since he left the manufactory at the age of twenty-two, he represents a loss to its artistic development which cannot be overlooked.

In 1736, the year that he left Meissen, a trend began which gave form greater importance than painted decoration. Although the decoration had derived new inspiration from a large supply of prints sent from Dresden, truly original work such as that executed on the Swan Service could hardly be expected with Höroldt in charge. Had Löwenfinck occupied a position of some influence, he could have given porcelain painting an importance which would have made itself felt well into the eighteenth century. If we read carefully the letter which Löwenfinck wrote from Bayreuth to Damian Pflugk, a member of the commission, on November 6, 1736, a few weeks after his flight, we are impressed by the fact that he had by no means left Meissen without forethought.[34] He knew that he was taking a chance in offering his services to less famous manufacturers of porcelain and faience. The uprightness of his character is illustrated by the fact that he fulfilled his promise to honor all his debts. But what makes this letter remarkable is the description of the disagreeable conditions in Höroldt's workshop. In similar criticisms and complaints put forward by Wildenstein, Kaendler, and Reinhardt the same inadequacies are mentioned, so that we may believe Löwenfinck for the most part. To have a team of painters satisfying only current tastes resulted in a routine approach to the business of painting that could only cause a complete developmental standstill. Löwenfinck quotes the following objectionable practices: Höroldt took on people without any kind of training and, what is more, without the slightest spark of artistic ambition. He let the newcomers practice until they could copy the so-called blue model mechanically, and then put them into the production line as apprentices who received only 50 percent of the assessment for each piece. Narrow drilling in one special aspect of the work without any prospects of promotion served in place of proper training. Indeed, Höroldt could not have found suitable instructors to carry out this activity because they would not have been paid properly. Höroldt looked upon ambitious people with great mistrust. Löwenfinck had always been most eager to learn, but every opportunity of learning something new had been denied him. If he worked on a painting for longer than was normally necessary, he faced financial disadvantages, and this was the cause of the insupportable increase of his debts.

Examination of the wage basis for the 1750s shows that there were directives with regard to the job of painting, but these were interpreted in a very personal fashion. Until 1725, Höroldt's painters were paid a fixed monthly wage, the sum involved being decided by Höroldt himself. Subsequently, piece-work was introduced by the manufactory commission, but did not come into force for the painters until after the review of 1731. The workers' dependence on the subjective evaluation of some individual or other was not, however, eliminated.[35] Clerks tried to value the individual pieces objectively but, as Löwenfinck states, Höroldt's judgments on his occasional inspections were entirely dependent on his mood at the time. Since very few of the Meissen paint-ers had enough outside experience as faience painters to know what their work was worth, Höroldt, his painting overseer, and his clerk were easy winners of disputes on value. Indeed, in cases of doubt they would remind the craftsmen of their duty to support their king's interest. When it came to the distribution of work, pieces of varying degrees of difficulty were lumped together, so the clerk could pass on the easy pieces to his friends and the tricky ones to his enemies. The number of pieces judged so difficult as to command a higher sum was very small, and even this was dependent upon the goodwill of the clerk. Löwenfinck reported with just indignation that there was no special reward for the artistic transformation of themes from engravings into painted decorations. The ap-prentices' lot was thoroughly lamentable. Höroldt had fixed the duration of apprenticeship at six years; this was a long time during which the young people were exploited to the full. They received a guaranteed but absolutely mini-mum wage which could, after a period of probation, be increased by additional piecework. Since this was based on the assumption that they could only pro-duce second-rate work, they were only allowed half the sum at which it was assessed; they had to work very hard in order to earn enough to live on. It is repeatedly stated that their work generally attained a standard of quality equal to that of the older craftsmen well before the six years had expired. Here and there a particularly gifted one would be promoted, but only when his talents lay within the normal repertoire. Höroldt considered general training in the art of painting a waste of time and would have nothing to do with it, although the commission often recommended such a course. The suggestion that general artistic training should be provided was probably the king's. The commission tried to introduce it repeatedly as, for example, in the hiring of the modelers Kirchner and Lücke, whose tasks included instruction of apprentices. The course was always no sooner begun than it was abandoned; Kaendler was the first to take this sensible provision seriously and give regular drawing lessons to all the apprentices. Indeed, he introduced annual prizes for the three best efforts. Hö-roldt, far from being pleased that his apprentices won the prizes, complained to the manufactory commission because Kaendler gave the lessons at his home and not on the factory premises.

To sum up, though, at the end of the 1720s, Höroldt was most happy about the surprising degree of independence he was allowed, even if this involved certain risks and considerable responsibility.

PORCELAIN DESIGN FROM IRMINGER TO KAENDLER

Johann Jacob Irminger was responsible for the design of articles made in porcelain during the Böttger period. His work continued to inspire production long afterward until, at the end of the 1720s, it became obvious that gradual replacement of the old designs was needed. A few individual pieces, statuettes, Far Eastern figures, and animals had occasionally been modeled and were used in production. Judging from the large numbers of them to be found in museums and various collections, they must have sold well. The plastic decorative elements for vessels of all kinds, derived from silverware, were carved in wood or hammered in copper by one of the sculptors employed for this purpose (such as Gottfried Müller, frequently mentioned in the records of 1725) and the plaster molds were made from them. "Free," that is, original, pieces by the above-mentioned Meissen sculptor are recorded once: on October 6, 1725, he delivered to the manufactory two commissioned pieces, a *Bajode* (pagoda figure) and a winged dragon, both carved in pear wood, receiving an honorarium of ten talers for the work. On the whole, though, the manufactory stuck to the range of designs that had sold consistently throughout ten years. If a new look was really required, good use was made of the embossers' skills. Höroldt himself once produced some designs for decorative features on Meissen ware but they were not carried out since they were only presented as drawings. The delay in obtaining new designs was mainly due to the fact that almost all the sculptors were busy during these years (1710–1725) in the often storm-tossed efforts to complete the Residenz in Dresden. Another reason was the manufactory's hope to manage with the few skilled embossers in its employ. Of these, George Fritzsche, born in 1698, had shown an independent style of working. He had joined the manufactory in 1712 and, in spite of his youth, the feeling for the difficult task of assembling a piece of porcelain was already in his bones. He brought his skills in modeling to bear on such difficult pieces as an elaborately ornamented porcelain clock case.[36] In addition he is mentioned as being able to create statuettes without being given a design. Although this is often referred to, it was also noticed that he never rose above a certain level of uninspired effort, and never succeeded in producing an artistically satisfying piece. Unfortunately, the records contain no details of his pieces apart from the above-mentioned clock case. Since no one else was active at this time, he must have been responsible for a small number of extremely primitive-looking figures among which are various *Nationalitäten* and two miners. At all events he gave incalculable service as an independently working molder. He was skilled in handling his material, and his knowledge of his craft later proved of great assistance to newly employed sculptors such as Kirchner and Lücke.

When a sculptor accustomed to working in stone and on a large scale turned his hand to small-scale work in such a different material it could lead to unexpected difficulties: Johann Gottlieb Kirchner experienced such problems. At the end of March, 1727, the manufactory commission had obtained the services of two sculptors suitable for work at Meissen. One of them, Kirchner, was personally interviewed by the commission, and he accepted the annual salary of 220 talers. He did not receive his terms of contract until six months later. We may assume that the inspector first wanted to acquaint himself with Kirchner's capabilities and qualities so that he could work out the terms accordingly. He was required to design free statuettes and groups and, in addition, new plastic decorative elements. He had to keep to his hours of duty as did everyone else. Later he was asked to undertake the co-supervision, probably meaning the artistic supervision, of all the molders; but at the same time he had to gain the respect of the molders, throwers, and embossers. The fact that he neither gained their respect nor managed to establish the systematic training of apprentices lay in Kirchner's unstable and light-minded character and, above all, in his illogical work methods. The one-sidedness of his previous work meant that he had a lot to learn in his new position. Since the time of his apprenticeship he had been occupied with stone masonry on monumental pieces, whereas his new contract required him to execute the models both in clay and in wood; he found this difficult to master at first. He also failed to catalogue his work as required by the commission.

An important point in his contract was the protection of the arcanum, in this case regarding paste composition. Kirchner was to exercise the greatest care with the mixture, on no account to take any back to his quarters, and to report the matter immediately if any was missing. A part of the large throwing room was sectioned off for him so he could work there undisturbed. He received a potter's wheel, a sufficient number of modeling tools, good French drawing paper, and Venetian pastels. Finally, he asked for a textbook for teaching the apprentices. The administration did everything to ensure a successful beginning for the manufactory's first regular sculptor, but it appears that Kirchner could not adjust to things. Inspector Reinhardt clearly, if reluctantly, reported that the results of Kirchner's first attempts by no means came up to the commission's high expectations. The translation of his craft into an unfamiliar medium seems to have progressed so slowly that Fritzsche often had to step in and help him. Kirchner's unsureness and nervousness seemed to increase rather than decrease after this bad start. He spent many hours shut away in his workroom to avoid the mockery of the other craftsmen, claiming he could do original work only in absolute seclusion. Finally he fell into disorderly habits of life and contracted an embarrassing illness. After four weeks the doctor announced that he was cured, but on March 15, 1728, the commission had already decided upon his dismissal.

Although Kirchner had not succeeded in overcoming certain weaknesses in his work in this new field, the output of his first period in Meissen forms a fairly well-rounded group. His first pieces, which Count Lesgewang, a member of the commission, wanted to be copies of Far Eastern originals, were cups decorated with fine Japanese figures. Then came a temple of Venus decorated with figures and foliage work, which took two months to complete. Of quite a different nature was the artistic creation commissioned by the wife of the crown treasurer, described as a drinking vessel in the form of a shell, where instead of the usual handle or foot a stag's foot was to be used. After Kirchner had made enough progress with the clay models of table lamps with ornamentation so that they could be executed in porcelain by Fritzsche, there followed a clock case with figures and elaborate decorations of his own invention. A curious order which had to be filled immediately after Christmas of 1727 was for porcelain masks glazed or unglazed. Shortly before his illness he was working on an elaborate clock case and had made the first sketches for a large washbasin, which was later molded by Fritzsche. Most of these works required the skill of an experienced sculptor who could create a harmonious appearance and could master the architectural elements of splendid clock cases and table centerpieces. The manufactory had employed no one of this stature before Kirchner, so it was depressing that the hopes of having found a useful designer for this purpose had been dashed.

In February, 1728, however, before Kirchner had been dismissed, a sculptor from a Dresden family of ivory carvers had offered his services. He was Johann Christoph Ludwig Lücke, born in 1703. He was extremely self-confident, having received a grant from the king to travel to Holland, England, and France in order to study the sculpture of those countries. In his letter of application he described his skills as an ivory and wood carver. He claimed to be able to model in clay and would therefore like "to be engaged at the manufactory, without taking Kirchner's place." In April, 1728, engaged surprisingly enough from the very start as a master sculptor, he began his guest performance: it was to end ignominiously after one year. He then left for North Germany and Denmark. His first successful work, which brought him a certain measure of fame, was not produced until 1750 in Vienna and 1752 in Fürstenberg. He appears to have been in England in 1760 and shortly afterward settled for a longer period in Dresden where he carried out his real métier of ivory carver. His wanderings ended in Danzig in 1780. His Meissen period was not blessed with success. His small output and the obvious lack of pleasure he found working there disappointed his employers far more than Kirchner's failure to master the technique. In September, 1728, only months after his engagement, they were already so dissatisfied with him that it took all his ingenuity to defend himself against the many criticisms leveled at him. He was accused of not being able to model in clay or to carve in wood. He could not even draw well enough, they said, to set down his designs, which anyway were often not even of his own invention. The modelers and embossers who were there to execute his designs expressed their scorn for the work of the *Herr Modellmeister*. Although he made an enthusiastic start on one project after another, and tried to make use of some of the sketches done on his travels, he could no longer be tolerated in such a position. He was informed that the manufactory would have to dispense with his services. We have a certain idea of what he produced in Meissen from the catalogue he made at the end of the year 1728 which comprises altogether forty-eight pieces.[37]

Thus Lücke's period of employment had no effect on future production in Meissen. His work was, however, valuable for its innovation and experimentation. Lücke received his requested honorable discharge and, much to his surprise, was allowed to retain his title as master sculptor at the Meissen manufactory. After Lücke's departure, Inspector Reinhardt was relieved when a model of a large clock case was received from an Augsburg merchant and new models and designs for many vessels from the Paris merchant Rudolphe le Maire, since this would tide them over until the hiring of a new sculptor.

In fact, negotiations had already been opened between Dresden and Weimar for the return of Kirchner to the Meissen manufactory. He was now married, had been working in Weimar, and was pursuing his real profession of sculptor. The building accounts for the ducal palace of the Belvedere show that he worked on relief portraits for the interior and exterior decoration of this palace. The Duke of Weimar was most unwilling to let him return to the Saxon court. Nevertheless, in 1730 Kirchner arrived in Meissen with family and household effects.[38] After a few problems had been dealt with, he appeared punctually on May 1, 1730, at his workbench in the *Weisse Stube* (white room) on the second floor of the Albrechtsburg, to start, with the best intentions, to carve models for relief decoration on tableware. According to a work report he designed thirty handles, finials, feet, and various relief ornaments. The salary he received at first was below that of his previous engagement. The honorarium for teaching the apprentices

was separately accounted for and could be paid only after he had given the agreed lessons. When he complained of these provisions, he was allowed a further five talers a month, but only in form of a bonus based on work done. He did not receive his contract for his second term of employment until fourteen months after it had begun. Not until Kaendler was engaged at Meissen a year later at a starting salary of 400 talers did Kirchner rightly complain to the court chancellery. Augustus the Strong then granted him a salary of 420 talers; this not only set him above Kaendler in earnings but also in status since he was in addition made master sculptor. He enjoyed this position for only two months, as the new arrangement came into effect only just before he finally left the manufactory in February, 1733.

From the spring of 1731 onward, as a result of a new scheme of a monumental nature, Kirchner's work was to clash with, indeed at times overlap, that of Johann Joachim Kaendler. We must examine the circumstances which led to this unique situation. The realization of a gigantic plan was the burning issue: the creation of a wonderful palace of porcelain, the likes of which would not be found anywhere else in the world. This idea had arisen when festivities for the electoral prince's marriage were being arranged. Work on the interior of the Dutch Palace had been held up for many years, however, and not until 1730 was it begun in earnest. Since 1727 the Dutch Palace, originally a three-winged building, had undergone a complete change. The central courtyard had been closed in by the building of a fourth wing, and the center emphasized by a dome. A consortium of the *Oberlandbauamt* (supreme building authority) including the most important court architects, Pöppelmann, Knöffel, Longuelune, and de

Bodt, was entrusted with these additions, and the individual parts of the building allotted according to the particular talents of each man. The overall effect of the resulting building is stately, but in relation to the Dresden style, too cold. Nevertheless, some elements of this Japanese Palace, as it was named after the change, such as the concave lines of the roofs and the chinoiserie sculpture of the inner court, are delightful clues to the eventual use to which the building was to be put. The interior, which was never completed, may be imagined to the smallest detail from the many drawings made by the architect Zacharias Longuelune. It was described by a contemporary of his, Johann Georg Keyssler, as follows: "The rooms on the first floor will be decorated with Chinese and Japanese porcelain. In the rooms of the second floor will be placed nothing but Meissen porcelain, and the first room will contain all kinds of native and foreign birds and animals in their natural size and their natural colors. The pieces that are already finished cannot be admired enough for their art and beauty. However, so that the animal pieces will always remain rare and costly, their molds are to be broken. The second room is to be occupied by all kinds of porcelain of celadon color and gold, and the walls lined with mirrors and other ornaments. The third room will be furnished with yellow porcelain with gold decoration. The fourth is a hall where dark-blue porcelain decorated with gold will take its bow. The fifth room will have porcelain of a purple color."

The realization of this gigantic plan was to be achieved by two people of great accomplishment who had enough enthusiasm and logical foresight for the task to enable them to unite the innumerable decorative elements into a whole. The first was the architect Zacharias Longuelune, who had to adapt the supporting moldings and consoles for the porcelain to the different rooms and to fill them with vessels and figures according to the plan. The man of next importance was the one who could serve as liaison between the interior designer and the artistic director of the porcelain manufactory: this was the *Bettmeister*, the major-domo of the Dutch Palace, Martin Teuffert, who visited Chladni, the director of the Dresden branch, countless times, and often came personally to the Meissen manufactory to ensure that the work would be carried out according to his requirements, would be of perfect quality, and would be delivered on the appointed date. In spite of the ruthlessness his position required, he seems to have been such a friendly, helpful person that Inspector Reinhardt recommended he be given a complete coffee service as a token of appreciation.

The newly housed porcelain collection was to be divided into three sections:

1. The collection of Far Eastern imported ware, which was the largest collection of its kind at any European court;

2. Meissen porcelain in imitation of this, but also the new and original branch of animal sculpture;

3. Architectural porcelain and functional porcelain such as door frames and archways, altarpieces, a Glockenspiel (porcelain chimes), organ pipes, and sacred sculpture.

The Far Eastern exhibits were already at hand, whereas most of the Meissen pieces had not yet been made. Considerable reorganization was necessary to provide the facilities for the manufacture of these articles. The difficulties involved were greater than had previously been imagined. Höroldt, who was far from enthralled by the influx of sculptural work, offered no support. Nevertheless, the work continued. As the first step they began to make models of a considerable number of large and medium-sized animals, mainly birds. At the same time large quantities of complete sets of vases were produced, and an energetic attack was made on the monumental apostle figures that were to flank the altar. The finished pieces appeared in November, 1731.[39] They were mainly exotic and native animals. Models on which to base their designs were not hard to come by, for Dresden itself offered many possibilities, including the stuffed animals in the electoral collection and living specimens in the Zwinger. The aviaries at the hunting seat in Moritzburg and the abundant game in the extensive forests also helped. The records of traveling allowances state where the modelers made their initial sketches.[40]

Preparations for the monumental pieces had already begun during the last months of Kirchner's first stay in Meissen. It must be emphasized that Kirchner pioneered these new and technically extremely difficult pieces, but the silent contribution made by Obermeister Stöltzel, after his earlier setbacks in the face of Höroldt's constant bickering, must not be underestimated. In July, 1732, faults in the firing were noticed and thenceforth technical limitations were allowed for in the modeling;[41] this partly accounts for the unusual appearance of Kirchner's large pieces. This is, however, the reason in only a few cases. The fact that Kirchner's animals and also his Apostle figures differ so profoundly from Kaendler's in conception is due to the pessimistic inclinations of this often underestimated sculptor. Theatrical pathos was foreign to Kirchner. The dynamic quality which so spiritedly pervades Kaendler's work is not to be found in the other's creations. He produced a work which generally does not express movement but instead expresses the concentration of power shortly to be unleashed—the still before the storm, so to speak. In his figures of stationary animals, such as the cat preparing to spring, the bear licking itself, and the glowering fox, we see the moment of tenseness before attack. It is not hard to imagine, however, that such a conception of animal life did not correspond to the ideas of the person commissioning the work, hence the arguments and refusals and the accusations of incapability heaped upon the artist as a result of his work. The difference of interpretation between Kirchner and Kaendler is most evident in their treatment of the same subject, such as the monumental figure of St. Peter the Apostle. Whereas Kaendler shows him in an unengaging pose with the conventional expression of his time, Kirchner brings out what he feels to be the most important aspects in an interpretation of this Apostle and the traits of character that appealed to him personally: passion and defiance. While the Peter figures represent a straightforward case of competition between them, there is a group of large animals which has generally been considered the joint work of these artists. Neither work reports nor stylistic points lend any support to this thesis.

Kaendler's arrival at the manufactory not only speeded up Kirchner's work but also changed his style. He was, after all, only twenty-five, and capable of change. Kaendler's amazing talent, his versatility, and the speed with which he developed an idea had the effect of shortening Kirchner's route from thought to sketch and of revealing to him new sides to his own artistic gifts. The Pietà group is a fine example of this. The fact that Kaendler later changed the rock base into a cloud (which, incidentally, did not improve the composition) gave rise to the opinion that this group, which people hesitated to ascribe to Kirchner on account of its harmonious proportions, represented the joint work of both sculptors. A work report of March, 1732, however, proves that Kirchner alone was responsible.[42] It must be concluded, therefore, that the co-employment of both sculptors was fruitful, especially for Kirchner who, at least at first, surprised everyone with a spurt of activity. Unfortunately he could not keep up Kaendler's pace. Consequently, at the beginning of 1733, the manufactory commission ordered that Kirchner be penalized with a decrease in salary. In a statement of January 19, 1733, Kirchner protested this harsh treatment. He made illness his excuse and also claimed that his ideas came much more quickly in the quiet of his home than in the hubbub of the manufactory. When his excuses were rejected, he asked to be relieved of his post, secretly hoping that he would nevertheless be kept on. In his letter of resignation he stated that he wanted to see something more of the world and perfect his craft in order to be able to serve the king better than before. All the same, he was dismissed at the beginning of March. It was agreed, however, after a reappraisal of the penalty that had caused him real hardship, to offer him some relief since he had to handle the final affairs of the Dresden studio of his cousin Johann Christian Kirchner, who had died suddenly. Four years later, in 1737, the commission once more allocated a piece of work to him.[43] It may be stated without any doubt that Kirchner played a considerable part in the success of large-scale works during the three years of his second period at Meissen. Work on the monumental animal sculptures must have been accelerated incredibly during the months that preceded Augustus the Strong's death. In a collection of bills for porcelain from the years 1725–1735, the value of the animals and birds delivered to the Dutch Palace is quoted as 10,134 talers and 20 groschen.

Although Kirchner's contribution to the artistic development of the manufactory's production should not be underestimated, the honor of having provided the style of European porcelain with an epoch-making breakthrough must go solely to Johann Joachim Kaendler who, after Kirchner's departure, inherited all the privileges and duties of his predecessor.

THE YEAR OF REFORM: 1731

In the long history of the Meissen porcelain manufactory, the year 1731 deserves a chapter to itself. The reason is its wealth of decisive events and the radical reform it witnessed, the beneficial effects of which continued to make themselves felt for decades. In that year the manufactory acquired the character by which it is still known.

Since the king was often away for months on end, the manufactory commission had to be headed by someone who would put the royal interests first when any major decision was to be made. Since 1729, this influential post of senior director had been occupied by the prime minister, Karl Heinrich Count von Hoym. He had been Saxon ambassador to the court of Versailles from 1725 to 1729 and was therefore closely acquainted with the state of affairs and commercial opportunities in France. A frequent visitor to his Dresden mansion in the Moritzstrasse was the Parisian businessman Rudolphe le Maire. On July 22, 1729, le Maire had concluded a favorable contract with the manufactory commission, according to which, against a monthly security of 1,000 talers, he was to take Meissen porcelain to France and Holland to sell on commission. He was always ready with immodest requests which even his patron, Count von Hoym, could not fulfill: he requested that white porcelain with Chinese marks be supplied him. Naturally enough, this could not be allowed and neither could he sell on commission in electoral Saxony or the other countries not specifically mentioned in the contract. There le Maire was trying, on the basis of his friendship with Hoym, to raise even higher his already considerable income. Owing to both his position and his connections with Versailles, Count von Hoym was able to inform the French court regularly about Saxony's political agreements with Austria and Prussia. This was discovered by the Viennese court in March, 1731. Since it was in Saxony's interest to appear obliging toward mighty Austria, the king had his prime minister placed under strict house arrest at his castle of Lichtenwalde until the end of the investigations. While his town residence in Dresden was being searched and many works of art confiscated, new and more serious charges were made that appeared well founded. A trivial incident accidentally brought to light curious irregularities. The Meissen castle garrison commander, Captain Schäffer, had reason to believe that firewood was being pilfered. He had the watch doubled at night. They captured not a wood thief but the maid of Manufactory Controller Nohr, who was standing with a box of white clay in the garden below the fortress. Secret dealings, which had been going on for weeks, led to the Palais Hoym in Dresden. Since Stöltzel had also been seen there on many occasions, he too, like Nohr, was immediately arrested. The real truth was never known, but various statements made and, above all, the fact that porcelain paste was found at the Palais surely indicate that Hoym and le Maire planned a betrayal of the arcanum to France. Stöltzel could not be proved an accomplice. The fact that he repeatedly visited the chief director of the manufactory, although this was not the proper way of going about his duties, could not be considered incriminating. A written explanation that Stöltzel sent to the king shows that Count von Hoym, who had not been told the arcanum, had exerted great pressure on the *Obermeister* to make him reveal the composition of the paste. Since Hoym was Stöltzel's supreme authority, the *Obermeister* had in his fear been compelled to cooperate but had given him a false recipe. In 1734, Hoym was taken to the fortress of Königstein, where, in 1736, he hanged himself in his cell. Le Maire, who had the audacity to ask for a renewal of contract in 1731, was deported. The business was then handled in part by the Parisian merchant Huet. Stöltzel remained in prison. His house was searched but no incriminating evidence found. Some notebooks, however, containing formulas for a paste and enamel colors caused the commission to order Stöltzel, Schuberth, and Hoppe to set down their knowledge, under military supervision, in the arcana books specially provided for this purpose. On April 12 they began their difficult and unusual task. On the twenty-seventh of the month the arcanist Schuberth was able to report that they had finished it. These books, bound in parchment and embossed in gold, are among the most precious of the Meissen Manufactory Archives. In spite of the similarity of their titles they differ from each other completely. Schuberth's information is set down clearly and logically. We cannot fail to notice his concern to produce an exhaustive report on the theory and practice of porcelain making. Hoppe's careful script reveals not only his way of writing but also that of his thinking. Stöltzel's contribution clearly shows the self-confidence he derived from his position. His information is by no means as thorough as that in his private arcana book dating

The fortress of Königstein

from 1723 to 1732. When the books were handed over to be examined in the *Nachtigallenstübgen* (*Nachtigall:* nightingale, *Stübgen:* little room), the strongroom for the safeguarding of the archives, the arcanists were given strict orders not to keep in their homes notes on experiments but to put them into the compartments in the secret cupboards reserved for the purpose. Since the commission thought it necessary to secure the arcanum for future craftsmen at the manufactory, it was decided to introduce a fourth man to its secrets. The only possible choice was, of course, Johann Gregorius Höroldt, who was acquainted with all practical aspects of production anyway.

On May 1, the king paid a visit to the manufactory, not with all his retinue but with only a few attendants. He carried out a brief inspection, and from May 19 took over the manufactory directorship personally. Stöltzel was set free, and the existing commission, which included Wichmannshausen, Pflugk, and Fleuter was reconstituted. The king's first act was to order that each manufactory employee be given individual instruction. One other matter which needed clarification: the sum demanded by the independent court painter, Johann Gregorius Höroldt, for his own work and for the running of his studio had risen sharply year by year until the manufactory commission could no longer tolerate it, so in February, 1731, Höroldt was asked for suggestions for a possible reorganization of the painting section. The commission hoped to merge his studio into the manufactory and employ the court painter on a permanent salaried basis. Höroldt responded with a long, carefully worded memorandum on February 24, 1731, which contained the following requests and recommendations. First, he emphasized that he had built up Meissen porcelain painting from almost nothing. With its twenty-five craftsmen and eleven apprentices the studio was an effective instrument in the manufactory's production, but ever-increasing demands necessitated expansion. He asked to be allowed to continue to engage and dismiss his own staff. Since the employment of experienced painters, such as those who had been working on Delft faience, had been a failure in many respects, he wanted to retrain people from other trades such as weavers, pursemakers, carpenters, and glovers, continuing a policy which had already been very successful. He suggested that the apprenticeship should last, as before, for six years. The apprentices could be used in actual production after a probationary period and would be paid only half the wages agreed upon for the journeymen.[44] The day's work was to begin not later than six a.m. and end at eight p.m. in the summer, and last from dawn to nine p.m. in the winter. No one was to travel or be absent from work without his permission. Spare-time work, with which the painters had supplemented their weekly wages, was to be strictly forbidden. Weekly wages, with a few exceptions, were to be abolished and replaced by piecework. The individual pieces of work were to be judged on a stricter basis, their value in wages being determined by him. In the case of bad pieces, corresponding reductions in earnings were to be made. A guaranteed wage was to be allowed for gilders, some of the blue enamel painters, certain apprentices (Löwenfinck and Eschenbach), and, above all, for his brother-in-law, Keil, who Höroldt claimed was clever and had learned quite a lot from him. Keil was to take over the supervision of the painting shop from the obstinate Augustin Dietze. He also suggested that the different groups of workers be split up, with blue underglaze painters, gilders, polishers, ground color painters, and enamel color painters each having a different room. The two additional rooms for this purpose were to be built in his residence, for he himself was thinking of moving. The rooms were to have new floors laid and be supplied with new lead glass windows. Sufficient furniture was also to be provided, and he was to be reimbursed for that which was already there, since it had been paid for out of his own purse. All in all he intended that these extensions of the manufactory should make a good impression when local or foreign people came to visit. As far as his personal conditions of employment were concerned, Höroldt suggested the following: a yearly salary amounting to 600 talers, plus free accommodation and heating, a completely free hand in matters of staffing, direct access to the court administration, admission to all parts of the manufactory, business trips to the places where the raw materials were obtained, a fixed sum for the acquisition of color and materials, and his own laboratory, which could be locked, within the painting workshop.

Höroldt's *Propositionen* did not lead to any definite decision. Clearly, the court painter intended to establish a hold over the entire manufactory. In the end he was provisionally engaged from March 1, with an annual salary of 600 talers and a fixed amount of firewood, in the capacity of technical artistic inspector. He succeeded in obtaining reimbursement for his expenses for colors,

gold, and tools and special remuneration for his personal artistic efforts. It was discovered that these additional concessions resulted in a net income for this cunning craftsman far in excess of 1,000 talers a year, so the king, after having the matter investigated, decided that Höroldt should receive only free accommodation and heating plus his expenses for essential business trips, in addition to his fixed salary of 1,000 talers and not a penny more. Payment of raw materials was to be effected by the manufactory treasurer. When Höroldt applied for reimbursement for furnishings he had bought for the painting shop he only received the secondhand value of the items. This he accepted. In any case he had met with remarkable success in his demands: besides an annual salary the likes of which had never been known at the manufactory, in June, 1731, he received the rank of court commissioner. His apartment in the electoral suite of the Albrechtsburg provided him, as highest-ranking employee, with a correspondingly distinguished setting. He had these reception rooms fitted with huge tiled stoves. Moreover, at his command the stone bench which ran all around the rooms and which, incidentally, had a constructional function in the architecture of these late Gothic vaulted halls, was removed in order to gain space for entertainment and banqueting. The cost of this operation, amounting to 375 talers 14 groschen 9 pfennig, was borne by the manufactory. On hearing of the matter, Augustus the Strong was less angered by the expense than by the outrageous damage done to the ancient building. Höroldt was at the height of his power, yet we can deduce from the terms of his contract that a further increase in power was to be withheld. The terms embraced the following points:

1. As inspector, Höroldt was to be responsible for all aspects of production.

2. He was to be first and foremost director of painting. He was responsible for the engagement and dismissal of those employed in his department.

3. He was to fix the contract terms for each new employee and these would subsequently be authorized by the manufactory commission.

4. He was to further technical and artistic developments in porcelain painting. A reliable record of experiment results was to be kept.

5. The scale of remuneration for painting was to be determined by him alone. The quality check on individual works was to be carried out by specialists named by him.

6. The unpainted porcelain needed by his department was to be delivered at all times without delay.

7. He was to undertake the supervision of the *Einbrenner* (the man in charge of the final firing). He was also to work toward improvements in matters of firing.

8. Spare-time work was strictly forbidden.

9. Höroldt was to be completely responsible for the resulting improvement of piecework.

10. Work he did on his own designs would continue to be paid for on a separate bill.

11. From June 1 of that year, Höroldt would have the status of arcanist and observe the relevant regulations.

12. In addition to his annual salary of 1,000 talers, he was given free accommodation, a quantity of firewood, traveling expenses, a retirement pension, and a pension for his widow.

In July, 1731, he had already taken action to see that the best-quality ingredients were supplied for his paints. The quality of underglaze painting, as we learn from Höroldt's *Propositionen*, had varied, even after 1723, when Köhler's recipe for blue was first used. So Höroldt, Fleuter, and Stöltzel set out for the mountains to examine the quality of the minerals *in situ*. Fleuter was included in the party because he was an equal match on legal points with the owners of the Weisse Erden Zeche St. Andreas in Schneeberg and also with the owners of the many cobalt mines, as well as being the only person authorized to conclude contracts without delay. The detailed report of the trip provides a vivid description of the state of the mineral sources and of the cunning dealings of the Schnorr heirs, who were represented by the executor of the Schnorr and Fischer families, Nikolaus Biel. The visit by the factory representative obtained results which even the liveliest correspondence could not have brought about. It was arranged that the dilapidated mining installation would be improved, that the washed china clay would remain constant, and that a favorable price for transportation would be worked out with the carters themselves. More than anything else, however, their surprise visit was a nasty lesson to the obstinate Schnorr family, who were occasionally tempted to sell china clay abroad. After ten days' absence the three gentlemen were able to ride home, their saddlebags full of cobalt ore samples, entirely satisfied with their work.

The protection of the arcanum continued to be a major concern of the administration, although since 1719 Meissen had not been the only possessor of the secret. In 1731, the commission was faced with the serious question of how many people could be admitted to the secret without endangering it. This dilemma was occasioned by the proposal to engage a number of scientists, who would necessarily have to know it, for the study of health problems involved in work at the kilns. The health of the compounders Hoppe and Schuberth was so poor that their life expectancy was not great. For the moment, however, only Höroldt was allowed access to the secrets, and the idea of including anyone else was rejected. Not until after the death of Hoppe at the end of 1731 and of Schuberth one year later did they take the inadequate step of appointing Dr. Petzsch, a Meissen physician, as both technical and scientific adviser to the factory. In a neat and minute script he filled page after page with his recipes. The old hands, however, noticed a measure of uncertainty on his part during firing inspections, and as far as artistic judgment was concerned he showed himself a complete ignoramus when, as Wildenstein humorously recounts, he took a camel deformed during firing for a crocodile. Höroldt was, of course, pleased to incorporate people with no particular ambition into his team of workers.

As a further precaution in the protection of the arcanum, an eye was kept on the illegitimate arcanists. Reports in the manufactory archives refer to the misdeeds of the Mehlhorn clan, of "Doctor" Meerheim and his son, and of the laboratory assistants Donner, Rothe, Christiani, and their cronies. Mention of them takes up considerable space in the Meissen archives, for they sent the manufactory lengthy memorandums for the improvement and better use of the arcanum.

When they cunningly hinted at their alleged possession of secret knowledge, their silence would sometimes be bought for considerable sums. In this way Gottfried Meerheim, Conrad Christoph Hunger, and the Mehlhorn family regularly, and for many years, drew pensions which equaled the salaries of master craftsmen, and for which they were required to offer no services except those of keeping their recipes to themselves and not leaving the country. The year of reform, 1731, saw a breaking of their stranglehold when Stöltzel persuaded the court commissioner to order the above-mentioned "arcanists" to give concrete evidence of their claims in the form of the submitted results of their experiments. This meant an additional task for the already busy *Obermeister*, but it offered the chance of bringing the whole matter into the open and, should the investigation prove negative, would permit them to dispense with agreements of this nature. In some rare cases, however, the manufactory

benefited from the activity of outside arcanists. When J. G. Mehlhorn senior, working on the problems of achieving perfect underglaze painting, produced stunning results, this competition had the effect of spurring the manufactory on in its own efforts. In any case the meddlings of outside arcanists caused no real damage other than financial loss. Concern for the secrecy of the arcanum was soon an anachronism.

The king's exorbitant wishes for an inestimable amount of monumental pieces necessitated expansion of the manufactory. First and foremost this meant construction of new kilns, rearrangement of rooms for the paste compounding, and a considerable enlargement of the fuel yards. The idea of building a timber escalator from the landing place of the timber rafts directly into the castle precincts was conceived by Stöltzel and all its technical details worked out by the civil engineer Simon. Since all these plans meant a considerable attack on the structure of the Albrechtsburg, Simon and the manufactory management felt that they could not begin without first consulting an expert. They sent for the famous Dresden master, George Bähr, builder of the Dresden Frauenkirche, and Fehre, the Dresden master mason, so that they could get competent opinions on the subject of the necessary extensions to the building. The manufactory commission agreed with the king that the ancient castle of the Saxon margraves should in all circumstances be preserved in its architectural originality. This feeling of respect for the monument was preserved throughout the entire 150 years that the Albrechtsburg housed Europe's oldest porcelain manufactory.

Before extension was embarked upon, complete relocation of the manufactory was considered. It was hoped to convert the ruins of the ecclesiastical foundation of the Holy Cross, which lay about a mile downriver from Meissen, into a factory which would eventually allow room for further expansion. The weight of arguments to the contrary, however, soon defeated this plan. A start was now made on filling the space between the Albrechtsburg and the so-called *Kornhaus* (storehouse) with technical buildings. A larger kiln house with two *Verglühöfen* and one *Gutbrandofen*, a workshop for the throwers, a laboratory for the arcanists, and an apartment for Richter, the manufactory's regular mechanic, were to be erected as soon as possible. Richter, who was also authorized to undertake the complete renewal of fire-fighting equipment, purchased a large fire engine with pump made at the bronze foundry of Wedel in Dresden. He built a turner's wheel and must also have constructed the second crusher so urgently requested by *Obermeister* Stöltzel. In spite of the manufactory's ever-increasing operating expenses, in spite of questionable investments and, above all, in spite of the fact that in 1731 porcelain to the value of 31,286 talers had to be delivered to the court without payment, the net profit of that year amounted to more than 16,000 talers. Measured against the purchasing power of the taler, this was a princely sum; measured against the extravagance of Augustus the Strong, it was but a drop in the ocean. The workers' efforts reflected in these figures can only be described as tremendous.

The manufactory's balance of payment figures between 1720 and 1731 impressively show the steep rise in profits during the ten years of Höroldt's management:

1720	Income	9,694 talers	Expenses	9,560 talers
1726	Income	23,463 talers	Expenses	17,451 talers
1730	Income	25,930 talers	Expenses	21,363 talers
1731	Income	43,952 talers	Expenses	27,890 talers

Business with the Residenz was very lively of course. A second permanent branch was established before the end of 1731 in Warsaw, but the place where continual and successful selling and advertising was done still remained the Leipzig Fair. Here, too, there was a considerable increase in turnover during the reform year:

The New Year's Fair brought	264 talers	6 groschen
The Easter Fair brought	3,306 talers	12 groschen
The Michaelmas Fair brought	3,498 talers	21 groschen

The number of active employees is quoted as eighty-six in the staff list of 1731. If we include their dependents, this meant an increase in population of 264 people for the town of Meissen.

The attitude of the townspeople of Meissen and their council toward the *"Porzelliner"* was by no means overflowing with goodwill. The employees of the Meissen manufactory were rated socially higher than ordinary citizens and were exempted not only from the meat tax, but also from the bridge toll. The manufactory was a social and economic imposition, a source of jealousy and envy.

To lighten the burden of the porcelain worker's working day, which was really quite arduous, a longer midday break was allowed in 1731, so that they could partake of a warm meal in the castle precincts or at their homes in town.

Thus we see that no aspect of factory life remained untouched by the reforms of 1731. For its day the manufactory was a shining example of a modern progressive enterprise. Now that it was self-sufficient, it benefited the balance of payments of the feudal state of Saxony. It had also been recognized that improvements to the financial and social standing of employees paid off in production terms and it must be repeated that in that year, which saw only the beginning of technical improvements, the achievements of the eighty-six employees were gigantic.

The work of one hitherto unknown sculptor completely astounds us with its wealth, power, and audacity—the astonishing pieces executed between June 22, 1731, and the end of that year by the young Johann Joachim Kaendler. Born the son of the pastor of Fischbach near Arnsdorf on June 15, 1706,[45] Kaendler was introduced at a very early age by his father to the world of ancient mythology. This stimulus to his imagination, together with a great store of general knowledge, direct observation of nature, and manual dexterity all provided an ideal foundation for his work. When Kaendler expressed the desire to become a sculptor he met with no parental opposition. Indeed, his father apprenticed him to the famous Dresden court sculptor and owner of an extremely busy altar-piece carving workshop, Benjamin Thomä, also a pastor's son. It is also probable that Pastor Kaendler remembered that his forebears had been stone masons in the Vogtland. Kaendler's period of apprenticeship evidently passed quickly and successfully. He soon showed such an unusually lively power of interpretation and technical skill that he was entrusted with independent work much earlier than his fellow apprentices, who included, by the way, Gottfried Knöffler of later fame. The task of furnishing the royal treasury (*Grünes Gewölbe*) with console tables, mirror frames, frames of showcases, and coats of arms was allotted to Thömä's workshop because of the amount of carving involved, and a large part of this fell to the young Kaendler.[46]

This young craftsman's swift yet careful manner of working must have often been observed by Augustus the Strong on his visits. Without the usual inquiries and formalities, he brought the hopeful young sculptor to Meissen. Kaendler's interpretations of heraldic beasts showed so much elegance and vitality that the king could not desire a better artist for the design of his monumental porcelain. Not once do we hear Kaendler complain, as Kirchner did at the beginning of his employment, that he was not used to modeling in clay, that he could not deal simultaneously with artistic and technical problems, that he could not tie himself to fixed working hours or permit the molders to watch him at work. The first major work that Kaendler undertook with élan and joyous boldness was the large eagle with spread wings, which breaks away from the traditional form of heraldry.

It is easy to understand why Höroldt, who according to the rules should have had right of approval over all new engagements, viewed the sudden arrival of an independent artist ten years his junior with suspicion. He must have scented the competition, which was bound to present him with many problems as far as design was concerned. He therefore engineered the speedy engagement of another sculptor, Carl Friedrich Lücke from Dresden, who was assigned the task of designing tableware, as an ally against the ambitious young newcomer. Kaendler, however, was completely absorbed, after making the appropriate studies from life, in the modeling of a *Fischadler* (osprey), a white-tailed eagle swallowing its prey, an owl, a monkey eating fruit, a water hen, and the monumental group of a bison and a wild boar locked in battle. Probably, he had also already made, as the first of the figures for the porcelain altar in the Japanese Palace, an early version of St. Peter the Apostle. In September, 1731, Kaendler received a command from the court chancellery to sketch the king on horseback on three consecutive days in the Dresden stables, indicating that an equestrian statue of Augustus the Strong was planned. Kaendler was by no means employed as Kirchner's assistant, nor were joint works expected from the two artists. Each was to work independently of the other, even when both had to treat similar subjects within the framework of a larger plan. The two never undertook study trips together to Dresden or Moritzburg. In the manufactory itself their places of work lay apart. Kirchner worked in his room sectioned off from the throwers' hall, and Kaendler received the so-called modelers' room on the third floor of the castle in order to work undisturbed. When this was stated by the manufactory inspector in his report of June, 1731, the question of Kaendler's remuneration had not been settled. Kaendler had asked for an annual salary of 400 talers. Since Kirchner, however, who still had the rank of a *Modellmeister*, received only 300 talers, Kaendler could only be awarded 300 talers officially and the remaining 100 talers were paid through Chladni from the funds of the Dresden branch. Of course Kirchner discovered this secret relegation of his work and was justifiably outraged. He did not attack Kaendler, but his attitude toward him became, understandably enough, distinctly cool. Kaendler, for his part, soon realized that the unhindered pursuit of his career depended less on a good relationship with his fellow artists than with the technical and administrative employees. It was essential for him to be friendly with Stöltzel, for the quality of modeling clay, especially of the paste for monumental sculpture, was crucial in large works. Neither could he dispense with the help of the molders Krumbholtz and Lohse, or that of the modeler George Fritzsche. During his forty-four years' employment with the manufactory, Kaendler, who was from the start socially superior to most of the employees, always found the right approach for profitable cooperation based on mutual respect and sympathy. His bearing compared favorably with that of Höroldt and his friend Fleuter. Thus the future master of European porcelain was firmly rooted in the organization of the manufactory after only a few weeks, and as this memorable year in the manufactory's history drew to a close Johann Joachim Kaendler had fallen under the spell of porcelain with the same passionate enthusiasm as some of the oldest *Porzelliner*.

THE GREAT PERIOD OF MEISSEN PORCELAIN

The decade following the year 1731 was decisive for the maturing of European porcelain style. It also established the Meissen manufactory's world reputation. Everything that had been promised in the few months from June to December, 1731, was now fully realized. Indeed, the Meissen manufactory reached an artistic climax in this decade, never to be surpassed. Occasional later attainments of high standard were only a reflection of these brilliant years. The late Saxon society may be seen at its zenith in this decade. The last years of the reign of Augustus the Strong passed during a period of peace in Europe. The elector had indeed succeeded in establishing himself as an absolute ruler in Saxony, though the constitutional rights for the Estates still existed. In Poland Augustus had to be content with his title. Lavish display and extravagance increased. In 1728 the king of Prussia wrote of the Saxon court: "The magnificence here is so great that I believe it could not have been greater at the court of Louis XIV and, although I have only been here two days, I can truly say that I have never seen the likes of it." At the palaces of Dresden and Warsaw the king erected sumptuous and costly buildings, and his favorites followed suit. Artists with

Kaendler's silhouette,
c. 1740

new evocative names were kept busy; architecture, painting, and the applied arts achieved new heights, nor did music and poetry fail to join in this *concerto grosso*. Porcelain, most significantly Meissen porcelain with its crossed swords, played a major part in this upsurge, the flowering of Rococo.

To be sure, there were weightier manifestations of this artistic phenomenon: these had their roots not at the court but among the ordinary citizens. The inhabitants of Dresden built their magnificent protestant Frauenkirche, which once stood like a firm reprimand to Chiaveri's elegant Hofkirche (Catholic court church). In Leipzig the music of Bach resounded, and alongside the delicate stilted verse of the court a new, more virile, poetry was germinating. During these years the Saxon economy was able to revive and this was reflected in further achievements at the Meissen manufactory.

Augustus the Strong resigned himself to the fact that his captive alchemist, Johann Friedrich Böttger, was not able to produce the gold he had dreamed of. Contrary to every commercial necessity and all mercantile good sense, in the last years of his turbulent reign Augustus personally took over directorship of the manufactory and drained it of all it could offer technically and artistically in the fulfillment of his plans for the porcelain palace. Members of the administration were probably greatly puzzled when they received specifications from Teuffert, the court administrator of the Japanese Palace. Chladni and Höroldt must have viewed the decrease in salable porcelain for the benefit of special pieces for the court with great concern, calculating the consequent loss of profit. Production must have suffered repeated upheavals through sudden rearrangements in matters of staff, kiln space, and use of material. Discontent and a sudden welter of problems resulted. At times there was stagnation in production. In spite of all this the difficulties were not only overcome, but it was also seen that greater demands made on the staff brought incredible achievements on their part. Yet, although the vitality of Kaendler's work quickened the tempo of design at the manufactory, Höroldt applied the brakes to any excessive speed in production on the artistic-technical side. Between these two extremes were the employees, who were bound to wonder how such unusual demands could be made and how the corresponding technical difficulties could be surmounted. When Inspector Reinhardt recognized that they were moving toward an increased output and decided to support Kaendler's efforts, he had to pay dearly for his opinion. Stöltzel, who had learned caution from the failures of independent effort, seldom expressed an opinion. He did not always approve of Kaendler's optimistic plans for a new type of craftsmanship, but he openly despised Höroldt's conservatism. One of Böttger's first employees, with a good many years' experience behind him, he remained skeptically aloof from bitter arguments and until his death in 1737 remained the reliable expert in matters of the constantly guarded arcanum.

The peak of the manufactory's achievements in the fourth decade of the eighteenth century was by no means reached through the harmonious cooperation of all concerned, but in the tense and quarrelsome atmosphere of factory life. It did not, however, break into an open quarrel before the death of Augustus the Strong. The king's personal interest, which was demonstrated by his energetic intervention in the manufactory's difficulties, did not decrease during the last years. He made even more frequent appearances, often unannounced, in the Albrechtsburg to see that business was carried out properly or to check on the progress of the gigantic pieces he had ordered. The work of the triumvirate of the manufactory commission, which still consisted of Johann Georg von Wichmannshausen, Damian Pflugk, and Johann Friedrich Fleuter, was encouraged by him in every possible way. A directive for the manufactory commission which came into effect on May 19, 1731, fixed the number of inspections to be made and limited the functions of the commission members.[47] It is of major importance for the history of the Meissen Manufactory Archives that this directive contained detailed information about the storage, guarding, and use of the files. The commission also had to determine instructions for the employees and make decisions about applications to visit the manufactory, stating which sections could be seen by an applicant. Permission to visit could be granted only by the governor of Dresden, who at the time was Count Wackerbarth. Such visits were rarely allowed. Even when the king arrived with his retinue he was politely reminded of the dangers of showing his Porcellain Fabrique to unknown foreigners. The last thorough visit, which the king, accompanied by Counts Brühl and Looss, made on November 8, 1732, toured the painting department, the old and new kilns, and the large storeroom still in the course of construction in the great hall on the first floor. The king witnessed a

trial firing at one of the kilns. Presumably this reminded him of Böttger's first experiments and successes, for shortly afterward he ordered a new bust of himself in brown Böttger porcelain. He was never to see this, for he died in Warsaw on February 1, 1733.

In the first days of March, 1733, the manufactory inspector was informed that until he received further instructions he was to continue production as before. Meanwhile, the commission undertook an analysis of the state of the business. Chladni, director of the Dresden branch, was the first to be questioned. He sorted out the unpaid bills for the porcelain delivered to Augustus the Strong from the Dresden branch during the period 1725 to 1733 and arrived at the astronomical sum 47,926 talers. The report on the state of the manufactory was presented to the privy council on April 28, 1733. The following subjects were mentioned: the staff employed at the time; the output of the manufactory; the extension of the market (especially to the Orient); reliable customers; the actual state of the finances (12,900 talers); the new conditions of employment for all works employees; the not quite perfect quality of table porcelain (iron spots); a query about the marking of porcelain to be delivered to the court; the new storage room and its guardian (the clerk Heymann); the laying of cobblestones in the manufactory yard, which was still in progress and estimated to cost 170 talers; the firewood lift and its constructor (the Dresden engineer Johann Christian Simon, who most humbly requested an *ex gratia* payment of 100 talers); the effected dismissal of Kirchner and proposed dismissal of the sculptor Carl Friedrich Lücke; the quality of work done by the *Modellierer* Kaendler, who could easily do the work of the two previously mentioned; and finally the question as to whether the considerable quantity of *Delphter Guth* among Böttger's property should be broken and removed, since it took up a lot of useful space and anyway was not true porcelain. The new elector, Frederick Augustus, the king's successor, studied these points and commanded that the porcelain intended for the court be marked FA until further notice, for he had not yet been elected king of Poland.

Frederick Augustus II did not possess the vitality and energy of his father. He left the running of the country to the Counts Sulkowsky and Brühl, and when Brühl succeeded in having Sulkowsky removed the king fell entirely under Brühl's influence. Augustus the Strong's foreign policy had already seen to it that Saxony lost importance in the Empire. Now the country was to be completely eliminated as a contender in the power struggle among the German princes. There was initial success in the suppression of French influence in Poland and in this matter Saxony was able to use the rivalry between Russia and Austria against France and obtain their support for the Saxon claim to the Polish crown—not without, however, once more giving rise to Prussian suspicions. The Polish nobility who had elected the French candidate, Stanislas Leszczynski, were bribed to the tune of three million Polish guilders to act in favor of the Saxon candidate after all. The War of the Polish Succession followed,

Stanislas lost, and he fled to the protection of his father-in-law, the French king, Louis XV.[48] To secure its authority in Poland, Saxony badly needed a land link, since Prussian or Austrian territory lay between the two countries. Saxony's aim in the 1740 war initiated by Frederick II of Prussia was to obtain this land link, but she thereby lost the Polish crown and with it all hopes of regaining her former political position in the Empire. In spite of all the suffering and deprivation left by the wars in the territory of Frederick Augustus II, he and his court resumed their extravagant way of life.

Frederick Augustus II (as king of Poland Augustus III) was an enthusiastic collector of Italian High Baroque and Dutch genre paintings; he was interested in the establishment of the Dresden opera and considered no sum too high if it were spent on a magnificent production. The cost of mounting one performance of *Solimanno* by Hasse was the same as that for building the Dresden Frauenkirche, a round 100,000 talers. He had not inherited his father's *"Porzellankrankheit"* (porcelain disease), but he respected Augustus' ambitious plans for the Japanese Palace and ordered the work on it to continue. Indeed, this work was speeded up so that the finishing touches, according to the plans of Zacharias Longuelune, could soon be made. It may nevertheless be assumed that this zealous behavior was suggested to the king by his favorite, Prime Minister Sulkowsky. It was Sulkowsky, too, who now had far-reaching influence on the direction of the manufactory's production. He initiated the development of the wealth of magnificent Meissen tableware. His desire to command respect by an extraordinary show of grandeur was, however, vehemently opposed by his enemy and rival, Count Heinrich von Brühl. After many years of

maneuvering for the king's favor, victory finally came in the spring of 1738 to von Brühl, who had now, moreover, replaced Sulkowsky as prime minister. In the same year Brühl was made supreme director of the Meissen manufactory.

The work commissioned for the Japanese Palace, the special requirements of Sulkowsky and Brühl, and the increased demands of the branch offices necessitated the utmost efforts be made by the craftsmen. Yet even during these busy years Kaendler managed to work out in detail the design of the monumental equestrian statue, the *Reiterdenkmal*, which was presented to the privy council on Brühl's recommendation. Although, to Höroldt's secret anger,

The Albrechtsburg and the timber lift

Kaendler took every opportunity of creating new and original works in porcelain, Höroldt did all he could to increase the production of salable ware, for he believed that a profitable undertaking would find greater favor with its owner than one which had to be subsidized. In this he was mistaken. Indeed, the extraordinary creations pleased the king most, for they added to the splendor of his court. The manufactory was expected to act not so much as a source of revenue as of fine artistic works. Saxony no longer had to import costly porcelain, and had indeed gained international prestige as the only country in Europe able to manufacture porcelain of excellent quality and in prodigious quantity. The manufactory extensions embarked upon after the reform of 1731 took about two years to complete. Engineer Simon, initially only called upon from time to time, was in 1732 engaged for building parts of the royal manufactory, and carried out with extraordinary devotion and consistency the many tasks allotted to him. At first he was adviser on all repair work affecting the basic structure of the Albrechtsburg. He always worked out the cost estimates and drawings in meticulous detail, purchased and allocated the finest materials, and supervised the preparations. The kiln house, built at a cost of 4,000 talers between the west wing of the Albrechtsburg and the Kornhaus, contained, apart from the arcanists, laboratories, the mechanics' workshop, and other important rooms, five *Gutbrandöfen* which came into use in November, 1733. The *"Holzmaschine"* (the lift from the landing stage where the timber rafts arrived) crossed the Leipziger Strasse directly to the castle hill and into the basement of the edifice. Its final cost was well under the original estimate of 892 talers, and savings on carting amounted to 286 talers per year. It had been in use since November,

1732. The necessary facilities for storing, preparing, and guarding the wood supplies on the Elbe were agreed upon by September, 1736. Several spacious sheds, a wall to protect the side from flooding and also to keep out thieves, and finally a cottage for the guardian were built. Since the two-kilometer pipeline from the *"Kynastgut"* (estate) was a considerable liability owing to rent and repair expenses and had to serve at the same time all the inhabitants of the castle precincts and cathedral square, a well was sunk in the castle garden in 1733.[49] It cost 28 talers 14 groschen. In 1737 a second well, serving the manufactory exclusively, was bored and walled on the slopes of the Meisa valley. The last project of the first great period of building was the renovation of the square between the cathedral, castle, and kiln house. In 1741 it was given the appearance it would retain until the nineteenth century. Between the Fürstenkapelle and the Kornhaus the manufactory yard was shut off by a high wall with two gatehouses.

While supplies of wood, after much hard bargaining, continued to arrive in sufficient quantity and on time during this decade, problems were encountered in the obtaining and above all in the quality of china clay from the St. Andreas mine. Secure in the knowledge that he owned the only practical source of china clay, Hans Enoch Schnorr conducted his affairs with such cunning that, in spite of being under suspicion of exporting clay abroad, he triumphed again and again. He demanded excessive payment, then delivered only how and when it suited him. He cheated on the weight, sending clay that was too damp or was impure. He was often late with deliveries and blamed this on the unreliability of the carters. Höroldt had to go to Schneeberg many times to put the manufactory's case to Schnorr and the Fischer heirs. So that they could threaten them with the use of other sources of supply, the commission had clay deposits from Grünhain, from Luppa near Oschatz, and from Schwarzenberg analyzed. The degree of impurity was too high, however, to make mining worthwhile. Stöltzel, who was best equipped to draw up a basis for these agreements owing to his long experience and daily handling of his material, was extremely reluctant to share his knowledge and, when he thought fit, dealt so independently that Höroldt's distrust was repeatedly aroused.

In the spring of 1735, Stöltzel secretly drew up plans for a subsidiary factory in Dresden. The so-called Falkenhof stood in a state of semiruin, having served for a time as a place for the Meerheims' experiments, near the Wilsdruffer gate on a level site between the Weisseritz and the Mühlgraben. Here Stöltzel intended to found a subsidiary of the manufactory capable of future expansion and which would have the advantage over the Albrechtsburg of an adequate source of power as well as easy access for transportation. He himself was to be in charge of the works, Johann George Heintze was to be in charge of painting and, if possible, Kaendler was to assume the position of *Modellmeister*. The administration and policy for development was to remain in the hands of the commission.

At first the commission did not take Stöltzel seriously. His proposals were taken for one of his habitual expressions of discontent. When he refused to admit defeat, however, he was seriously warned not to create further unrest. But Stöltzel then worked out the details of his plan with such precision and presented such weighty arguments in its favor that no further objections against a thorough investigation into it could be raised. Simon was asked to report on the condition of the Falkenhof and the cost of renovating it. He produced an estimate, purely for the building work, of approximately 20,000 talers. Based on the expectation of quick returns, such an outlay would not have been too high, but against the advantage of a higher degree of profitability over the Albrechtsburg premises, certain disadvantages had to be measured. Administration of the artistic-technical side, which had finally been united, would have to be split up once more. Moreover, the question remained as to which products should be made in which factory. Above all there was greater danger that the arcanum would be discovered at the Falkenhof. Stöltzel's argument that the rooms in the Albrechtsburg were inadequate for rapid expansion was met by the alternative suggestion of a rearrangement to make greater use of existing space. Finally, therefore, the project was rejected and Stöltzel was firmly told not to raise the matter again. Höroldt, who always tried to discourage initiative in his employees, was greatly relieved. He would tolerate nothing that threatened his own reputation, and in September, when the Meissen organ builder Johann Ernst Hähnel had completed the beautiful keyboard for the porcelain Glockenspiel in the Japanese Palace and had, moreover, submitted a plan for the construction of a potter's wheel on which oval shapes could be formed, Höroldt rejected it with the arrogant comment that he himself could construct one far better.

In spring, 1734, came the first bitter quarrels between the two groups that had arisen since Kaendler joined the manufactory. Höroldt's rejection of Hähnel's plan, although the model had proved functional, was only one of the many criticisms against the artistic and technical director. With blatant misuse of his powers, Höroldt held back the development of porcelain design. He considered that the production of large statues, all kinds of architectural elements for the Japanese Palace, the making of a Glockenspiel and an organ in porcelain, were pushing his own activity, painting, into the background. In addition—and he was undoubtedly right on this point—these time-consuming special items hindered the regular production of salable goods. His fears were justified insofar as the increasing use of relief ornament on tableware was making a free-painted decoration unnecessary. He argued that an item which had proved popular should continue to be produced in as large quantities and in as bright colors as possible. This corresponded with the views of Chladni, who was responsible for sales. Fleuter, Höroldt's closest friend, was naturally also on his side, although Fleuter had to play his cards carefully since the commission, to which he was secretary, was interested in the present state and possible development of the manufactory.

The mining officials von Wichmannshausen and Pflugk did not wholly concur with this reliance on traditional styles. As widely traveled men they were aware that an exporting concern run on mercantile principles must be sensitive to contemporary taste. Fashion trends, especially in the culture of the dining table, were determined by Paris. For a long time the French had favored accentuated relief decoration, and a large proportion of the manufactory's ware was exported to Western Europe. In addition there were the requirements of the court. These too had to be fulfilled despite any inconvenience to the normal running of the manufactory, and these wishes seemed to favor a wider variety of design in the sculptural rather than in the pictorial aspect. In the quarrels between the two groups we see the opposing points of view of the reactionary feudal aristocracy and the new elements brought in by the porcelain manufactory. In many cases Kaendler's complaints were either too general or were exaggerated and could not form the basis for a thorough investigation. Who could prove, for example, that Höroldt's management was responsible for an annual loss of 20,000 to 30,000 talers?

The only concrete complaint put forward was that Höroldt had directed that cracks which appeared during the firing of life-size figures were to be filled in with a mixture of resin, sawdust, and plaster of Paris and then painted over in lacquer colors. Wildenstein's uncovering of Höroldt's peculiarly dictatorial behavior, as well as his alleged neglect of duty, were not sufficient for an investigation. The accusations by Inspector Reinhardt again brought up the matter of Höroldt's illegal appropriation of Köhler's recipes. Furthermore, they stressed that Höroldt's instructions contributed directly to the spoiling of large figures. The painters' main objections concerned his fickle assessments of their efforts, the highly offensive manner in which Höroldt's brother-in-law, Keil, carried out his supervisory duties, and the inadequate training of the apprentices. All in all this thick volume of complaints presented a considerable embarrassment for the technical-artistic director. It could not be pushed aside since every worker was bound by his conditions of employment to report irregularities of any kind. What happened next was evidently the result of Fleuter's efforts. With Chladni's help, he had Inspector Reinhardt arrested on the ground of irregularities in the accounts and thus put out of harm's way. Reinhardt was subsequently able to prove that the accounts were in order but was not reinstated until four years later, in 1739, as inspector of the cobalt quarries in the Erzgebirge at an annual salary of 1,000 talers. For the time being, however, he had been rendered silent by his imprisonment, and Fleuter and Höroldt were jubilant that this most dangerous opponent had been silenced.

At Sulkowsky's command, the commission was now reconstituted for the examination of the "*Gravamina*" compiled against Höroldt. The *Geheimrat* Ernst Ferdinand von Erdmannsdorff was the chairman of these proceedings, and the *Justitien Rath* Johann Friedrich Henckel took over Fleuter's functions for the duration of the investigation. In this way a biased judgment which, at its most extreme, would have meant Kaendler's dismissal, was avoided. The commission did not see fit, however, to revoke Reinhardt's imprisonment. Neither did it give the defendants any opportunity to defend themselves point by point. On the contrary it dismissed the matter as trifling, maintaining that it could be set right by reorganization here and there.

Above all it cautioned Kaendler and the molders Geithner, Rehschuh, and Wildenstein. To prove that production was rising rather than falling, it had the director of the Dresden branch present the balance of the accounts for the few preceding years. There was a pleasing upward trend. The proceedings could therefore be terminated on an optimistic note. In a subsequent tour of the works, during which complete frankness on the part of the employees had been requested, the commission not surprisingly met with nothing but embarrassed silence on the part of the workers. Even Höroldt kept quiet, preferring to present his side of the argument some months later, in an equally lengthy statement in his defense. It was not until five years later that he tried in earnest to get his revenge for what had been done to him earlier. This time, however, in 1740, the supreme director, the almost omnipotent Prime Minister Count Brühl, responded personally. After a thorough inspection of the works, Brühl had certain of Kaendler's designs, which Höroldt had rejected for no good reason, carried out immediately. He then summoned Höroldt to his Dresden residence for a personal talk in which he made it clear that arrogance would not, in the future, be tolerated. The atmosphere in the manufactory grew calmer, and an equilibrium of powers was established.

Although Höroldt and Kaendler were never again involved in face-to-face controversies their secret rivalry did not cease. Höroldt repeatedly tried to use

his position to undermine Kaendler's instructions, to put business and technical difficulties in his way, or defeat him with petty bureaucratic matters. Their mutual dislike remained, and they avoided any kind of social intercourse. The rivalry of these two great craftsmen was less damaging to the manufactory than might be imagined. Each of them gave his utmost in order to make the best impression on the commission and the court. Höroldt reacted to the complaint that the quality of the painting had declined by imposing harsh discipline. In his list of February 18, 1734, are mentioned fourteen painters who had been found guilty of absence from work as well as of unevenly applied paint and who could therefore expect a deduction in wages. These included such well-known names as Friedrich August Zimmermann and Johann David Kretzschmar, the best painters in blue underglaze of the time, and even Johann Ehrenfried Stadler, whose independent spirit Höroldt tried to dampen.

In the same year the worst-paid workers, the wood choppers, made a demand for higher wages and when their mere pittance was not increased went on strike. Payment of outstanding wages was made but their other wishes were inadequately complied with. Nevertheless, the manufactory could not avoid a thorough reform of the wage scales. Surviving records show that the increases were based on information obtained by questioning individuals about their requirements. Kaendler, who up to this point was still receiving 400 talers, asked for double that amount, but his salary was only raised to 696 talers. The sculptor Eberlein, who worked completely independently and, in spite of his trouble, with great industry and originality and who was always eager to please, had until then received not one groschen more than the molder Wildenstein—only 144 talers a year. His modest request for 240 talers was granted. Ehder, who was occupied on the Swan Service for Count Brühl to the same extent as Eberlein, doing more or less independent modeling work, asked for an annual salary of 184 talers, since the sum of 112 talers which he had been receiving was by no means a just reward for his achievements. He received henceforth all of 180 talers which, compared with the painters' salaries, still seemed a very small sum: Wagner, the miniature painter, for example, had had an increase from 254 to 348 talers. Heintze, on the other hand, who was still being paid 313 talers in 1740, had his salary reduced by Höroldt to 288 talers. At all events it is very interesting to note that the opinion that painting should be valued much more highly than design obviously prevailed into the forties. It seems incredible that a craftsman such as Schlicke, one of Kaendler's most reliable molders, had his earnings raised to a mere 84 talers from 72 talers although his work constantly presented him with difficult problems.

In the course of the disagreements between Höroldt and Kaendler the matter of the inadequacies of the painting workshop was raised repeatedly. Höroldt should have dealt with the problem, but he avoided doing so. He preferred to draw attention to new colors and glazes he developed. He reported that he had invented a "pleasant-looking" yellow glaze, that he had improved the white glaze, and could now make wider use of the blue underglaze. Unfortunately, he claimed, the number of good painters at his disposal was too small and not in proportion to the many exacting commissions. The progress reports from Höroldt were not very impressive. His studio was well organized and carried out its task as well as it was able. If there were too few excellent painters among the others of average talents, it was a direct result of his own policy. The fact that painting played a smaller part than the development of form in porcelain during the years 1730 to 1741 rendered the former's stagnation less obvious. The various elements of decoration were executed by specialists in a deft manner, especially the painting of Kakiemon designs. It must be added that harbor scenes, landscapes, and battle paintings in this period reached the height of subtlety and harmony. They enjoyed great popularity with a public eager to buy. Skills learned in this particular type of painting prepared the way for development of Watteau painting.

In 1741, the painting team had increased to ninety, including thirty-one apprentices and three color chemists, but the newcomers included very few able to rise beyond average achievements. When those with talent realized that better-quality work would not bring them promotion, they tried later, when Europe had a number of similar factories, to find better situations elsewhere. In this way Meissen lost the brilliant battle scene and landscape painter Johann Balthasar Borrmann (1725–1784), who did excellent work in Berlin on the delightful service for Catherine II from 1761 onwards. Johann Benjamin Gerlach (1714–1786), a brilliant flower painter whose services were continually in demand since the invention of the *Deutsche Blume* (German flower) decoration, left in 1747 to become miniature painter to Frederick II of Prussia, worked in Vienna from 1758, a year later was in Neudeck (Nymphenburg), and went to Ansbach two years later to devote himself to faience painting. Nevertheless, he was one of the rare artists who was later, in 1768, able to regain entry into the Meissen establishment. Another loss for Meissen was occasioned by the departure of Carl Wilhelm Böhme (1725–1795), who had earned himself a name as a specialist in *feine Figuren* but left for Berlin in 1761 and soon became court painter and royal supervisor of paintings there. An Augsburg painter, Johann Elias Heyde, who had been engaged by Höroldt in 1733, was evidently quite unable to endure the regimen in Meissen and returned without any explanation to his own town. It seems that painters engaged on superior work only remained in Meissen if Höroldt accorded them special fees and the necessary independence within their own special field.

With the 1731 reform, the separation in production of special commissions and ordinary ware grew wider. A difficult portrait painting was not ordered every day, but the studio had to be in a position to execute such a work as well as carry out its daily tasks. The bulk of production consisted of pieces with underglaze painting, since they were fired only twice and were executed by the cheapest labor. Disruption of this line of production meant a loss of income for the manufactory, yet it was this very line which was most subject to technical mishaps; the cobalt ores delivered were of inferior quality, or the glazing was not properly mixed, or the fire in the kilns adapted for the large statuary was much too *"flattricht"* (fluttery), to employ Stöltzel's colorful word. In April, 1733, a new white glaze had been discovered.[50] A leap forward was also made in blue underglaze painting and by the end of the forties the so-called *Zwiebelmuster* (onion pattern) based on certain Japanese examples had been developed. This had the advantage of being quickly executed and it possessed an astounding adaptability to any type or shape of vessel. It would be incorrect to name an "inventor" of this pattern since dependency on Far Eastern examples had been required by the court, as is shown by some very early pieces (*c.* 1728). The blue ware, in contrast to the tableware, which was painted in enamel colors, was often signed, since the success or failure of the color application depended on the firing. The underglaze painting was mainly executed by apprentices. According to the standard they achieved in this, Höroldt would decide which apprentices could be put on to colored painting. Each of them had to sign his work with the first letter of his surname. The letter *K* occurs very frequently, which shows that the blue underglaze painters Peter Kulmberger, Johann Paul Krause or Johann David Kretzschmar worked on the *Zwiebelmuster*. This pattern, developed from stylized peony flowers, very quickly and permanently replaced similar motifs from the Oriental store of decorative elements. It proved to be of lasting popularity and has been admired throughout the world to the present day. Underglaze painting was employed for European motifs much later than other techniques. Only after 1745, for example, did the *Deutsche blaue Blume* play a more important part in production.

Not every lover of Meissen porcelain wanted colored specimens. Certainly they were admired, but variety had been achieved in colors and was at last required of form also. An order by the chamberlain von Friesen for a service decorated purely with raised ornament came as early as 1731.[51] The execution of the work on this service presumably took a very long time, for in April and in September, 1736, Kaendler sculpted the plaster mold for a chocolate beaker and small bowl belonging to it after a Japanese model which bore a stylized flower motif. Although the decoration of the Friesen Service was to be based on Oriental designs, which would seem to be retrograde rather than progressive, it marks the beginning of a development in which modeling was to oust painting as chief decorative element. Although great demands were made of Kaendler to complete the large statues of animals for the Japanese Palace, he approached the problem of the plastic ornamentation of tableware with all imaginable keenness and an amazing thoroughness. He began in October, 1732, with a design for the huge handles of an ornamental vase, and he soon realized that the shaping of the simplest form of a vessel, a handle, a finial, or a spout should embody the inventiveness of the craftsman and the sculptor's feeling for style. His source of inspiration, as far as he had need of one, was Far Eastern porcelain or Southern

German or French silverware derived from the tectonic elements of the Renaissance. Kaendler was not, however, totally enveloped by one or the other of these. After a few years of experimentation with new material he developed completely new creations which are still admired today. Höroldt must have felt the chill wind of change when he saw the new forms porcelain was taking. The smooth, continuous surfaces were ruthlessly split up, the walls of the vessels were curved in and out, indented, or covered with relief ornament resembling basket weave. Free-representational painting was limited to reserves and was totally absent in some cases. Höroldt considered functional painting of relief ornament and the heightening by color of the projections and the hollows beneath his artistic vocation and he was in fact not so wrong in this. Kaendler was so intensively occupied with the task of designing vessels in the years 1732 to 1738 that he simply had to make time for his creations in plastic decoration. Both fields of artistic activity, however, were later to be united.

For the time being it was sufficient to satisfy the demands of an eager public and provide all kinds of cups, pots, and tureens with the *"rechtschaffen"* handle. This description of Kaendler's is to be interpreted literally; the vessel should be "right," *i.e.*, made to suit its function of containing food or drink, and all its features should make it easy to use. The shape dictated by this principle should in turn dictate the proportions and rhythm of the ornament. That the style of the time, Rococo, made lavish use of growing organic forms, and that Kaendler adapted this can be seen in every piece of the Swan Service. Before this style was to reach its zenith, intermediate stages were passed through. For a time the influence of silverware continued. It was not a rare event for

silver vessels to be sent to the manufactory with the request that they be imitated in porcelain. The bias in favor of porcelain as the most refined material still held sway. In 1734, Kaendler stated his principle that handles, finials, and so on should be designed so that the vessel could be easily grasped, but in the meantime he executed work to suit other people's wishes, which were far removed from such practical considerations and which left little scope for his own imagination—such as the two teapots in the shape of cock and hen. In March, 1735, the lion from the Sulkowsky coat of arms was first modeled to ornament a vessel. In October the first large commission came from Sulkowsky for a banqueting service. Preliminary work on this brought Kaendler into contact once more with his old teacher, the court sculptor Benjamin Thomä, who had been allotted the task of sketching designs for a large service after the elaborate kettles of the Augsburg silversmith Biller. Kaendler was to make models from these designs, that is, to carve the individual pieces in limewood. The basic form of these vessels, among which were a number of oval tureens, was octagonal, and handles, finials, and feet had to be richly decorated. The main motif was the one which appears again and again: a lion bearing a coat of arms. It sometimes sits disproportionately on a tureen lid, proudly drawing attention to its martial heraldry. This was certainly not Kaendler's idea and he cannot be held responsible for the vain fancies of an upstart. He must have found it tasteless that the various parts of the massive tureens, candelabra, and sauceboats bore too little relation to the whole, but, as we note in the curling feet, the handles in the form of old men's faces, and so on, they too had an independent existence. The overall effect of this, with the large amount of gilding that had been requested, does not show porcelain at its best.

The pieces commissioned in the second half of the year 1736 reflect the struggle between Sulkowsky and Brühl for the supreme position in the State. From August onward Brühl ordered a series of costly pieces in the form of candelabra, sweetmeat bowls, and tea caddies, culminating with an order for an elaborate washbasin. Sulkowsky, uneasy as a result of the originality and number of Brühl's commissions, doubled his own requests, which consisted principally of large caryatid candelabra. In response, Brühl had Kaendler complete a few designs for a completely new kind of table centerpiece, representing some park cottages lit from inside and a hunting party. The first designs were, however, set aside, since the king's up and coming favorite ordered a dinner service with plaited borders for his own use. Sulkowsky's commissions decreased. His last order came in November, 1737, for a large sweetmeat holder. Brühl's orders correspondingly increased.[52] His next idea was not a complete dinner service, but a table centerpiece. A good month later, however, Kaendler was summoned to the Palais Brühl for a discussion and asked to bring with him sample plates, for which he had already submitted the sketched designs. The plan for a large service, later to gain world fame under the name of the Swan Service, was to be carried out as soon as possible.

For three days Kaendler made drawings in the natural history collection of the royal palace of various rare shells in order to design the service more naturally. The attributes of water, shells and reeds, swans and herons, occur in relief on all the pieces in different combinations, but these applied ornaments are integrated with the shape of the vessel.[53] The body of the vessel is often in the form of a shell, an oyster, or a swan. Most imaginative of all, however, is the modeling of the feet, handles, and spouts. Kaendler describes some of the handles as follows: "...in the shape of a dolphin ... in the shape of a shell, out of which creeps a little snail ... like a coral segment ... the handle represents a merchild."

The populous world of water flowed with ideas that Kaendler could design harmoniously into the functional elements of a vessel. All the vessels he designed were stable and easy to use. Special comments on function, as found in his early reports, do not appear in those he wrote concerning his work on the Swan Service from December, 1737, to May, 1743. Yet this commission, comprising more than two thousand pieces, contained a number of functional items that had been thoroughly discussed with the French chef of the Brühl household, such as stands for serving oranges and other more exotic fruits, dishes for oysters and snails, containers for new spices, and other much larger dishes. The master appears to have welcomed all these problems as opportunities for interesting and entirely new designs. Although these completely new tasks certainly inspired Kaendler, the possibility of making figures was much more to his taste. We see in the variations of the handles and similar parts that the design of the vessel itself and all its functional parts brought to mind the flora and fauna of the sea.

In many cases these parts went beyond being merely functional and existed in their own right. Glaucus holding a shallow cup, the beautiful nereid carrying the shell, and many mythological groups crowning the tureens become independent works of art. In these efforts to transform a functional piece into the variable world of organic life, Kaendler shows himself a child of his times in the same way that Baroque architecture and its parkland setting interact so that the geometrical forces its strict logic into surrounding nature and the organic softens the architectural order. Kaendler succeeded in re-creating the spirit of his time in the new material, porcelain. The Swan Service has therefore become a unique example of how each epoch must find the material which expresses its spirit most sublimely. It would be an exaggeration to speak of a "porcelain era," but it may be concluded that the Rococo period would certainly be the poorer without porcelain and without the Swan Service in particular. The two thousand pieces of the Swan Service give a better insight into an epoch than all the store of mid-eighteenth-century porcelain figures. The artistic merit of this commission lies above all in the synthesis of overall design and sculpted parts — in the merging of the functional with the purely aesthetic. If Kaendler had done nothing else but design this service, it would have been the most challenging task ever achieved with European porcelain. The raison d'être of this most costly ensemble of pieces is the glorification of the owner, symbolizing his power and wealth. This unique service manifests the last great moments of feudalism in which the prime function of the artist was to give expression to an uninhibited pleasure in luxury and to underline absolute power. It is amazing that Kaendler completed this overwhelming task while applying himself to other demanding commissions. This would have been impossible, however, if not for the fact that he had built up in a short time a cooperative work team.

Kaendler's vitality assured the success of his designs, but the early death of the king gradually pushed completion of the Japanese Palace into the background. The last piece made for the palace was a porcelain Glockenspiel in 1736. In 1735, when Kaendler had obtained the services of the congenial Friedrich Eberlein, a revival of large sculpture occurred. In that year Kaendler modeled, for example, a cock pheasant and a hen with her chicks, a bittern, a guinea fowl, a crane, and a she-wolf with her cubs in actual size, and his *"Adjuvante,"* Eberlein, produced an owl seizing a pigeon, a he-goat, a sheep lying down, and a turkey. These statues, which were to be the last for the palace, were ready by the end of October. On the insistence of the interior designer, Zacharias Longuelune, a start was then made on some of the architectural elements in porcelain. Parts of chimneypieces and doorposts are mentioned in Eberlein's notes of 1736 and 1737, though these were later installed in Augustus III's favorite palace in Hubertusburg. Fortunately, however, an important work of Kaendler's, the porcelain Glockenspiel, was transported to Dresden by boat in December, 1736, under the personal supervision of the master, and assembled in the Japanese Palace under his guidance and that of the master organmaker Hähnel. Plans for fitting the palace with a mechanical Glockenspiel had been in existence since 1721. When efforts to tune the bells were somewhat successful, Hähnel made a start in 1736 on the construction of the mechanism in the form of a double manual; the case was first modeled in clay by Kaendler after a sketch by Longuelune, and was later built up by a carpenter. The task of carving the *"ornamenta"* was a long and arduous one for Kaendler and Eberlein. There were still, however, a few imperfections in the tuning, and their correction occupied Kaendler on occasional visits to Dresden during the first few months of 1737. Not until a year later was the seal of approval given by the master of the king's music, Pantaleon. He expressly praised the carefully thought out design and fine execution of the work, but was not at all satisfied with the tuning. He was especially disturbed by the lower notes. Höroldt's envious reaction to the Glockenspiel is interesting: he was very reluctant to put his signature to Hähnel's statement of working hours.

At the same time that the idea of building a Glockenspiel was conceived, the plan for an organ with porcelain pipes was considered. When the arcanists had given a positive answer to the court chancellery's inquiry as to whether this plan was technically possible, and Hähnel had estimated the cost at 460 talers, the production of fifty good pipes annually was authorized. Although we read repeatedly—for example at the end of 1732, in April, 1733, and finally in 1736—of the delivery of some organ pipes to the warehouse, there is no mention of a start being made on the assembly of these parts. This leads us to the conclusion that some of the ambitious plans for the fitting out of the Japanese Palace were abandoned in their early stages. Kaendler instinctively opposed any perceptible revision of gigantic projects. At every opportunity he tried to see that sculptural work was executed on a large scale. When the work on the large statues of animals drew to its end, he put forward the suggestion for a monumental equestrian statue. The Swan Service at least had the advantage of being a massive unified work in spite of all its embellishments; but he probably could have wished porcelain away at times, with the unlimited possibility of reproducing a subject by means of molds, with the restrictions enforced by its commercial aspect, its vulgar colorfulness, and indeed the whole factory with all its contradictory aims. It is therefore understandable that this descendant of stonemasons took on and carried out, in spite of considerable lack of time, several commissions for monumental tombs. These should not be overlooked, if only for the reason that sculpture similar to these is found in his work in porcelain. The figure of Time with the appropriate attributes, scythe and hour glass, appears in the memorial plaque carved in limewood for Pastor Malsius in Gröbern and in the stone memorial to Maria Rebekka Schlegel in the Meissen Town Museum. Kaendler created a dramatic and original memorial tablet in 1738, consisting of a rectangular inscription on a sarcophagus which jutted out at an angle from the rocks and vine branches flanked by Fate on the one side and Saturn on the other. Kaendler signed it. Also in the Meissen Municipal Museum is a Chronos column made for Herr and Frau Keil, conceived as a free-standing sculpture. It shows the ambiguous Chronos supporting the column of life with his right hand and attempting to break it with his left. Both monuments suggest Kaendler's familiarity with the evangelical rhetoric of his time, which is natural enough since he was a pastor's son. The influence of his work in porcelain after 1731 is evident in these large sculptures executed between 1738 and 1750. But just as we detect his penchant for large-scale works in his small creations, we are bound to notice the satisfaction which he took in the sculpting of large statues. More conventional than the above-mentioned memorials is the stately epitaph to the electoral prince's former major-domo, Count Alexander von Miltitz, in the church at Naustadt near Meissen. It has obviously been executed after an existing design, namely Richelieu's tomb in the Eglise de la Sorbonne in Paris, for apart from the traditional requisites—draped sarcophagus, figures of Faith and mourning Justice—it shows the dying man drawing his last breath, while on a background of drapery billowing up to the elaborate architrave a haloed angel points toward heaven. The conception is based on the principles of sweeping diagonal movement. But this work too, signed with Kaendler's full name and title of *Modellmeister* and executed in fine-grained sandstone, can be imagined as a glazed and painted table centerpiece in porcelain. Finally, mention must be made of a small limewood altarpiece which von Wichmannshausen, chairman of the commission for many years, presented to the church in Tauscha, of which he was patron. The figures of Love and Faith flanking the centerpiece were, according to the signatures, designed by Kaendler and executed by one of his carvers.

A considerable additional quantity of work is represented by his sculpture outside the range of his duties for the factory and gives rise to the impression that Kaendler was actually working in two different fields. We must not forget, however, that Kaendler's work in porcelain involved a wide range of varied tasks and the uniting of many dissimilar elements and that his experience with different materials during his apprenticeship had proved of great value to him. His versatility came to fruition in the richness of the countless groups and innumerable figures. There is hardly any theme to which his inexhaustible imagination did not give fresh and apt interpretation. We know from various work reports that he did not rely entirely on his powers of imagination but took advantage of every opportunity to study exhibits in the royal natural history collection, the cabinet of curiosities, the menagerie of the Jungfernbastei, and the aviaries at Moritzburg. In some cases there is evidence of his use of engraving and painting collections. His main aim was to create an impression of reality. His comments reveal that he knew how to express himself well verbally on many varied projects. His frequent contact with Weisse, a teacher of the Fürsten- und Landesschule St. Afra, who was a natural historian, mathematician, and musician, throws light on this gift and reveals the important place he gave to general knowledge as a source of his inspiration.

The transition from the huge Japanese Palace pieces of the early years to the small figures, which were to hold Kaendler under their spell until the end of his creative life, was effected through the sculpting of countless animals—small mammals, dogs, cats, squirrels, beasts of prey, mice, native songbirds, and the like. These were soon very popular and gave rise to many special commissions of

this nature, such as portraits of pug dogs. This was some three years after Kaendler's engagement at Meissen. In 1735, however, the production of figures began with the miniature representation of a Chinese couple, succeeded in 1736 by a number of Tyrolean musicians and Harlequin figures, by a peasant playing a zither, and a beggar woman with her lyre. One of the first small groups, a pair of rustic lovers, began a rich and varied tradition of small sculpture: the hand-kissing scene, the first court crinoline group, and the couple making music on the sofa already represent a remarkable climax in this the most charming and indeed most popular aspect of Kaendler's creativity. Here we see for the first time what porcelain could offer when held up as a mirror to the colorful life of that era. The question as to who was responsible for the countless ideas for the thousands of porcelain groups which were made in the eighteenth century in similar large quantities to the Tanagra figures, whether it was the persons who commissioned them or the artist himself, cannot easily be answered. It was the spirit of the times that produced this variety of pieces, and the previously mentioned supplies of engravings no doubt had their influence. Naturally, Kaendler was expected to produce original designs, for very seldom, according to the archives, did customers submit more than vague ideas. Kaendler probably knew how to convince an indecisive customer of the merits of a theme he happened to have in mind.

Apart from this development was the 1735 commission from the Roman Curia for the modeling of all twelve Apostles on as large a scale as possible. As the first series ever executed by Kaendler, this commission is not without interest, but in the individual figures, 42 centimeters high, we notice the strictly conventional interpretation laid down by the Vatican as far as pose, gesture, and dress are concerned. They bear a strong resemblance to Mattielli's work in Chiaveri's Hofkirche in Dresden.

A small statue which often appears as a key figure in the rich variety of small animals is the 40-centimeter-high Bologneser Hund which belongs to the large figure groups since it is almost life-size, yet in its entirely undramatic realism seems to be the origin of the scores of similarly sculpted animals. In addition its pose reminds one of the snarling Fu dogs of Far Eastern ceramics. It must be stressed, however, that in spite of the realism, Kaendler was able to interpret it, silky curls and all, in a Rococo manner. The fact that the material offered so many sculptural possibilities led Kaendler to the most daring experiments. He had not yet grasped the fact that the more complex a piece of ceramic work is, the more susceptible it is to damage during firing. Nevertheless, his understanding co-workers did their best to see that his figures would succeed. Only Inspector Höroldt repeatedly mentions, in his reports and complaints about Kaendler's independent way of going about things, the latter's failure to take into account the difficulties of the firing process. By resorting to all manner of official warnings and reprimands he tried to make him give up these "fripperies." But after a few mistakes Kaendler showed his ability to appreciate the technicalities and he learned how to compensate for distortions when making his figures. The designs for the bases of his bird statues, for example, are usually built up to support the body of the creature, adding a certain local color with the details of the bird's habitat and, not least, rounding off the composition to a pleasing compactness. No one else in the factory at this time had Kaendler's wealth of ideas. The master, unperturbed by occasional opposition, continued on his chosen path, and soon progressed from the animal kingdom to the colorful world of costume and social behavior.

An aftereffect of the 1731 African expedition initiated by Augustus the Strong is seen in the many figures and groups of foreign peoples, extremely naïve in their conception, resembling the grotesque hardstone figures made during the reign of Johann Georg III for his cabinet of curiosities. The progression to folklore, to the numerous costumed figures of musicians, at the market, or at the costumed court balls, seemed an entirely natural development. From these figures it was easy to take as subjects groups of craftsmen. Here Kaendler rendered true impressions, from miners to the humblest itinerant scissor sharpeners. He provided us with a rich store of material for the study of the development of costume or the dress of workingmen and for the study of tools and how they were used.

No less realistic are Kaendler's representations of the court's favorite pastime, the hunt. Here Kaendler could unite people and animals in groups full of movement. From 1739, complicated hunting groups are often mentioned in his journals, especially in the well-known *Taxa*, his own catalogue of his additional work from 1740 to 1746. These groups were executed with the utmost skill. The anatomically correct representation of man or beast presented him with as little difficulty as their personal characteristics or the convincing depiction of facial expressions and gestures. The compositional elements, particularly their interaction within a scene, were logically and skillfully developed. The son of Augustus the Strong was a fanatical devotee of hunting and even at table wanted to be reminded of its pleasures. Hence the countless groups and figures on this theme which were delivered to the royal court pantry in the 1740s. They decorated the long tables, with a large centerpiece dominating the scene. The military figures may be associated with the above-mentioned groups, although no series of these is mentioned in the work reports. Single soldiers, usually cavalrymen, were occasionally made.

A much greater role is played in Meissen porcelain by the grotesque figures of the Commedia dell'Arte. Although other themes had been commercial successes and attracted collectors, customers were even more eager to own the Italian Comedy figures, even the full set. Kaendler was acquainted with the characters: Isabella and Octavio, Lucinda and Pierrot, Lalagé and Mezzetino, Leda and Capitano Spavento, Donna Martina and the Doctor, Julia and Pantaloon, Columbine and Scaramouche, Corine and Anselmo. He had quite obviously based his models on Callot's engravings of the individual characters. To obtain further information about the costumes of the Italian Comedy characters, Kaendler referred to Watteau's paintings, but he let neither that artist nor Callot, nor Engelbrecht nor any of the others determine his own spirited interpretation. The way the Italian Comedy was played was usually adapted to the customs of the country where the company performed. This explains its popularity. It was in keeping with the spirit of the time to want to be reminded of happy hours by these small porcelain figures.

If a person did not want or could not afford the whole series, a pair from the group formed a satisfactory unit. In these pairs of figures, or *Gegnern* as Kaendler called them, he was faced with another artistic problem, to which he found a solution in hundreds of variations. He linked the gestures of a figure to those of its opposite number, but he took care that this movement outward turned in on itself again so that each figure had a unity of its own. The urge to own a complete set was not thereby diminished. Whether the Italian Comedy, the Monkey Band, or the Street Vendors, a series of twelve to twenty-four single figures always attained the level of a harmonious piece of music. Since the Italian Comedy figure of Harlequin in his diamond-patterned costume was especially popular, Kaendler modeled it in different grotesque postures and produced a considerable number of witty variations.

This paved the way for the true-to-life models of the two famous Saxon court jesters, the postmaster "Baron" Schmiedel and the master of the Company of Fools, the court jester, Joseph Fröhlich. There are two scaled-down

Title page from Kaendler's
Taxa

busts of them dating from 1737 and 1739, showing Schmiedel as a troubled melancholic and Fröhlich as a fearless skeptic. These show Kaendler at his best as a portraitist.[54] In the statuettes of Fröhlich dating from 1736, one of which shows him sitting like a head-nodding Buddha, although in his case he is not nodding but shaking his head from left to right in despair, Kaendler has caught and immortalized the rough features of the most famous of all Saxon court jesters. Some groups refer to actual incidents, such as the one showing Fröhlich and Schmiedel at the royal sleigh race, or the one showing the presentation of a mousetrap to Schmiedel. These groups date from 1741, a year which also saw the making of the Quack Doctor, or Market Crier, group and shortly afterward the Public Dentist group. Who is lurking behind the figures of the quack doctor but Fröhlich, who performed with the small Harlequin, Johann Christoph Kirsch, in many taverns.

Court life now dominated the entire range of small- and medium-sized figures and groups. The painters of ornament were now afforded the opportunities to work more intensely and independently. The richness which painted porcelain could attain is best illustrated by the crinoline groups, where the ladies' wide stiff skirts were painted with brocade-like flower arrangements on a yellow or black ground. The majority of these groups, inspired by the intoxicating, colorful social life of the aristocracy, are not intended as portraits of particular nobles and courtiers; they are generalizations aimed at showing joys and sorrows, usually of love-stricken young people. In rare cases they derive from Watteau's work, as Kaendler states in his reports. On his business visits to Dresden and Moritzburg, however, Kaendler was overwhelmed by teeming impressions of the colorful court life and was quickly able to capture and transfer them into his enchanting porcelain creations. His delight in telling a story finds expression in certain other groups of anecdotal content, which are also culturally and historically informative, as in the case of his ironic criticism of the excesses of fashion.[55] Kaendler sometimes used a figure from one mold in subsequent groups, making only minor changes in its appearance, an economical method which had already been practiced with success by the *"böotischen Koroplasten"* in their variations of the Tanagra figures. Sometimes he would put two simple groups together to create another scene with completely different content. An amusing example of this is the Group of Lawyers, which was merely intended as a general criticism of the loose morals of the time and by no means referred to a particular scandal at the Dresden court. [56] Similarly, the so-called Podagragruppe (*Podagra* = gout), which was for a long time thought to represent the aging Augustus the Strong comforted by his natural daughter Countess Orzselska, shows nothing more than an everyday family scene.[57]

From roughly 1740 onward, allegorical figures and groups were produced in increasing quantities, in many cases requiring complicated settings from ancient mythology. This vogue was no doubt sparked by Baroque park statuary. Symbolic representations of the season (showing how Kaendler follows in the Bernini-

Permoser tradition), the entourage of Neptune in his grottoes, the quarrels of the goddesses (this theme furnishing piquant parallels with the intrigues of court life), and most of all the amorous activities of Cupid were apparently adapted from corresponding sandstone sculpture and transformed with great success into Meissen porcelain. Add to these the additional charms of color. As long as the color followed Kaendler's recommendations and was as decorous as that of the Swan Service, the porcelain remained within its own bounds of good taste. The demands of the purchaser, however, often had to be taken into consideration. Figures often appear more exuberant than aesthetic. Yet the unity of style between the modeling and its color decoration was retained throughout the Rococo period. Seldom was there conflict between the color and movement of a piece.

As a boy, Kaendler had been introduced to the world of ancient mythology and was closely acquainted with the most intimate characteristics of the gods and goddesses. His naïve re-creations of the ancient legends burst with life. The ideas come so swiftly that the craftsman's hands, most certainly not slow at their work, must have found difficulty maintaining the pace. He therefore developed, with the aid of members of his studio, a method of producing speedy and successful work. He would prepare a sketch or model so that the movement, drapery, and facial expression were already determined, pass it on to Eberlein, Ehder, and later Reinicke for execution in wood, and then carefully go over it once more himself with the carving tool for the main purpose of heightening its expressiveness—before it was cut up for the molding of the separate parts. With the orders for porcelain rolling in, the studio craftsmen became more independent and responsible. The reports show that a large number of their pieces were their own original work. Kaendler was evidently free from professional jealousy and applauded his colleagues' artistic successes. One is constantly aware—at least until Acier's arrival—of the willing cooperation among all the employees in Kaendler's studio.

Many of the numerous god figures lent themselves well to artistic interpretation with their accompanying legends, deeds, and sufferings. These took the form of complicated "*Musenbergen*," which Kaendler built up in the style of the hillocks and grottoes peopled with statues to be found in famous parks and gardens. An ornate Apollo hillock, a cliff strewn with dead animals and human corpses as a drastic representation of the labors of Hercules, and similar table centerpieces, considerably laden and of immense dimensions, were made. At the same time we sense a certain coldness in Kaendler's allegorical pieces. We also feel his lack of inner involvement in some of his religious groups and figures, which were in greater demand with the increase of Catholic influence at the Saxon-Polish court. The large crucifixion group, carried out intermittently between 1741 and 1743, shows an admirable richness of expressive individual figures, but Kaendler did not succeed in uniting this wealth into a clear composition. Out of what seems like a confusion of actors on too small a stage rises the realistically conceived crucifix. In contrast to this, the 1743 Hubertus group commissioned by the king looks as if it were molded in one piece, and is a complete success, being well suited to the material in its filigree-like splendor of branch and foliage work. Despite a certain freedom of interpretation, we are aware of a relationship between this and Dürer's engravings of St. Eustace.[58]

The third and fourth pages from Kaendler's *Taxa*

Since these complicated pieces were additional to the ever-increasing orders pouring in for Kaendler, it is clear that his staff must also have worked on them or they would not have been possible. Kaendler organized his studio on entirely different lines from Höroldt's. Höroldt, who had been responsible for all artistic-technical aspects since 1731, never tried to understand the steps Kaendler took to obtain the maximum effort from his craftsmen in porcelain design; indeed, he may have made many attempts to defeat Kaendler in his objectives. Kaendler would engage only well-trained artistic and technical staff. Höroldt showed no understanding for this necessity and even complained about it in a letter to the highest authority, objecting to Kaendler's request that all who were willing to learn and gain experience should be given general artistic training. Although Kaendler approached the training problem in a generous way, he insisted on obedience to his personal authority in the carrying out of pieces destined for the market. Since he could not possibly supervise the many different pieces being made, he would place his staff according to their talents on unsupervised work. It sometimes happened, however, that a skilled Bossierer would be working on the application of decoration or shaping the handles of parts of services while an employee with the status of sculptor would be repairing figures for months on end, even though he was capable of more difficult tasks. Thus entries in the work records may sometimes lead to false conclusions. There is frequent mention of George Fritzsche, the experienced molder of Böttger's day, who was the bes substitute when Kirchner left and who received the same salary, 144 talers annually, as the sculptor Johann Friedrich Eberlein. Andreas Schiffer, Friedrich August Albrecht, Johann Georg Schlicke and the master's own brother, Christian Heinrich Kaendler (1711–1766), employed at the manufactory from November, 1733, first as Bossierer then as overseer of the *"Weissen Korps,"* whose job it was to look after the mold collection, were among the most reliable technical workers in Kaendler's studio. This was reflected in their salaries, which still were far lower than those of painters. Artistic work had to be done by specially trained craftsmen.

In 1734, Kaendler visited the studio of the French metal founder Vinache to personally engage a sculptor of remarkable ability, namely Johann Friedrich Eberlein, born in Dresden in 1696. Eberlein had presented himself to the commission with a claim that he had mastered the arts of drawing, molding, and modeling in lead, brass, and iron, and sculpting in marble and ivory, having worked on statues in the *"Grossen Garten."* He had made further studies during journeys to Northern Germany and England and gained experience from working on the copper-gilt equestrian statue of Augustus the Strong, so much so that he felt confident he would be able to work in the new material. Although Eberlein was ten years older than Kaendler, from the beginning of his employment in Meissen on April 18, 1735, he offered no objections to his subordinate position, cooperating on certain large animal statues, important pieces of the Swan Service, and on many figures and groups. The records he kept from May, 1735, to December, 1747, begin with the work he did on large and small birds, indicate his keen cooperation on the Swan Service and on the development of further tableware designs, and on the whole do not differ greatly from those of his master. The most important part of his work seems to have been on sculpted decorative elements of ceremonial tableware. The prolific *Modellmeister* must have valued Eberlein's willing and independent assistance greatly. The last report deals exclusively with work on figures. Eberlein's figures are essentially softer and more passive in their movements than those of Kaendler, and his faces are easily recognized by their narrowness and their slightly sloping eyes. But even Eberlein's zeal was not enough to meet the ever-increasing demands.

In October, 1739, Johann Gottlieb Ehder, born the son of a Leipzig stonemason in 1717, was engaged as a sculptor. His work consisted less of independent pieces than of the equally necessary modeling of the manifold additions to tableware. From the nature of his commissions, however, we can appreciate the immense dexterity and the reliability with which he carried out his work. In March, 1747, for example, he received an order for a watch case in openwork and decorated with all kinds of delicate ornaments. In May of the same year he did some remarkable work on a set of dentures.[59] Another of Kaendler's closest colleagues was Peter Reinicke, a sculptor born in 1715 in Danzig, who joined his studio on April 1, 1743, and quickly developed a talent for figure modeling. Kaendler could entrust him with almost all the figures from the numerous cycles such as the Italian Comedy, the Paris Street Cries, the *Nationalitäten*, the Exotic pieces, the Allegories, and the Continents, entirely confident in his ability to create them independently or touch up worn molds. In 1743 and 1767 Reinicke did considerable work on the two versions of the Monkey Band. The Apostle cycle and many busts created in the mid-1740s also passed through his busy hands. The fact that he took on particularly *"mühsam"* (laborious) work which demanded incredible patience and great skill is proved by the numerous orders for porcelain houses which he received from Count Brühl as well as from Knöffel, the chief architect.[60] These years saw a new sensation at the tables of the aristocracy, and most particularly at that of Count Brühl. Instead of candelabra stood splendid miniature porcelain buildings illuminated from within, sometimes in imitation of Dresden architecture. They were arranged in long streetlike rows. When he died Brühl possessed no fewer than sixty-seven such buildings. Such work, however, could be entrusted without reservation to Peter Reinicke. He died on May 2, 1768, at the age of fifty-three, after twenty-five years' service to the Meissen manufactory.

The year 1736 marked the final domination of sculptural design in the field of porcelain ornamentation. With the development of everyday tableware, the design department grew in size and importance. Some of the designs in tableware which, like the Sulkowsky and Swan Service, date from the 1735–1745 period deserve mention.

In the Swan Service there was not the smallest area left free for separate painted decoration. The plastic ornaments were spread over the entire surface of the vessels, and any further development in this direction appeared impossible. Nevertheless, the Vases of the Elements, designed by Kaendler as a gift from Augustus III to the French court, prove otherwise. The allegories of Fire, Water, Air, and Earth were designed in an artful mixture of low and high relief to suit the bulging shape of these massive pieces. Kaendler was attempting to go beyond the limits of the material's possibilities. These costly pieces were not intended for any kind of use but were valued, as Kirchner's grotesque vases once had been, as pure showpieces for the state rooms, where they would also offer the courtiers scenes from the world of ancient mythology interpreted in the bombastic contemporary manner. In the same year, 1739, a coffee service was made for the electress Maria Josepha; it was called the Schneeballblüten Service (*Schneeballblüten:* flower of the Japanese snowball tree) and was considered the most artistic Meissen service of the Rococo period. In the Swan Service all the ornamental elements, insofar as they had certain functions to perform, such as handles or feet, were entirely suited to their purpose; but in the Schneeballblüten Service the harmony between basic shape, function, and decoration was lost. The entire body of the pieces is evenly covered with small individually sculpted flowers. The overall impression made by the large sugar bowl from this set is pleasing in its serenity; an effect obtained by the methodical application of these tiny ornaments. Double rows of flowers that spiral around the body of the cream jug give a still tolerable effect, but the coffeepot has a handle in the form of a branch sprouting twigs with leaves, and songbirds emerge from the mass of flowers which encase the body of the piece, so that one hardly dares to touch it. The realism of individual decorative elements is so far removed from the conception of the decoration of the whole—not to mention its functional aspect—that now, although the high degree of craftsmanship cannot be disputed, the boundary between the extravagant and the absurd has been well and truly crossed.[61] The origin of this attempt to "naturalize" items of tableware lay in the custom dating from the Middle Ages of turning the feudal table, by means of the art of the court pantry, into a display of pomp. Stuffed pheasants or even peacocks, boars' heads with lemon slices in their mouths, artistically garnished vegetable dishes, and similar items were a feast for the eyes as well as the stomach. Naturally, there was a desire to make such a magnificent but short-lived display somewhat more permanent. Neither metal nor any other material had succeeded in even approaching the satisfactory fulfillment of this wish. Ceramic materials inspired by the works of Bernard Palissy, most particularly porcelain, first offered a satisfactory solution. From 1740 onward there is an increase in the number of Kaendler's reports referring to vessels and containers in naturalistic guise. There are butter dishes in the form of ducks, hens, and even snails; teapots in the form of fruits; drinking beakers shaped like lilies. The banquet services ordered by members of the court reveal a certain hesitancy on their part to follow the new fashions. The best example of the new style is the service made for the major-domo of the Brühl household, Count Hennicke. Here fruits, flowers, and small birds sculpted in the round are scattered over the pieces without any consideration for the basic shape.

The service for the Russian Generalissimo Hünnich shows excessive use of plastic ornament only in the table centerpiece. The other pieces show less of it, except for one fanciful spout: it is in the form of a nobleman's head, and the water spurts out of his three-cornered hat. A service made in 1741 for the archbishop-elector of Cologne, Clemens August, shows an intricate and fascinating interplay of painted and sculpted flowers. The putti which serve as finials can in some cases be ascribed to Eberlein. Quite naturally, this elimination of fixed and dominating decorative elements gives painting a new importance in the form of scattered flowers, fruits, and insects.

Modeling and painting meet each other, as it were, halfway. Whereas the plastic elements have eliminated the last remaining tectonic unity in their efforts to represent movement and resemble painting, the motifs of the painted decoration clearly aim at a three-dimensional effect, rejecting flatness in the light-and-shade handling of the fruits, flowers, and insects. The attempt to use both decorative techniques together in this manner was not always a complete success, but the confident pursuit of this genre went a long way toward solving the problem. All the same, subjects for imitation, taken around 1740 from the now more readily available natural history works with their numerous copper engravings, were still indispensable. On the advice of the king's agents for works of art in Paris, Amsterdam, and Frankfurt, as well as of Brühl's artistic expert, Count Hennicke, the commission ordered some copper engravings which could only have been intended as examples for the painters. In 1742 alone, the then supervisor of painting Johann George Heintze was provided with three bound illustrated works and no fewer than 314 loose copper engravings. Although the flowers illustrated in these *"Herbaria"*[62] were already arranged in arabesque-like ornamental fashion, they had to be rearranged to suit the various shapes of the vessels for which they were destined. Therefore the so-called "dry" Meissen flower had a predominantly stylized character for many years to come. As greater efforts were made to give all objects their natural appearance and correct proportions in relation to one another, and as colors began to be broken up into degrees of light and shade, giving birth to the so-called "shaded German flower," the stylistic unit of form and decoration was placed in the balance and a harmonious combination was not always achieved. Observation of the independent life of the vessel's painted decoration on the one hand and of its plastic ornamentation on the other led to the realization that aesthetic unity was endangered. In these years around 1745 there was an increase in the demand for simply shaped tableware decorated with views, battle scenes and, above all, with the popular Watteau paintings. The delicacy of these paintings was as impressive as the richness of their content. A discriminating public demanded ever more subtle brushwork, a still wider variety of subjects, and all kinds of time-consuming elaborations in the backgrounds of these landscape and genre paintings.

This could be done only by painters of long training and experience. Höroldt was forced to relax his principle and try to engage skilled miniature painters such as Wagner or Heinrici. These two were roughly the same age and nearly simultaneously obtained privileged positions in Höroldt's team of painters. Johann Jacob Wagner, who was born in Eisenach in 1710 and died on January 2, 1797, in Dresden, was engaged by the factory on March 11, 1739. He described himself as a *"Migniatur-Mahler"* and demanded, with Höroldt's support, special remuneration for his pieces. He was employed on a piecework basis and paid monthly on his engagement, in 1739 receiving 16 talers, for example, for a *tabatière* with portraits painted on it. By 1740 he was already receiving an annual salary of 348 talers. Johann Martin Heinrici, who was born the son of a Lindau surgeon in 1711 and died in Meissen on April 21, 1786, is also specifically called a miniature painter. He was employed by the factory from 1741 until his death, obtaining the rank of court painter in April, 1756. His remuneration of 300 talers (from 1743) was on a level with that of an inspector and acknowledged him as an expert in the field of refined taste. He is also mentioned as a color chemist, and his abilities in the application of gold and silver to porcelain were especially invoked in his request for a fixed salary.

In the first years of the Watteau groups shortly after 1740, an attempt was made to reproduce the colorfulness of Gobelin tapestry. The restrained brownish-green tones were a noble match for the surrounding gold lace decoration, which in its turn served as a link with the delicate outline of the most varied designs in tableware. These colorful executions were later often abandoned in favor of monochrome painting. The fresh color of the blue-green copper oxide was favored and, except for the flesh color of face and hands, was used in all its shades for robes, bushes, and trees. Finally the lacy background was simplified or disappeared completely as in the Gotzkowsky and Marseille designs; at the most it was replaced by arrangements of scattered flowers. Some scenes on plates may be traced to copper engravings but there are many which have no traceable precedents.

It has already been said that the nature of the plastic ornamentation could determine the nature of the painting. Therefore, it seems appropriate to describe some of the most important designs, especially since they are still produced today as typical traditional styles of Meissen porcelain. The basket-weave motif which, incidentally, goes a long way back in the history of ornament, appears in the so-called Ozier Pattern borders. The radial ribs dividing up the border later became spiral ribs, taking the name of *Neuozier*, the radially ribbed pattern now being termed *Altozier*. When the weave alternates at right angles and diagonally in the sections of the border, it is known as the *Alt-Neubrandenstein* pattern, because it was first ordered by the master of the royal household, Count

Brandenstein. There are rocaille and flower spray borders on the plates in the Gotzkowsky, Dulong, and Marseille patterns, playfully reaching out toward the center of the plates at intervals. Sometimes they overrun the entire surface of the pieces, as we have already noticed in the Swan Service. These new trends in decoration presented the painters with many difficult problems but led to a practically unlimited choice of original designs. The choice could not be wide enough, for the demand for Meissen products rose—since there was no competition worthy of mention—year by year during this period. The public demanded a product as near perfection as possible, so inspection of all pieces was essential, especially before they could be released for the final firing.

The impressed molders' marks had been in use since 1711 to facilitate control, and they had a certain similarity to the craftsmen's internal marks. Kaendler found them unsuitable and he asked the commission to replace them with molders' numbers. Although Höroldt objected, Kaendler's request was granted.

That the bulk production of so-called Turkish cups, exported in tens of thousands to the Balkans, could lead to careless work is proved by complaints from the dealers. These complaints were set down in great detail because the ten representatives of the Balkan market—the most famous of these being Athanas Manasses of Sofia, who bought Meissen products in bulk for many years, and his successor Cosman Demetri in Belgrade—quite rightly feared a decrease in their market.[63] Presumably Meissen had underestimated the traditional intuition of their Oriental customers for shortcomings in craftsmanship.

The numerous addresses of trade representatives regularly recorded from 1728 that much quality ware was also exported. The 1740 list mentions the

following places and some of the dealers: Amsterdam (Dulong); Augsburg, Berlin (Gotzkowsky); Breslau, Belgrade, Brunswick, Erfurt, Frankfurt-am-Main, Geneva, Hamburg, Hanover, Leipzig, London, Magdeburg, Marienberg, Macedonia, Paris (Huet); St. Petersburg, Peterwardein, Tockaj, Vienna, Warsaw (own warehouse), Wolfenbüttel, Zöblitz (five representatives, export to Bohemia). Since two to five representatives or correspondents were allotted to each place, it seems that sales had already reached remarkable heights in 1740. Thus a contract, delayed for a long time by the administration, was signed on July 17 with the Paris merchant Jean Huet for the delivery of porcelain to the value of 20,000 talers. This exceeded the unpaid deliveries to the king, which nevertheless amounted to 13,762 talers' worth for 1740, Count Brühl purchasing 13,151 talers' worth also. Measured against the balance of payments for the whole year (70,932 talers' income to 61,893 talers' expenditure) these sums seem extraordinarily high. These latter figures represent, however, the income and expenditure of the factory only, including the income of 26,807 talers from the Leipzig Fair. If the balance in favor from the previous year, the stock in hand and the not inconsiderable amounts outstanding are taken into consideration we arrive at assets to the value of 153,231 talers, compared with liabilities of 141,213 talers.

Apart from the porcelain he commandeered, in 1740 at the beginning of the War of the Austrian Succession and the First Silesian War the king extracted 68,713 talers in cash. Compared with the 100,000 talers he spent on a single opera performance, this sum seems small, but it shows that the manufactory was not only a status symbol but also a source of income for His Majesty. The net profit for 1740 was a mere 9,655 talers, but it showed that the Royal Porcelain Works was no lame-duck industry, as many other enterprises intended as profit-making ventures proved to be. There was satisfaction with this result, but no appreciation that behind this relatively small sum was the sweat, suffering, sometimes ruined health, and hidden deprivation on the part of the employees.

The yearly increase in sales was not only the consequence of greater demand, but resulted essentially from the perceptiveness and energetic dealing of the director of the Dresden branch, Samuel Chladni, who had almost fallen victim to a somewhat obscure intrigue at the time of the 1731 reform. His temporary transfer to the post of director of the royal salt refineries was canceled, however, when his substitute at the Dresden branch, one Otto, admitted after a time that he was not suited to the position. The branches in Dresden, Leipzig, and Warsaw had to offer a rich choice of ware. Their stock was constantly maintained at a level of 300,000 talers' worth of porcelain. The greatest sales were to be made at the three Leipzig Fairs, however, at New Year's, Easter, and Michaelmas. The value of sales effected in "Auerbachs Hof" was three times that of a month's business in all other places combined. Selling was not done in Meissen itself although there was an extensive and representative collection of porcelain which could be shown in the largest room of the Albrechtsburg. Presumably it was not thought desirable to attract any doubtful visitors who might have taken too close an interest in the arcanum. Kaendler succeeded in getting permission for *Brac*, deformed but usable porcelain, to be sold at low prices in a shed in front of the Kornhaus. Höroldt's father-in-law, Johann Gottfried Keil, innkeeper, shopkeeper, and Meissen councilor, wanted to take "*Mittelguth*" on commission for sale in his shop not far from the Elbe bridge. In addition the Meissen council requested the opening of a salesroom on the Jahrmarkt, the present-day Theaterplatz, since many prospective buyers congregated there. Both of these requests were shelved. This reluctance was occasioned by the continuing concern for the secrets of making porcelain, the firing processes, and the color compounding. Only those parts of the Albrechtsburg could be viewed that contained nothing pertaining to the arcanum. Foreign visitors to the town were very closely watched.

Until 1736, the Albrechtsburg had a military guard made up of members of a company of soldiers invalided from active service. However, the expansion of the factory, the increasing number of visitors and, above all, the possible means of access via the timber escalator necessitated a correspondingly strengthened guard which would command respect. On July 20, 1736, at about eight o'clock in the morning, the quaint old guard was unexpectedly relieved by a regular military unit from the Löwenthal regiment under strict command.

Auerbachs Hof during the Leipzig Fair

The arcanists objected to these surprise precautions and lodged a serious protest, for they interpreted this as an expression of mistrust. But the new commandant, a Lieutenant Pupelle, merely listened in arrogant silence and in the days that followed took unheard of liberties. Visitors were not merely accompanied to the doors of rooms they were free to visit but were followed inside. The soldiers aroused particular hostility because at the sounding of the tattoo they would extinguish the candles of the spare-time workers, who were then taken into custody. Thus the zeal of the guard was seen less as a protection for the factory than as an intrusion. Not until three months later were these excesses curbed by a new set of orders. Permission to visit the Albrechtsburg was very seldom granted, according to the regulations not more than ten times a month. The rooms that could be visited were clearly indicated on the visitor's pass. The nobles, foreign diplomats, scholars of international repute and, not least, the members of the House of Wettin itself were often interested in seeing the world-famous manufactory at work, but many were most certainly disappointed at only being allowed to see the stockroom. People who ordered large quantities of tableware, such as the master of the royal household, Brandenstein, or Baron Grossschlag, the electoral attaché of mines, made frequent visits to keep an eye on the progress of the commissions. Visitors' comments on the porcelain were seldom recorded, but Monsieur Siegel, master of the Danish royal pantry and a connoisseur of Chinese and Japanese porcelain, said that he had nowhere seen porcelain as beautiful as that made in Meissen.

In the spring of 1745, plans were embarked on for engaging a fully paid drawing master, so that the seventy apprentices could receive regular tutelage. In the recommendation, presumably submitted by Höroldt, it was demanded that the drawing master be an already well-known artist, that the apprentices receive six hours' daily instruction, and that painters who wished to qualify themselves further should be given the opportunity by special courses. Besides this—and it is important because by this method artistic development was not to come from within, but was decisively controlled from outside—the new drawing master was to classify the commissions and comment fully on the subject to those who had to decide on new designs. He was to be free to make any criticism of any of the factory's products and permitted to state his own price for the occasional pieces of porcelain he painted himself. For this extremely influential post the Dresden painter Carl Heinrich Jacob Fehling was chosen. He had gained a good reputation with his drawings of the great procession of miners in the *"Plauensche Grund"* in 1719. He was engaged at a salary of 400 talers on March 9, 1745, and, since he was no longer young, he was allotted an assistant, Augustin Hoffmann, with a salary of 200 talers. Their first task was to present their independent suggestions for the organization of the courses of instruction, which were to take place in Kaendler's house on the cathedral square, probably in a ground-floor room. In the meantime the number of students had risen to ninety. Fehling consequently recommended a maximum of one hundred apprentices and the division of classes into beginners and advanced pupils. Moreover, he asked for an additional consignment of copper engravings suited to the various stages of progress. The lessons were to be given to groups of fifteen, each lesson to last two hours. Individual progress was to be examined twice a year and outstanding effort rewarded with a prize. The recommendations were put into effect without delay. Numerous copper engravings were supplied and the groups arranged as agreed. The archives of the following year contain the lists of the outstanding, good, moderate, and also unsatisfactory pupils, together with comments on their behavior. Some apprentices had to be expelled for obvious incapability, sometimes on account of a *"blöden Gesichtes"* (literally, a stupid face) that is, an eye defect. Nothing is mentioned about the actual methods which were used, but it is assumed that they were only educated to imitate the work of others. This training was certainly thorough, but it was modest and narrow. Kaendler had envisaged a more general, humanistic, or at least more artistic approach.

The year 1740 saw the beginning of military action among the large absolutist states in Europe in the struggle for supremacy. Saxony was involved both through her geographical position and the treaties binding her at the time, but it was the corrupt aristocratic government and Brühl's contemptible policies which resulted in Saxony's political, economic, and military decay. She was only a pawn in the hands of the other contenders and emerged from the conflict in 1763 ruined and forever eliminated as a major power in German politics.

Seventeen hundred and forty had seen a change of ruler in both Berlin and Vienna. In Prussia Frederick II became absolute monarch, inheriting a nation that had been transformed into an efficient, highly organized military state. In contrast the succession of Maria Theresia was fraught with doubt and difficulty. Austrian absolutism was by no means so rooted and the throne was also claimed by the Bavarian elector. Frederick saw how he could take advantage of this dispute over the Austrian succession, thereby gaining territory at Austria's expense. In December, 1740, he attacked Silesia. Although Saxony was bound by treaty to Austria she sided with Prussia in the hope of gaining tracts of Bohemia and Silesia, thus establishing a land link with Poland. The war was to involve all Europe , turning not merely on the Austrian succession nor even on the rise of Prussia and her position relative to Austria in Germany, but on France's influence in Germany and on Franco-British relations. With the Peace of Breslau in 1743, Frederick succeeded in retaining Silesia but Saxony gained nothing. She changed sides, joining Austria, with the result that in 1744, when hostilities were resumed, Frederick marched into Saxon territory. In 1752, he made known in a "political testament" his intentions to enlarge Prussia by annexing parts of Saxony, among other areas. After the invasion, the Prussian king made his entry into Meissen: this was on August 19, 1744, and he inspected the manufactory with great interest. In the course of the war, Prussian troops were repulsed by Bohemia into Silesia, but in June, 1745, the great defeat of Austria and Saxony near Hohenfriedeberg occurred. In December, Saxony was the theater of war and Meissen was at the center of the action.

The commission was anxious to review the situation in November, 1745, for it seemed that the enemy would penetrate into the Dresden, Meissen, and Freiberg regions and force a decision. Besides, it feared that Frederick II's keen interest in Meissen porcelain would lead to the appropriation of the production secrets; consequently a full sitting was called for December 7. By that day Höroldt, Dr. Petzsch, Schertel, and Dr. Schatter, as arcanists; Keil and Lehmann, as color chemists; and Kaendler, as *Modellmeister*, had already traveled to Dresden under orders from the highest authority. On December 6 the commission again visited Meissen, where, after a tour of the factory, they dismissed but kept on full salary 286 workers and ordered the demolition of the enameling kilns, the dismantling of the grinding machines, and the hiding of pastes, glazes, and other materials. Finally, on December 7, all kilnmasters, compounders, and laboratory workers were transferred to Dresden.

On December 12, at about one o'clock in the afternoon, the vanguard of the Prussian troops, led by Count Leopold von Dessau, entered the town by way of the Fischergasse below the Albrechtsburg, arriving at the closed watergate. The town was surrendered without resistance and without conditions, although the Albrechtsburg and the Afranische Freiheit part of Meissen remained under the jurisdiction of the regional government. An envoy was sent to the fortress blindfolded and accompanied by a trumpeter. Its commandant, one Captain von Dost, had long departed together with his guard, so Fleuter surrendered the castle precincts without formality. The remaining factory officials, Inspector Auenmüller and the accountant Heymann, waited fearfully. Forty thousand Prussian troops streamed into the town. On December 14, the Prussian king made his headquarters the Roter Hirsch on the marketplace. Major General von Polentz issued orders from the king himself to the effect that the manufactory premises were not to be altered by anyone and stated that he was authorized to obtain certain porcelain items for His Majesty.

Since Polentz had to return to the front on December 14, he was relieved by the newly arrived general intendant of the royal palaces and gardens, Baron Georg Wenzeslaus von Knobelsdorff (1699–1753). In the freezing cold Heymann had to sort out, according to precise instructions from the baron, large quantities of porcelain, mainly tableware, make an inventory of them, and have them packed into fifty-two cases. This hard work came to an end on December 21. The next day a procession of Saxon carts set off with their fragile load along the wintry roads to Berlin, Charlottenburg, and Potsdam. Meanwhile, on December 15 the Austrians and Saxons had been annihilated at the bloody battle of Kesselsdorf west of Dresden. The so-called Porcelain Regiment of Wuthenow saw action at this battle. These were Saxon dragoons who had been purchased by King Frederick William I for forty-eight pieces of Ming porcelain. They fought on the Prussian side with ferocious animosity after the early part of the battle in which their former compatriots, initially victorious, deprived them of their kettledrums and flags. Within a few hours the Albrechtsburg had received 453 wounded. In spite of the thirty-man guard on the porcelain, officers and common soldiers forced their way into the storehouse and tried—threatening Heymann and his packer with sticks and drawn swords—to carry off pieces. Knobelsdorff had been empowered to make presents of porcelain, the quantity determined by rank, to the generals, to the counts Podewils, Lehwaldt, Stille, Kyaw, Gessler, and Rochow, and to Major von Aulock. These presents, too, were listed piece by piece and signed for by the recipients.

The requisitions had been registered to the last detail and counted in the peace negotiations as a valid contribution. Direct damage came about as a result of other factors, mainly the cessation of production for one month along with full payment of all salaries. The theft of firewood worth 9,042 talers was felt very keenly, and tedious discussions on replacement of or reimbursement for it took place the following year. In addition, materials such as timber, tools, nails, and rope, amounting to 544 talers, had been requisitioned. Finally, considerable repair work and cleaning would have to be done as a result of the Albrechtsburg's having been used as a hospital, and this, together with the reconstruction of the kilns and machines, meant extra work and required materials difficult to obtain. On January 7, work was started again. Three days later, Kaendler and the other arcanists were ordered back to Meissen. Amazingly enough, the first successful firing was recorded as early as the seventeenth of that month. Since the prepared pastes and color ingredients had been well hidden and the deliveries of fuel were soon back to normal, production was again running so smoothly that the commission decided to grant considerable wage increases to a large number of the workers. There were still many sick and wounded men in the town to be cared for and a Prussian relief detachment was not recalled until April, 1746. A consignment of porcelain was sent to the Easter Fair as usual, and the astounding recovery of the Meissen manufactory was reflected in a proud remark by Inspector Auenmüller.[64]

The balance for the year 1746 is brilliant proof of this statement: the assets carried over from the previous year, in spite of the war, amounted to 65,552 talers. Although the turnover for the first few months was very modest, the Easter Fair had already resulted in dealings worth 33,707 talers. The total income for this year amounted to 254,414 talers, the expenditure standing at 209,875 talers. Included in this expenditure total was the porcelain delivered to the royal court, royal pantry, etc., delivered gratis to the king at a value of 53,696 ta-

lers. Furthermore there were 35,895 talers paid in cash to the king. The expenses incurred by the three fairs in Leipzig which brought a total turnover of 64,532 talers seem very low, amounting to only 1,300 talers. Production costs, for February 2,861 talers, for December, however, 13,337 talers, nevertheless reached the total of 94,401 talers. This signifies an enormous collective achievement.

Various individuals were lost to the war. Not before March did Inspector Auenmüller, after careful inquiries, find that five men who disappeared had been pressed into Prussian military service and forced to leave the country. Four others had made use of the chaos to leave and try their luck elsewhere. At first there seemed no need to mourn their loss, but later messages were sent through relatives left behind in an attempt to win them back, as in the case of the mold carver Kayser, who fled to Berlin, a man dexterous in the assemblage and operation of machines. Christian Daniel Busch, an extremely skilled painter who had been employed since 1741, having absconded to Vienna, embarked on a restless, nomadic, yet ultimately successful career, of great benefit to himself and other parties, but highly damaging to Meissen.

The inventory of porcelain delivered to Frederick II shows the rise and fall in popularity of certain shapes and decorations. In tableware, pieces with the basketwork border and with applied flowers and openwork were particularly admired, a clear indication that large, rounded-off compositions were being abandoned in favor of playfully scattered decorative motifs. The amount of chinoiserie in the pattern decoration is rather small and reflects the decline of the Chinese fashion in the 1740s. Thus *"kleine indianische Bluhmen"* are only found once; *"grosse indianische Bluhmen"* three times; *"japanische Figuren"* only three times; whereas *"Teutsche Bluhmen,"* the so-called German dry flowers, occur twenty-three times; landscapes thirteen times; battles eight times; shaded naturalistic flowers eleven times; and colored Watteau groups four times. In references to underglaze painting the term *"blaue Teutsche Bluhme"* (blue German flower) is mentioned. The craze for the simple life, the pastoral, the quaint, is noticeable in the small porcelain sculptures. Very popular were the craftsmen, gardener, and vintager statuettes and the innumerable medium-sized and small birds, not correct, however, in every zoological detail. Ancient mythology is presented less in its heroic than in its arcadian aspect. Now nymphs, fauns, satyrs, and Bacchantes were commissioned by customers who had spent half their lives on the numerous battlefields of Europe as idyllic motifs for the adornment of their tables and mantelpieces.

The transition from stylistic creation to pure adaptation was slow but fluid. The extreme differentiations of the rocailles, expressive of a lively dynamism, gradually evolved into natural forms. At the age of forty, having progressed from *Modellmeister* to court commissioner, Johann Joachim Kaendler was now at the height of his creative powers. Since he was sure of the support of the manufactory members, he could make decisions that would otherwise probably have had to be discussed by all the arcanists. The design department met, more often than the painting department, with problems that had to be solved quickly. The effect of fashions emerging from Paris was strongly felt in this department. In the period between the Second Silesian War and the Seven Years' War, Kaendler was often presented with commissions which were novel not only artistically but also technically.

The most elaborate work of this period is without doubt the large *Trumeau*. This ornamental mirror, three meters high, allowed Kaendler application of motifs used in other works and rearranged to become an organic part of a completely new whole. The figures of the Muses, which he had modeled for Frederick II as individual seated figures on high pedestals, now rise gracefully with supple movement from the ornate rocaille frame of the large oval mirror. The whole piece shows what the artist dared attempt with porcelain, the most versatile material of the Rococo period. While he previously had decorated all structural parts with sculpture, carved flower garlands, and shell ornaments, as in the large architectural table centerpieces, here the console table and the colossal oval of the mirror frame seem entirely and almost haphazardly composed of rocaille ornament, figures, flower garlands, and shell motifs, all fusing into a functional whole. The main impression intended was one of imaginative improvisation rather than of a deliberately constructed piece of architecture.

In the late summer of 1750, this ornate mirror was transported to Paris by Kaendler and Michael Helbig as a present from the king to the dauphine, his daughter Maria Josepha. Unfortunately it was destroyed during the French Revolution, so it is not possible to say whether it differed essentially from the later

cast, which survived until 1945. Since the second piece showed the insignia of the Polish crown and the monogram AR in the cartouche crowning the frame and on the electoral arms on the front of the console table, and since Kaendler mentions work on the large mirror frame in the report of January, 1745, long before Richelieu's overtures regarding the hand of the Saxon princess, it may be deduced that this was not made as a wedding present. In that case the arms of both the houses of Wettin and of Bourbon would both have been shown. The mirror presumably was intended to furnish the Warsaw palace, but the king made other use of it, partly because of the uncertain times and partly for reasons of prestige. The fact that he sent its creator and the esteemed Helbig to Paris to hand it over ceremoniously shows that the costly gift was to be accorded the dignity it merited. For Kaendler this, his only journey abroad during forty-four years of service for the manufactory, must have been an exciting experience.

A commission involving very great difficulty was the continuation of the cycle of emperor busts that had been interrupted by the war. Queen and Electress Maria Josepha, proud of her Habsburg lineage, cared deeply for this project. A large number of these portrait busts, based largely on rather unsatisfactory engravings, fell to Peter Reinicke. There is proof that he modeled the busts of Emperors Ferdinand I, Matthias, Leopold, Charles VI, and Joseph and later improved them when better visual representation of these emperors' features came to hand.[65]

Evidence that Prime Minister Brühl's love of ostentation had not been moderated by the lost war is furnished by his order for a large grotto of Neptune intended as a table fountain. A free interpretation of the Mattielli fountain in the garden at Ostra was planned. In the autumn of 1745, a few weeks before the battle of Kesselsdorf, Kaendler made sketches of parts of the fountain, still being erected in the Friedrichstädter Park, in order to translate the wealth of statues from a group dominated by a powerful Neptune figure as faithfully as possible. From his work reports we learn that he used the same architectural elements, even to the smallest detail, as conceived for the sandstone sculpture by Longuelune and Mattielli.[66]

Of the many small figures that were produced singly or in cycles during these ten years of peace, The Monkey Band (1747) gained the public's immediate affection. Shortly after its appearance it had become so popular that one of Meissen's manufacturing descendants, Chelsea, copied it in 1756. This, and the fact that the Meissen molds had become blunt from constant use, convinced Kaendler to reproduce the monkeys in a second and enlarged version. His and Peter Reinicke's new versions were so successful that the efforts of competitors soon failed.

Designs in the form of natural objects grew fashionable after the Second Silesian War. Sometimes orders were received that left little scope for artistic interpretation. A case in point was the Duke of Anhalt-Dessau's request for a large tureen in the form of a stag: he sent in his own sketch of the antlers of the stag he had killed and insisted that they be copied exactly.

Historians will notice the break in Kaendler's thorough and interestingly written work reports between December, 1748, and July, 1764. Only occasiona pieces of new or other entries can be used as a basis for cautious dating of the work of this time. On a loose sheet of paper, for example, there is mention of four groups of two-figured representations of the Seasons, which, after an earlier version (probably 1748), were being entirely remodeled in September, 1755. There is no doubt that the amount of work Kaendler was doing was increasing rather than the reverse, partially because Eberlein's health deteriorated considerably beginning in the autumn of 1747. He died on June 20, 1749, only fifty-five years old, of tuberculosis.

The reports of December, 1746, mention, apart from countless orders for tableware, no less than seven *Musenkinder* (*Musen*: muses, *Kinder*: children) as allegories of the Arts and Sciences, and three statuettes of Cupid. Eberlein had previously worked intensively on the statues for the copy of Mattielli's fountain. Unfortunately Kaendler makes no mention of special creations by his colleague. Shortly before his death, Eberlein appealed for a charge of troublemaking against him to be dropped. Evidently his ill-bred son had troubles with the authorities. Whether or not Eberlein's relations with Kaendler, ten years his junior, ever deteriorated, we do not know. We do know Kaendler's aims had always guided Eberlein.

Johann Gottlieb Ehder was also lost much too early. In October, 1750, he made a reckless leap from the castle wall to avoid the watch after he had tarried too long at an inn, and died shortly afterward of his injuries.

On May 10, 1748, Friedrich Elias Meyer, born in Erfurt in 1724, entered Kaendler's studio as a sculptor. It seems remarkable that he was immediately offered a special position. From remarks in connection with a travel allowance in the summer of the same year, we gather that he worked independently from the very beginning. He carried out his modeling in Kaendler's private studio on the cathedral square, until a special room could be allotted to him in the Albrechtsburg. Unlike the other sculptors who had immediately obtained a contract, he was until 1754 employed on a piecework basis. Nevertheless he did not fare too badly, for an entry in the accounts shows that in the second half of the year 1748 he had already received the lordly sum of 415 talers. In spite of this, he experienced great financial difficulties in 1754 when he was ill for three months. After this he requested a fixed salary such as he had received as sculptor to the Weimar court, namely 200 talers in addition to the payment for piecework. In his request he used the same argument as other members of the manufactory, such as Kirchner, Christian Friedrich Herold, and others had used.[67] Meyer was obviously engaged as a substitute for the hopelessly ill Eberlein. The style of his sculpted figures was, however, quite different from Kaendler's. Meyer derived the movements and niceties of a figure's facial expression from the theme of the piece. There is a certain tension about them, but he avoided giving them meaningless gestures. Thus their slender forms were endowed with sinewy elegance, great sensitivity and, above all, authenticity, which even in allegory appeared realistic. His integrity by no means led him to a ponderous naturalism, however. He remained throughout a child of his times, clothing reality in grace and charm. His figures move with astonishing elegance and suppleness, more characteristic of the French mentality than the German. In this way he seemed predestined to fulfill Frederick II's wishes. His departure to Berlin in 1761 must be judged from this point of view. Before it came to this, however, he had a mountain of work to do. Since he was not allotted routine daily work like the other sculptors, we may assume that he was exclusively employed on designs and models. Ascribing specific work to Meyer is difficult. Since his years of employment at Meissen coincide with the gaps in the archives, we can find no record of this successful sculptor's activity. Indeed there is practically no written reference to his work in Meissen. Although Helbig records a complaint from Kaendler on the small heads of Meyer's figures, all such figures should not be attributed to Meyer. The only means of identification left is to study the figures dating from 1749 to 1761 for certain characteristics of style, and even then they should be ascribed with caution. The characteristics mentioned above are probably most evident in a cycle known as the Orchestra of Gallants, in which each individual player possesses a character so well related to the instrument of his choice and is rendered in so convincing and so restrained a fashion that the artist in question is unmistakably Meyer. The emotions expressed in the attitudes of two dueling cavaliers are most effectively put across: the duelists are so individual in character and the handling of their costumes is so similar to that of the Orchestra of Gallants that they must be counted among Meyer's work.

In the many mythological figures which were enjoying an increased popularity in this period, the handling of drapery, which often helps scholars determine attribution, shows many characteristics of Meyer's hand. The long, flowing ancient garment, the peplos, is molded by Kaendler in the softest possible lines, with the folds of the robe grouped diagonally following a fixed scheme. Meyer, on the other hand, lets the garment emphasize the shape of his figure and does not hesitate to use the drapery to accentuate the silhouette and deepen the mood of the piece. Meyer's individual approach to sculpture is further evident in the shape of his rocaille bases, the rhythmic movements of which become the counterpoint of the gestures or are thrust up into the group composition. This interplay, especially in the male and female Bird Catchers, gives the whole work a certain charming tension. If we did not know that Franz Anton Bustelli began to work five years later in Nymphenburg quite independently and with no influence from elsewhere, we would be tempted to assume that his first inspiration came not so much from Kaendler as from Meyer. A clear change in Kaendler's character is shown by his attitude toward Meyer. The burden of many responsibilities had turned this once carefree artist into a skeptic. It frequently happened that one or other of his workers, such as the Dresden sculptor Körner, or a molder, a plaster worker, or an unskilled laborer, would through some minor incident incur the master's displeasure to such a degree that the only possible response could be dismissal. On the other hand, these tendencies also had a more positive effect: he would show excessive concern for the well-being of the manufactory and of his employees. He repeatedly used his influence to gain better wages for all his staff or for certain individuals. When the factory workers' wages proved inadequate for the higher cost of living in 1752, Kaendler made urgent recommendations for an increase. He energetically supported the tireless molder Albrecht's request for a raise, claiming Albrecht was without doubt the best molder and always had to mold the largest, heaviest, and most artistic pieces. Since claims often lay unattended to in Dresden, Kaendler had either to insist vehemently on action, as he unfearingly did, or show great patience. He was also able to practice patience. The number of molds had increased to such an extent that additional storage rooms and a certain amount of reorganization were needed to permit easy inspection to be carried out. Neither the shelves nor the floor space would suffice much longer to house the molds satisfactorily and in such a way as to make them easily accessible. Kaendler suggested the floor of the Kornhaus and even the vast gallery of the cathedral as extra storage space. It was almost seven years before the molds were systematically sorted and arranged in grades, according to the urgency with which they were needed, thus meeting with Kaendler's suggestions set down on eight closely written pages.

The factory commission was appallingly slow to realize that regular care and inspection, careful registration and, most important, storage of molds in a safe way would mean considerable savings for the factory in the long run. It seems incomprehensible that the commission did not at first see the need to employ two people for this purpose: the brother of the *Modellmeister* and Friedrich August Albrecht. Kaendler must have spent considerable nervous energy before all the prejudiced views on this subject were overcome. His suggestions for technical and administrative changes were indirectly, however, the preparation for a gigantic undertaking. In 1751, with Brühl's full support, Kaendler managed to get work started on the "Reiterstandbild," the long-planned equestrian statue of Augustus III.

The history of this monumental work, which was never to see completion, is one of the best examples of the many giant undertakings of the Baroque period that became anachronistic even before their manufacture, and were abandoned in their early stages. In the case of Kaendler's intended masterpiece, however, these early stages had been worked out to the last technical detail in countless sketches, unfortunately mostly lost, and even expressed in concrete terms in a porcelain model that, happily, still exists and is so brilliant that it stands out from all his other works as does the Swan Service. In September, 1751, Kaendler was summoned to Dresden to model the king on horseback from life.[68] Two months later, the execution of the work, which we must assume to have been a statuette, is recorded. Since this has been lost we do not know what it looked like. Whether the plan for a massive version was already under consideration cannot be established from the mere existence of this model, but the fact that Kaendler's main duties in Meissen were to help Kirchner in his

work on the large animal statues would seem to indicate that Augustus the Strong had already conceived the idea of a large equestrian statue.

Three years later, in 1734, this idea began to take very definite shape. Kaendler put a very bold interpretation of it on paper and submitted it to Augustus III.[69] This important letter was occasioned by accusations brought before the commission of his alleged libel against Höroldt and of his having issued orders counter to the interests of the manufactory. Kaendler was obviously anxious to dispel the discreditable impression made by these accusations, so he sent the sovereign his suggestions, couched in flattering terms, for the proposed statue. By chance, in the spring of that year the copper gilt equestrian statue of Augustus the Strong had been erected on the Neustadt marketplace. Kaendler's writings reveal that he recommended making two equestrian statues. The reason for this was as follows: among the many sketches made by the chief architect, Longuelune, showing various possible locations for the copper equestrian statue of Augustus the Strong, there was a plan to emphasize the beginning of the main avenue of Neustadt at the castle bridge by gatehouses on each side. Instead of a roof, the one-story buildings here were to have a kind of pyramid surmounted by the statue of Augustus the Strong on the western side and of Minerva on the eastern side. We may assume that Kaendler knew of his plan and proposed that Minerva be replaced by a second equestrian statue.

Kaendler was destined to see this project put aside for many years. The master, however, continued to work on his plans in secret. A few statues of mounted hunters, cavalrymen, and other equestrian groups prove how deeply he was engrossed in the problem of creating a harmonious representation of rider and prancing horse. The February report of 1741 indicates that Kaendler has begun modeling "the large statue in clay."

In July, 1745, there appears in a work report by Eberlein the first clear reference to their work, although still very sporadic, on the problems of the equestrian statue.[70] They became, however, increasingly occupied with these problems, for in 1746 the first model of Augustus III appears, showing the monarch in Roman dress mounted on a neat boxlike base, which bears an extraordinary resemblance to the final version. Five years passed, however, before Kaendler was officially commissioned. In 1751, he received a total of 15,000 talers, 12,000 for the large statue and 3,000 for the small one. Meanwhile he was concentrating on the overall plan for the memorial, the details of which are preserved in many sketches, written descriptions, and clay models. Much of Kaendler's free time was spent with this exploratory work. But many visits to Dresden were necessary too, in order to confirm Count Brühl's opinion that Brühl could do nothing wiser than convince his royal master of the desirability of such a wonderful opportunity to show the world his glory. Nevertheless, it proved a difficult task to keep the king's interest in this project alive. At last Brühl was successful, for in the spring of 1751 the court chancellery finally gave consent.

Kaendler approached the work systematically and sent in a request for a building suitable for the erection of a plaster model.[71] The clerk to the state building department, Simon, now hastily calculated the estimated cost for this special project and came up with the sum of 508 talers 13 groschen and 9 pfennig. After Kaendler had approved a design for a building on a site leased from the Cathedral Chapter, and after this had been built, another 110 talers 15 groschen had to be paid by the manufáctory to decorate the interior of the house. Kaendler had meanwhile devoted more attention to his small equestrian model. He had made further studies from nature, sketching an extraordinary Lippizaner horse from the royal stables.[72]

In 1752, Kaendler had already engaged six sculptors and three carpenters, so that work on the large version, as well as on the small piece which he and Eberlein were presumably tackling alone, could be started. From the later reimbursement of expenses it is clear that these workers, whom Kaendler initially paid from his own pocket, were not only lodged in his house on the cathedral square but also received food and other services there.

In 1753, the smaller version, 1.40 meters high, was finished. It has survived and provides us with an exact impression of the elaborateness of the large statue. From a rock base, apparently of natural forms, rises a slender pedestal, its facing side decorated with coats of arms. The horse rears up on this, bearing the proud imperator. To secure the horse, Kaendler at first introduced the allegory of Envy trampled beneath the animal's feet. But this solution failed to satisfy him. so he tried to make use of an iron device, invented by him earlier in 1734, which was to pass from the base, through the tail, and into the body of the horse. On the rocky base was a mass of allegorical figures arranged so that their gestures led the eye up the soaring architecture of the entire conception. The figures of Virtue, Justice, Courage, Peace, and Fame, popular at the time, appear together with the personifications of the Elbe and the Vistula and representations of the arts and sciences. Kaendler handled the Baroque interplay of a multitude of individual independent figures with almost casual ease, in the Bernini tradition, but in view of the catastrophic reality of contemporary conditions in Augustus III's country the effect is of a hollow and even ridiculous pathos. For Kaendler, however, this work represented the crowning of all his artistic efforts, until he gradually began to realize that not only had the circumstances changed but also that monumental art had been replaced by intimate art.

In November, 1754, there were already signs of the difficulties Kaendler had run into: his promise to have the actual-size plaster model ready by spring, 1755. Höroldt, who had meanwhile been promoted to the rank of a *Bergrat* (mining councillor) and was therefore more unapproachable than before, had no intention of helping Kaendler obtain an additional weekly one to two zentners of porcelain paste. The production of special mold containers for the details which were unusually formed and of hitherto unmatched size was beyond the means of Kaendler's special studio. The growing number of molds which would have to be safely stored for many years was becoming a burden. Even the factory commission, which rightly viewed the making of the equestrian statue as an impingement on normal factory production, now refused the importunate Kaendler any help, so that he had to appeal to Brühl again. Brühl ordered space to be provided in the large storehouse. The local management offered the unused floor space of the Kornhaus, but the floors could not support the weight of the molds, and because of their weight they would not be readily available there. Kaendler therefore gave notice to the tenants on the ground floor of his own house to provide accommodation for the huge reliefs of the monument base. The smaller version had been erected in the largest room in his house, for which he asked 60 talers a year rent.

In 1755, after the court had viewed the large completed plaster model in its shed on the cathedral square and befittingly marveled at it, interest in the project vanished quickly and irrevocably. With the outbreak of the Third Silesian War and the beginning of seven anxious years for the safety of Saxony, it was suggested to Kaendler that he abandon all work on the statue. In 1756, a payment of 2,700 talers was made, then all funds were cut off. Neither Kaendler's current expenses—for he had decided, of course, to carry on—nor his request for reimbursement of previous expenses, for the most part justified, were met. He did not relax his demands, and the more he was treated as a nuisance, the more ill-tempered and obstinate he became in his claims for reimbursement.[73] His stubbornness created considerable indignation in Dresden, and in Meissen his own colleagues formed a veritable cabal against him. One day the frustrated Kaendler innocently remarked, "How would it be if I were to put the king of Prussia on the horse?" This remark, recorded in the archives, was interpreted in higher places as unpatriotic. His compliance with the many varied wishes of Frederick II was, furthermore, seen as treachery, so that the worthy master fell into disfavor when peace was concluded. Even after his death his widow and five children continued negotiations until, in 1798, they received an *ex gratia* donation of 500 talers from the elector. The plaster model remained for some years in its separate house. Then, after the usual bureaucratic hemming and hawing, it was destroyed and the house, already rotting away, was demolished. Of this great project only the small version and an actual-size cast of the extremely flattering "imperator head" remained. During the ten years of peace between the Second and Third Silesian Wars there had been a period of active building in the factory and on the Albrechtsburg. Most of the rooms had new floors, the painting shops were provided with wooden planks instead of the dusty tiles, stoves were installed everywhere, damaged chimneys and turret roofs replaced and, most importantly, an effective fire precaution system was devised. In 1749 the factory's technical expert, Jürgens, had every floor supplied with running water by constructing a special pressure device. This system was not meant for daily need but was to be used in the event of fire. The massive wall built in 1748 between the castle and the cathedral was to prove a godsend in 1773 when the only conflagration in the Albrechtsburg's history occurred.

The lighting of the courtyard, the approach, and the castle steps also had to be improved upon since the painters had sent in a report which quoted an alarming number of accidents, particularly on the badly lit steps. A kiln house, a guardhouse with roomy stables, the protective building for the equestrian statue, and a considerable lengthening of the so-called long corridor between the castle and the Kornhaus also date from this time. The Kornhaus was given thirty-eight new dormer windows so that the large attic space could be used. This building had been used for miscellaneous purposes for many years, and now it was entirely at the disposal of the factory. All these improvements, extensions, and technical innovations (Jürgens constructed among other things a grinding mill for plaster) were carried out under the authority of *Landbaumeister* Simon.

In the production of regular ware for export to all parts of the world, painting played an important role. Specialists of considerable renown ensured a high level of quality. The portrait painter Johann Martin Heinrici (1711–1786), who had been with the factory since 1741 working on special commissions, deserves mention. When Höroldt realized that Heinrici was going his own way, probably with Dresden's support, he left him to continue with this special work.[74] Surprisingly enough, Kaendler proposed Heinrici as overseer of color chemistry in 1751. This is remarkable, as it shows that Kaendler took an interest in the progress of all departments of the factory while Höroldt was reluctant to contribute to any activity that could compete with his own. From 1756 to 1763, and again in 1775, Heinrici was in Frankenthal, although he had been made court painter shortly before the outbreak of the Seven Years' War and in Meissen had been allotted his own workroom with a permanent young assistant named Johann Friedrich Bader. In 1765, Heinrici made his first experiments with a dark blue ground color with which he had become acquainted on a visit to Sèvres, but it was left to the Marcolini era to use this achievement to its best advantage in late eighteenth-century portraiture.

In 1753, the old drawing master, Fehling, died. Since his assistant, Hoffmann, could not stand up to the pupils, Brückner and Hentzschel, painting overseers, were both proposed as Fehling's successor. There was no concern for the psychological aspect of the apprentices' training, and apparently discipline was not all it might have been. The forty to sixty young boys were expected to spend twelve hours every day at their workbenches. They tended, naturally enough, to lark about during these lessons, if, indeed, they attended them at all. The porcelain painter Christian Gottfried Hahnemann (whose family name was to acquire world fame through his son Samuel Hahnemann, the founder of homeopathy) suggested that an official educator be engaged and a proper boarding school established. Hahnemann recommended that the young men be taught not only their particular craft but reading, writing, and gymnastics, and offered himself as teacher and his house for lodging. He suspected that his plan would be turned down for reasons of economy and begged the commission not to be put off by the cost, which would obviously only bring dividends in the end. His estimate of the proposal's budget provides interesting information on the cost of living around 1760.[75] Farsighted and carefully thought out though it was, Hahnemann's proposal was shelved.

In 1751, the reports showed that the manufactory had brought the town of Meissen 553 workmen, 398 wives, 719 children, and 138 servants, and a population increase of 1,808 inhabitants. The town councillors should have been well satisfied since these extra people would be buying food, clothes, and other necessities. Augustus the Strong's advisers had already mentioned the opportunity of bringing new commercial life to the town when there was talk of founding the factory. Yet many records, measures, and town bylaws reveal that throughout the eighteenth century the Meissen porcelain makers were treated poorly and despised, that attempts were made to charge them exorbitant prices for everyday items, that the highest rent was exacted from them, that the highest rates were demanded for their funerals, and that petty offenses brought down the heaviest penalties upon them.

The manufactory employees attempted to defend themselves, as in the so-called beer strike of 1752. Since the quality of the local beer, which was made and served according to medieval brewing laws, was atrocious, no porcelain worker would consume it, preferring to drink imported beer. In May, 1752, when the council stopped all imports of beer, especially the Freiberg brew, there was a demonstration by 400 workers and the order had to be revoked. After this comic-opera victory the workers raised more objections in the years 1752–1753, and in 1754 considerable improvements were made. Price regulations were established, Thursday was made a third market day, the school system was reformed and fixed prices for the most important medications were introduced. The population and the council gradually realized that more than 500 wage-earning heads of families contributed considerably to the township's prosperity.

THE MANUFACTORY DURING THE SEVEN YEARS' WAR

After a few years of peace another test of strength took place between Austria and Prussia and once more their quarrel extended to other nations of Europe. Austria and Prussia went all out to strengthen their positions administratively and militarily after the Second Silesian War. Prussia was intent on securing its unlawfully extended frontiers; Austria was determined to regain the lost territory. Meanwhile Saxony's leaders unconcernedly reveled in the splendors of court life. It is true that the country recovered quickly from the war. Mining boomed and new industries were blossoming, but the people who benefited most from this new prosperity were the nobles. Brühl had supreme control in matters of government and well understood how to make the king totally dependent on him. He maneuvered to increase Saxony's political influence, but did nothing for the security or strength of the State. It was not prepared for further warfare and fell blindly into Frederick's carefully prepared holocaust. On August 29, 1756, 70,000 Prussians entered Saxony. It remained under Prussian occupation for almost seven years, the scene of many bloody battles. As an economically productive land it financed Frederick's military enterprises to a large extent.

Meissen was continually occupied from September 6, 1756, until the end of the war, and its inhabitants underwent much suffering. The town had to provide military supplies and was required again and again to provide money for the war effort. The townspeople chafed under the burden of having Frederick's troops billeted among them and were often required to help build fortifications. Plundering by Prussian troops was not unknown. Fighting often took place in the environs of the town and on occasion the Austrians, Saxony's allies, gained entry, but their behavior brought equal misery.

At the outbreak of the Seven Years' War the commission gave orders for the archives, especially the arcana books, to be moved to the basement rooms of the Dresden branch. After the war it was officially stated that in Frederick II's artillery bombardment of Dresden on July 19 and 20, 1760, the Meissen porcelain accounts, tableware, and other items, together with all the files, had been lost in a fire. In fact only the archive material for the war years was lost. Perhaps the archives for the war years were deliberately destroyed because certain circles desired to conceal the nature of activities at the factory. In the forefront of these was the royal *Kammerrat*, Georg Michael Helbig (1715–1774), who rose amazingly quickly from the position of accountant of the Dresden branch to that of *Kommerzienrat* (commercial adviser) and who during the Seven Years' War became a court official. He worked for the manufactory from 1735 to 1764.

In one of the first postwar volumes of the manufactory archives there is a short historical outline of its history from 1709 to 1763, which was undoubtedly written by Helbig and signed by von Nimptsch, Helbig, and Ernst, members of the commission.[76] Many of the dates and pieces of information in this account are incorrect, and its sole raison d'être would appear to be a justification of Helbig's dealings. It is quite correctly reported that Frederick II considered funds of the Electorate of Saxony, its armaments and food supplies, as booty of war, which he intended to appropriate according to his needs. Since he needed cash there and then, he sold the porcelain stores in the Dresden, Meissen, and Leipzig branches to a corn merchant, the privy councillor Schimmelmann, for 120,000 talers. Since income from the various branches would, in normal times, guarantee the Meissen manufactory the necessary money for production, Helbig, as he stresses in the account, with no small danger, from his own means, mainly however with credit from elsewhere, bought back the stock of porcelain for 160,000 talers.

The manufactory had been forbidden to continue any production, which paralyzed it indefinitely. Wilhelm Caspar Wegely, who had founded a porcelain factory in Berlin, had arrived quickly with authority from the Prussian king to visit the works with a view to transferring the enterprise to Berlin, but although an expert accompanied him he obtained no information about the secrets of porcelain making. As in the Second Silesian War, the kilns had been destroyed and the paste hidden. No equipment of any kind was in use and, above all, no one was there to give information, for the arcanists had left the country for Frankfurt-am-Main on the orders of Augustus III. Wegely returned to Berlin unsuccessful. Production was nevertheless restarted by Helbig, and the Prussian minister von Borck made a complaint, but as some of Frederick II's commissions were still in the making at Meissen, work was allowed to continue. Helbig correctly supposed that this uncertain situation could only turn to the disadvantage of the manufactory. So, more or less at Brühl's instigation, he decided to lease it out. This too was only possible through Schimmelmann, who rented it for a monthly sum of 2,000 talers and then sold this lease under the same conditions to Count Bolza and Helbig. In the course of the war, after Frederick became convinced of the capabilities of the enterprise, the rent was raised to 5,000. In 1762, it was raised again, 7,000 reichstalers. When Helbig declined to pay such a high sum, the Prussian war official Flesch threatened the manufactory with Prussian control. At this, Royal Polish Chamber Commissioner Lorentz, head of the Leipzig depot and the manufactory's legal adviser, agreed on a lease with the Royal Prussian War Administration that contained the following terms:

1. The manufactory was to be at Lorentz's entire disposal under the following conditions:

2. A monthly rent of 7,000 talers, and from January 1, 1763, 10,000 talers.

3. All porcelain delivered to Frederick from November 24, 1762, to the end of April, 1763, was not to be included, as previously, in the rent.

4. The workers were to be exempt from compulsory military service.

5. Passes were to be issued for the transportation of raw material and finished wares.

6. The parties to the agreement were under an obligation not to take part in intrigues against one another.

In the autumn of 1762, Frederick came to the conclusion that the manufactory, having withstood this test, could now endure further burdens: he therefore ceased to recognize the delivery of porcelain to the value of 20,000 talers in lieu of rent and, in spite of the agreement, demanded a monthly rent of 12,000 talers beginning January 1, 1763.

In November, 1762, Dr. Justus Lorentz reacted by sending a report describing the pressures to which he was subjected. When he refused to accept this increase, Frederick's agent, Lieutenant von Anhalt, threatened him with the immediate transfer of the manufactory to Berlin and confiscation of all Meissen porcelain stocks. Since Lorentz remained steadfast in his refusal, the lieutenant, waving his drawn sword, agreed to negotiate and lowered his demands by 1,000 talers. Lorentz was adamant. He was immediately surrounded by soldiers with fixed bayonets and was escorted to the guardroom. There he was left to cool his heels in the hope that he would relent. When the agent came back with a revised contract for a lease of 10,000 talers a month with a clause that all the porcelain delivered from November 24, 1762, to April 31, 1763, was to remain unpaid, he decided to sign. In his report to the manufactory commission, however, Lorentz complained that this brutal behavior was only made possible through the attitude of certain employees. He accused the former accountant and current court commissioner, Haustein, of servility toward the Prussian king. Even Kaendler was accused of base venality, for he had allegedly persuaded Frederick to order new pieces so that he could increase his income.

The restarting of production was no easy matter and was made particularly difficult by various circumstances. The transport of raw materials and finished ware could hardly be carried out in view of the changing battle scene. The employees became more and more discontented as in 1759 Helbig reduced wages by 30 percent. The money they received had little purchasing power since it was part of the Prussian king's wartime measures to mint Saxon coin with a greatly reduced silver content. Food prices had shot up and consequently most of the factory workers—although they, unlike men in other trades, had remained employed—were in great need and burdened with debt. In February, 1761, when wages had not been paid for more than three months, the painters threatened to take their services elsewhere if relief was not forthcoming. Inspector Auenmüller had been able to provide a certain amount of relief through the purchase of large quantities of wheat and the fair distribution of bread, but these occasional measures could not eliminate the poverty. The health of the people deteriorated with the increasing lack of food and firewood.

Discontent among the workers was mainly directed against Helbig, who had been allocated the apartment of the mining consultant von Heynitz in the Albrechtsburg and who continued to lead the life of a gentleman. Being generally held as the favorite of the hated Count Brühl, he was so unpopular that he hardly dared show his face. In a demand for an immediate increase of wages made by the molders it is stated that they would have to leave their work if things did not soon improve, for Helbig was out to see their ruin. Helbig's reputation was not at its best at the court either, and he was even accused of black marketeering in foodstuffs. The electoral princess called him the biggest villain of his time. Without excusing the weakness of his character, it must be said that it was a mark of his versatility and personal courage that the manufactory survived the war better than any other institution in the land, and that its output was relatively substantial in spite of increasing competition, thereby assuring a considerable number of families of at least a minimal income. This, however, led in the end to overproduction and a warehouse overflowing with wares increasingly more difficult to sell.

The agents of the Wegely factory made the most of this situation, putting many of the specialists into a quandary as to whether to remain or not. Through their efforts the following craftsmen were lost to Meissen at the outbreak of the war: Gottlob Albert and Johann Gottfried Besser, two painters who had been suspected of carrying out secret *Hausmalerei*, and the blue glaze painter Christian Friedrich Engelmann, who was sent by his father to Berlin undoubtedly in the hope of better rewards. They were followed in 1761 by the landscape and figure painter Carl Wilhelm Böhme, who succeeded in becoming court painter and supervisor of painting, and the irreplaceable, highly gifted Johann Balthasar Borrmann, who painted views and battle scenes in Meissen and who was essentially responsible for the painting on the dessert service which Frederick II had made for the Empress Catherine of Russia. The gravest loss was Friedrich Elias Meyer. When in 1761 he was offered the opportunity of a better-paid post in Berlin, he immediately accepted the offer. Meissen lost an important artist who could have bridged considerably more ingeniously than any other the period of Baroque and the new Classicism of the late eighteenth century.

In 1763, the following craftsmen left the Albrechtsburg for Berlin: the molders Johann Heinrich Müller, Gottfried Benjamin, Bergmann, and Johann Gottfried Klügel, the painters David Büttner, Johann August Horn, Elias Gottlob Lohse, Meerheim the younger, Carolus Toscani, and Carl Jacob Christian Klipfel, who was highly rated in Meissen as a mosaic and flower painter. He was especially patronized by Frederick II and soon rose to be second supervisor of painting by way of the post of painting accountant: eventually, in 1782, he became *Hof Kammerrat* and in 1786 *Geheimrat* and codirector of the Berlin factory.

In spite of losses of this kind and in spite of the most difficult material conditions, the manufactory was not hamstrung. The opposite was the case, for Helbig, a versatile businessman, knew how to reopen business channels. Neither did he fight shy of selling Meissen porcelain below standard if necessary in order to keep these channels open. The factory was not only working at full capacity, but was also able to take on more manpower. This apparent boom could only be achieved at the expense of the employees. On March 31, 1760, Frederick II had arrived in Meissen and had made the Hachenberg House on the cathedral square his headquarters for a whole month. Together with Prince Heinrich, he made a tour of the porcelain factory. The Albrechtsburg was to be surrounded with a palisade. The population was forced brutally to build fortifications, since a strong defense line for the Prussian army had to be established along the elevations from Nossen to Meissen. The battle for the Elbe line reached a dramatic climax with the bombardment of Dresden in July, 1760, and with the Prussian victory near Torgau. Meissen suffered particularly. Each side tried, when the town fell into its hands, to deprive the population of every possession and to render useless anything that remained to the enemy. From November 24 to December 8, 1760, Frederick was once more at the Hachenberg House. Two years later in this house the discussions between the Prussian king and Thomas von Fritsch, the representative of the Saxon monarch, began. These discussions led to the peace treaty of Hubertusburg in February, 1763. The population of Saxony had decreased by one hundred thousand. Fifty million reichstalers had had to be paid in reparation to Prussia. Not until March 2, 1763, did the Prussian troops finally leave Meissen. From March 17 to 19, 1763, Frederick II stayed at the Hachenberg House for the last time and on the twentieth the musical society of porcelain makers held a big concert in front of the house. These peace celebrations resounded joyfully in Kaendler's rooms, where a party for forty guests was being held. There was every reason for their sighs of relief. Although the manufactory had demonstrated an amazing resilience in face of all the oppressions, the possibility that Saxony would lose it for good had loomed dangerously large.

In spring, 1763, it seemed high time that a stop be put to the conqueror's unlimited demands. Frederick, nevertheless, took hold of all he could get. One hundred crates of porcelain embarked on their journey to Berlin. In the summer of 1763 Frederick II not only forbade the importation of Meissen porcelain but also its transit through his territory. He hoped that these measures would benefit the Berlin enterprise. Wegely had closed down his porcelain manufactory in 1757. Two years later a businessman by the name of Gotzkowsky took it over and it was bought from him by Frederick II at a price of 225,000 talers. From then on the manufactory was styled the Königliche Porzellan Manufaktur and its ware bore the scepter mark.

To gain an impression of the manner in which the paths of Frederick II and Kaendler crossed during the time Frederick II was staying in the Hachenberg House, let us refer to the latter's own report. According to this, on November 11, 1762, Haustein, the local inspector at the Meissen manufactory, brought a letter from Frederick stating that His Majesty wanted some new table services, groups, and exclusive pieces to be made as soon as possible, and requesting Kaendler's presence in His Majesty's quarters that afternoon at two o'clock. During the morning, however, the king decided to pay the manufactory a visit to acquaint himself with the variety of work produced there. He arrived at eleven o'clock accompanied by General Krockau. Without comment he made a thorough tour of the large and small colored ware stockrooms and several painting rooms. When Kaendler attempted to speak to the silent sovereign he was curtly reminded of his visit arranged for that afternoon. Nevertheless, around midday *Kammerhusar* Rüdiger brought him a *Voraus-specification* so that he could prepare himself for the ensuing discussions.[77]

Kaendler found himself obliged to inspect the painted work during Höroldt's absence, for the king occasionally complained that it was too coarse, that it was not executed with sufficient concern for the individual piece in question. The fact that Frederick had silver plates from Paris delivered to the manufactory to be used as models, although around 1760 Meissen itself had a wealth of designs for plastic ornament, shows that he had very personal views on the question of design. He appears to have preferred an emphasis on details of literary inspiration to showy overladen pieces. At first he commissioned great quantities of porcelain for his own use, but then he took to giving it as precious presents, so that new-style Meissen work found its way to various lands. There is no documentary evidence to support the suggestion that Kaendler, who had handled the manufactory's technical and artistic activity by himself during the Seven Years' War, had tried to impose his own design ideas on the Prussian king. It is highly improbable that Höroldt, who had emigrated comfortably in his own coach to Frankfurt-am-Main and who, on full salary, led the easy life of a royal pensioner, would have changed places with him. What Kaendler had to endure in war troubles as director of an enterprise being made to serve the enemy cannot be imagined vividly enough.

148

THE MANUFACTORY AFTER THE STATE REFORM OF 1763

The Prussians withdrew from Saxony, leaving behind them an impoverished and plundered land. The elector and his prime minister, Brühl, had spent the war years in comfort in Poland and had shown little concern for Saxony's miseries. The peace treaty was none of their making but was brought about by the electoral prince who was, like the electoral princess, opposed to Brühl's policies. The choice of Thomas Fritsch, an opponent of Brühl's, as the Saxon king's representative at the peace negotiations was also due to the electoral prince's influence. Even members of the king's entourage began to realize that a continuation of Brühl's policy could only contribute to their downfall. When Augustus and his prime minister returned from Poland, the Estates began to show their discontent. But the king died during the ensuing discussions and Brühl, who must have felt that his days of power were numbered, tendered his resignation. He himself died shortly after the king on October 28, 1763. Later, when the papers pertaining to his period of office were studied, among other abuses enormous personal misappropriations of money were discovered.

Under the new elector, Frederick Christian, a policy of reform for Saxony was undertaken which was to have far-reaching effects. It did not change the feudal constitution, but laid the foundations for the development of the country along capitalist lines. Between 1763 and the French Revolution, many lands with feudal industrial organization saw the bourgeoisie becoming aware that it must do away with the constraints of society's feudal structure. The aristocracy was obliged to take the new attitudes of this class into consideration, but managed in states where enlightened absolutism existed to gain advantage for itself by reaching a compromise with the middle classes.

Saxony even went so far as to invite men who represented the bourgeois-enlightened point of view to assist in proposed reforms. Of greatest influence was Thomas Fritsch, the son of a Leipzig publisher, and who himself had been a book dealer in Leipzig. He had been in the Saxon civil service, had been ennobled, but had left the civil service as a result of the conflict of his ideas as an ordinary man with those of the feudal-absolutist system. During his travels he had become acquainted with the constitutions and economics of several Western European countries, was in contact with the French Encyclopedists, and had studied the English political economy.

Other considerable personages in the Saxon *"Rétablissement"* such as Gutschmid, Ferber, and Lindemann, were of non-noble background. Behind the reformers was the strength of Saxony's bourgeois capital, which lent the reform all the opportunities for further success. Even though a drastic change in the feudal constitution was unthinkable in the eighteenth century, nevertheless the reform "undoubtedly assisted in the channeling of monarchical despotism after 1763 into enlightened bureaucratic absolutism," as Schlechte writes.[78] Foreign observers made mention of a so-called Republican Party founded by

Ferber and Lindemann, which aimed at the reform of the constitution favorable to the middle classes on the English model.[79]

After the early death of Frederick Christian in December, 1763, Prince Xaver was regent for the infant heir until 1768. The reforms were continued during his regency. In October, 1765, Saxony renounced all claims to the Polish crown. Later, however, there were disputes between Xaver and the Estates when he tried to push through army reforms without consulting them. On this issue Fritsch and von Einsiedel, a cabinet minister who also belonged to the reformers, resigned from office.

Among other measures intended to benefit the nation was one to improve the financial system and to further industry. The Economic, Industrial, and Trade Deputation was formed in 1764. Industry, which had been sadly neglected by Brühl, was the special concern of the reformers. In 1763, Fritsch had already made proposals for the setting up of new manufactures, and now they were encouraged by awards and subsidies. "The period between 1763 and the beginning of the nineteenth century saw the flowering of Saxon manufactories," Forberger writes.[80] The law concerning foreign enticement of managers, craftsmen, and other useful citizens was strictly applied. Those who were proved accessories to this received five to ten years' imprisonment; repetition of the offense and very serious cases of it were punishable with death by hanging. To discourage defections by craftsmen, drastic reforms of the totally outdated guild laws were initiated. This promising beginning of a new era gave fresh impulse to the Meissen manufactory. In 1765, the number of employees reached its peak for the eighteenth century, standing at 731. It did, however, fall to 606 in 1769. Sales were not matching the somewhat overheated rise in production and, in spite of improved transport arrangements and extended trade relations, and in spite of the rich choice of porcelain items available in the Meissen, Leipzig, Dresden, Kassel, and Spa outlets, representing a sum of 40,500 talers, profits had in fact decreased most alarmingly. The manufactory commission, then consisting of von Fletscher and von Heynitz under the chairmanship of von Nimptsch, decided to launch a thorough investigation of the European market, the trends in taste, and the potential of rival manufacturers. On the basis of their discoveries they would undertake drastic reforms. As a result we have reports dating from 1764 to 1766 on exploratory journeys, from Johann Christoph Hummitzsch and Johann David Elsasser (Paris, Chantilly, Nancy, Strasbourg, and Ludwigsburg: October, 1764), and from Johann Friedrich Otto (Genoa: September, 1766, and Marseilles: August, 1766). Hummitzsch and Elsasser were to investigate artistic and technical innovations, and Otto the commercial possibilities. Their daily expenses were paid and they were supplied with ready money to buy details of working methods or drawings—in other words for nothing less than industrial espionage. Elsasser, for example, in addition to his expenses for his journey to Paris, received a sum of 320 talers. He used these funds when he had gone no farther than Höchst, where for money and persuasion he was told almost all the secrets. Elsasser appears, according to his vivid reports, to have been the most active of all the Meissen spies. He had to decide in which places an increase or decrease in trade would be necessary. A particularly important duty of the investigator was to persuade ex-Meissen craftsmen to return to the factory. In Frankenthal, Elsasser was successful in regaining the Lücke brothers, Johann Friedrich and Christian Gottlob, a not insignificant triumph, for the elder of them possessed besides great skill in his craft all the secrets of porcelain making. In fact, Johann Friedrich Lücke (1727–1797) disliked Frankenthal so much that he had soon decided to serve his former "most gracious" government faithfully again. He also demanded an annual salary of 300 talers, his fare home and, above all, a guarantee of safe conduct. Lücke returned without penalty to Meissen, where he became overseer of the *Weisse Corps*.

Another of Elsasser's functions was to ascertain as precisely as possible the price of porcelain from other factories. In many different places he bought pieces for examination. He happily reported that the citizens of Frankfurt knew the supreme beauty of Meissen porcelain.

The first journey made by this observant and knowledgeable representative of the Meissen manufactory was in June, 1764. He visited Erfurt, Frankfurt-am-Main, Höchst, Frankenthal, Ludwigsburg, Mainz, Mannheim, and Strasbourg. In Paris, the decorative styles of vases, tableware, furniture, stucco work, and so on were systematically studied and it was concluded that the so-called *goût grec* was still in fashion but that the silver workers were not bound to the Greek taste and were eager to find new styles of decorating. The works of Watteau and Lancret were no longer used to the same extent as models for the painted decoration, but more spiritual and historical topics, landscapes, and portraits were favored. The measure of influence of these new subjects on the increasingly popular low-relief decoration is then discussed. Boucher's shepherd scenes were highly regarded. In Sèvres statuettes after Boucher's groups were being produced in biscuit porcelain, without glazing and decoration: the Meissen representative praised Sèvres without reservation. Although the work, which was carried out "very slowly and very laboriously" in Sèvres was worthy of admiration, it was reassuring for the Meissen manufactory to be informed that nothing was to be seen there that was not already known in Meissen.

The report hinted that during the immediate past Meissen had neglected to see that it remained competitive. No attempt had been made to accommodate the refinement of French taste, especially seen in the expression of landscape motifs. Apart from this the spreading vogue for the *goût grec*, with its extreme austerity, quite the opposite of an atmosphere of sweetness and softness, would have to be taken into consideration. This stylistic parting of the ways and apparent contradiction of tastes reflects the whole dilemma of the late eighteenth century. It resulted in a conscious direction of the painting method. The original lack of inhibition in Meissen work was lost. But this report's advice was not acted upon on the scale and in the methodical manner that was necessary. On April 15, 1763, Höroldt had returned to Meissen and made immediate inquiries among members of the commission about matters concerning the running of the manufactory.[81] He did not issue any orders to change the running of the manufactory, but merely compiled a list of private expenses for reimbursement.[82] Kaendler, who had stayed at his post working under most difficult conditions, and who had been forced to weather difficult disagreements with the domineering, unpredictable Prussian king, who had seen most of his molds for the equestrian statue destroyed and who was finally accused of disaffection, at Höroldt's return was subjected to the following. At a sitting of the commission on February 16, 1764, Höroldt made stinging accusations on the subject of Kaendler's alleged negligence during the Seven Years' War.[83] We clearly see in Höroldt's behavior his resentment that Kaendler had taken over, as a matter of necessity, many of his duties and had received credit for having adapted them to the difficult times of war. Naturally it was by no means easy to sort out anew the various responsibilities and to reestablish the course of production as it had been before the war. Höroldt could not simply take up matters again as he had left them in 1756. Circumstances had changed drastically, especially now that the design of porcelain and its decoration was controlled by the Dresden Art Academy. Höroldt, who had never liked the idea of an authority over him, was unwilling at the age of sixty-eight to make concessions, and applied for his pension on September 18, 1765, with the additional request for permission to leave his rooms in the Albrechtsburg and to move to his estate on the Plossen near Meissen. The request was granted, on condition that he set down all his knowledge on paper and hand it over sealed and that he on no account leave the country. He was granted an annual pension of 600 talers. Kaendler, who had replied to his accusations in a memorandum, breathed a sigh of relief as soon as Höroldt left the manufactory. His immediate task was to restore order to his personal finances, and in a lengthy explanation to the commission he asked for the payment of outstanding debts. He accounted for his demand for 8,600 talers as follows: 3,000 for outstanding payment for the small version of the equestrian statue, 3,600 for extra work done during the war, 1,000 for teaching duties, and 1,000 for the invention of new supports for the ware during the firing process. He justified these claims individually, and indicated the enormous reduction in damaged ware achieved since these supports had been used.[84] His requests were only partially met. His expenses for work on the Reiterdenkmal, as already mentioned, remained mostly unpaid. Added to these problems, the commission itself cast doubt upon his professional honor, even calling his superior ability into question.

As a substitute for Friedrich Elias Meyer, who had left for Berlin, and at a higher salary than Reinicke, the Dresden sculptor Carl Christoph Punkt was engaged in 1761 and made court sculptor in 1763. Although he was probably a good craftsman, he could not equal the imaginative powers of his predecessor.

He is seldom seen in the forefront of activity during his four years of work (he died in 1765 in this post). On the other hand, Kaendler had less cause to worry about his employment than about that of the Parisian sculptor Michel Victor Acier (1736–1799), who was eventually engaged in 1764 after long negotiations over salary and pension, on the recommendation of Dietrich, who as member of the Academy made the decisions about the engaging of staff.

At first Hummitzsch and Elsasser, given the task of finding a suitable sculptor, had been successful in coming to an agreement with the Parisian sculptor of small works, François-Nicholas Delaistre. Shortly before the contract was signed, however, Delaistre withdrew his acceptance. The two agents were glad to obtain the services of Acier, who was at that time working in Versailles. Although he had been offered 600 talers to cover the expenses of his transfer from Paris to Meissen, and a starting annual salary of 455 talers, he too wanted to withdraw from the agreement: only when he was assured of the title of *Modellmeister*, an annual salary of 800 talers, and a pension of 400 talers, did he decide to remain in Saxony. In 1781, he retired, as required by his contract, went to Dresden, and there claimed the chair of sculpture at the Academy which had become vacant on the death of Gottfried Knöffler.

Acier's self-confident behavior was not entirely justified, for Kaendler, whose official equal he was, was undoubtedly the superior craftsman in spite of the decline in his powers. Like all newly employed sculptors, Acier had no idea of the difficulties that the medium of porcelain could present. He was fortunate enough to have the cooperation of a skilled sculptor, Schönheit (1730–1805), who had been employed at the manufactory since 1745. Kaendler's displeasure at

seeing one of his pupils drawn toward his rival was as bitter as his realization that the authorities were no longer so respectfully accommodating toward him. Prince Xaver took his special orders exclusively to the French sculptor. Acier's work, it is true, did conform to the contemporary Parisian style. The vitality and comparative lack of conventional prettiness in Kaendler's work no longer appeared refined enough for aristocratic taste. All expression in the sculpted figures had to follow the rules of etiquette: artificial grimaces were preferred to restrained individual features. This resulted in a stereotyped art of cramped brittleness and disturbing falsity. Sentimentality and moralizing didacticism cast out the expression of genuine feeling. The tendency, or rather the dictum, to "dress up" each theme led to an increase of allegorical interpretations and generalizations. Winkelmann's misunderstood thesis of quiet simplicity and noble greatness began to spread into the applied arts. In the case of porcelain making, its interpretation often resulted in an arid hollowness. Nevertheless, since the choice of themes and the variety of form and color at the artist's disposal were still so rich and, indeed, had increased through technical innovation, we cannot speak of an impoverishment of porcelain work, but rather of an insipid uniformity. Yet if Meissen wanted to withstand the advance of rival factories it had to follow the vogue established in Paris. For this reason the investigations into current tastes made by Elsasser and Hummitzsch and the employment of Acier were quite justified, indeed very necessary, since Meissen found it more difficult each year to maintain its leading position among European porcelain manufactories.

It was evidently believed that Acier's employment would encourage Kaendler to produce more fashionable work. The authorities were sadly mistaken. Kaendler viewed the work of his rival, thirty years his junior, with both suspicion and scorn. When the two sculptors were required to cooperate on larger commissions, it is probable that the vexed and grumpy old craftsman did not repress his obstinacy. Prince Xaver, delighted with Acier's previous allegorical groups in praise of the House of Wettin, commissioned a huge table centerpiece comprising no fewer than forty elaborate allegorical groups. Both Acier and Kaendler were to be employed in this. In October, 1772, Kaendler submitted the plan, which showed the entire Olympus, figures representing the arts and sciences, allegories of Catherine II's deeds of war and peace, and the power of her realm symbolized by Russia's mightiest rivers.

The plan met with Prince Xaver's full approval, and in November, 1772, Kaendler began work on the model of the first group. The entire conception of the centerpiece is a revival of long-outmoded Augustan festive cavalcades of splendidly ornamented chariots with thronelike superstructures composed of mythological groups. Here Kaendler's approach to his art found its full expression for the last time.[85] It took many months to make the huge groups, which involved the most laborious and intricate work, technical difficulties being overcome mainly through the skill of the Bossierer Carl August Starke. Acier's willing cooperation on the Russian commission may in some respects be compared with Eberlein's on the Swan Service. Other pieces, however, were to show that while Acier had significant influence on Meissen production, he had none on Kaendler's work. At the beginning of 1774, a year before Kaendler's death, this gigantic cyclic piece, the last of its kind to be made in Meissen during the eighteenth century, began its journey to Russia.

Although it had been hoped that Acier's engagement would give the manufactory an artist with his own creative imagination, the ideas from Paris remained an essential part of the inspiration for successful Meissen work, even for that done by the Frenchman from Versailles. An extraordinary aspect of the transmission of ideas is the fact that it was a German, Johann Elias Zeissig, known as Schenau (born in Grosschönau near Zittau on November 7, 1737, the son of a damask weaver), who made sketches of useful designs in Paris and sent them on to Meissen. Schenau had been a pupil of the younger Silvestre in Dresden and had gone to Paris during the Seven Years' War. There he came under the influence of the genre painter Jean Baptiste Greuze. Schenau seemed inexhaustible. Single figures and groups of a sentimental, moralizing, gaily jesting nature, the personification of human vices and virtues as putti-like child figures called *Devisenkinder* were executed by Acier, Schönheit, and Jüchtzer more or less freely in Meissen porcelain. They found, and continue to find, a ready market, especially the Devisenkinder, which show on their base a motto revealing the meaning of the figure. The same may be said of the Gardener (or Vintager) Children, collectors' series which express, in their prettified, slightly erotic sweetness, a trend whose literary equivalent is the shepherd poem. Acier's original work, however, was concerned with themes on a somewhat larger scale. Yet these, too, often derive from available engravings, such as the Anette and Lubin group, after an engraving by Debucourt. Even in the porcelain version one finds a portrait-like depiction of the actors Cailleu and Madame Favart, both very popular at that time. The scenes showing the commonplace joys or mishaps of bourgeois family life were now designed as groups in the round as opposed to Kaendler's conception based on one viewing side. In spite of the most meticulous attention to detail and most careful decoration, these elaborate groups seem staged and lifeless. Yet their faithful reproduction of costumes, tools, and domestic utensils provide an accurate and attractive illustration of the manners and customs of the late eighteenth century.

In this category are such pieces as The Promenading Couple, The Gentleman with the Telescope, The Lady with the Letter, The Young Bride and, of course, the touching and universally popular Happy Parents. Scenes showing a dramatic incident such as The Broken Eggs and The Broken Bridge are also didactic. After Kaendler's death, Acier was required to execute more exacting works, mainly large allegorical groups for the tsar's court, as, for example, the groups entitled The Goddess of Justice, Glory of the Duke, Flourishing Happiness, and Flourishing Trade, all of them rather questionable choices as themes in view of the times. It is interesting to note that Schönheit undertook the model-

ing of the horse in the equestrian statuette of Frederick II in 1778. Acier finally created a miniature monument to the poet Gellert which, in the same way as the statuette of Frederick, shows Acier's ability to produce a sculptural portrait.

The cooperation of Schönheit, son of a machine operator, and Acier led to a fruitful exchange of knowledge. Schönheit, who imparted the technical knowledge and absorbed the artistic, was employed as a sculptor working independently within the manufactory. His versatility was a great asset since he could be assigned to many tasks, such as the groups still to be executed after Acier's retirement, which he successfully completed according to the latter's specifications, but not, however, without leaving his own mark upon them. His skilled hands created works of clear expression and originality such as The Four Seasons, in 1782; The Grape Harvest, The Winepress, and The Gentle Postponement, in 1787; and Love and Reward and Love and Forgiveness, later.

Since the reform moves of 1764, the regeneration of modeling had been facilitated by enforced adoption of contemporary tastes. No effort was spared to improve the apprentices' training in painting. That this was only partially successful was indicated by the requirements of the pampered Parisian customers. They demanded, over and above spontaneous virtuosity, that a piece should remain unique and inimitable. In contrast new technical breakthroughs were achieved in color development. In 1768, there is mention of a beautiful aquamarine blue, a brilliant purple, and a much improved yellow.

The Albrechtsburg fire, 1773

Der Brand in der Albertusburg zu Meißen den 30 Januar 1773

The quality of Schnorr's china clay seems to have varied during this period. It would by no means have been out of character for him to send, in 1764, impure clay from an almost worked-out deposit, while smuggling better clay over the border. At any rate there is mention in 1765 of the seizure of a consignment of clay near Oberschlema in the Erzgebirge and of a fruitless investigation. It is not surprising that the search for clay of good quality had started once more. Specimens from Welbsleben in the county of Mansfeld and from Reinsdorf near Wittenberg had proved unsatisfactory, so there was obviously considerable delight when in 1764 the painter Hahnefeld discovered china clay a few kilometers northwest of Meissen near the village of Seilitz. The arcanist Schertel gave a good report of it based on his analyses, and Hahnefeld, employed in Höroldt's studio since 1736, was awarded 50 talers. In 1765, Hahnefeld was made overseer of the washing and compounding of china clay with a monthly salary of 18 talers. The new deposit was at once fenced in and prepared for excavation by the miner-carpenter Grüssel. In addition, a building for the minehead was bought in Königstein and transported by water to Zehren near Meissen. The first pieces made in the new material proved unsatisfactory as far as the color was concerned, although the actual paste seemed more durable than the Aue variety. After four years of experimentation a satisfactory paste was eventually obtained, so that by 1768 nearly four thousand Zentner were ordered from Seilitz and only five hundred and sixty-three Zentner from Aue.

As important as the best possible raw materials and the vast quantities of firewood was a steady and adequate supply of water. An agreement had been made in 1766 with Johann Wilhelm Schönhals, owner of the *Kynastgut*, situated about two kilometers southwest of the manufactory, to the effect that he and his heirs would allow the manufactory access to the spring on his property for an annual fee. This supply proved insufficient, however, for the households on the cathedral square also drew on it. Neither did the well sunk in the northeastern garden of the castle some thirty years earlier yield enough water, so diviners were consulted and finally a nearby underground spring was found which Grössel drilled. In May, Grössel completed the installation. The water was not only intended for manufacturing processes but also for the extinguishing of any fire that might break out in the Albrechtsburg. Since the fire in the Bischofshof in 1720 and the terror of the cataclysmic thunderstorm of 1756 when lightning struck the brass buckles of some of the painters' shoes, there had not been any major conflagration. On January 30, 1773, however, a fire broke out, obviously as the result of carelessness, which could have enveloped the Albrechtsburg, the cathedral, the deanery and, quite possibly, a large part of the town. But a change in the direction of the wind and the excellent fire precautions prevented the worst. A few brave manufactory workers and courageous craftsmen from the town managed to bring it under control, but it took them eighteen hours to finally extinguish it. The castle and town were declared out of danger at one o'clock in the morning of January 31. Surprisingly, this is the first time that the reports clearly indicate that the townspeople of Meissen and the manufactory employees considered themselves united.[86]

Production was suspended for a time since the throwing room and some painting rooms had been rendered unusable, but emergency measures were undertaken with all possible speed and after eight days production was again running smoothly. Attempts to fill all orders were successful, so rumors circulated by its rivals that Meissen was unable to cope were ineffective. Shortly after the fire a member of the commission, Ernst Haubold von Miltitz auf Oberau, developed precise proposals to avoid a repetition of the disaster and to improve the fire-fighting methods if it should nevertheless occur. He proposed that firewood be stored in small and separate quantities away from the kilns, and submitted a detailed account of the extra expenses that would be incurred by the employment of additional staff for this task. But, above all, an adequate supply of water was to be at all times available and for this purpose a large covered cistern was supposed to be constructed on the site of Kaendler's building for the Reiterdenkmal model. The rebuilding of the northwest rooms where the large storerooms for the molds and the workshop for mold turning were situated was not completed until 1775.

In spite of all efforts, but undoubtedly as a result of the break in production caused by the fire, the sales for 1774 were lower than the period following the Second Silesian War, having dropped to 134,069 talers, after the interim recovery to the value of 220,000 talers for 1766. The warehouse manager, Otto, had an astonishing amount of success with his auction sales, which brought an income of 13,000 talers, but since these merely involved the sale of second-rate goods in smaller towns, they did not recommend the Meissen product to the more desirable markets. On the contrary, as subsequent business showed, they reduced Meissen's prestige. The manufactory workers themselves were particularly aware of the decline. The cost of living had only come down slowly and to a very limited degree after the end of the Silesian wars, whereas wages—although they had occasionally and in special cases been raised on application—remained the same as in the prewar period.[87] This represented an unbearable discrepancy. The manufactory commission did not feel empowered at this point to redress the balance.

Already one year after the end of the Seven Years' War, the administrator of the Electorate of Saxony, Prince Xaver, recommended that the wives and daughters of the manufactory workers be employed and paid one-third of the accepted wage. The year 1764 therefore marks the beginning of the employment of women in the manufactory, but it was kept at a ratio of some five hundred male workers to some thirty female.

THE INFLUENCE OF MEISSEN PORCELAIN
IN THE EIGHTEENTH CENTURY

What was the extent of Meissen porcelain's influence throughout Europe? Efforts were made from the beginning to ensure that Meissen retained the monopoly for making porcelain. It is interesting to note, however, that by 1746 records were kept of the experiments of others with the arcanum, noting where they were being carried out and with what degree of success. One entry mentions unsuccessful experiments in St. Petersburg; there are also references to experiments by a Dr. Pott in Berlin, to a manufactory in "Stafford in Engelland," to another in the mountains in the Kingdom of Naples, and to Höchst and Freywalde in Brandenburg. Incidental mention is made of the defection of the Meissen flower painters Klinger and Hietzig to Vienna. Vincennes porcelain draws the sole comment that it is superior to all the others. Countless scraps of information about attempts to make porcelain and about attempted foundings of new factories demonstrate Meissen's constant watchfulness and efforts to keep itself informed.

In spite of this, Meissen did not succeed in keeping its monopoly. It retained its reputation, however, as the most important, most versatile, and most adventurous of all the European porcelain manufactories. If we study the dates of the main eighteenth-century porcelain manufactories—about twenty-five in all— we note that they were founded in three different periods. Two factories deriving from Meissen existed before 1720; then, by 1751, after a space of twenty-three years, there were a further seven; the rest followed in the period between 1755 and 1767, although Limoges and certain Thuringian factories appeared late on the scene, bringing us up to 1777.

All European factories directly or indirectly, often unconsciously, imitated or were influenced by Meissen. Whether it was in its adoption of recipes, its workers, or its artistic inspiration, in all cases there exists some link between Meissen and successive manufactories. On the other hand, certain technical achievements and special artistic facets developed or were pursued at other places, and Meissen was eager to profit from these outside achievements.

A particularly clear case of this reverse effect is shown in the relationship between Meissen and the Vienna manufactory. In the same year that Hummitzsch and Elsasser visited Paris, Meissen sent, at Kaendler's instigation, a representative, Carl Gottlob Müller, to Vienna to investigate how that manufactory was working and what it was producing, how great the influence of the ex-Meissen painter Klinger was, how extensive the export to Bohemia was, whether china clay was still being obtained from Aue, and whether Augsburg silver was still the basis for the design of Viennese tableware. Müller reported that he made only one tour of the Vienna works and observed that most of what he could see there was like Meissen's work. He brought back for Kaendler an oval, very delicately shaped salt cellar which the *Modellmeister* promptly proceeded to copy. Also, based on information a Meissen embosser had gathered from Vienna, in 1764 a new mixture for paste and innovations in making molds were attempted. There are, however, much earlier indications of reciprocal influence. In 1734, the factory commission gave orders for inquiries to be made in Vienna as to the type and quality of ware that the manufactory there was producing and what experience had been gained in the making of larger pieces and vases. These inquiries were probably linked with the commissions for the Japanese Palace.

Not until 1736 did Johann Martin Kühne in Vienna, expressly for this purpose, provide exact information about the number of employees, the organization of the works, prices, and special creations. Special mention is made of a service worth 2,000 crowns, which was painted prettily in imitation of black copper engravings, and of two large mirror frames as a present from the Viennese to the Muscovite court. As for the rest of their production, it was modeled on Meissen work. The Viennese manufactory was especially dependent in matters of sculpture. Kaendler's figures had been copied since the 1740s. With customary disregard for original rights, copies were made of the pastorals, garden figures, all kinds of animals, including the large statue versions and, of course, The Monkey Band, which always sold well. The Monkey Band was a favorite item in the repertoire of the Chelsea factory, founded in 1745. Indeed, the pieces bore the Meissen sword mark, as did the innumerable scent bottles, snuffboxes, and other toilet articles. Since Chelsea was taken over in 1769 by the successful porcelain maker William Duesberry, who owned a factory in Derby, the favorite Meissen pieces were, of course, imitated there also.

In Höchst, a new porcelain manufactory was founded by the two mirror makers Göltz and Clarus on March 1, 1746, by appointment to the elector of Mainz; the technical-artistic direction was undertaken by none other than Adam Friedrich von Löwenfinck. No information about Löwenfinck's work, however, could be given by the anonymous author of a report dated April 9, 1746, from Frankfurt-am-Main, but this correspondent was certainly concerned about the danger of new competition. It remains an open question whether Löwenfinck, who could hardly contribute more than a few color recipes, was able to launch this factory on the road to success. Only three years afterward his employers showed their lack of confidence in him and initiated a legal action against him for alleged breach of contract. Löwenfinck won the case, but he lost his post as director in Höchst and with his brother Christian Wilhelm, who had followed him there, went to Hannong's in Strasbourg. There is no evidence of artistic influence of Meissen at Höchst in the years 1746–1749. The art of making porcelain was presumably first mastered when the arcanist Johannes Benckgraff arrived and another arcanist, Joseph Ringler, supplied kiln designs from Vienna. Then the Höchst manufactory became a serious competitor, even more so when two good painters, Hoffmann and Rothe, and a skilled molder, Gottfried Becker, arrived from Meissen.

In 1764, Elsasser gave an estimation of the capacity of the Höchst establishment.[88] He mentioned the adverse effect of high prices on business transactions. The Höchst manufactory could only keep its hold in the saturated porcelain market with the greatest difficulty and went into liquidation in 1798. The influence from Meissen felt by the Fürstenberg factory, founded in 1747, was of no great importance. In 1752, Johann Christoph Ludwig Lücke arrived there from Vienna. He presumably started there as a *Modellmeister*, but left as little trace of his activity in Fürstenberg as in Meissen. Simon Feilner, figure modeler at Fürstenberg from 1753 to 1768, was able to report to the director of the manufactory, von Langen, in 1757 that the molds sent by Meissen repairers and engravers had arrived safely.

The Meissen flower painter Georg Christoph Lindemann was working in Nymphenburg around 1770, but he did not achieve recognition for his personal interpretation. The flower painting of his day had a fairly fixed character, strictly imitating the well-known engravings from botanical works.

The porcelain manufactory at Frankenthal has achieved renown for its unusually wide repertoire. It was founded by the Strasbourg faience manufacturer P. A. Hannong in 1755, and taken over in 1762 by Elector Karl Theodor of the Palatinate. Under Joseph Adam Hannong, son of the founder, the sculptor Johann Wilhelm Lanz carried out work in the traditional styles of faience making, but Johann Friedrich Lücke created his pieces in the image of the Meissen product. The famous Meissen miniature painter Johann Martin Heinrici worked at Frankenthal for a considerable time. It is therefore not surprising that Hummitzsch and Elsasser gave this manufactory special attention. They stated objectively on June 18, 1764, that they had seen fine pieces of Frankenthal work as far as the quality of the porcelain and the modeling was concerned, for the sculptors were Meissen emigrants.

The departure of the elder Lücke was not too disconcerting for Frankenthal at first, for they thought they had found in the sculptor Konrad Link a substitute of equal merit. After the former had left, his brother, Carl Gottlieb Lücke, took over the position of chief modeler. At this, Meissen influence grew stronger, which made itself felt in a sales increase.

The popularity of the Frankenthal figures and groups made it possible for some of these figures to be made and sold in Grünstedt, after the final closing of the manufactory on May 27, 1800, by its last owner, Johann Nepomuk van Recum. In spite of other influence in the field of figure-making, Meissen was most strongly reflected in the work here.

The founding of an imperial porcelain manufactory in St. Petersburg is also related indirectly to Böttger's discovery. The leaseholder of the "*Delffter Stein- und Rund Bäckerey* in Dresden," Peter Eggebrecht, later Kaendler's father-in-law, was invited by Peter I to St. Petersburg in 1718 to organize the founding of the manufactory for "*Delffter Gut*." Eggebrecht's correspondence gives no clear idea of how far he progressed with this project. When Conrad Christoph

Hunger, the itinerant arcanist, heard in Stockholm of the plan to found a porcelain manufactory in Russia, he offered his services to the imperial court. After four years he was expelled from the country, accused of being a fraud, and it was left to the imperial mining expert, Dmitri Winogradow, trained in Freiberg, to discover, after much tedious experimentation, the secret of making porcelain. Winogradow died in 1760, and Catherine II summoned the Saxon arcanist Gottfried Müller to St. Petersburg as technical director. In spite of these links with Saxony, and although the Meissen modeler Karlowsky entered into employment at the imperial factory in 1768, Meissen had no artistic influence worth mentioning. From 1780, Sèvres porcelain was the model. Flat areas of color and excessive gilding were applied to tableware in order to obtain the desired luxurious effect.

The Sèvres manufactory was indeed the only one to remain free from Meissen influence. Entirely the opposite was the case when Meissen imitated the *"bleu royal"* first used in Sèvres in 1753. In 1765 the Meissen factory commission applied to the administrator of the Electorate of Saxony, Xaver, for a reward for the court painter, Johann Martin Heinrici (1711–1786), in acknowledgment of his successful trial piece, a cup in the "French blue." To strengthen its request, the commission sent along a Sèvres cup for comparison, and from that time royal blue enjoyed increasing popularity. Modern Meissen production cannot be considered without it.

It is certain that this achievement came as a result of Elsasser's information. Subsequently detailed reports of the fine Sèvres biscuit porcelain were received from Paris and the ware was made and perfected to an amazing degree in Meissen. In the nineteenth century the Meissen manufactory sent its craftsmen to work in Sèvres for long periods in order to profit from the latter's achievements. In this way the *"pâte-sur-pâte"* painting technique was adopted and further developed by Meissen. The fact that Sèvres, the first manufactory to do so, opened its own Musée céramique led Meissen, in the twentieth century, to organize its own large representative collection of models in the Schauhalle.

In 1758, a year after the Ludwigsburg manufactory was founded, Gottlieb Friedrich Riedel (1724–1784) arrived and soon proved himself so superior to his co-workers that he was made artistic director of the factory. He had worked under Höroldt in Meissen from 1743 to 1756 and had then spent a very successful three years in Höchst and Frankenthal. In 1779, when Ludwigsburg ran into commercial difficulties, Riedel traveled to Augsburg where he made a number of copper engravings for the use of porcelain painters. The investigators make no mention of him in the report of their short visit to Ludwigsburg in 1764. The manufactory made no great impression on them, apart from its good sculptural work. The porcelain was, they said, by no means as white as that of Frankenthal, it broke easily, and was poorly decorated. This harsh judgment was hardly valid. It is possible that the two suspicious-looking visitors were not shown the best pieces, and Riedel probably stayed out of sight for obvious reasons. Riedel's influence and the resulting Meissen-like character of Ludwigsburg ornamentation was very long lasting. Although Riedel's greatest talents lay in the field of landscape painting, he also was a master of figure and flower painting. He also had the gift of communicating his ideas on vessel design and every kind of plastic ornamentation to the modelers in such an attractive and convincing fashion that many particularly delightful pieces were produced under his direction.

From 1757 to 1758, the factory in Ansbach, founded in 1710 for the production of faience, was enlarged by Margrave Karl Alexander to include the making of porcelain. A nephew of Meissen's Kaendler, Johann Friedrich Kaendler (1734–1791) from the Vogtland, and the flower painter Johann Benjamin Gerlach (1714–1786), employed as miniature painter to Frederick II from 1747, together developed the arcanum. The factory needed credit, and its stocks swelled year by year, for the porcelain market was saturated. Its best customers were the Balkan countries, which by 1784 had purchased no less than seventy thousand Turkish cups in Ansbach. This fact, and the ability of the Dresden modeler Carl Gottlieb Laut, who was employed to produce figures of a deceptive similarity to Meissen's ware combined to make Ansbach a source of competition for the Meissen manufactory.

Ludwig VIII, Landgrave of Hesse-Darmstadt, also decided that he could not manage without his own porcelain factory. As a result the Kelsterbach works were founded in 1761, also around an existing faience factory, with the Meissen painter Christian Daniel Busch as director. Busch was a restless artist who traveled from place to place in the hope of meeting with greater success. He left Meissen in 1745 to travel to Vienna, Munich, Künersberg, Sèvres, and eventually to Kelsterbach: from 1765 until his death in 1790 he was employed at Meissen.

The increased demand for everyday items led to the flowering of the industry in Central Germany and particularly in Thuringia from 1760 onward. Conditions were favorable there. There was an abundance of cheap labor, raw materials, and kiln fuel. In contrast to the usual founders of porcelain manufactories, who were financially overburdened, capricious, illogical, and bankrupt sovereigns, here energetic businessmen and their families launched thriving businesses. One such family were the Greiners, who eventually came to own six works (at Volkstedt, named Älteste Volkstedter, founded 1760; the others at Kloster Veilsdorf, 1760; Limbach, 1762; Wallendorf, 1764; Ilmenau, 1777; and Gera, 1779). Independent of Böttger's invention, Wolfgang Hammann of Katzhütte (1760), Georg Heinrich Macheleid (1760), and Gottfried Gotthelf Greiner of Limbach (1761) succeeded in the reinvention of hard-paste porcelain.

Gotthelf Greiner, the senior member of this famous family of ceramic workers, founded the small Limbach factory in 1762. They were relatively independent of Meissen in technical matters. As far as output was concerned, however, public taste had to be taken into consideration. Customers visualized Meissen examples when ordering tableware and figurines. They demanded a similar article at a lower price. This resulted in the copying of Meissen ware, and a mark consisting of crossed forks was applied by the Volkstedt factory, Wallendorf, and Limbach to deceive the buyers.

In the case of Volkstedt, the Saxon elector made an energetic protest about the crossed forks in 1787 and succeeded in getting this factory to mark its products henceforth with one fork only. Meissen's artistic influence held sway in Central Germany, where there were numerous larger and smaller establishments, until the Thuringian factories began to concentrate on a purely industrial production and develop their own styles as a result of extensive mechanization and mass production.

After unsuccessful attempts by Elias Vater, windowglass maker, known as a fraudulent arcanist in Meissen, porcelain making was eventually established in Copenhagen in 1760. Certain preparatory work may have been done by a member of the Mehlhorn family, Johann Gottlieb, and by Johann Christoph Lücke in 1754 before production was started by Niels Birch. Apart from these doubtful links through individual craftsmen who had made little impact on the Meissen manufactory, Copenhagen's production seems to have remained relatively free from Meissen influence.

The impressive range of small later-eighteenth-century Meissen figures, the popular collecting pieces such as the Gardener Children or the Devisenkinder, were initiated at the Fulda factory (founded in 1765) under the supervision of the chief modeler Laurentius Russinger. They were carefully made and beautifully decorated in a porcelain of perfect quality.

Brisk trade was done in the northwestern parts of Germany via Kassel; as early as 1735, the Meissen representative there thought it his duty to report on an alleged project for the foundation of a porcelain manufactory. This did not materialize until 1766 and the factory closed in 1788. One Meissen painter, Carl Gottlieb Grahl, took up a post in Kassel in 1769 and became overseer in 1780.

No other factories tried to imitate the creations marked with the blue swords during the eighteenth century. Jealous interest was always shown by Meissen in the production and sales of these daughter companies. Voluntary reports were sent in by Meissen sales representatives from various locations. Pieces made by other factories were bought occasionally in order to assess their standard of quality. Above all, expert craftsmen were sent out as investigators.

Repeated mention has been made of outside spare-time work: as far as painting was concerned this consisted of *Hausmalerei*. This was naturally disapproved of and, in extreme cases such as that of Heintze, punishable by imprisonment. It was not always for financial gain that the painters ran this risk. Many a talented artist was so frustrated by Höroldt's insistence on narrow specialization that he wished to find a way of giving his artistic urges free expression. Artists with a liking for independence would not allow themselves to be tied by employment contract clauses. This had been Höroldt's own approach. There was nevertheless a difference between the craftsman who worked exclusively for the factory and whose pieces were sold only by his employers, and the one who obtained Meissen *"Mittel-Guth oder Brac,"* as was possible until 1728, painted it with his own colors, fired it in his own muffle kiln, at his own risk, and then sold it at considerable profit for himself. This kind of free-lance enterprise demanded supreme skill, for the public had become very discerning through familiarity with the original pieces bearing the blue swordmark.

In this field the members of the two Dresden families Meerheim and Mehlhorn were less successful than the Augsburg specialists, who produced works of such delicacy that they now arouse the greatest interest in collecting circles. The splendid gold and silver decoration done by the Augsburg goldsmith and engraver Johannes Auffenwerth is well known. He not only did occasional work for Meissen, but he also independently applied his gilded lace ornament and chinoiseries to Böttger porcelain, Far Eastern ware, and Delft faience.

Another artist of the first order was Bartholomäus Seuter (1678–1754), the head of a prolific and artistic family business. He became a rich and famous man, partly owing to Meissen, partly owing to his own great ability. The author of travel descriptions, Johann Georg Keyssler, writes of Seuter's activity: "Seuter sold the most beautiful pieces of porcelain, many of which he had sent in a white state from Dresden and had rendered much more precious with the addition of fine painting and enamel work." Naturally enough, the factory commission was not prepared to contemplate this highly questionable practice for too long, and the same author reports in October, 1730: "For one and a half years the sale of plain white porcelain has been forbidden in order that the profit which outsiders gain with painting and gilding should be made by the factory itself and for this purpose forty painters should be maintained."

There were, of course, other sources of white porcelain, even if of inferior quality, most of it coming from northern Bohemia, so *Hausmalerei* continued even after this restriction. Among those who continued to carry it out successfully were Johann Friedrich Metzsch, Johann Christoph Jucht in Bayreuth, Johann Philipp Dannhöfer and, above all, Ignaz Bottengruber in Breslau (whose work is eagerly sought by collectors today), with his two pupils, Carl Ferdinand von Wolfsburg and H. G. von Bressler, who also made names for themselves around 1740.

Unique work was produced by Ernst von dem Busch, a canon in Hildesheim. Between 1748 and 1775, he produced diamond etchings, based on copper engravings, on the white glaze of Meissen vessels and rubbed soot into them afterward. Although this unceramic technique went against all principles of suitable treatment for a material, his skilled work found appreciation and continues to do so today.

CLASSICISM AND THE MEISSEN MANUFACTORY

The rapid development and growth of manufacturers contributed to the emancipation of the middle classes. In France it culminated in the casting off of feudal chains by the revolution of 1789. The Saxon *Rétablissement* was a concession to these forcibly obtained developments. Similar compromises in other German states warded off actual revolution. Popular opinion was strongly influenced by the thinkers of the Enlightenment. In art these social changes were reflected in the rejection of Rococo for Classicism, and these changes are evinced by the Meissen ware of that period even though the pieces are derivative in character. Original artists of the period were closely linked with feudal society and its style, and the manufactory itself was part of the establishment. This period in the history of the manufactory is often referred to as the Marcolini period after Count Camillo Marcolini, who on August 20, 1774, took over the management of the manufactory and retained his position as director until his death in 1814.

Marcolini was of Italian origin and at the age of thirteen came to the Dresden court to be a page. He became friends with the elector (from 1807, King Frederick August I), who was eleven years younger, and remained his confidant all his life. Marcolini was given several court posts, and was also director general of the arts and of the Art Academy. He became a cabinet minister in 1809.

As with every previous change of management, proposals for reforms were made after a thorough investigation into the artistic and commercial state of affairs. Marcolini had no illusions about the extent of the manufactory's downward trend. Alarmingly, the ever-increasing sums it had to invest in its production appeared in an inverse ratio to sales. In order to introduce effective measures, Marcolini questioned all employees on their particular observations of defects in the system. No one except Kaendler, however, had the necessary overall view of the difficulties and their origins. In the final months before his death on May 18, 1775, Kaendler was preoccupied with the problem of the manufactory's survival, a concern that found its expression in countless memorandums to the factory commission.

In the first, on January 18, 1775, Kaendler drew attention to the frequent theft of white unpainted porcelain and to the chaos in the main warehouse. He called for an arrangement of porcelain stocks that would allow them to be checked easily.[89] On February 1, Kaendler took up his pen once more, mentioned the stealing again, and recommended that a porcelain controller be engaged to strictly supervise the buying and releasing of ware. The factory's transport methods were highly uneconomical, he alleged. These costs could be greatly reduced if four retired horses and two carts could be obtained from the electoral stables. Further economies could be made by constructing a short canal from the Elbe to the woodyard so that wood could be delivered directly into the hands of the choppers. He pointed out that unnecessary expense in production was incurred by the willful attitude of some department heads who were incapable of guaranteeing smooth passage of work from one process to another. Kaendler also found it disadvantageous that reports of insufficiencies, introduced in 1731 as an obligation on the part of all employees, were no longer the custom. If they were reintroduced, material for the Trade Fair would be properly prepared, would be in ample supply, and would suit the public taste.

The wisdom of employing female workers was, to his mind, highly questionable, and he criticized their being placed on the third floor, removed from any effective supervision. He recommended that a permanent fire officer be posted on the attic floor and that spare-time work, which meant that the rooms were occupied well into the night, be forbidden. But since fire could, nonetheless, break out a skilled master plumber should be engaged to supervise work to ensure a constant flow of water at high pressure. On April 18, exactly one month before his death, Kaendler reminded Marcolini how the 1731 reform had bound the arcanists of the time to set down in writing their knowledge and skills, and how their information was then sealed and handed over for keeping in the "*Grüne Gewölbe*" as if it were a holy relic. Later, Fletscher, unfortunately, had moved the writings to Meissen, because he was of the opinion that porcelain making was no longer a secret. Kaendler asked Count Marcolini to prevent the distribution of the secret of the Meissen paste and recipes at any price. It was necessary, however, as Kaendler concluded, to ensure the expansion of the factory along its traditional lines: a few days before his death he asked the directors to grant regular private instruction to his two faithful "*Scholare,*" Jüchtzer and Starke, every Wednesday and Saturday from eleven to twelve o'clock, so that his art and acquired knowledge would not die with him.

It is amazing that Kaendler, while considering all the problems involved in the factory's survival, continued to work at his craft until his final collapse. If we look through the pages of his work reports, we notice that the artist continued to give each piece of work his serious attention, whether it was as comprehensive as, for example, the big Russian commission, or as simple as a sketch for a new type of tureen foot. His massive repertoire, all his detailed knowledge of mythological and religious themes, remained with him to the last, as vivid in his mind as ever, always ready to be expressed in tangible form. He himself was probably aware that certain of his ideas were not merely slightly worn but frankly out of fashion, that here and there the Baroque pathos had a hollow ring about it and sometimes caused sympathetic smiles among his fellow artists, but he refused to accept this, just as he refused to accept the undeniable fact that the Meissen manufactory no longer held the European monopoly in porcelain making. In certain respects he had fallen victim to senile obstinacy. He would not admit that creations that had met with great success over the decades no longer found universal approbation, that the times no longer favored the making of monumental statues, and that the engagement of a second highly paid *Modellmeister* from France was a necessity. The incentive for his passionate exertions during his final years came no longer, however, purely from a desire to give his ideas artistic expression. His stubborn resistance to change often resulted in routine empty pieces. He is another example of the tragedy of the aging master, unaware of the weakened effect produced by the repetition of earlier triumphs. Nevertheless, if we compare most of his work of this last period with that of other European factories in their prime, we must acknowledge the higher quality that raises it above the rival product. The old craftsman was still interested in the possible variations in the style of tableware. Prince Xaver repeatedly engaged him on design in the rising Neoclassical mode, and certain interesting pieces resulted, such as the special tureens for the serving of snails, a similar dish for strawberries, an oval glass cooler, and an intricately woven breadbasket.

In stark contrast to the austere shapes of early French Classicism are the vessels, especially the lidded tureens, in the form of naturalistic inventions from the plant and animal kingdoms, which Kaendler modeled with devotion to the finest detail. Without complaining that his personal powers of invention were being overlooked, he undertook the making of the "most graciously" commissioned special items for the court, such as imitation of Japanese porcelain bowls sent from Holland, or of a Parisian service in silver. On the whole Kaendler relied more and more during his last years on motifs he had realized were effective and used decades before. In many of these late works we miss the originality of the earlier pieces. On the other hand, it is remarkable that Kaendler lost none of his talent for presenting a figure or situation in a most attractive manner. While most of the Italian Comedy figures, single shepherds, and vintagers no longer have the appeal they had at the time of the wars with Frederick II, Kaendler's wit reveals itself once more in certain situation pieces, such as the Cherry Group (January, 1765) and The Old Woman in Love (March, 1765). A particularly humorous piece reflecting immoral customs is A Painful

Situation (1770), in which a young woman is shown at breakfast with her husband, who has left off reading his paper to stare in amazement at the little dog which is barking at a lover hiding under the bed. A cycle of religious sculptures and the so-called Small Crucifixion Group make up the large "Roman commission" which Frederick Augustus III intended as a gift to the Vatican.

Kaendler's last work reports date from March, 1775. They mention a wide variety of figures. Along with some of the Italian Comedy figures, there is a Doctor, a Gondolier, and a Tartaglio. Kaendler had also been occupied with the serious wishes expressed by the educated public for a monument worthy of the "*praeceptor Germaniae*," the pious and learned poet Christian Fürchtegott Gellert, who had died on December 13, 1769. Kaendler made a few busts and medallions in various designs to get a good likeness, so that the best could be used in a monument. On the Classical-style base, which he changed many times, were seated figures representing Faith and Adoration as previously seen in the Miltitz memorial. His vast output therefore came to an end not with a glorification of absolutism but with the expression of middle-class intellectual achievements.

On May 18, 1775, Johann Joachim Kaendler died. His death is mentioned in the May report as follows: "On May 18, the court commissioner and first chief sculptor of this electoral porcelain manufactory died. Herr Johann Joachim Kaendler, a skilled artist, whose memory will never fade in the manufactory, in the 69th year of his life, after serving the factory for forty-four years ..." On January 26 he had been preceded by his old rival, Höroldt. The question as to who was to replace Kaendler went unanswered, and as a temporary solution his work was distributed according to ability among his experienced fellow craftsmen.

At the time of his death the manufactory did not lack skilled modelers. Mention has already been made of the cooperation of Acier and Schönheit. They were joined in 1768 by the sculptor Jean Troy from Lunéville, who had followed Christian Gottlieb Berger from Sèvres. We cannot form a picture of the work of these two sculptors, who remained only a short time at the factory, since it is not mentioned in work reports. It was most probably Berger who brought the biscuit porcelain technique to Meissen from Sèvres. Unglazed porcelain was first used for the making of statuettes at Vincennes by Bachelier, head of design there, and after the takeover of that factory by Sèvres, it was produced to an extraordinary extent in the latter. The aim to produce an "antique" porcelain was partially fulfilled when, as a result of a special compounding, the paste achieved the appearance of marble. The imitation of Classical themes, as well as the modeling of busts and medallions, was much more convincing in biscuit porcelain than in the white glazed variety, especially when the soft, waxen, and dry effect desired by English connoisseurs was obtained. Glazed porcelain was not so suitable for true-to-life representations since the facial characteristics were softened in the glazing process. The fact that porcelain's special quality had been cast aside did not, on the other hand, appear to trouble the public of the day.

Biscuit porcelain must be seen in the context of its period in order to appreciate its aesthetic charms of impressive delicacy and cool precision. The ways in which it may be used are, of course, limited. Its practical value seemed questionable to the two Meissen agents when they saw the biscuit porcelain statuettes kept under glass domes in Sèvres. But the economic necessity for Meissen to create a well-balanced paste for this biscuit porcelain, in soft tones and the mat shimmer of its surface, led to results of remarkable artistic maturity.

Even in this lesser period Meissen produced masterpieces. Among the many works by Schönheit, Jüchtzer, Matthäi, and Schöne is many an excellent creation and many a successful translation of an antique model in the new material. In 1796, the management sent Jüchtzer to Dresden to study the plaster cast collection of ancient statues. Whereas Matthäi put down roots there, eventually becoming an inspector of the plaster cast collection, Jüchtzer returned to Meissen, under the spell of the ancient world.

Christian Gottfried Jüchtzer (1752–1812) joined the manufactory in 1769 as an apprentice embosser. Kaendler frequently chose him to cooperate on intensive work. On the death of his first master, Jüchtzer avidly worked for Acier, and was in 1781 himself made *Modellmeister* because of his proficiency. Eventually he became chief director of design. His thorough study of the electoral collection of antiquities tore him decisively away from Kaendler's influence and led him to make an artistic choice along the lines of Winckelmann's principles. His strength lies in his single figures, calm silhouettes approaching the Classical ideal.

While Jüchtzer's works were for the most part of his own design, Johann Gottlieb Matthäi (1752–1832) worked exclusively from copies of ancient sculptures which he transposed in miniature into Meissen biscuit porcelain. He had started work in Meissen in 1773, disappeared for some months in 1776, allegedly to Copenhagen for the purposes of study, but returned to Meissen in the same year. He served the manufactory well until 1795 when he became inspector of the electoral collection of casts of ancient statues in Dresden.

The third member of this group of biscuit porcelain specialists was the modeler Johann Daniel Schöne, born in Meissen in 1767. His career began in 1783 and followed the course already established by Jüchtzer and Matthäi. A report shows that in 1810, the centenary year, he was working on a portrait medallion of Böttger. The rest of his pieces are hardly distinguishable from those of his colleagues—indeed this period was the least conducive to individuality in artistic creation. From 1780, the manufactory decided to imitate Wedgwood ware. Meissen and other European manufactories recognized a fierce competitor in this new ware invented by Josiah Wedgwood at Etruria, Staffordshire, in 1769, consisting of marbled pottery, basalt stoneware, and a particularly satisfactory stoneware, colored brownish-red to sepia, known as Jasper ware, made in pieces of Classical shape. When the younger Wedgwood began to produce soft-paste porcelain in 1795, Meissen could only get a foothold in the market by ruthlessly imitating Wedgwood ware. This cool, mat, extremely severe material was more suited than any previous for the expression of Classicism. The tableware made in it, with its acanthus-leaf ornament, beadings, and finely cut antique profile portraits, found great public approval in 1800, although it lacked certain characteristics of the glossy eighteenth-century china, namely its colorful decoration and simple hygienic advantages.

Reliefs in the ancient Greek manner, portraits in the style of high Roman sculpture, and the almost forgotten art of gem cutting led to technical achievements of outstanding merit. Together with the style in furniture and the fashions of dress also imported from England and inclining toward discreet elegance, they made for a refreshing unity in the applied arts. All this had to be taken up by Meissen, tried out in its own very different material, produced economically, and finally launched on the market at competitive prices. This was often done unsatisfactorily and, from the point of view of fashion, too late. Compared with the variety of form and decoration offered by Wedgwood, the choice of Meissen examples of this kind is very narrow. Nevertheless, this portion of Meissen's output stands out and reveals attractive and delicate specimens.

The cool language of Classical style has the warm breath of sentimentality breathed into it occasionally in the form of flower garlands, symbols of friendship and fondness, and written mottoes. On the whole, however, the repertoire of decorative elements may be described as impoverished and limited to a few motifs from antiquity, such as rams' heads, acanthus borders, beadings, snake handles, and ribbon ornament. This recalls similar situations in the Böttger period almost a hundred years before, when shapes and ornamental elements of a formal character, which had been developed for other materials and were

hardly suitable for porcelain, were used. We are amazed at the lack of vitality exhibited after seventy years by these formal elements. Only the art of the portrait reached remarkable heights, almost comparable with late Roman work. The tendency toward naturalistic design found its fulfillment in these occasionally excellent examples of the miniature relief and in a group of animal carvings, an aspect of work in porcelain that had faded into the background. Insects, reptiles, and various small animals were modeled in white biscuit porcelain and placed on a blue or reddish-brown plinth. Their grotesque postures are particularly effective as in a realistically displayed fight between a frog and a crab. All forms of the tectonic, which demands the uncluttered straight line, the right angle, and the curve, show themselves, however, most unsuitable for the medium of porcelain. The stereometric elements, which in all other materials afford precise reproduction, are the very ones that were seldom executed satisfactorily in ceramic work. Most pieces show aberrations from the mathematical conception, and although these are relatively slight they spoil the overall effect in some cases. In this respect Kaendler had an easier task working during the Baroque and Rococo periods.

From the period between 1780 and 1790, there exist some tableware designs, grading, and mold lists which supply exhaustive information on the complexities of production. According to this information there were about one hundred plate designs with different rim treatment and different relief ornament which could be matched with all the other parts of the service in the same pattern and which were all still part of the production. If we multiply these designs by the numerous painted decorations, we realize that by 1780 an enormous variety was available. However satisfactory this richness might appear, it was in fact a liability in times that were bad for business, for it could never be anticipated what would be rejected and what would sell particularly well. The manufactory always had to be prepared to beat competitors in all fields. A sudden change of fashion, however, could result in a catastrophic burden of unsold stock.

Although the change to Classicism in the figure production had been effected by this time, tableware was slow to follow suit. Silhouettes with straight lines, large smooth surfaces, and handles in the form of a right angle first appeared in 1790 and it was a long time, almost decades, before they established themselves. The unbroken surfaces offered a large area which could be filled with painting in disregard of artistic principles. For this reason the team of painters was engaged on separate specialized tasks. And if already in Höroldt's time switching battle painters to work on the *deutsche Blume* was avoided when possible, by the Marcolini period such change had indeed become an impossibility.

Since the time of the commissions of Frederick II of Prussia, judged purely on a quantitative basis, flower painting was undoubtedly in the lead. Since the Berlin and Vienna manufactories had developed flower painting to an extraordinary degree with the help of specialists from Meissen, and had acquired an excellent name in this art, Meissen itself was compelled to make efforts to catch up with its competitors. One of the most able flower painters of the early Marcolini period was David Friedrich Weller (1759–1789), who started work at the manufactory in 1781 but soon moved to Dresden where he occupied himself with still-life painting of flowers, working not only on porcelain but also on large pastel and gouache paintings. On his deathbed this highly gifted man was accorded the title of court painter. Although Weller left Meissen after a very short time, flower painting was continued by Christian Adolf Heynemann, also court painter, who took up employment in Meissen roughly at the time of Marcolini's arrival and whose excellent work raised the standard of flower painting in the manufactory.

Closely related to the flower painting, the depiction of fruits in combination with representations of birds ("*Federviehmalerei*") was extremely popular. One of the earliest Classical tableware designs, with an openwork border and cornflower-blue stripes was, at the request of the Saxon court, decorated with excellently painted fruits and native birds. Toward the end of the century the "*Federvieh-Spezialisten*" were increasingly in demand, since the public showed a preference for colorful naturalistically painted birds above all other motifs. There was also an increased demand by the wealthy for portraiture, as on porcelain cups. For these paintings calm Classical silhouettes on cylindrical cups were the best vehicle. Johann Georg Loehnig (1745–1806) revealed from the very first days of his employment at the manufactory in 1763 an extraordinary talent for these. His main period of activity lies around 1780. Since the discovery in Stuttgart of some cups initialed by him, we can recognize his handiwork on other items. Besides this painter it is possible that Johann Jacob Wagner, who died at a great age in Dresden in 1797, and Heinrici may both have applied their skills in the field of miniature painting.

It is interesting to note that the colored Watteau motifs enjoyed a second spell of even greater popularity in the last quarter of the century. One of the most brilliant miniature painters of this genre, Isaac Jacques Clauce (1728–1803), who had been allowed to leave Meissen in 1754 after one year's work there, was now working in Berlin. In Heinrich Christian Wahnes, born in 1700, the manufactory found a painter who is still mentioned in 1778 as a specialist in putti styled after Boucher.

Since the delicate tints of these paintings were all too easily lost on the white porcelain ground, a strong background color was provided for them in the Sèvres manner with the *bleu royal* already mentioned. The transition from background to painting was modulated by an extremely fine gold lace border. Gold lace painters were scarce; much depended on the subtlety of their art.

The acquisition of an unlimited palette of ceramic colors led to the extension of this imitative work to the wholesale reproduction of particularly treasured paintings in the electoral gallery. Heinrici, the versatile miniature painter, made a start on a copy of Raphael's "Madonna della Sedia" in 1763, and various

Meissen painters, such as Heinrich Gotthelf Schaufuss (1760–1838) tried to equal him in this test of artistic skill. Schaufuss, who had been employed with the manufactory since 1781, was later made supervisor of painting. He repeatedly proved his ability as a creative artist, as in October, 1807, when he received a special fee of 25 talers for two allegorical pastels. A Dresden academician, Georg Wilhelm Grünwald (1749–1831), at Meissen from 1775, made copies of copper engravings by Jean Baptiste Greuze that were true to the last line.

The battle painters, too, began to receive more frequent commissions some time after the Prussian wars. Specialists in this field during the Marcolini period were Johann Gottlieb Friedrich Tiebel (1750–1796). who worked in Meissen from 1773 and supervised painting from 1782, the porcelain painter Grossmann, sent as an industrial spy to Sèvres in 1766, and finally the battle scene painter Christian Heerfurth (born 1786). Heerfurth, incidentally, belonged to that group of painters who worked outside the manufactory. He made the picture Bibles for the library of the House of Wettin. The same is the case with Karl Gottlob Ehrlich, painter and drawing master (1744–1799), with the manufactory from 1763. Although no piece of porcelain painting can be ascribed to him with certainty, his works in other fields have become well known, such as the huge modular watercolor showing a view from the Albrechtsburg, now in the Meissen Municipal Museum, the uniquely realistic and atmospheric etching of the fire in the Albrechtsburg, and the documentary gouache painting showing drifting ice on the rising waters of the Elbe in 1789.

Apart from him, there was a whole group of landscape painters, such as Johannes Karl Mauksch (1754–1821), at the manufactory from 1775, whose work around 1780 included a signed cup with a shepherd scene, and the painter Christian Gottlieb Naumann. Some painters came to the fore with above average creations sometimes of more universal significance, who while with the manufactory trained the succeeding generation of artists, or who as supervisors set standards for the painting department. The successor of the versatile artist Johann Elias Zeissig (Schenau) was Johann David Schubert (1761–1822). Apart from scenes from *Werthers Leiden* which were of his own design, he painted copies on porcelain of the most popular pictures from the Dresden Gallery. Deserving mention as drawing masters during the Marcolini period are Carl Gottlieb Grahl (1740–1782), August Johann Ernst Mehner (died 1832), and Christian Lindner (died 1806), although they never produced any noteworthy work of their own.

The production of the Marcolini period may be judged of extremely variable quality. In spite of a few voices raised in defense of certain individual successes, numerous criticisms reject this epoch as inimical to the medium of porcelain, decrying its imitative production in particular. One must also take into account both growing competition and the unhappy economic conditions in Saxony after the eighteenth-century wars. The taler never recovered its 1756 level. Although the manufactory workers' standard of living had nearly sunk to subsistence level, as a result of economy measures introduced under Marcolini their wages were further reduced by a third. The workers made repeated united protests and organized strikes. The commission saw these as dangerous revolts and imprisoned the ringleaders. In these movements too there was also evidence of the tensions boding revolution. In August, 1790, one year after the outbreak of the French Revolution, these tensions were released in varying ways and in various places, most markedly in the uprising of the Saxon peasants who were rebelling against their state of serfdom. In many places the landowners were put to flight and the soldiers sent to put down the rebels were disarmed. During the disturbance in the Meissen region some two thousand peasants set free their leaders, who had been imprisoned on the Burgberg. The revolts soon collapsed, however, since the peasants stood almost alone in their struggle and lacked the support of other antifeudal factions. It is not recorded how the employees of the porcelain manufactory felt about the events taking place at their door. One contemporary report quotes the fear that the poorer classes of the town of Meissen might join forces with the peasants.[90] Any sign of growing solidarity among the employees was viewed with extreme suspicion. In spite of this, certain developments could not be impeded. For instance, the commission could hardly disapprove of the founding of a woodworkers' burial fund to help the neediest pay these fees in hard times, since electoral subventions could not be counted on.

Consideration of the manufactory's commercial development during these forty years, in which it self-consciously added a star to its sword mark, shows the growing problems that confronted Marcolini. He often despaired of overcoming them. When he took up his post in 1774, and as his first act ordered a work analysis, he received the following balance of accounts: sales of 188,697 talers had

to cover expenses amounting to 151,908 talers, so the resulting profit was far from satisfactory. The 24,743 talers distributed in wages to the 144 workers in the modeling department meant on average 130 talers. More highly paid were the 257 painters, with the total standing at 38,200 talers, and the average at 149 talers. The annual average income of an employee on the commercial side lay at 151 talers, while the manual workers rarely received more than 70 talers. Nevertheless, the pensioners and the sick were provided with a sum of 4,940 talers in 1773.[91]

The problem of how to economize remained unsolved during the Marcolini period. Control could not be introduced at those points where money might have been saved, for this in itself would have involved additional expense. In his last analyses Kaendler had proposed the doubling of officials in key posts and additions of supervisory staff, in order to end crippling wastages of time, but this would have resulted in an undesirable increase in the number of employees. An attempt to obtain outstanding sums and assess the amount of porcelain given on commission was also made. This list of debtors all over the world names the following cities: Amsterdam, Ancona, Archangel, Bern, Bologna, Bordeaux, Brussels, Cadiz, Constantinople, Copenhagen, Cracow, Dublin, Genoa, The Hague, Hamburg, Kaluga, Kiel, Liège, Lisbon, London, Lubeck, Madrid, Marseilles, Milan, Moscow, Naples, Narva, Nuremberg, Palermo, Paris, Pest, St. Petersburg, Reval, Riga, Rome, Rotterdam, Smolensk, Stockholm, Strasbourg, Thorn, Utrecht, Venice, and Warsaw.

In order to boost sales and popularity at any cost, the manufactory returned to the questionable means tried out in 1765 in Amsterdam, St. Petersburg, and Constantinople: the auction. A report dating from November, 1773, states that the first experiment with this method of selling was made at a time when, owing to unrest in Poland, the Turko-Russian war, and the universal high cost of living, it seemed that there would be a decline in the porcelain trade and that payment for deliveries was so far behind that the manufactory's finances threatened to be thrown out of balance. The success of the first auctions held in Hamburg encouraged repetition of the experiment. An analysis dated October 6, 1775, however, revealed that auctions did not improve the smooth conduct of business, since the wares sold below their actual cost. Before the year was out, 385 crates of porcelain were sent abroad for auction as a means of obtaining speedy cash. No other course was open to the manufactory in the last decade of the eighteenth century in order to extricate itself from the problem of the enormous surplus of totally outdated ware. Marcolini granted the court commissioner and mining official Dr. Carl Wilhelm Poerner the concession for holding three large auctions in 1790, 1791, and 1793. For these auctions Poerner obtained wares worth 50,000 to 60,000 talers at a discount of 12.5 percent to 25 percent. Presumably, he made a profit. What made this highly respected scientist and author take such a risk at his age is not known. He died in 1796 at the age of sixty-four. His various publications on natural science, medicine, and chemistry include such works as *Anmerckungen zu Baumés Abhandlungen über den Thon* (1771) and *Mineralogisches im Neuen Schauplatz der Natur* (1775–1781), fields not far removed from the matters of the arcanum to which he was admitted in 1768.

At the end of the Marcolini era, auctions became impracticable owing to the hazards of transportation in wartime. They were immediately begun anew when the roads became reasonably safe. At the end of the eighteenth century the bulk of the sales of Meissen porcelain consisted of large consignments of tableware to Russia. This was mainly cheaper ware, exported mostly as a result of the Leipzig Fair. Sales to Turkey also rose, although they never equaled the Russian orders. All went well until November, 1806, when an embargo on all European porcelain was ordered by the Russian court and trade with Turkey almost ceased during the Turko-Russian War. The damage caused by these two blows is represented by figures showing the decrease in profit for these years:

1805	156,000 talers
1806	132,200 talers
1807	65,500 talers
1810	51,000 talers
1813	24,400 talers

The number of employees dropped from 521 to 395 during the same period. In spite of this decrease, conditions for the workers hardly improved. On the contrary, food prices rose rapidly. The manufactory commission found itself with no choice but to allow not only a cost of living bonus for the poorest, but to order eighty bushels of grain to be delivered from the Dresden warehouses and made into bread.

Saxony, including the old town of Meissen, was destined to suffer the direct effects of the Napoleonic wars. The year 1807 proved particularly fateful for the Electorate. Although Napoleon had succeeded in winning over Frederick Augustus III to the Confederation of the Rhine by making him king of Saxony, the country was made to pay a war contribution of 7,000,000 talers. The Meissen district had to pay 1,300,000 of this. The manufactory employees made a contribution according to income, payable in two installments. Thus an arcanist paid 4 talers, a painter 6 groschen, and a yard worker 2 groschen.

In 1809, the disruptions of war were again felt keenly. The psychological effects must not be underestimated here; the ebb and flow of French troops on the one hand and of the allies on the other brought changes of occupation. People's sympathies were confused. Although the accounts for 1809 show no deficit, complete closure of the manufactory was being considered by the management at the beginning of 1810, exactly one hundred years after its foundation. The current archives did not mention this, nor did they mention the journey of two cartloads of manufactory workers to Dresden on April 3, 1810, to protest the threat of closure. The deputation fortunately succeeded. Production continued and a few weeks later the centenary of the oldest European porcelain manufactory was celebrated with the dignity it deserved. From the detailed reports of the centenary celebrations two important facts can be established: for the first time the manufactory and the townspeople joined in a common harmonious celebration without any petty jealousies. The pride felt by the inhabitants of Meissen at having within their midst an establishment of such strong tradition and world renown showed in the decorated streets, extravagant illuminations, fanfares from the towers, and the common service of thanksgiving in the cathedral. Secondly, we learn that the program of festivities was arranged as a real *Volksfest*: feasting at table in tents set up on the Schützenwiese proves that. The following people were invited: 412 workers, employees, and artists; 22 female employees; 28 pensioners; 350 manufactory workers' wives; and 154 employees' widows. On the meadow between the tents and the colossal busts of Böttger, Augustus the Strong, the reigning king, and Marcolini, a masque called *The Expression of Gratitude* was performed. Altogether 944 people took part. Wine presented by the members of the town council propelled the general air of merriment well into the night. Approximately ten thousand people streamed into the decorated town from all sides. These festivities seemed to impart a new courage for further work, otherwise the purchase of a new clay field in the plain around Colditz would not have been contemplated. Yet a mere two years later the town, and with it the manufactory, was once more threatened by war. Meissen formed a bridgehead in the field of conflict.

A full account of the way in which the storm of battle raged round Meissen cannot be given here. However, as during the Silesian wars, an employee of the manufactory kept a chronicle of events. According to the records of Manufactory Controller Herrfahrt, the turbulence and threats reached their height in September and October, 1813. Although the manufactory had lost more than forty employees through a typhus epidemic and fifteen through military call-up,

production was fairly well maintained. Later, however, circumstances necessitated the cessation of all work. Prussian and Russian officers requisitioned various items of porcelain to the total value of 824 talers 4 groschen. More keenly felt was the loss of work materials, tools, firefighting equipment and, most of all, considerable quantities of firewood, which had grown more and more expensive. The castle precincts were also gradually occupied by 1,500 wounded of all nations, among whom no discipline was maintained.

A few months before it came to this dismal pass, no less a person than Johann Wolfgang von Goethe had visited the town. He arrived on April 19, 1813, at the *Gasthof* "Goldener Ring," and on April 20 wrote to his wife thoughtfully describing the exhaustive tour he made of the manufactory: "Tuesday the twentieth was a very pleasant and instructive day. We first went up to the castle and visited the porcelain manufactory, mainly the stockrooms. It is strange and almost unbelievable to find there very few things which one would like in one's own home. The reason is that there were too many workers (twenty years ago there were over seven hundred) so they had to be kept busy and were allowed to build up large stores of things that were fashionable at the time. Fashion changed, but the stocks remained. They were afraid to auction these objects or send them to distant parts to be sold cheaply. And so they remained in storage. It is a most splendid exhibition of things which no longer please, and this does not apply to merely one piece, but to masses, hundreds, indeed thousands."

These explanations of misplanning may not be altogether valid. Goethe was probably given some false information, and of course his taste lay exclusively with the Classical, while most of the pieces he saw in the overflowing storerooms were in the late Rococo style.

It would be unfair to blame the manufactory's accelerating decline during the 1774–1814 period solely on its *Oberdirektor*. From the very start he felt inadequate to his overwhelming task and frequently made his views known to Frederick Augustus. In 1791, he urgently requested to be relieved of his post, but the elector and later king of Saxony again persuaded him to continue as supreme director of this languishing concern. Due to his sober nature, he tried to fight the manufactory's decay by administrative means, neglecting any initiative on the creative side. He had little appreciation for porcelain. Patrons such as Brühl were a thing of the past. Count Marcolini was nevertheless the first man in the State and the representative of his country, and for this reason he commissioned a certain amount of porcelain. Apart from a service showing his arms in an old-fashioned rocaille cartouche, and a second one showing the arms uniting the Marcolini and O'Kelly families, there are very few personal pieces, such as some portrait cups in biscuit porcelain, cylindrical cups with excellent miniature paintings of his estate and vineyards, and a bust made by Andreas Weger on the occasion of the centenary celebrations.

THE MANUFACTORY IN THE FIRST HALF
OF THE NINETEENTH CENTURY ·

The first half of the nineteenth century in Germany was characterized by popular antifeudal movements, struggles for a democratic constitution and a
united Germany, and by the industrial revolution.

Class structure was swiftly changed by the advent of the industrial revolution in Saxony. A new class, the industrial proletariat, emerged. In the Meissen
manufactory the industrial revolution had made itself felt through the reorganization of the managerial side and by the improvement and mechanization of
the manufacturing processes, but Meissen's special character as a manufactory
had not been lost.

After Marcolini's death in 1814, *Bergrat* Carl Wilhelm von Oppel became
director. Under his leadership the manufactory began its revival after the difficult years of the Napoleonic wars. The Leipzig businessman Martini was made
trade supervisor. In 1814, authority over all technical matters was granted to
Heinrich Gottlob Kühn (1788–1870) as production inspector. Kühn was without a doubt the most outstanding personality connected with the manufactory
during the nineteenth century. He had studied mining in Freiberg, law in Wittenberg, and chemistry in Berlin. Only two years after his engagement by Meissen his salary was increased from 500 to 800 talers, since he had made an important innovation—the circular, or story, furnace. Story furnaces enable a double
use to be made of each firing, so that the lower part is used for the first and the
upper for the second firing. In 1816, a second, and in 1817 three additional story-
furnaces were built. A production analysis for 1827 reveals that, compared with
the output of 1814, four times as many plates could be produced as a result of
these new kilns. In addition the staff in charge of the firings could be reduced to
nineteen and better use made of the extremely expensive kiln fuel.

Building activity during these years consisted of extensive alterations to the
kiln houses, the enameling, and eventually all other departments. Kühn was
most concerned to cut down the distance covered between one process to another. In order to avoid too much disruption of production routine, this project
had to be carried out from the ground floor upward. Kühn had the scattered
laboratories united under one roof as one modernly equipped laboratory, and he
obtained the permanent engagement of two smelting assistants, Friedrich
August Köttig and Karl Friedrich Selbmann. After a short probationary period,
both were made arcanists; the laboratory supervisor was Christian Gottfried
Leberecht Holtzwig, an arcanist who had been employed as color specialist
since 1802.

The next problem was the quality of the china clay. The clay from Aue and
Seilitz were compared. In 1817, a clay had been found, on the property of the
Sornzig convent near Mügeln, which was equal in quality to the best consign-
ments of the Aue variety, but which was not regularly used in the paste until

1842. Four years later Schletta clay was discovered which, since it was open-cast mined only five kilometers away, could be delivered to the manufactory quickly and cheaply, but this material was not used in regular production until 1861. The deliveries of Aue clay gradually decreased until their final cessation in the middle of the century.

The manufactory commission decided in August, 1814, that the Hubertusburg castle stoneware factory and the Döhlen pottery works should be amalgamated for administrative purposes with the Meissen manufactory, but this experiment had to be abandoned after two years. Artistic influence from Meissen continued to dominate the decoration of Hubertusburg stoneware especially in flower painting, until the Hubertusburg manufactory finally failed in 1839.

A horse gear that had been installed to power some engines is first mentioned in 1732. Since around 1790, it was in operation under the north front of the Albrechtsburg, it was covered by an onion-shaped roof and drove most machines by a transmission system. New *Ovaldrehscheiben* had been constructed for the molds. These labor-saving alterations permitted a reduction in manpower.

The reorganized work routines gradually functioned smoothly, and even the most recalcitrant skeptics had to admit that the changes had brought about the beginning of a clearly profitable production. A factor contributing to this improvement was substitution of monthly and annual accounting for the earlier occasional method.

When Kühn welcomed the considerable savings made by the abolition of original painting which had become possible in 1814 through the use of copper engravings, he failed to see that an important facet of the manufactory's work had been discarded. He was also mistaken in the assumption that a new store of copper engravings, models of other manufactories' tableware, and other bases for design would revive artistic ability.[92]

The artistic life of the manufactory underwent a revival as a result of the activity of Georg Friedrich Kersting, who was born October 31, 1785, in Güstrow, and died July 1, 1847, in Meissen. He was a well-known painter of the Dresden Romantic school. Kersting had received his artistic training in Copenhagen and Dresden, and settled in the latter, where, on account of his upright character, he was welcomed into the circle of Carus, Friedrich, and von Kügelgen. From 1813 to 1815 he took part in the wars of liberation in a volunteer corps and then for three years was tutor in the household of Duchess Sapieha in Poland. It was there that he received his offer from Meissen. He took up his new post on July 1, 1818, and stayed in it until his death. In his independent work he specialized in interior scenes charged with atmosphere. The Meissen manufactory was hardly interested in this, so his artistic influence in Meissen was negligible. His main contribution lies in the fact that he rescued the painting team from their dusty conservatism and gave them a fresh, direct approach to their artistic duties. The work of many artists visibly improved under his guidance. A number of them later became known for their creativity.

A single important commission, offering the opportunity to compete with Sèvres, Vienna, and Berlin, restored to Meissen its rightful prestige. The so-called Wellington Service was made for Arthur Wellesley, who was created Duke of Wellington in 1814 for his victories during the Napoleonic wars. The

Heinrich Gottlob Kühn

gifts presented to him by the allies in recognition of his services included costly silverware and a porcelain service comprising many hundreds of pieces, made at Meissen, Berlin, Vienna, and Sèvres. The Meissen contribution, the so-called Saxon Service, was conceived as a dessert service and consisted of 134 pieces. These included impressive vases in the form of ancient amphorae, sweetmeat bowls, ice containers like craters, and a considerable number of dessert plates with various decorations. The conventional form of the items is not as important as the painting on them, which was probably executed under Kersting's supervision according to Arnhold's principles of painting technique. The working group for this commission was definitively chosen in January, 1819, and from then on was exclusively occupied on this task. It consisted of the painters Johann Samuel Arnold, Johann Gottlieb Böhlig, Christian Gottlieb Hottewitzsch, and Johann Friedrich Nagel. The entire commission was completed in 1820 and sent to London.

Johann Samuel Arnhold designed the green underglaze vine leaf pattern that first appeared in 1817 and is still very popular today. According to Kühn's report, the experiments to find a new underglaze color, chromium oxide green, had begun in 1814 and succeeded in 1817. After Kersting developed a more feasible type of gilding, Kühn succeeded a few years later in making even further improvements. In 1827, he succeeded in inventing an unusual gilding preparation of the highest degree of fluidity which, now generally used and having the same durability as the old type, took up only one quarter of the gold used in 1826 for covering the same surface. This was *"Glanzgold,"* a gold which had no need of polishing after firing.

Another opportunity for Meissen to regain a foothold abroad came with the decision to make considerable reductions in prices in 1824. For this reason and as a result of extensive investments in technical innovations, the manufactory had to rely for many years on large subsidies. The number of employed dropped to 354 in 1827, a situation that might have seemed alarming if viewed superficially. While the number of mold makers stood at 38 in 1814, 17 were sufficient in 1827. The number of workers needed for smooth firing decreased from 22 to 11, the men on the first, or light, firing from 19 to 8, the color compounders from 11 to 6, general staff from 60 to 44. On the other hand, the number employed in forming had increased from 57 to 71 and in painting from 110 to 121. The output improved in quantity and quality. Sales improved, too.

The industrial revolution in the first half of the nineteenth century reinforced antifeudal feeling already prevalent. It nevertheless heightened the differences between the groups interested in abolishing the feudal constitution.

The throwers' room in the Albrechtsburg, 1850

Property owners, craftsmen, apprentices, journeymen, and the new industrial proletariat were all ranged against the feudal system, but each group had a different aim. After the French July Revolution of 1830 and risings in many parts of Germany, the first contradictions among the various antifeudal factions

The painters' and gilders' room in the Albrechtsburg, 1850

became evident. In Saxony the disturbances started in Leipzig, the town with the most liberated middle class. A few days later there was trouble in Dresden, and the cabinet was reshuffled as a result of pressure from the revolutionaries. In 1831, Saxony obtained a constitution which created a constitutional monarchy whereby the representation of the classes was changed, but only insignificantly. This representation in no way reflected the new social structure. Workers and peasants were not represented.

Constitutionally, the private income of the sovereign and his entourage was separated from the national finances. In September, 1831, the manufactory became a nationalized industry placed under the control of the Saxon Diet. Since it needed continual subsidy—12,500 talers in 1831 and 10,300 in 1832—closure was considered in spite of encouraging signs, among them an event of decisive importance—the establishment of the German Zollverein in 1834, which seemed likely to boost the trade in Meissen porcelain. From 1834, the manufactory no longer needed government subsidies.

The surplus in the balance of payment began modestly with a profit of 1,500 talers in 1834; by 1847 it had reached an annual average of 14,000 talers. Nevertheless, expenses were to exceed income once more from 1848 to 1851, when money was invested in essential manufactory improvements. In 1855, the profit of 17,800 talers augured well. Since England exacted no import duty on porcelain at this time, trade with her became very lively, in spite of unfavorable newspaper comments on Meissen ware shown at the Great Exhibition of 1851.

Carl Wilhelm von Oppel had died in 1833. His post remained unoccupied until 1849, when Kühn was made *Bergrat* and manufactory director. The function of liaison between the administration and the government once performed by the manufactory commission, which had devolved upon Oppel, could be directly reported by the technical-artistic and commercial management.

At Kühn's promotion to director of the whole enterprise, the hierarchic system by which Meissen had a local administration and a supreme administration in Dresden was abolished. The director was wholly responsible for the success of the works and had to submit monthly reports to the Ministry of Finance. Kühn had a universal outlook. The fact that he gave precedence to technical necessities and developments lay as much in his training as in the contemporary advancement of science. In 1839, after repeated experiments begun as early as 1814, the kilns were adapted for coal firing. Small manufactories in northern Bohemia had been using local brown coal for years, which naturally lessened the cost of the firing since it gave more heat than the costly firewood, involved fewer transport difficulties, and required no expensive preparation. Rebuilding kilns, though, obviously involved a major expense.

In 1853, the clumsy and quite expensive *Göpelantrieb* was superseded by a steam engine in the northwest ground floor rooms of the Albrechtsburg. In professional circles it had been thought that the vibration and jerking of the eight-horsepower engine, as well as the enlarged transmission system which

necessitated breaking into the centuries-old stonework would endanger the structure of the Albrechtsburg considerably. But Kühn insisted, so a steam engine and a number of paste-compounding machines were purchased for more than eight thousand talers with money granted by the Ministry of Finance.

An accidental discovery made by Inspector Köttig, which was in no way connected with porcelain making and decorating, led to the invention of a synthetic ultramarine blue and the founding of a subsidiary factory for the production of this *"Lasurstein"* blue, which became very popular. In 1850, the profit from the sale of ultramarine blue reached 10,500 talers, but fell so quickly owing to spreading competition that not only were the plans to build the manufactory's own production department abandoned, but also in 1877 all making of this color ceased. All the same, the Ministry of Finance was able to quote an overall profit from this secondary activity of almost 315,000 marks.

Through the efforts of Kühn, Köttig, and Selbmann the arcanum had been stripped of all vestiges of medieval mystery and the Meissen laboratory had become a respected research institute.

From Kühn's entire approach we can see that he repeatedly tried to better the lot of his employees, but he had insisted on such large investments in the firm on the part of the Ministry of Finance that he had to limit himself to the introduction of certain safety precautions: free working clothes for workers involved in special processes and a protective mask to prevent the inhalation of substances detrimental to health. Silicosis was also prevalent at the time and was indirectly combatted as far as was possible by rotation of workers. Kühn's liberal thinking found expression in other matters. The popular unrest in Paris in 1830 had stirred the formation of a *"Communalgarde"* in Meissen which carried out military exercises under the command of Kersting in the park of the electoral school. But in 1848, revolution echoed even more strongly in Meissen.

The Saxon king's resistance to the Imperial Constitution that had been agreed upon by the National Assembly in Frankfurt in the early days of May, 1849, occasioned an uprising by the inhabitants of Dresden which led to the proclamation of a republic and the flight of the monarch. The inhabitants of Meissen also produced a majority vote in favor of a republic. Changes had taken place in the common consciousness of Meissen, hitherto a relatively small and unimportant town. A Workers' Society had arisen. The mayor of Meissen, Hugo Tzschucke, who had been a deputy at the National Assembly, gave the communal guard the order to show support for the provisional republican government by marching to Dresden. Among the first to volunteer for the march were workers from the Jacobi iron foundry.[93] Employees of the manufactory were also among the troops who marched out of the town. The porcelain painter Seidel had helped to carry wounded from the barricades in the Dresden Neumarkt under a rain of bullets. The Dresden rising was put down after a few days by Prussian troops borrowed by the king to use against his own people. Those who had taken part in the revolt were given severe prison sentences. Tzschucke was also condemmed. Kühn intervened on behalf of the manufactory's employees, getting their sentences reduced and organizing a committee to give financial aid to the victims of oppression.

The administrative and technical progress made by the manufactory in the second quarter of the nineteenth century did not signal an artistic revival. When the enthusiasm for the severity of Classical forms had burned itself out, style seemed to run riot in a way that could hardly have been worse. The so-called second Rococo period was born after attempts to reproduce the neo-Gothic style in porcelain failed, and the cheap *Glanzgold* was used to excess to obtain a brilliant effect which was, however, of doubtful taste. In 1851, an artistic commission was founded, consisting of the director of the manufactory, the heads of design in modeling and painting, and a triumvirate of professors from the Dresden Academy. Each of these experts was, however, far too entrenched in his opinions to see the problems objectively. The commission failed to recognize that the administration had neglected to cultivate a competent succeeding generation of both generally and specially trained artists which would have ensured an improvement of artistic standards. In 1814, with the best intentions, they had transformed the loose ties between the manufactory's art school and the Dresden Academy into a formal interdependence. The training of future Meissen painters became an extramural department of the Dresden Art Academy. The manufactory hardly benefited, since the Dresden experts did not take their task seriously and, considering the artistic activities of the manufactory to be second-rate, sent only superfluous staff to the Meissen teaching posts.

In this manner Adrian Ludwig Richter came to Meissen on March 1, 1828, and was engaged to give twice-weekly corrective drawing classes until December 24, 1835. Although the painter must have been greatly charmed by the unchanged appearance of the ancient town of Meissen, he must have felt deprived of the exchange of views with his Dresden friends. Since he taught only two days a week, he earned only 200 talers a year. He found his contact with the manufactory employees uninspiring. It was a contact made difficult by the stratification of small-town social life. He had domestic problems and an irrepressible yearning for Italy, struggling for higher ideals and better circumstances. Only when he succeeded in obtaining a traveling allowance to visit the Bohemian Elbe Valley with a group of his more talented pupils did he overcome his obsession with Southern impressions and produce pictures with native motifs. These reflect a spiritual return to his home country. None of this was evident in the work he undertook for the manufactory, which blind bureaucracy prevented him from actually executing. Regrettably, Ludwig Richter's seven and a half years' employment left few tangible marks, but his later rich output of woodcut illustrations do show the roofs, gables, and towers of Meissen and its enchanting surroundings.

The responsibility for artistic continuity now lay once more in the hands of the manufactory directors, who made painting teachers of the best trained and most talented artists among the employees. The instruction was limited to solid training in the commonest principles of painting and decoration, however. Standardization of artistic work extinguished the last spark of free interpretation. New designs and new models were introduced only by free-lance artists who were occasionally given work on the advice of the artistic commission.

Ernst August Leuteritz (1818–1893) succeeded Johann Gottfried Dressler, who had gained many awards for the few pieces he produced, as head of design. Appointed in 1849, Leuteritz had been a pupil of Rietschel. In spite of his adoption of the Classical style under the influence of the Dresden Academy, he supported the Rococo revival with all determination, producing complicated figure groups and table centerpieces which were intended to re-create the richness of the eighteenth century. These creations had no inner substance in spite of their technical excellence, a shortcoming due less to the artists' failure than to the outdated artistic expressions of the Rococo period he was imitating.

The pieces made by Leuteritz's former teacher Ernst Rietschel (1804–1861) on behalf of the manufactory for the great Munich Exhibition in 1854, such as a monumental vase in the antique style, show deep penetration into the objectives of an artistic undertaking. This is most evident in the free sculptures he produced in 1855, such as the bust of King John of Saxony and the statuette of Ganymede of which Rietschel himself requested a reproduction in biscuit porcelain. It should be pointed out that Rietschel, unlike Gottfried Semper, advised the manufactory against the revival of Rococo taste.

Semper had once expressed the opinion that the exuberance and richness of the sculpted ornament on the Dresden Zwinger was a derivative of the contemporary art of porcelain. This false conclusion came from his misconceived thesis that the development of an architectural style could be traced to the regional character of ceramic ware. Although Semper sensed the charms of the Rococo, he worked along entirely different lines, so that his exhibition vases decorated with mythological scenes after designs by the Nazarine painter Schnorr von Carolsfeld show the respectable style of the High Renaissance revival. Julius Schnorr von Carolsfeld (1794–1872) designed many friezes of mythological content, particularly in the years 1854 and 1862, for use on amphorae and craters in Meissen porcelain. Influenced by the impressions of his stay in Italy, he tried to execute his painting as in majolica ware, although this type of ceramic art is entirely different from porcelain painting. He was the child of a time which lived and breathed revival, and he was unable to free himself from historical interpretation.

A more sober and artistically honest note is found in the few pieces designed for the manufactory by the sculptor Christian Daniel Rauch (1777–1857) in the form of an excellent Goethe statuette and an idealized representation of Dürer carried out in biscuit porcelain. Mention must also be made of Johannes Heinrich von Dannecker (1758–1841) and his carefully thought out Classical work, Ariadne on a Panther. These exceptional contributions made by prominent artists were invaluable to the manufactory during this decade of this lowest creative ebb.

The Meissen manufactory's reputation gradually increased. At the great international applied arts and industrial exhibition which took place in Munich in 1854, only items based on the designs of prominent artists had been shown. A first prize was won there, and at the Paris World Exhibition in 1855 the Porcelaine de Saxe received universal acclaim. Seven years later, single artistic pieces of gigantic proportions were exhibited in London, and once more a first prize was awarded. Although they entailed a large sum in artists' fees and the special production of unusual and technically demanding monumental pieces, these successes eventually brought commercial rewards and laid the foundations for the manufactory's boom in the last quarter of the nineteenth century.

THE MANUFACTORY MOVES TO NEW PREMISES

When celebrations for the 150th year of the manufactory's existence were being planned in the spring of 1860, the decision had already been made to move from the original site. The condition of the Albrechtsburg had become so critical that full-scale restoration had to be considered. The Saxon Historical Association, which was also the Society for the Protection of Monuments, had cautioned against any further development of the manufactory's increasingly mechanized activities within the historical edifice.

The Albrechtsburg, built by Arnold von Westfalen in 1472, is the most magnificent and valuable Gothic lay building in German architecture. Although it was occupied by the manufactory for 150 years and suffered from fire in 1773, it has remained basically unchanged structurally down the centuries. Its interest architecturally stems from the fact that Arnold von Westfalen, using medieval stylistic features, conceived a building anticipating Renaissance principles.

The alternatives of giving up the manufactory or encouraging its profitable growth on a new site were therefore discussed in government circles. The Ministry of Finance finally assigned to Kühn the task of investigating proposals on this subject and making an estimate of the relevant costs. In 1858, the Saxon Diet finally, after lengthy debate, authorized the expenditure of 300,000 talers for a new building, new technical installations, and moving expenses. A petition on the part of the troubled employees, calling for the continuation of the manufactory at all costs, had influenced this decision.

On May 28, 1861, the foundation stone for the new manufactory was laid in the Triebischtal. The building, consisting of four wings around a rectangular works yard, was erected speedily. The order of completion of building was conceived to allow certain aspects of manufacture to be carried on in the Triebischtal before the firm's total removal to the new premises. In this manner, Kühn was able to ensure that not a day was lost. The move took place in the summer of 1863, and columns of bearers were employed to carry the costly wares. Not until 1865 was the changeover complete. Sometime before departing the Albrechtsburg, undue secrecy about the arcanum had given way to scientific research into ceramic raw materials and their use. The new building in the Triebischtal could be seen as a symbol of this change to rational work methods based on scientific knowledge. Kühn had foreseen and made provision for the expansion of all sections in the new premises. The kiln space had been doubled, and mechanically driven washing drums speeded up the preparation of paste. By the end of the century certain technical innovations had been made, such as the mixing machine in 1884. In 1891, the plane grate firing was discontinued in favor of the double sloping grate firing. This aided fuel economy. In 1873, the first filter press was introduced. The wooden frame press bought in 1884 was still operated manually with a diaphragm pump. Also before the turn of the century, crushing mills and wet grinding edge runners were installed.

To accommodate this extension of mechanization and to provide the necessary facilities for the boom which seemed to be on the way, a fifth wing and a spacious timber shed were built in 1871–1872. A further wing with two kilns was completed in 1873; another kiln was added in 1874. In 1878, the first part of the present-day boiler house was built. The mid-eighties saw the construction of various special buildings, some coal bunkers, the storerooms, the carpentry building, and the packing department. These extensions were carried out unhindered by building problems and without moving entire departments or equipment, and they proved the essential soundness of Kühn's conception of a central core of buildings.

Within seventeen years following the completion of construction, the capital invested in the new building had been recouped. The expenditure on these considerable extensions and technical installations amounted to 400,000 marks, which was covered by the manufactory's own profits. From 1875 to 1880, the manufactory's average annual net profit was 260,000 marks. From 1880 to 1909, the treasury received a total of 7,500,000 marks.

Kühn, however, did not live to see the results of his efforts. He died on January 10, 1870, having devoted fifty-six years of his life to the service of the manufactory. His place was taken by Moritz Oskar Raithel. When Kühn was made director in 1849, the workers had a sympathetic listener to their complaints. Wage reform and other improvements were made by him together with a workers' committee to correct hardships and insufficiencies, such as the arbitrary manner in which wage deductions were made and work was evaluated. Finally, the wages of female employees were raised. The right of the workers to form associations, establish committees, and meet in open gatherings, and the right to take part in consultations on wage and administrative questions was granted by the Ministry of Finance. The problem of guaranteeing a future supply of craftsmen was reexamined, and the period of apprenticeship fixed at six years. As soon as the apprentices were engaged in regular production, they were paid a modest wage, similar to the practice established in the eighteenth century. The drawing school, incidentally, was closed in 1896 and the more talented pupils were advised to enroll at their own expense at the Dresden Academy, grants occasionally being made for this purpose. The workers' exemplary self-help organizations founded early, such as

the General Burial Fund, founded 1736;

the Widows' Fund for the Painting Corps, founded 1756;

the Widows' Fund for the *Weisse Corps*, founded 1766;

the General Fund, founded 1766; and finally

the Burial Fund for Woodyard Workers, founded 1775, had proved valuable to the members and their dependents for decades. They were weakened by overburdening claims during the Napoleonic wars and by the catastrophic devaluation. In 1814, the deficit of the General Burial Fund amounted to 4,310 talers. In 1816, the government attempted to get the employees to amalgamate their five benefit funds. The stormy rejection of this proposal prevented a purposeless centralization. Over the years the finances improved, and a State investigation in 1826 revealed assets of 30,337 talers. These investigations, repeated in 1863 and 1867, alway showed that income and expenditure had been correctly entered. The State nevertheless tried once more to get the five funds amalgamated with the promise of tempting subsidies, in order to gain greater control of these self-help organizations. The employees successfully resisted these overtures, so the organization continued along the same lines. The available funds rose annually, reaching the admirable sum of 331,678 marks in 1878.

In principle, however, all five funds supplied only immediate aid, although it was possible in cases of special need to offer a short-term interest-free loan. Permanent help in the form of regularly paid pensions did not come until 1840 with the so-called Local Pensions Institute. Since, according to the State Service Law passed in 1836, only the inspector, cashier, accountant, supervisor of design, arcanists, and some clerical workers had pension rights, the rest of the employees were obliged to build up a pension fund with their own resources. The contributions consisted of a percentage of their income. The pieceworkers paid theirs on the basis of calculated average earnings. The sum obtained in this way was not sufficient to pay out the pensions, which amounted to one third of the last-drawn wage in the case of an employee with ten years' service, one-half for twenty-five years, and two-thirds after forty years, and it had to be supplemented by the State.

The manufactory in the Triebischtal, 1864

Sickness benefits had at first been paid by the manufactory accounts department, and later by the treasury in urgent cases. In the eighteenth and early nineteenth centuries this was already done, less on humane grounds than with the aim of retaining irreplaceable special craftsmen. In 1839, some measure of order was introduced into these arbitrary dealings. All regular employees who had been with the manufactory for at least two years could continue to draw their rather meager monthly salary for a period up to six months, and piece-workers were granted a steady monthly sum of 36 marks. Since experience showed, however, that domestic expenses increased in cases of illness, a sickness fund was established in 1875 which only required small contributions, and which paid out two-thirds of daily earnings in cases of necessity. This, too, was subsidized by the Ministry of Finance. In order to provide not only for the basic necessities of life in times of acute hardship, but also to raise living standards generally, and as a protection against the firm's commercial crises, 155 manufactory employees, on the advice of the modeler Wilhelm, initiated a cooperative society, from which the Meissen Consumer Association emerged on July 19, 1869. Meissen workers had already formed a linen and bread association in 1849, but it had disappeared in the same year as a result of the general ban on workers' societies.

The boom the manufactory enjoyed at the end of the nineteenth century by no means indicated its artistic standards. With the formation of the Zollverein, changes in constitutions, and the founding of the German Empire by Bismarck, the situation was favorable in Germany for the rapid development of capitalism, and this took place. The ground lost to other nations was very soon regained. In Germany, compromise had been reached with the feudal powers, and the bourgeoisie had succeeded only partially in freeing itself from feudal ideology. Indeed, it tried to accommodate the latter after it no longer had the need to oppose it. This accommodation delayed the development of a characteristic artistic expression and resulted in the all-time low and the eclecticism of official art in the second half of the nineteenth century. The manufactory director Raithel was an artistically totally insensitive man who took purely commercial approaches. His efforts were aimed at the widest possible production at the lowest possible cost, and the avoidance of any kind of risk. Never would he chance the expression of new artistic ideas in porcelain design. The fact that the revived Rococo led the field in contemporary crafts, but mainly in porcelain design, confirmed his view that only time-honored paths should be followed. Commercial success proved him right, but what was the position of artistic activity now? No manufactory in the world possessed such a rich store of eighteenth-century molds for Rococo figures and tableware designs. The molds were sorted out, freshened, completed and, unfortunately, also "beautified." This approach brought the manufactory a truly feudal commission: during the period from 1876 to 1877 the Bavarian royal palaces of Linderhof, Herrenchiemsee, and Berg were fitted out with mirror frames, console tables, wall brackets, massive clock cases, and door frames in Meissen porcelain (the designs being specially executed by Munich artists, however); and later, in 1884–1885, the interiors were re-created in the style of Augustus the Strong and Count Brühl. The extremely skilled and versatile head of design at that time, Ernst August Leuteritz, and his staff guided the production of these special commissions. A circumspect and resourceful worker, Leuteritz occupied this post until 1886. He was succeeded by the sculptor Emerich Otfried Andresen, who held the post until 1902. As a specialist on monuments, Andresen was artistically one-sided, but his work was entirely in accordance with the spirit of the times. If we compare Andresen's Böttger memorial with the bust made by Andreas Weger in 1820, which is far removed from a realistic representation, we are truly aware of the decadence to which this art had succumbed.

Toward the end of the century, the naturalistic presentation of animals found great favor. Among the sculptors who were able to adapt their art to the special difficulties presented by ceramic work, Karl Ringler takes pride of place.

The manufactory remained neutral in the last decade of the century during the controversies between the younger generation of artists striving toward artistic veracity, and their elders, who espoused conservatism and historical interpretation. Since the manufactory could not allow itself to fall behind a progressive trend, it was decided in 1895 to buy pieces made by the French sculptors Deloye and Bourgeois, and also an appealing group entitled Eulenspiegel and Nele executed by the Belgian sculptor Charles Samuel. In 1897, at its annual exhibition in Dresden, the Saxon Art Association showed two sculptures, the Hun on Horseback by Erich Hösel, and the Kugelspielerin by Walther Schott. The

copyrights of both sculptures were bought, and the Kugelspielerin was a best-seller for many decades. During the period from 1870 to 1900 the figures and their bases were unhappily painted over in enamel colors to obtain a "naturalistic" effect. The face and limbs were tinted in an almost waxwork fashion, much to the delight of the nouveau-riche public. Decorative painting, inasmuch as it did not repeat the traditional motifs, had no relation to the porcelain except that the latter provided it with a receptive surface. This was the basis upon which the painter Ludwig Sturm worked for twenty-five years, from 1880 to 1905, as supervisor of painting. There would have been almost nothing of more than contemporary value in this field if Július Eduard Braunsdorf, a renowned specialist in watercolor and flower painting, had not been hired in 1874. Braunsdorf, an artistically independent craftsman skilled in the composition of rich and tasteful still-life paintings, had such a mastery of the application of color that he succeeded in achieving just the right accent with it and in bringing his paintings into a finely balanced relationship with the porcelain on which they were executed.

In 1878, *pâte-sur-pâte* painting, with which the effect of low relief could be obtained by application of thin layers of translucent white on colored ground, was introduced from Sèvres. In 1883 Dr. Heintze, works inspector since 1875, developed a new red based on protoxide of copper which, along with the new crystalline glazes and "smear" glaze, enabled a new type of vase decoration to begin. The resemblance of these new decorations to similarly glazed inferior wares caused the rejection of these innovations and continuation of the pseudo-tradition.

Not until the turn of the century did revolutionary artistic elements come to the fore in an attempt to give a new appearance to Meissen products. All the same, at the Paris World Exhibition in 1900 the mark of the blue swords showed no sign of the new artistic movement being ushered in by French art. The director at the time, Horst Karl Brunnemann, persevered in the well-proven tradition, but there were no brisk sales to report, and the period from 1895 to 1901 proved commercially critical for the manufactory. Brunnemann's successor, Paul Gesell, therefore considered reducing the number of employees, but instead adopted shorter hours in the departments concerned, thus avoiding wholesale layoffs. At this time a special commission was received from the Saxon government: in 1876, the outer wall of the Stallhof, the east wing of the Dresden Palace, had been decorated with a 100-meter-long graffito by August Walther that now needed renovation. Dr. Heintze decided after lengthy experimentation to paint the mural on porcelain tiles in *grand feu* colors. The proposal was adopted, and in 1907 the 25,000 tiles produced within two years were fitted together so tightly that the mural survived even the terrible destruction of the night of February 13, 1945, without damage.

Meanwhile the battle raging between historical and realistic art in sculpture and painting was decided in favor of a direct interpretation of nature.

Sculpture, as is often the case in art, became the avant-garde element in Meissen. A rich variety of new figures and groups was created in an unrestrained style. Erich Hösel (1869–1953), who was called from Kassel to take up work in Meissen, was considered one of the most talented sculptors of his generation. In his memoirs Ernst Barlach, who was later to be of equal significance for the manufactory's reputation, describes how quickly and accurately the young Hösel could work. The main fields of inspiration that Hösel favored for his pre-1914 porcelain figures were the animal kingdom and folklore, the latter offering the opportunity for the most varied color decoration. The main point about Hösel's approach, however, was the fact that he not only avoided a one-sided preference for contemporary motifs, but also deliberately cultivated the feeling for cultural heritage. Professor Hösel was extremely cautious in his handling of damaged or worn Classical molds in the course of his study. He had casts of Kaendler's figures made from the molds in their actual state, then, having studied Kaendler's work reports on the models in question, tried to reconstruct their original appearance. He bore in mind the description of their details, and if this information was not available, he based his reconstruction on an understanding of the piece. In this manner he performed a great service for students of Kaendler's art.

Many of Hösel's gifted colleagues, such as Bochmann, Helmig, Lange, and Paul Walther, made attractive animal groups showing unity of form and understanding of the material. Paul Walther's many designs, particularly those for exotic birds, which afforded a vivid kind of decoration, were of a powerful and novel exuberance. The animal groups by Pilz or Fritz enjoyed widespread appreciation, and Otto Jarl's Polar Bear is still in demand. Well-known sculptors

from Germany, Austria, and Sweden occasionally did work for the manufactory. The variety of models offered was in this way considerably extended. In comparison with realistic sculpture, painting showed a tendency to reduce its design to symbolic motifs. Among the firm's independent designers, the painters Baring, Barth, Hentschel, Kretschmar, and the Voigt brothers pursued a line which came very close to the spirit of the Worpswede circle of painters.

Landscapes frequently appeared in which sharply outlined large areas of paint united the pictorial elements to give a heightened decorative effect. This heavy, noble, and distinguished effect was little suited to porcelain, but the underglaze painting was considerably enriched through this ambitious manner, which reduced the motifs to symbolic terms. Views of towns, portraits, souvenir and commemorative wall plates, especially those with Christmas themes, stirred the urge to collect in porcelain lovers. The traditional store of painting was plundered to a greater extent than form was. At all times the *Zwiebelmuster* was particularly in demand, so that from 1897, as a protection against the spreading competition (after the Meissen firm of Teichert had obtained a license for this pattern), the crossed swords appeared on the face of the plate or other item below the bamboo branch.

When Ludwig Philipp Georg Sturm died, his post remained unoccupied until 1909. In controversial matters decisions were made by the administration on the advice of Professor Hösel. The post was eventually assumed by Karl Ludwig August Achtenhagen, who was granted the title of professor in 1910. He was a painter of unique talent, the creator of numerous landscapes and still-life paintings in which harmony of color was consistently achieved. He was

responsible for the design for the Rococo ceiling frescoes in the exhibition hall of the Meissen manufactory in 1916. Under Achtenhagen's influence painting became much more ornamental.

The drawing school, which had been closed in 1893, was reopened in 1906 in a reorganized form. Above and beyond training in arts and crafts, there was a truly broad education. With this inauguration the educational ideals visualized by Kaendler, and even more strongly by Hahnemann, were realized.

In 1898, the porcelain painter Grust designed the Mozart vase, which deviated from the established style in form and decoration and showed the typical flowing lines of the *Jugendstil*. This vase is the first definite example of an article in the new style. Wisely the manufactory engaged two prominent outside artists in 1904 to provide the contemporary note: the architect Henry van de Velde and the interior decorator Richard Riemerschmid. The designs they produced were entirely different in character, yet both must be attributed to the *Jugendstil* movement. They show the wide range of expression found by the artistic revolt against the perversions of taste of the immediate past. Whereas Riemerschmid's table service (1905) derives from peasant craftsmanship, van de Velde bases his solution on the essence of function, which resulted in a brusque rejection of tradition and anticipated our changed world. Neither of these designs was popular.

Apart from the so-called Crocus Service by Konrad Hentschel, the manufactory's permanent artists now designed single fashionable pieces of the *Jugendstil* category, which in many cases represented a compromise between the popular neo-Baroque of the time and the "revolutionary" style of the period around 1910. A tendency toward a gentle, sensitive, and natural outline was establishing itself in the arts. On the whole Meissen kept aloof from fashionable excesses. This not only applied to tableware, but also to the considerable wealth of Meissen figures and groups of this epoch. They consist mainly of birds and mammals of decorative appearance. The human form taken from everyday life also appears, such as the woman in contemporary dress. The cut and color of her costume embodied the spirit of the time. In this way similar figures may be compared with costume figures from the eighteenth century. The cool elegance of Copenhagen porcelain influenced the overall character of the Meissen output in this period. Many valuable ideas were derived about the use of *grand feu* colors. The diversely shaped vases with shiny surfaces and calm outlines offered a new opportunity to experiment effectively with new crystal glazes as developed decades earlier by Dr. Heintze. The research into Far Eastern culture, gaining, for instance, inspiration from Japanese colored woodcuts, indirectly widened the choice of Meissen decoration.

At the same time the working conditions and living standards had changed and, measured against the precarious situation of the late eighteenth and early nineteenth centuries, afforded a measure of security. This is reflected in the healthy state of the benevolent funds at the end of 1909, whose total assets at the same period amounted to some 1,100,000 marks. The sickness fund, which like the pension fund was subsidized by the State to the extent of about a third of its own annual resources, had assets amounting to 32,963 marks in 1909. From surpluses in the sickness fund a plot of land was bought in the spa of Bärenfels in 1897 and a convalescent home built on it. These sums, aside from the State subsidy, were supplied by the employees, which indicates that wages had improved since the end of the nineteenth century. While the average income for a manufactory worker stood at 1,006 marks in 1878, it had risen to 1,540 marks in 1909. The cost of living had, however, also risen considerably as had the level of people's cultural needs.

On the occasion of the bicentenary, the State donated 50,000 marks to the reserve fund and raised the subsidies for the benevolent funds from 29,000 marks to 35,000 marks a year. The output for the Jubilee Year, incidentally, bore the dates 1710 and 1910 along with the crossed-swords mark.

THE MEISSEN STATE PORCELAIN MANUFACTORY: 1918–1945

When the aging director of the Meissen manufactory, Dr. Heintze, looked for a suitable successor he found the required personality in the director of the Schwarzburg Werkstätten, Max Adolf Pfeiffer (1875–1957). Pfeiffer began his employment in Meissen in 1913 as sales director, although he was a certified engineer for ceramic industry machines. Without delay Pfeiffer reformed the manufactory's accounts department, and while the First World War was still raging he began building a works museum that had been approved by the Saxon Diet before the outbreak of the war. In 1918, the year of the German November Revolution, Pfeiffer became manufactory director. In that year revolution swept the monarchy away once and for all. The revolution also brought a change in suffrage and improvement in the working man's position. A state mirroring the actual social structure was not, however, achieved. The changes in the class system of suffrage brought an absolute majority for the parties representing labor between 1918 and 1933. The greater part of the artists and workmen employed at the manufactory showed themselves to be of progressive opinion. After the revolution, the Royal Saxon Porcelain Manufactory Meissen changed its name to the State Porcelain Manufactory Meissen. In 1926, Pfeiffer was made director general. In the twenty years that he served the manufactory, Pfeiffer, while conserving a respect for Meissen's tradition, never allowed external events or a decline in sales to hinder technical or artistic innovations and, in spite of increasing commercial difficulties, put them into practice.

Pfeiffer was undoubtedly one of the ablest directors in the manufactory's history. He had mastered all aspects of the work that were important to the porcelain works and its further development. As a technician, businessman, and organizer he was a source of many valuable innovations. His greatest contribution was to bring artistic standards to the highest level, the only valid comparison being with the work of the mid-eighteenth century. He knew which artists to engage for the manufactory in order to give the material new artistic expression in harmony with the times and to make Meissen once more the center of influence in the world of porcelain design. He was himself artistically gifted. He made his own prints on the manufactory press for a circle of connoisseurs.

Besides the erection of new premises for technical purposes—for instance a new kiln house—Pfeiffer had the sculpture workshop considerably enlarged in 1922. In 1928, two wings had additional stories built over them in order to provide large and light painting workshops. In the same year a special house was erected to store the precious molds. Production of technical porcelain was increased and reached its highest peak between 1919 and 1939. The technical director, Dr. Willy Funck, developed a new, more resistant porcelain for this production. He also improved the brown "Böttger stoneware." As director of Unterweissbach, Pfeiffer had already been in contact with Paul Scheurich, who was born in New York in 1883 and died in Berlin in 1945. Pfeiffer now succeeded in obtaining the artist for independent work. The number of models he designed for the manufactory is an incredible 102. Not since the time of Kaendler and Bustelli had porcelain figures been so arresting in appearance and suited to their medium. Scheurich's genius embraced cool factual interpretation, theatrical eccentricity, and even the grotesque. The Pavlova group, The Lady with the Moor, The Herdsman, and Eve sold well. Scheurich's works are anecdotal in the best sense of the word, as is shown by such pieces as The Drinker, The Elopement, The Lady with a Doe, and even The Fallen Horsewoman. Although Scheurich continued a tradition begun by Kaendler, their work cannot be compared. Scheurich's works do not seek to disguise their twentieth-century origins. Their ironical note arises from a knowledge of psychology, while Kaendler's art simply depicts human passions and weaknesses in a serious or humorous vein.

From Scheurich's strongly expressive work it is only a step to that of Max Esser (1885–1943). He shares Scheurich's joy in artistic creativity but his repertoire is not so wide. He was the designer of a table service showing the fable of Reynard the Fox, in which the animals' various characters are wittily depicted. He also designed chessmen, such as a set made up of fanciful animal figures, along with a board with an ornamental border and an original box. Esser's Seagull, skimming a wave in flight, has also become one of Meissen's most popular pieces. More decorative in effect, however, are his monumental animal masks, the big cats, apes, rams, and bears, all in dark Böttger stoneware. Characteristic in his work is the tension created by the opposition of spacious open areas and lively realistic details, which give static figures an unusual inner dimension, new to Meissen porcelain. Modern Meissen without the work he did in the twenties and thirties would be unimaginable.

Esser was, incidentally, a pupil of the animal sculptor August Gaul (1869–1921). Some fifteen of Gaul's sculptures in his possession at his death were bought by the manufactory for execution in Böttger stoneware and white porcelain. The monumental compactness of Gaul's animal sculptures demanded large-scale reproduction. The much quoted objection that their surface treatment, their cubic and decidedly static character, was in conflict with the Meissen material must be rejected. The solemnity and size of Gaul's conceptions and the harmony of the compositions join with porcelain's noble effect to form an admittedly very unusual but consistent impression of unity. The figures of animals, forest creatures at rest, lions and bears, the sea lion and the massive beaver, show a timeless powerful vitality and are a demonstration of the wide range of artistic possibilities which Meissen porcelain and the redevelopment of Böttger stoneware afforded.

With the execution in Böttger ware and white glazed porcelain of works by Ernst Barlach (1870–1938) such as The Sleeping Peasants, which were originally conceived in wood and bronze, we see that Meissen porcelain can be used for works of art at the highest level. This artist was probably not pleased by the prospect of his work being reproduced, but when his friend Max Esser brought him into contact with the Meissen manufactory it was with the aim of making Barlach's work popular and thus improving his economic position. This suited Max Pfeiffer's intention of helping struggling artists during the years of inflation while maintaining Meissen's reputation as an institution which furthered the cause of art. He bought suitable works from prominent sculptors at a fair price and had as many reproductions made in porcelain as the demand warranted. The art lover could now afford to obtain a collection of the best in small sculpture by artists of repute. The cultural effect was of the greatest importance. Works that were not of immediate appeal but which deserved closer study on the part of the observer began to find an appreciative public. Evidence of this is Barlach's wonderfully compact peasant group.

Among the sculptors who worked in connection with the manufactory were Richard Scheibe, his pupil Gerhard Marcks, and—recommended by Paul Scheurich—Richard Langer. Although Scheibe's activity in Meissen was not a success, Marcks produced an original memorial, two well-known candelabra in the form of horsemen, the strange small figure of a woman sleepwalking, Reclining Figure, an expressive head of the Madonna, and a female bust called Erwachen.

The painter Willy Münch-Khe made an application for employment at the manufactory at the end of November, 1911, at the age of twenty-seven. He took up his post on January 2, 1912, and until his resignation on November 30, 1913, was mainly engaged on countless designs for the decoration of vases, bowls, and other containers. After the First World War (he had in the meantime successfully turned his hand to animal sculpture) he renewed his association with the manufactory, now as a free-lance artist, however, and offered attractive models of leaping or resting foals, donkeys, deer, and calves. From his graphic work a number of well-known figures were executed in porcelain: the Eulenspiegel in various interpretations, a Peter Schlemihl, the waggish figure of the archivist Lindhorst, and a Simplicissimus.

The most versatile and productive artist of the group that blazed the trail for Meissen's artistic development after the First World War, the artist who was of all the moderns most closely linked with porcelain, was the painter and sculptor Emil Paul Börner. He was born in Meissen on February 12, 1888, the son of a cabinetmaker employed in a local manufactory. At the age of fourteen he took up an apprenticeship with a small Meissen ceramic firm. The extraordinarily gifted and industrious young boy succeeded a few years later in being accepted to study at the Dresden Kunstgewerbeakademie and later at the Kunstakademie, where one of his teachers was Oskar Zwintscher. In December, 1910, after a period of study in Florence, he began his work at the Meissen manufactory. As early as 1912, German museums began to acquire pieces by him, but it was not until the end of the First World War and the passing of the *Jugendstil* that he found his most characteristic expression. In a few years he was surprising the world with works which put him on the level of the greatest artists in porcelain. In 1930, the artistic direction of the manufactory was entrusted to him.

Börner developed new vase and tableware designs which have become a standard part of the manufactory's output. He used porcelain to make medallions and plaques. He made the first working porcelain carillon. and his monumental memorial to the war dead in Meissen's St. Nikolai church is the largest and most unusual porcelain work ever made.

Börner's vases and other vessels are of classical beauty, well balanced, and of a striking simplicity. The decorative and functional elements, such as handles, form a harmonious whole. With such masterpieces as his, Meissen again became the leading manufactory within the porcelain industry. The decoration designed by Börner for his pieces, sparing or lavish, is always exquisite in coloring and follows the example of the "Indian" decoration of the first half of the eighteenth century when it is in the form of stylized plant motifs. Yet, in its expressive movement, it is incontestably of its own period.

Börner's sculptural pieces are influenced by the Expressionist movement, but while they are inspired by strong inner tension, the realistic form is not lost. Works by him before 1930 include a series of musicians, a number of putti, a dancer, an Eros, a gooseherd, portrait busts, and candleholders. His greatest work in the field of sculpture is his masterpiece in St. Nikolai church. The tablets and statuary form a memorial to the dead of the First World War and represent eight years' work. They were ceremonially given to the public in 1929 on the occasion of the thousandth anniversary of Meissen's founding. Mourning women and children flank the tablets, which bear the names of the dead. Beneath are two groups of weeping women and children, forming a block of porcelain, two and one half meters high and approximately 300 kilograms in weight. The ensemble of tablets and figures is very impressive in the modest interior of the Romanesque church. It is a powerful expression of grief and shows that porcelain is not only to be used in the expression of gaiety and frivolity.

Also in 1929, after many years of experimentation, the first working carillon in porcelain was ready. It consists of thirty-seven bells and hangs in the tower of the Frauenkirche in Meissen. The bells, designed by Börner, are tunable within certain limits and have a pleasant clear tone. Other carillons were made for the Dresden Zwinger, for Bremen, Nuremberg, Lüneburg, Gmunden in Austria, Hamburg, Schwarzenberg, and Bärenfels in the Erzgebirge.

Börner's development of coin-, medallion-, and plaque-making represented a new venture for the manufactory. Plaques and medallions with bas-reliefs had occasionally been made, but Börner was responsible for well over a thousand of these small artistic pieces. He also made porcelain emergency money at a time of great inflation for Saxony, Meissen, and certain other German towns. His lively imagination, his strong feeling for what is aesthetically good, the skilled allocation of decorative elements in a given area, and the superb carving of the smallest details make all his pieces valuable artistic creations.

Börner also designed some glass windows, and he modeled the decoration for two bronze bells in the Meissen cathedral, the largest bell of which, two and one half meters in diameter, was for a long time the most richly decorated bell in the world.

During the period of Pfeiffer's service not only were new developments sponsored, but care was also taken to see that Meissen tradition was continued. At his instigation unique pieces of early Meissen porcelain, some of the Dresden Palace vases, Kirchner's grotesque vases, Kaendler's large animal pieces, and almost all his figures and groups were recast. In this way we still have an impression of many pieces that were destroyed during the Second World War. This positive reflection of tradition did not directly activate artistic impulses, but it prevented a one-sided overemphasis on contemporary activities and helped to increase the artistic level within the team of painters, for the rapid sculptural development had not been accompanied by similar achievements in decoration. Moreover, this reflection of tradition had an influence on the training of the new generation of porcelain artists.

During these years of heightened artistic sensitivity, painting in underglaze blue also underwent a welcome revival. Wall plates, bowls, and floor vases designed by William Baring, Rudolf Hentschel, Hermann Limbach, Oskar Voigt and others were adorned with painted landscapes, seascapes, animals, and stylized flowers in great variety.

The thought of countenancing a less imaginative production during the years of crisis and the resulting loss of prestige was intolerable to Pfeiffer. He therefore had artistically valuable porcelain made, even though there was no market for it. At the same time the cost of fees to artists was relatively low. Expenses for the subscription pieces were usually covered. The expenses incurred for the purchase of new sculpture (8,130 reichsmarks in 1924 and 42,556 reichsmarks in 1927) appear rather modest if seen in relation to the general ex-

penses of the manufactory of 1,833,208 reichsmarks in 1924 and 2,473,551 reichsmarks in 1927. If we stroll past the many museum showcases exhibiting the varied and rich creation of these years, we are hardly aware of the dark side of these unsettled times masked by the Great Depression. The commercial position of the porcelain manufactory was deteriorating rapidly. The number of workers reached its peak in 1922 at 1,108, sank to 933 in 1926, and in 1933 stood at 612. This slump in the entire industry had such catastrophic effects in 1929 that of the seven porcelain manufactories in Saxony only three survived.

Between the years 1918 and 1933 good relations developed between the manufactory and the town of Meissen. The manufactory made friendly gestures toward the outside world, as is witnessed by the St. Nikolai memorial and the lottery it held to help finance the new library building in Meissen. Its artists were represented in public exhibitions and many a painter, graphic artist, or sculptor of worldwide reputation began his career at the Meissen manufactory, including Rudolf Hentschel (1869–1951), Oskar Burkhardt (1882–1960), and Rudolf Bergander (1909–1970), pupil of Otto Dix, one of the leading artists of the DDR and for many years professor and rector of the Dresden Kunstakademie.

With the beginning of the Nazi dictatorship in 1933, Meissen's promising development was stopped. Pfeiffer was dismissed by the Nazis. A series of Nazi *"Betriebsführer"* followed. They had no understanding of porcelain, with the exception of Wolfgang Müller von Baczko, who had been an assistant director under Pfeiffer from 1921 to 1925. He was made director in 1936 but soon made himself unpopular with the Nazis and was dismissed in 1940. Börner clashed with the Nazis in 1937, left the porcelain works, and went to teach at the Dresden Academy. Some designs were obtained from Scheurich: the pair of figures representing a Spanish guitarist and a dancer with castanets (1934), five grotesque musicians, and some dishes and lidded pots for smoking and toilet purposes (1937). In 1937 the manufactory was awarded the Grand Prix of the Paris Exhibition for Scheurich's sculptures entitled Elopement, Resting Figure, Lady with a Fan, Lady with Deer, Amazons with Cupid, Falling Rider, and for Esser's Fish Otter. When Pfeiffer was working for the Berlin porcelain works, he obtained for them in 1938 the services of Scheurich. Between 1935 and 1937 four designs—a swan, a guinea fowl, a hen pheasant, and an owl—were bought from Esser. The artistic élan of the Pfeiffer period was waning. Fortunately there remained in the manufactory people who were able to keep up the traditional production.

During this time Willy Münch-Khe had renewed his relations with the manufactory and had produced very marketable sculptures of a doe, a roebuck, a goat, and a foal in Böttger's stoneware. Some nude statues were obtained from Robert Ullmann, a free-lance sculptor working in Vienna: Girl Wrapped in Thought, Woman Gazing, and Spring. These were executed in both white porcelain and Böttger stoneware; the Woman Gazing was also made as an almost lifesize figure. The sculptor Erich Oehme provided a special note with his animal sculpture. He made use of his outstanding knowledge of anatomy and animal behavior to make convincing representations of individual creatures. Famous racehorses such as Alchemist or Packard, a bison and an elk from the Dresden Zoo, as well as a magnificent stag from the forest, to name only a few, were the creations of his careful hands. After the war, Oehme created two large bronze figures for the Berlin Tierpark.

A sculptor who gradually worked his way up from the craftsman grade was Alexander Struck, born in Meissen in 1902. He added to the range of the ever-popular fairytale and legendary figures, with the following works dating from the years between 1936 and 1940: the Eulenspiegel, Baron Münchhausen Riding the Cannonball, Tailor Wibbel, The Seven Swabians, various costumed figures, a chess game with pieces in the form of frogs, and a group of playing bears.

The curtailment of production during the Second World War threatened a gradual paralysis. In August, 1944, Meissen was declared one of the manufactories considered unimportant to the war effort. It carried on for a time, however, mainly for the production of war goods, with some six hundred employees, until in autumn, 1944, 107 women and fifteen men were transferred to war work. In summer, 1944, the removal of porcelain from the exhibition halls into the cellars of the Albrechtsburg was completed.

THE MEISSEN PORCELAIN MANUFACTORY
IN THE POSTWAR YEARS

Meissen remained unscathed until the last year of the Second World War. At the end of April, 1945, however, the Eastern Front had reached the northeastern part of the town. During the fighting the town center was subjected to artillery fire, which caused civilian deaths and damage to buildings. There was much destruction in the old quarters of the town when the Wehrmacht blew up the two Elbe bridges as well as two railway birdges. This demolition had no military advantages, since the Soviet troops had already crossed the Elbe a few kilometers below Meissen. A number of buildings at the manufactory had been destroyed by artillery fire. Normal work was rendered impossible by the action, and production was stopped.

It was during those dark days that the people of Meissen began to show their opposition to the continued war effort. The majority of the Meissen population had never embraced the Nazi cause. On May 6, anti-Nazi groups succeeded in getting the people of Meissen to assemble on the market square, and speakers attacked the order to defend the city. The result was a concerted effort to make the officers of the Wehrmacht and the Nazi town council flee the town. On May 9, a new anti-Nazi town council faced a difficult task. The first measures to be taken, if life was to proceed normally once more, included decisions affecting the future of the manufactory. The entire organization of the Nazi state had crumbled, so for the first time since its foundation the manufactory was taken over by the Meissen town council. On May 15, 1945, Herbert Neuhaus, who had been a participant in the first deliberations of the new council, was appointed director. Minutes of a meeting on May 20, signed by the mayor, Albert Mücke, and the councilor for industrial affairs, Gerhart Ziller, confirmed the council's decision.[94]

Herbert Neuhaus, who was now to see the manufactory through one of its most difficult periods, had already worked at the manufactory as a painter. There had been many difficulties in his life, but he had surmounted them with great energy. A smith's son, he was born in Dresden in 1897. Before he was called up for the war in 1916 he had worked for four years as a dairyman. A serious wound which rendered his right hand useless hospitalized him from 1916 to 1919. While in the hospital he took evening classes at the Dresden School of Arts and Crafts and learned to paint on porcelain, using his left hand. His efforts were so good that the Meissen manufactory engaged him as porcelain decorator in 1921. In his new capacity he so earned the respect and trust of his fellow workers that he was nominated as a member of a delegation to the Soviet Union in 1927, was made chairman of the manufactory's Trade Branch in 1928, and in 1931 became adviser on matters concerning the Meissen manufactory in the Saxon Chamber of Deputies.

In 1933, he was forced by the Nazis to resign from his posts and put under police supervision. Neuhaus continued his task of self-education in the most varied subjects, adding to his general cultural store a thorough knowledge of art history. In addition he was a well-known chess player and Esperantist.

He was the sort of person the postwar world needed. His energy, knowledge, and experience proved invaluable in the manufactory's reestablishment. On May 16, the employees met to affirm their will to set the manufactory in motion again. Production could only be undertaken on a limited scale, however. Many parts of the works had been rendered useless. There was a shortage of coal and electric power, of raw materials and of money. The first task was to clear up the rubble, and to paint and sell existing stocks of undecorated ware.

Since the manufactory had been used for arms production during the last years of the war, a firm of Dresden arms manufacturers having set up within its precincts, it was to be totally dismantled under the terms of the Allied agreement. On June 22, 1945, with heavy hearts but aware that the action was necessary as a sign of good intentions, the workers started dismantling. After the dismantling was declared adequate in September, 1945, a resumption of production in the remaining workshops could be considered. The problems looked insurmountable since much important machinery was lacking, but the rebuilding was undertaken with the greatest courage and optimism. In a radio broadcast at that time, Herbert Neuhaus said, "We shall go on, even if we have to prepare the clay with our bare hands."

At first 200 people could be employed, including fifty painters and thirty-one designers. The management consisted of Neuhaus, sales director Emil Wagner, chief accountant Willy Naacke, and chief painter Rudolf Lauschke. The manufactory obtained as chief designer Heinrich Thein, who had previously been employed in another Meissen ceramic factory where he had produced highly individual and expressive sculptures. Thus, in the autumn of 1945, the firm was already in a position to exhibit at an industrial fair in Dresden, the aim of which was to show what Saxony's industry could once more offer. In the spring of 1946, Meissen porcelain was also seen at Leipzig's first postwar fair. Until July, 1946, the number of employees remained at 600. Production figures continued to rise and at the same time artistic standards were maintained. The manufactory still had at its disposal the talents of well-established artist-craftsmen. It was a more difficult matter to guarantee the quality of the basic mixture and glazing, since the earlier sources of raw materials were no longer available and the alternatives proved less satisfactory. Designs and decoration consisted only of those already known. New developments could not be considered because of the heavy load already borne by the staff during the technical reorganization. One exception was the limited edition of a plate designed by Gerhard Schiffner celebrating the completion of the rebuilding of the Meissen Bridge on February 3, 1946.

The Soviet military administration was most effective in its support for the manufactory's rebuilding program. As early as May, 1945, good relations had been established between the Soviet authorities and the manufactory, relations which were not impaired by the decision to dismantle the manufactory. Help was given in the provision of raw materials, the importing of coal, and the purchase of electric kilns, new machines, and other apparatus. Among the Soviet experts who helped the management in those difficult days of regeneration, Major Dr. W. Flerow deserves special mention. It was at that time that Neuhaus changed the Meissen mark slightly. The addition of a small bow binding the sword handles symbolized peace between two swords formerly crossed in battle.

July, 1946, brought a change in the status of the works decisive for the following years. As part of the German war reparations, Order 186 of the Soviet military administration confirmed the Meissen manufactory as part of the Soviet enterprise AG Cement. This was on July 19, 1946. This measure aided further reconstruction. The German management under Herbert Neuhaus remained unchanged, as did its duties, the sole innovation being the introduction of a Soviet director general, N. D. Nikotin.

Regeneration was rapid both in the reestablishment and extension of production and in the setting up of social facilities for the employees. The canteens were modernized. A kindergarten was set up, and a medical center with facilities for massage, health baths, and sunray treatment was established. The convalescent home in Bärenfels once more opened its doors. In 1949, a number of rooms in the exhibition building were adapted to provide a social club with a reading room, music room, lecture theater and rooms for societies and exhibitions. The library, with its valuable book collection, was recatalogued and a professional librarian engaged. The old market garden was transformed by the voluntary effort of the manufactory employees into a sports arena 6,500 square meters in size. The manufactory choir, which had existed in one form or another for several hundred years, gained a new lease on life. A youth choir was formed, and amateur music groups and circles for various cultural activities came into existence. The manufactory became the cultural focus of Meissen. In the House of Culture and the Exhibition Hall, public performances of various kinds, exhibitions, and concerts took place. Good relations of a kind not seen before developed between the manufactory and the townspeople. Help was given by them to the town theater and they took part in the activities of the League of Culture. As tourism came back to the town, the manufactory proved one of its chief attractions.

During the Soviet administration all departments were started up again. Between 1947 and 1950 production rose by 41.2 percent, and trade relations with foreign countries were revived. The number of employees had risen to 918 by 1950. The director general, Mr. Nikotin, not only succeeded in restoring to the manufactory its earlier production power and good reputation, but also gained the respect and affection of the employees. After his duties in Meissen were over, he was often invited to return to the manufactory on special festive occasions.

Reorganization brought with it a change in working procedures, which at first was expected to have an unfavorable aesthetic effect on the product. The manufactory began to work according to plan, and it was soon seen that Meissen porcelain would retain its famous high quality.

The training of future craftsmen posed a particular problem. The training scheme was changed. The apprentices no longer received their training in a particular section, but were taught in central workshops by professional teachers. A hostel was provided for apprentices who lived far away.

The production was limited to known design during the period of Soviet administration. One of the few original pieces of this period was a large pyramidal group, the joint work of Schulze, Struck, and Voigt after an idea by Herbert Neuhaus, which represented the story of the Russian workers' movement. Plaques and medallions were also made to mark special occasions, but their artistic merit was not always satisfactory.

Following the founding of the German Democratic Republic on October 7, 1949, the Soviet Union recognized the sovereignty of the new German state and transferred all powers, obtained by the unconditional capitulation of Nazi Germany, to the authorities of the DDR, at the same time returning those industries which had been taken over as war reparations. Thus the Meissen manufactory was returned as a State industry under the name VEB Staatliche Porzellan-Manufaktur Meissen.

THE VEB STAATLICHE PORZELLAN-MANUFAKTUR MEISSEN

After the manufactory had been returned to the German Democratic Republic, Herbert Neuhaus remained director for four months and then took over the management of a Thuringian porcelain manufactory. His successor was Waldemar Wüstemann, who had been a salesman for several porcelain manufactories in Thuringia. The rise in output continued. By 1960, export contracts had been obtained from more than forty countries, and from more than seventy a few years later. This easily surpassed prewar figures. As well as continuing the manufacture of the traditional product, it was decided to introduce new lines on a larger scale. The policy of providing social facilities, begun during the manufactory's time as part of AG Cement, was maintained. As a source of information and discussion for the staff of the manufactory, a newspaper called the *Manufaktur Echo* was started.

The manufactory once more became active in scientific research. For the reorganization of the archives, the services of the Meissen historian, Dr. Helmuth Gröger, were obtained. His research formed the basis for this book. After his death in 1957, Otto Walcha became chief archivist. Dr. Gröger was also responsible for the layout of the exhibition hall, the displays being drawn from pieces owned by the manufactory. A display comparable with the original one could not be achieved until 1958. The manufactory's own collection, kept in the cellars of the Albrechtsburg until 1945, had been removed to the Soviet Union along with other German art treasures. This measure undoubtedly saved many pieces from destruction, as the lack of local accommodation would no doubt have had ill effects. At the end of the war there was no facility for a comprehensive exhibition, since many of the buildings where the pieces had been housed had been destroyed. On the return of art treasures to the DDR in December, 1958, the Meissen collection was found to be in perfect condition, so that in 1960 the Exhibition Hall was able to show its renewed splendor for the 250th anniversary celebration. It was arranged according to modern principles of museum presentation and was opened as one of the great collections of the DDR.

The celebration marking the 250th anniversary of the manufactory's foundation took place in June, 1960. The participation of the government of the DDR, its guests from all parts of the world, and above all the people of Meissen, transformed the celebrations into a genuine popular festival and a major event in the manufactory's history. This splendid occasion showed that the manufactory had regained its old reputation as an artistic institution of note and that its activity and latest developments were fully supported at all levels. A new porcelain carillon was set up in the manufactory courtyard, and at the same time a demonstration workshop was opened to show the manufacturing processes of Meissen porcelain to interested visitors. The town of Meissen erected a fountain as a monument to the greatest eighteenth-century craftsman in porcelain, Johann Joachim Kaendler, ornamented by one of his own animal sculptures. The highlight of the celebrations was the speech by the prime minister of the DDR, Otto Grotewohl, given in the courtyard of the Albrechtsburg before thousands of Meissen inhabitants and other guests.

As already mentioned, Meissen's artist-craftsmen had turned their attention to new developments. Its young artists were interested in new trends. It is true that Willy Münch-Khe had been appointed at one time, but his artistic talents proved to be unsympathetic to the qualities of porcelain. The manufactory renewed its links with Professor Börner, who designed the anniversary plaques and a number of skillfully executed services and vases that were more in the old tradition than in the new spirit. Subsequently Börner worked in both Berlin and Thuringia. He was active until a few days before his death on November 7, 1970, and one cannot tell that the small sculptural groups are of his late period, some having been made when he was over eighty years old. They are usually satirical groups showing human weaknesses, but there are also beautiful mythological figures. For the Berlin firm he completed a service started by Scheurich, who died in 1945 before completing it. In the years following the Second World War, Börner modeled well over a hundred figures and groups for execution in porcelain while also producing paintings, graphic work, and window designs.

Mural design, a branch of porcelain making to which little attention had been given, gained a new lease on life. The mural in the Dresden Palace stables, made up of porcelain tiles dating from 1905–1906 and known as the Prince's Procession, had been a solitary example of this art, but the 1953 mural covered wall by Professor Max Lingner on the State Ministry buildings in Berlin met with such approval that many requests were received for similar murals for public buildings, hotels, and clubrooms. Most of these were designed by the painter Gerhard Clauss, who died in 1966. Since then decorated tiles have been an important item of Meissen output.

In 1966, the director of the manufactory, Waldemar Wüstemann, retired. His successors were Rudi Richter, and in 1969, Professor Karl Petermann. Under Petermann's guidance a far-reaching reconstruction and extension of the works began, commencing with the erection of a large modern kiln house.

To meet the demands for stylistic innovations, designs were purchased from free-lance artists such as Professor Fritz Cremer, Professor Heinrich Drake, the sculptress Elfriede Reichel-Drechsler, and the industrial designer Professor Horst Michel. A new venture for the social development of the DDR is the collective work of a group of young artists of whom the most active are Rudi Stolle, Peter Strang, Heinz Werner, and Ludwig Zepner. They have developed forms and decorative motifs which are original and modern in spirit and yet succeed in remaining within the Meissen tradition. The groups based on Shakespeare's *Midsummer Night's Dream*, J. Schwarz's *Dragon*, and Brecht's *Dreigroschenoper* (Threepenny Opera) touch themes new to Meissen's sculptors, beginning a dynamic new phase in the artistic development of Meissen porcelain. Their greatest effort was the Chase Service (1973—250 pieces), which can be ranked with some of the best works in porcelain. The new artists justifiably regard Meissen porcelain as an exquisite material with which to satisfy a luxury demand. Their rich artistic forms and decoration surprise and delight with an exuberant *joie de vivre*. New, yet true to the original Meissen, Meissen's contemporary work seems to have reached its logical conclusion. The makers of these objects do not have to consider mass production or marketing power, since another branch of the porcelain industry takes care of everyday ware more quickly and more cheaply. Meissen continues its original vision—that of being an art center first and foremost, that of producing original porcelain art, not utilitarian ware; works that are the result of artistic activity; which appeal to our aesthetic sense and enrich our lives. The artistic work of the past few years has been somewhat narrow and yearns to be pursued in a number of different directions. This is inevitable. It is certain that the future development of the Meissen porcelain works will include new and marvelous achievements.

PLATES

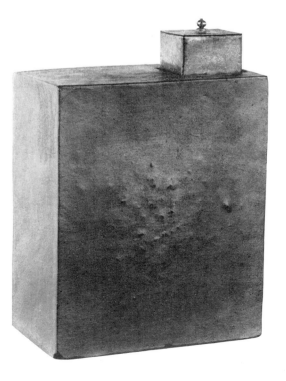

7 Mounted tankard in marbled
   Böttger stoneware, *c.* 1711
8 Vase in marbled and faceted
   Böttger stoneware, *c.* 1711

9 Polished and covered vase
  in Böttger stoneware
  with applied decoration
  by Johann Jacob Irminger,
  c. 1712
10 Teapot and coffeepot
  in Böttger stoneware, *c.* 1712

11 Covered tureen with acanthus decoration in Böttger stoneware
   by Johann Jacob Irminger, *c.* 1714
12 Polished bowl with foliage decoration in Böttger stoneware
   by Johann Jacob Irminger, *c.* 1712
13 Black glazed pot in Böttger stoneware
   with lacquer painting, *c.* 1715

14 Black glazed bowl in Böttger stoneware
   with gilding, c. 1715
15 Four-sided pot in Böttger stoneware with enameled decoration
   studded with precious stones, c. 1715

16 Portrait medallion of King Frederick I
   in Böttger stoneware, *c.* 1710
17 Harlequin figure in Böttger stoneware, *c.* 1710
18 Statuette of Augustus the Strong
   in Böttger stoneware, *c.* 1710

19 Relief of Judith in Böttger stoneware, *c.* 1714
20 Head of Apollo in Böttger stoneware, *c.* 1714

21 Sugar bowl with lid in Böttger porcelain, *c.* 1713
22 Reticulated goblet in Böttger porcelain, double-walled,
   openwork on the outer wall, *c.* 1716

23 Covered vase in Böttger porcelain
    with vineleaf decoration
    by Johann Jacob Irminger,
    after 1714

24 Key-shaped vessel in Böttger
    porcelain with vineleaf motif
    by Johann Jacob Irminger, 1714

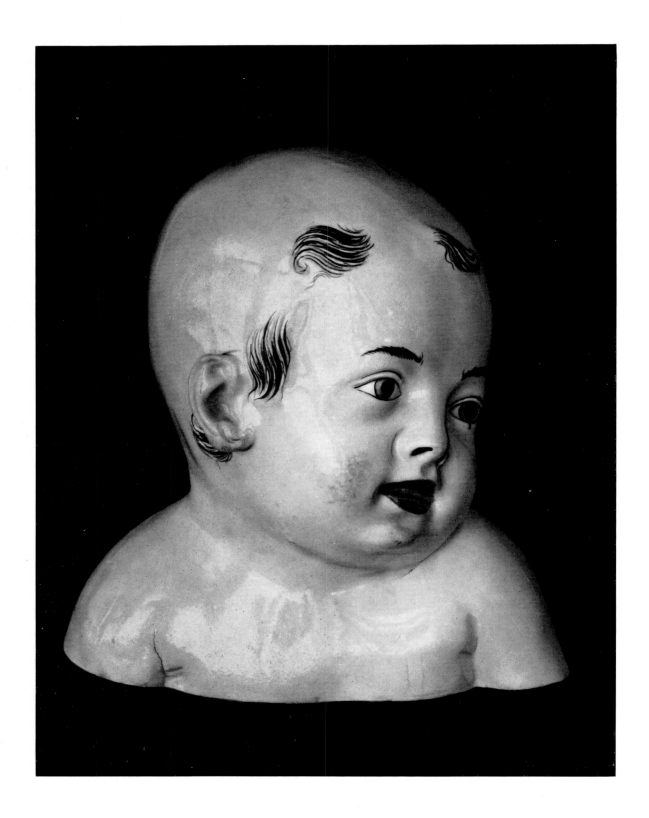

25 Child's head in Böttger porcelain, *c.* 1715
26 Pagoda in altarlike setting
   in Böttger porcelain, after 1715

27 Small cup in Böttger porcelain with gold luster decoration, *c.* 1718
28 Beaker-shaped vase in Böttger porcelain, *c.* 1715

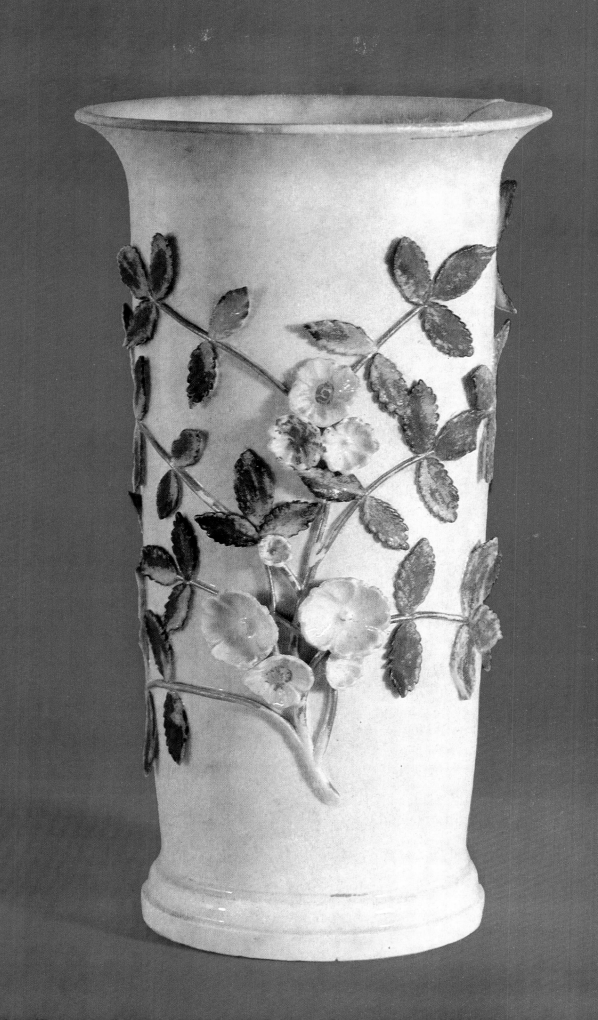

31 Bouillon cup with Augsburg gold chinoiserie decoration, *c.* 1722
32 Teapot with lace decoration, *c.* 1720

35 Teapot with lambrequin decoration, *c.* 1725
36 Teapot with fish and billows, *c.* 1725

37 Vase with colored ground, chinoiseries
and indianische Blumen *c.* 1730
38 Gourd-shaped bottle with indianische
Blumen *c.* 1732

39 Pen drawings from Höroldt's sketchbook, 1725–27
40 Vase with blue ground, chinoiseries and indianische Blumen
  by Johann Gregorius Höroldt, 1726

41 Mantelpiece clock, model by Johann
   Gottlieb Kirchner, decoration by Johann
   Gregorius Höroldt, 1728
42 Detail of the Höroldt painting
   on the clock by Kirchner, 1728

43 Oval dish with red dragon from the Court Service, *c.* 1730

44 Covered tureen with the *reicher alter Löwe*
   decoration, *c.* 1730

45 Small lidded basin with green ground
   and chinoiseries, *c.* 1730
46 Goblet with chinoiseries, *c.* 1725

47 Plate with Far Eastern decoration,
    painted by Johann Ehrenfried Stadler, *c.* 1725
48 Lantern with painting
    by Johann Ehrenfried Stadler, *c.* 1725

49 Large covered vase with Indian
   branch motif, *c.* 1730
50 Octagonal two-handled cup
   with Kakiemon decoration, *c.* 1730

51 Lidded jar with scale decoration, *c.* 1725
52 Reserve of a yellow ground vase with motif
      of Fabeltiere, *c.* 1730

53 Octagonal sake flask
   with indianische Blumen decoration, *c*. 1730
54 Four-sided sake flask with chinoiserie decoration, *c*. 1728
55 Globular vase with rich indianische Blumen
   decoration, *c*. 1730

56 Plate with wheat-ear decoration and checkered ornament,
c. 1728

57 Plate with wheat-ear decoration and phoenix, c. 1728

58 Leaf dish with checkered decoration, c. 1730

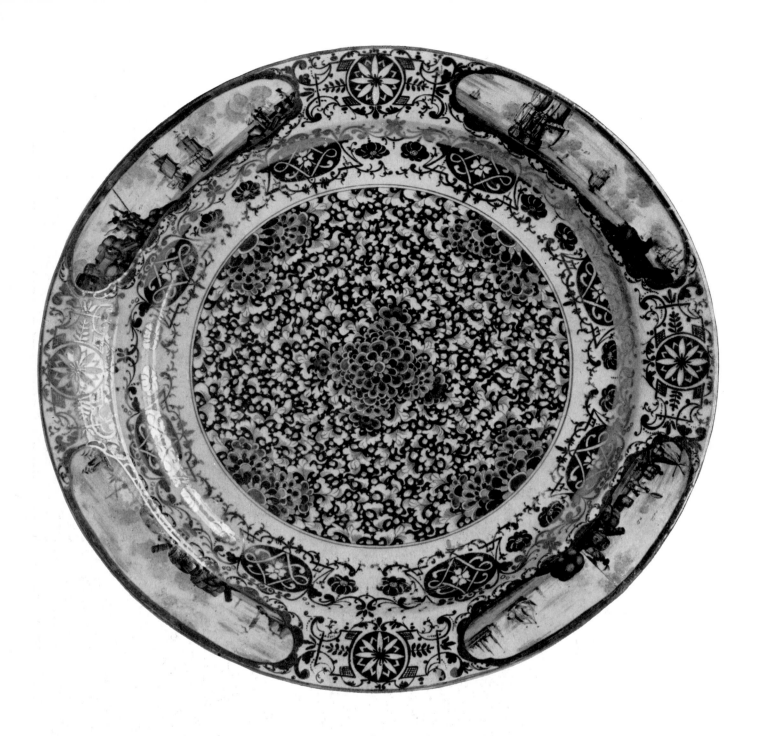

59 Richly decorated bowl with harbor scenes,
   c. 1730
60 Barrel-shaped coffee container supported by caryatids,
   richly decorated, *c.* 1728

64 Saucer with painting
of a farm, *c.* 1723

65 Bouillon cup with landscape,
c. 1723

66 Pot with I-shaped handle,
landscape decoration, *c.* 1740

67 Pot with spout in the form of a cavalier's head and
landscape decoration around the body, c. 1740
68 Lidded caddy with coastal landscape decoration,
c. 1745

69 Circular covered bowl with battle painting
   by Christian Friedrich Herold, *c.* 1740

70 Mounted jug with cover bearing a portrait and
   a view of Leipzig, *c.* 1730

71 Reserve painting showing a hunting scene, *c.* 1740
72 Bowl on scroll feet adorned with putti,
   by Johann Friedrich Eberlein, *c.* 1740

73 Pagoda after a Far Eastern example made *c.* 1720
by the molder George Fritzsche
74 Grotesque vase modeled by Johann Gottlieb Kirchner
after an engraving (Stella), 1728

75 Elephant by Johann Gottlieb Kirchner, 1731
76 Heron by Johann Joachim Kaendler, 1731

75 Elephant by Johann Gottlieb Kirchner, 1731
76 Heron by Johann Joachim Kaendler, 1731

77 Hen with chicks by Johann Joachim
Kaendler, 1732
78 Vulture by Johann Joachim Kaendler, 1734

79 Paduan cock by Johann Joachim
   Kaendler, 1732
80 Pelican by Johann Joachim Kaendler, 1732

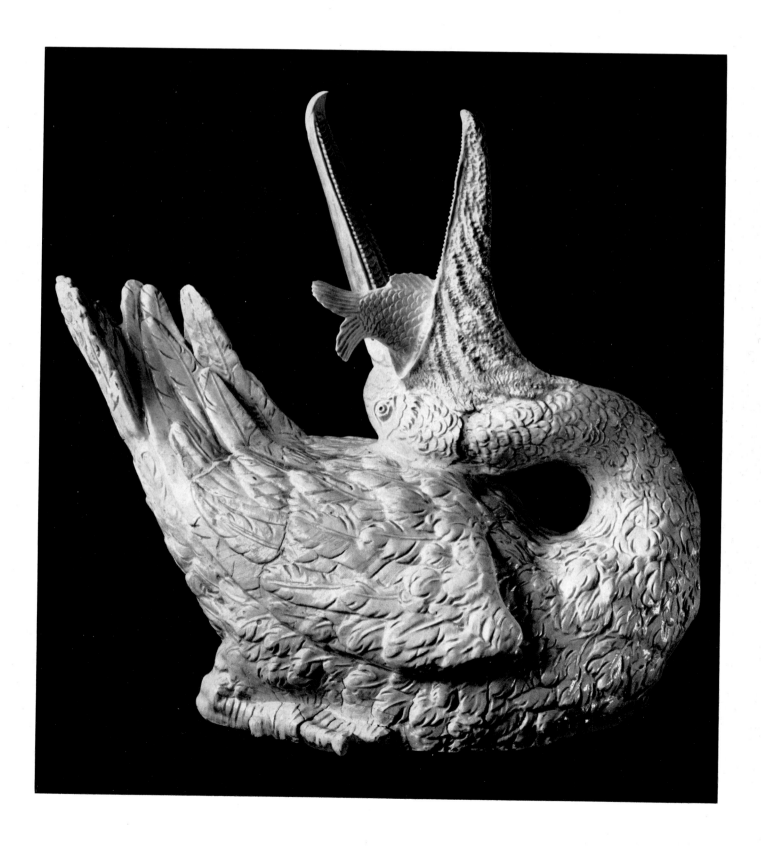

81 Chamois buck by Johann Friedrich Eberlein, 1735
82 Monkey taking snuff by Johann Joachim Kaendler,
1732

83 *Bolognese Hund* by Johann Joachim
 Kaendler, *c.* 1770
84 *Mopshündin* (pug bitch) by Johann Joachim
 Kaendler, *c.* 1745

85 Spouted vessel in the form of a monkey with young
   by Johann Joachim Kaendler, 1735
86 Marmoset by Johann Joachim Kaendler,
   c. 1732

91 Candlestick from the Swan Service
by Johann Friedrich Eberlein, 1739
92 Tureen handle from the Swan Service
by Johann Joachim Kaendler, 1738

97 Apfelsinenbecher (orange stand) from the
   Swan Service by Johann Friedrich Eberlein, 1738
98 Finial from the large tureen
   of the Swan Service by Johann Joachim
   Kaendler, 1737–41

99 "Element" vase by Johann Joachim Kaendler, 1741
100 Vase with Japanese snowball tree decoration
by Johann Joachim Kaendler, c. 1740

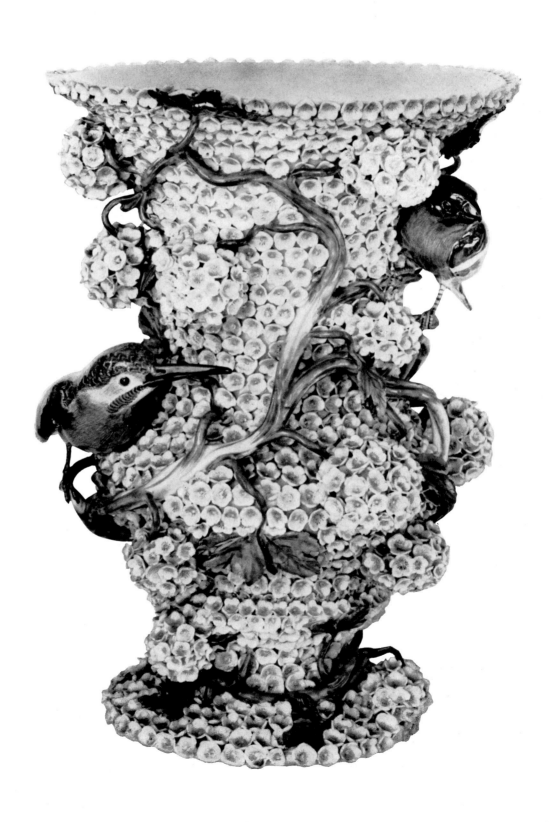

101 River god from the table centerpiece for Count Brühl
by Johann Joachim Kaendler, 1744
102 Companion piece to 101
103 The Apostle Matthew by Johann Joachim
Kaendler, 1738

104 Fröhlich, the court jester, by Johann Joachim
Kaendler, 1737
105 Fröhlich and Schmiedel
by Johann Joachim Kaendler, 1741

112 Woman from Malabar by Friedrich Elias Meyer, *c.* 1750
113 Man from Malabar by Friedrich Elias Meyer, 1749
114 Harlequin by Johann Joachim Kaendler, 1738

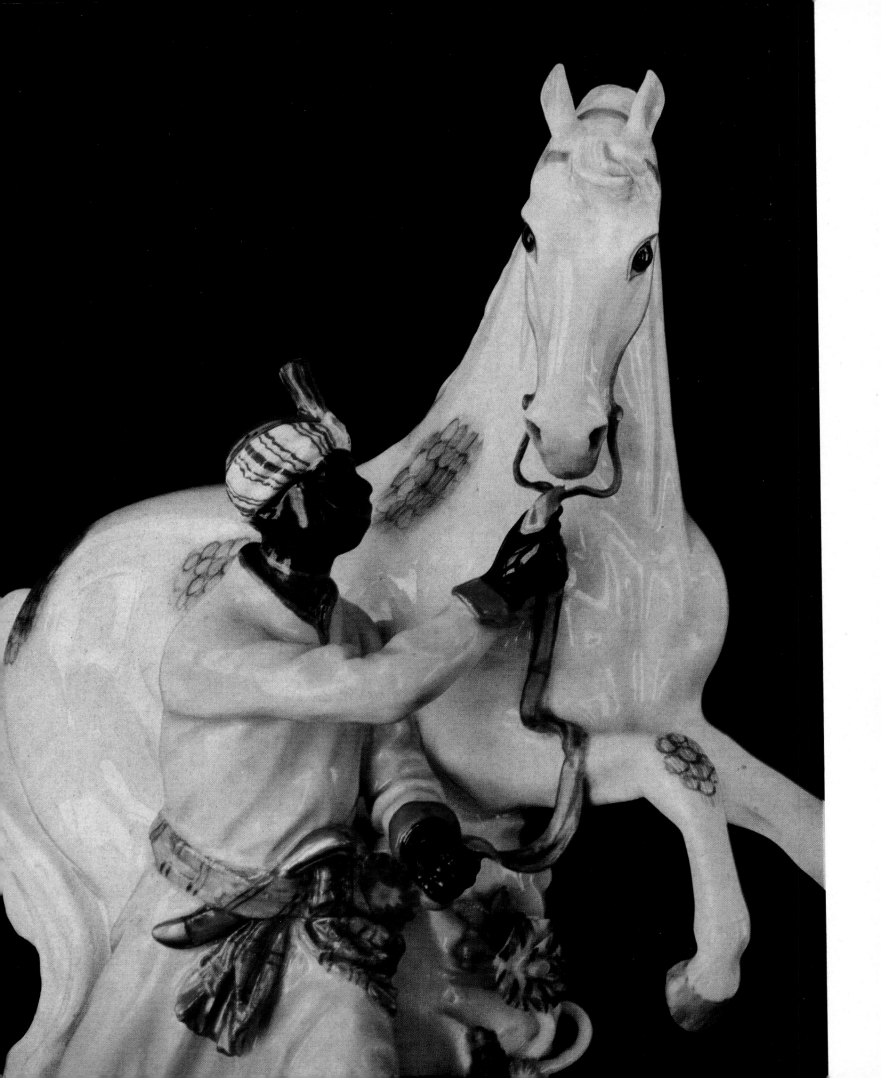

122 Persian by Johann Joachim Kaendler,
     c. 1748
123 Hungarian hussar by Johann Joachim
     Kaendler, *c.* 1750
124 Beltrame and Columbine by Johann
     Joachim Kaendler, *c.* 1740

125 Shepherdess by Friedrich Elias Meyer,
  c.1752
126 Tailor's wife riding on a goat
  by Johann Friedrich Eberlein, 1740

127 Sea swallow by Johann Joachim
    Kaendler, *c.* 1750
128 A hunting group by Johann Joachim
    Kaendler, *c.* 1758
129 Aviary vase by Johann Joachim
    Kaendler, *c.* 1732

134 Shepherd group playing instruments by Johann
    Joachim Kaendler, *c.* 1755
135 Shepherd group beneath a tree by Johann
    Joachim Kaendler, *c.* 1750

145 Tankard, mounted, underglaze decoration,
     c. 1722
146 Mounted tankard with underglaze
     chinoiseries, *c.* 1725
147 Mocha pot with underglaze decoration,
     c. 1728

155 Tureen with shaded flower painting, *c.* 1745
156 Four-sided cup with flower painting, *c.* 1745

a . Leucojum incanum majus flore ex
purpureo et albo pleno.
b. Leucojum incanum majus flore ex coc,
cineo et albo pleno.
c. Leucojum hirsutum minus.
d. Leucojum bisentatum asperum majus et minus.
e. Leucojum foliis et siliquis hirsutis.
f. Leucojum luteum Sylvestre.

a . Anemone aurea striis rubris notatis.
b. Anemone semiplena flore albo et pallido variegato.
c. Anemone lutea magna flore punctata .

157 Pages from the Weinmann *Codex*, 1735
158 Tureen (*Neubrandenstein* type) with figure of maiden
     and bouquets of flowers, *c.* 1760

159 Reserve from a tankard with flowers adapted from woodcuts,
   c. 1745
160 Reserve from the same tankard as in plate 159

161 Tureen with branch handles and stylized flower decoration,
   c. 1760
162 Coffeepot with stylized flower decoration, *c.* 1765

163 Cup with stylized flower decoration, *c.* 1760
164 Wine jug with relief flower ornament heightened
   in enamels, *c.*1740

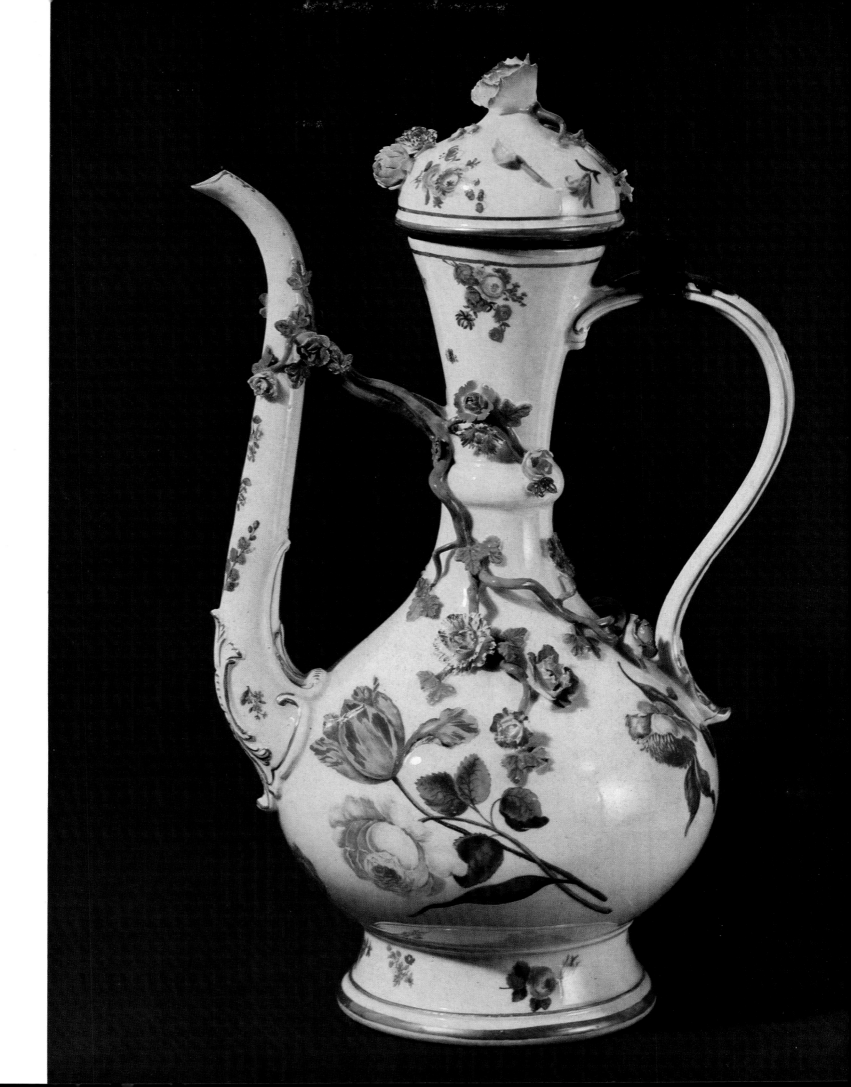

165 Covered vase with gold ground and rich
     flower decoration, *c.* 1750
166 Vase with gold lace and rich
     flower painting, *c.* 1745

167 Needle cases with landscape
  and flower painting, *c.* 1740 and 1745
168 Cane handle with Watteau painting, *c.* 1740
169 Cup and coffeepot with Watteau painting,
  c. 1745

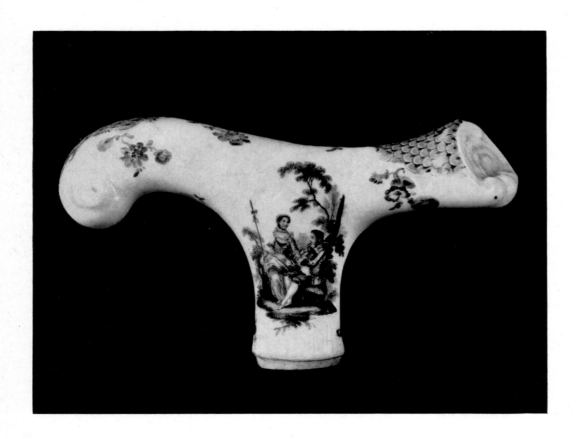

170 Tureen with raised decoration
    and diamond point etching, 1774

171 Mounted *tabatière* with battle painting
    in the manner of Christian Friedrich Herold, *c.* 1745

172 Portrait of Augustus III by Johann Martin
    Heinrici, 1753

173 Lidded cup with scenes from Goethe's
Die Leiden des jungen Werthers
by Johann Georg Loehnig, *c.* 1780
174 Chocolate pot of the Marcolini period
with alternating stripe decoration, *c.* 1780

175 The Good Mother, group by Michel
    Victor Acier, 1774
176 Children at the Cradle, group by
    Michel Victor Acier, c. 1775

177 Portrait bust of Count Marcolini
   by Andreas Weger, 1809
178 Amphora by Michel Victor Acier
   with sepia painting, 1780

183 Dice thrower by Christian
    Gottfried Jüchtzer, 1798
184 Dying Gaul by Johann
    Daniel Schöne, 1814
185 Miniature of Aristotle as Hermes
    by Christian Karl Schiebel, 1793

186 Amphora with snake handle
and gold ground, engraved, 1810
187 Cup with relief portrait,
interior gilt, c. 1820
188 Allegorical plaque in the style
of Wedgwood, c. 1800

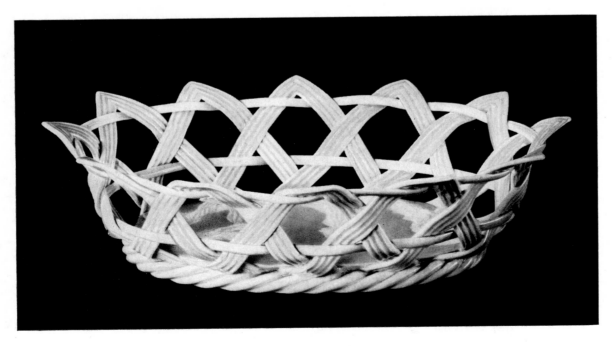

189 Dinner plate with
vineleaf decoration, *c.* 1820

190 Oval wicker basket, *c.* 1800

191 Jug with swan handle
and vineleaf decoration,
c. 1825

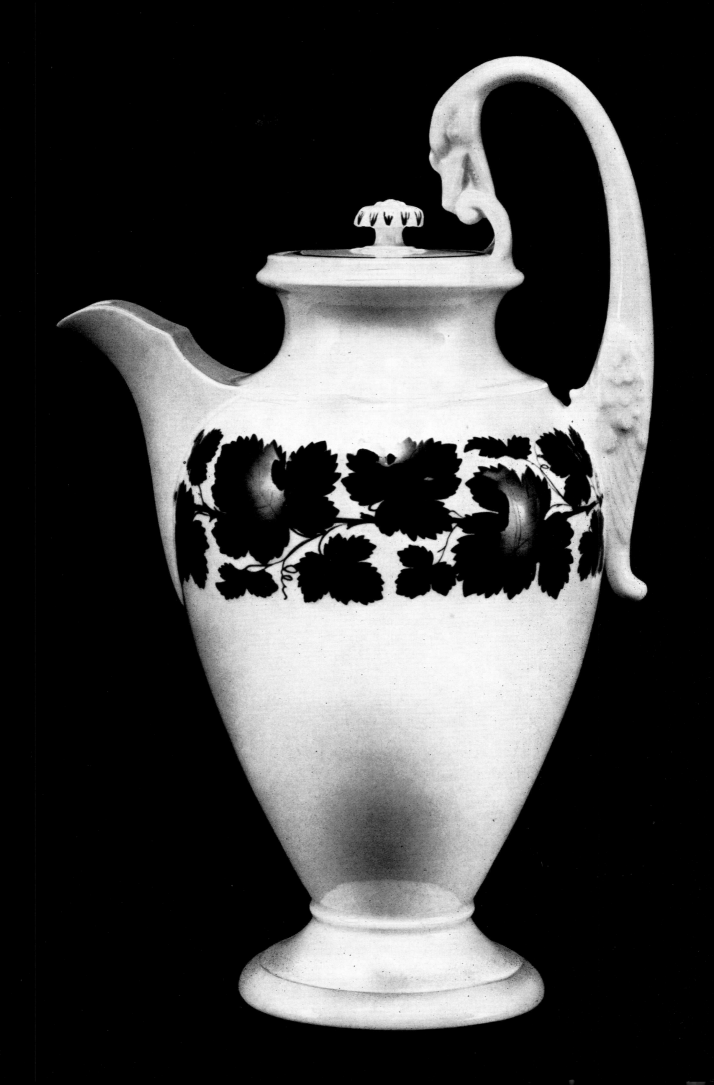

192 Cylindrical cups with portrait painting, 1807
193 Cylindrical cups with portrait painting, *c.* 1810

194 Plate from the Wellington Service, 1818
195 Portrait medallion by Georg Friedrich
 Kersting, c. 1825
196 Plate with landscape from the
 Sächsische Schweiz, c. 1820

197 Ariadne by Heinrich von Dannecker, *c.* 1820
198 Statuette of Goethe by Christian
     Daniel Rauch, 1830

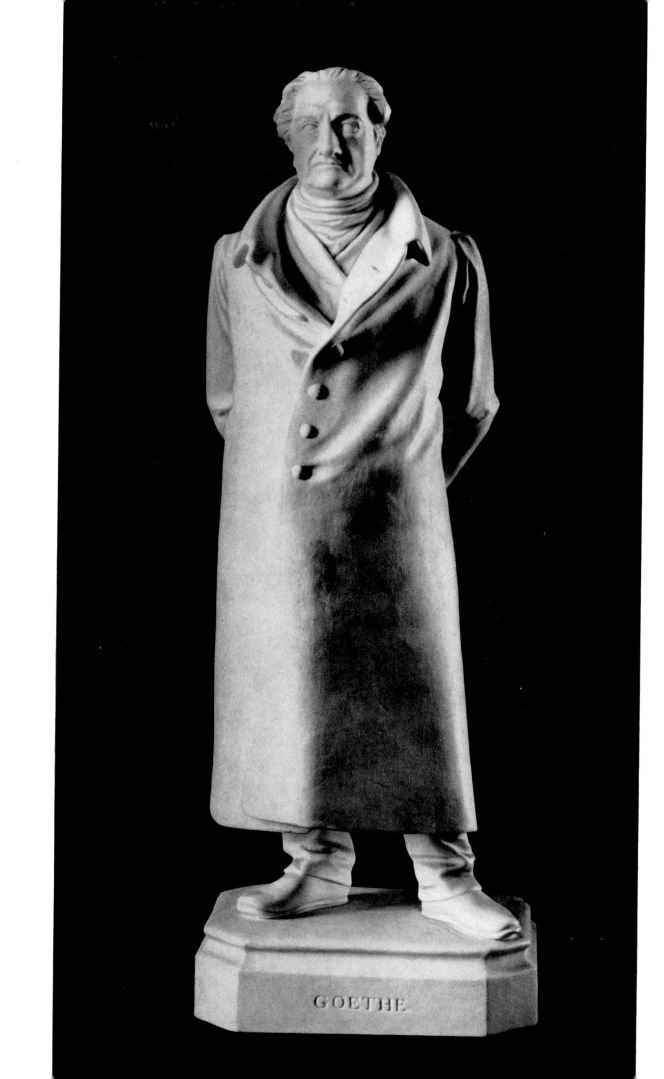

GOETHE

199 Wall plate with landscape
and flower painting, *c.* 1860
200 Cup with neo-Gothic decoration,
c. 1855
201 Coffeepot in the style
of Capo di Monte porcelain, *c.* 1872

202 Ornamental vase with gold
    and platinum painting, *c.* 1875
203 Lidded bowl with medallion
    in *pâte-sur-pâte* technique, 1870

206 Vase richly decorated with flower painting
by Julius Eduard Braunsdorf, *c.* 1900
207 Cup with *Jugendstil* decoration by Konrad
Hentschel, 1906

208 Wall plate with early
    Jugendstil ornamentation, *c.* 1900
209 Lady with bouquet
    by Theodor Eichler, 1904

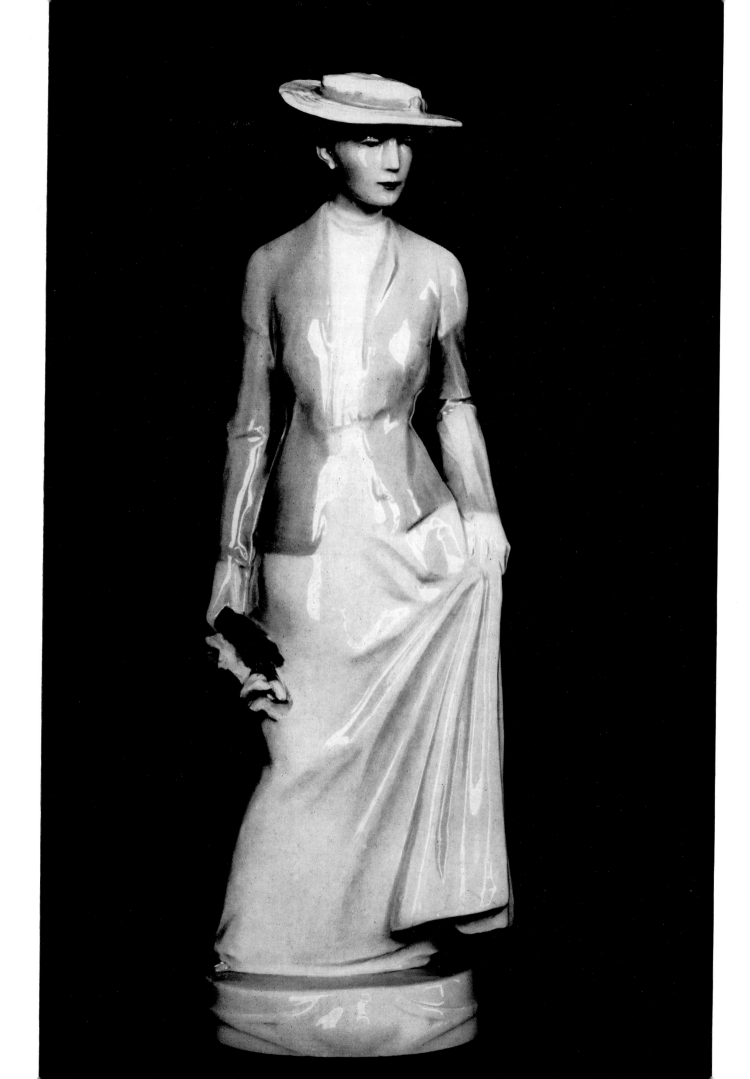

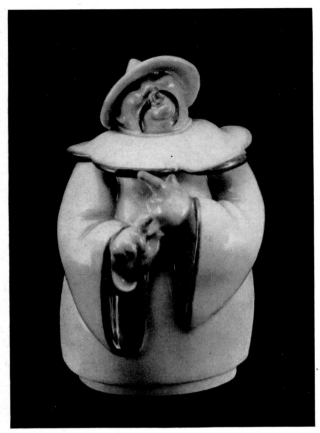

224 Floor vase, design and decoration by Paul Börner
225 Pot from a coffee service by Paul Börner, decoration
by Arthur Findeisen, 1932

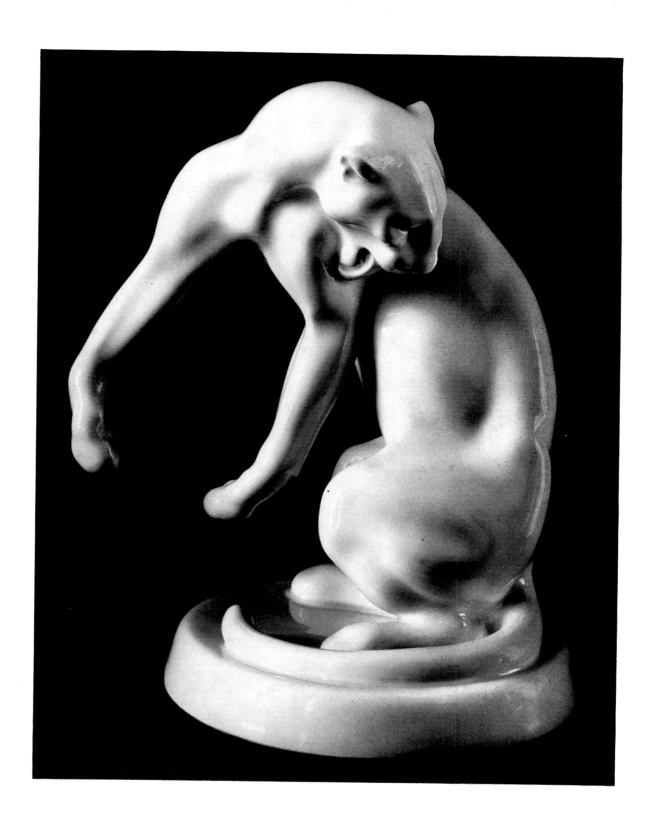

257 Baron Münchhausen by Alexander Struck, 1941
258 Flamingos by Elfriede Reichel-Drechsler, 1960

239 Angel for a tomb by Gerhard Marcks (detail)
240 Angel for a tomb by Gerhard Marcks, 1920
241 Sleepwalker by Gerhard Marcks, 1920

242 Candelabrum in the form of a rider
    by Gerhard Marcks, 1920
243 Sleeping Peasants by Ernst Barlach, 1925

244 Shetland pony by Heinrich Drake, 1956
245 Vase by Hans Merz, 1958
246 Vase by Ludwig Zepner, 1965

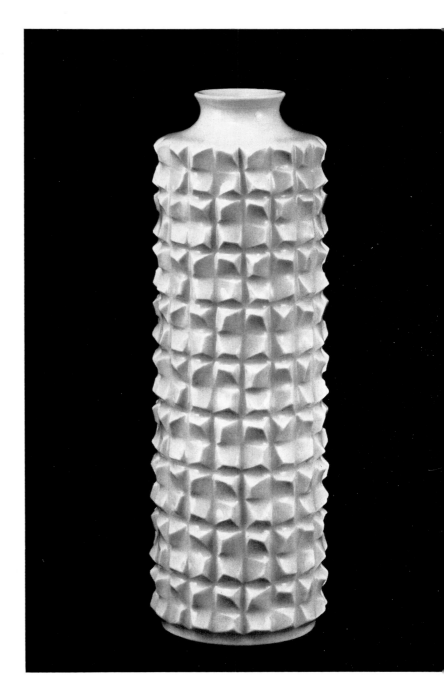

247 Cake dish by Ludwig Zepner, 1965, flower painting
    by Heinz Werner
248 Coffee service by Heinz Werner, 1964

249/250 Details from the memorial in St. Nikolai
church in Meissen by Paul Börner, 1929
251 Altar in the Dresden cathedral
(former Hofkirche) by Friedrich Press,
1973

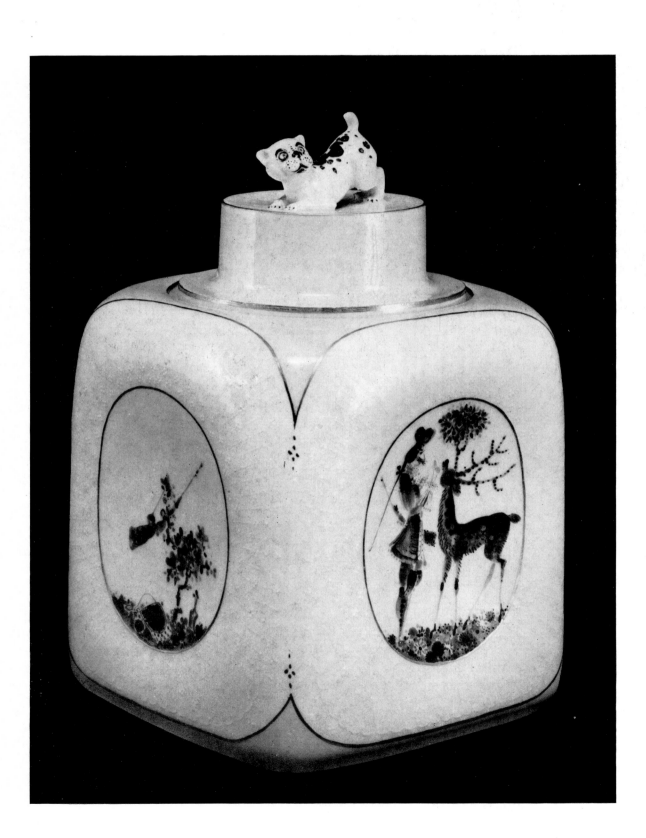

256 Container by Ludwig Zepner with painting
     (Baron Münchhausen) by Heinz Werner, 1968
257 Wall plate by Heinz Werner, 1967
258 Goblet by Ludwig Zepner, 1967

APPENDIX

NOTES

WA = the Werkarchiv of the VEB Staatliche Porzellan-Manufaktur, Meissen.

1. Schilfert, G.: "Deutschland von 1648 bis 1789." In *Deutsche Geschichte*, volume 1, Berlin 1967, page 652.

2. Sturmhoefel, K.: *Illustrierte Geschichte der Sächsischen Lande und ihrer Herrscher*, volume 2,1, Leipzig 1908, page 399.

3. Voltaire: *Le siècle de Louis XIV*, chapter XXIX.

4. Forberger, R.: "Die Meissner Porzellanmanufaktur in der Sächsischen Manufakturgeschichte." In: *250 Jahre Staatliche Porzellan-Manufaktur Meissen*, Meissen 1960, page 42.

5. Forberger, R.: *Die Manufaktur in Sachsen vom Ende des 16. bis zum Anfang des 19. Jahrhunderts*, Berlin 1958, page 210.

6. Forberger, R.: "Tschirnhaus und das sächsische Manufakturwesen." In: *E. W. von Tschirnhaus und die Frühaufklärung in Mittel- und Osteuropa*, edited by E. Winter, Berlin 1960, page 214 ff.

7. Forberger, R.: *Die Meissner Porzellanmanufaktur*, page 23.

8. The great service rendered by this scientist in the advancement of exact scientific methods in the beginning of the Age of Enlightenment is mentioned in a contemporary appreciation by Burchard Menckem, *Compendiöses Gelehrten Lexicon*, published in 1715 by Gleditzsch in Leipzig: "Von Tzschirnhausen, Ehrenfried Walther, Lord of Kislingswalde and Stoltzenberg, Royal and Electoral Privy Councillor, one of the most illustrious persons of recent times, comes from an ancient line of Bohemian counts. He was born on the 10th of April, 1651. He studied in Leyden in Holland where, owing to his great interest in mathematics, he devoted himself to the study of physics, especially mechanics. He traveled throughout Europe and made good use of his travels for his observations. His erudition was so highly appreciated in France that in 1683 he was appointed a member of the Royal Academy. He spent his fortune on many valuable inventions in the field of optics, one of which was an astonishing burning mirror, as well as in the areas of metallurgy and mineralogy. In Saxony, he discovered deposits of coral and agate. He founded three remarkable glassworks. Furthermore, he showed how to make porcelain from a certain kind of clay found in Saxony. His desire to penetrate even deeper into the secrets of Nature's realm was interrupted by his sudden death on the 11th of October, 1798, in his 57th year of age."

9. Frit porcelain belongs to the group of the

pseudoporcelains, since it contains a lime marl as plastic ingredient instead of china clay, and as condensing fluxing agent a frit rich in alkalis. It is coated with a lead glaze. The relatively low firing temperature (below 1250 °C) permits the use of a varied palette. Claude Reverend and Louis Poterat are considered to be the inventors.

10. One of Johann Friedrich Böttger's first helpers was a Freiberg miner, Paul Wildenstein, who in 1736 presented a comprehensive report to the manufactory commission (WA I A 24 a/ 312 ff.), giving a lively description of his activities in the laboratory of the inventor of porcelain. Engelhardt, in *Johann Friedrich Böttger—Inventor of Saxon Porcelain* (Leipzig 1837), utilized portions of this material for his biography. Here are some selections:

"... in 1706, I came to Meissen to the Baron Böttger, to the secret laboratory, and we were shut in there for 18 weeks. Even the windows had been walled up to half of their height, and Herr von Tzschirnhaussen [sic] from Dresden was often with us as well as the mining councillor Pabst from Freyberg. We had a laboratory with 24 kilns, and the baron and Tzschirnhaussen had already made specimens of red porcelain in the shape of small slabs and marbled slab stones.

"... After we had been there for 18 weeks, Herr von Tzschirnhaussen came to us together with Herr Burghardt, the bailiff of the late Prince of Fürstenberg. They brought us the news that we should pack up the baron's belongings and ours. We had to leave because the Swedes were invading. We had to have everything ready within two hours. The other things we possessed had to remain in two rooms which were locked up and sealed. The baron then took three of us with him; the other three had, however, to go to Freyberg again. So we went, accompanied by a strong convoy, to the Königstein where we were watched much more closely. Each of us had his special duties. Moreover, we had been told to have good care that the baron not speak to anybody."

While Böttger was imprisoned in the Königstein, preparations were already being made for his future work: "... Meanwhile, on the so-called Jungfer [the Eastern Bastion of the Brühlsche Terrasse in Dresden] a house had been built, to which we came later on. The appearance of the vaults was very untidy, and we had to work quite hard to make into a laboratory. There Herr von Tzschirnhaussen, too, was giving instructions, and they began

to research. Among other things, specimens of red porcelain were made, as well as white. Köhler and I had to stand nearly every day by the large burning-glass to test the minerals. There I ruined my eyes, so that I now can perceive very little at a distance.

"When, however, the master saw that the specimens were turning out better and better, he asked His Majesty for permission for his men to go out in order to fetch materials and other things he required for his work, for we, too, had been locked up again. This permission was readily granted.

"Then Herr von Tzschirnhaussen fell ill, and every night two of us had to take turns sitting up with him, since his health grew worse and worse. His Majesty had commanded that he be informed if Tzschirnhaussen died. This happened at midnight. The king mourned over him. We, however, worked on, and the specimens became better and better."

Since difficulties had developed with the kilns they were using, a much larger one was quickly constructed. But this was to no avail:

"... We couldn't manage to make a strong fire in the new kiln; all our toil was fruitless and the fire remained weak. While it was burning, we had to make the fire walls sometimes higher, sometimes lower, but it was no use until we finally discovered the fault in the casing. The coals wouldn't burn all the way down, so we had to pull them out every thirty minutes. We had to toil like cattle. This lasted for six days and six nights, for there was no draft, since we couldn't build a fire wall up the vault, which was just beneath the pleasure pavilion. The fire rejected everything, and big stones were pulled loose and burst from the vault. They are still to be seen. Our hair was scorched and the floor had grown so hot that our feet were covered with large blisters. Moreover, the room was filled with fumes owing to the extreme dampness, and enormous silver-colored masses were hanging from the vault, which had been scorched in this way. The baron, however, had the kiln fed again without delay, and this time it operated better and the coals burned well.

"His Majesty had the baron informed he would come as soon as there was a good fire in the kiln, and so he did. His Majesty arrived with the Prince of Fürstenberg, but when they entered the laboratory and felt the terrible fire, they would rather have turned back. Since, however, the baron—looking

440

like a sooty charcoal-burner—was so close to him, His Majesty entered and urged the prince to come in, too. The baron told us to stop firing for a while and to open the kiln, and during this time the prince said several times, 'Oh, Jesus.' The king, however, laughed and said to him that it was in no way to be compared to Purgatory! The kiln was opened, and all was bathed in white heat so that nothing could be seen. The king looked in and said to the prince, 'Look, Egon, they say that porcelain is in there!' The prince said he couldn't see anything either but finally the kiln grew red, since it was open, so they could see the porcelain. I had to draw out a specimen, which was a sagger containing a small teapot.

"A tubful of water stood nearby, so that the glowing iron could be extinguished. The baron immediately seized the tongs, drew the teapot out, and threw it into the water. Suddenly a loud bang was heard, and the king said, 'Oh, it's smashed.' but the baron replied, 'No, Your Majesty, it must stand this test.' He then rolled up his sleeves and took it out of the tub. It indeed proved to be intact; only the glaze had not yet entirely run; then it was covered with snow and again put into the kiln. After that His Majesty gave instructions that the kiln not be opened again until it was thoroughly cool and could be emptied, and said he wanted to be present then.

"This happened a few days later. The firing had gone very well, and the king was pleased. He took the teapot for himself and said that it was just to his liking. But the baron cut him short and said, 'I know very well what Your Majesty is thinking—I am a mortal man and it might please God that I died today. But there are my men, who know how everything is done. I don't hold back back anything—you can ask them to reply in accord with their consciences.' And this was done.

"The king said, 'It is impossible that the men can tolerate such toil,' but the baron answered, 'My men will do anything for Your Majesty's sake, and they will spare no pains in their work.' The king laughed and said rather cheerfully, 'Then they shall have my blessing and their livelihood.' And soon after it was arranged that we got new clothing.

"The baron engaged potters and workmen in order to move ahead more quickly. The work was done in the house of Bartholmäi, the physician in the Moritzstrasse, but the mass was composed in the fortress, and was also fired there. The medicus himself collaborated, composing and plugging. He spoke to the workers in such an unassuming manner that we would have worked day and night for him."

11. Number 44 of the Pretiosen of the Meissen Archives consists of seven loose pages (eighteenth-century writing paper) in an extraordinarily hasty hand, of which six bear Johann Friedrich Böttger's handwriting (according to a graphologist's opinion). These notes were written during the time of his experiments on the Jungfernbastei in Dresden. The most interesting of these pages is dated January 15, 1708, and besides seven different ceramic recipes contains the following remark: "...has probas eodem die hora 12 imposimus ignisque datus, quo continuatim usque ad horam 5 (Quin-)tam vespertinam tunc crucibuli extracti et patellulae inventae uti superius ad signatim Numerum notatum invenies ..." Since in four of the seven results of the experiments the ceramic product is described as "*album et pellucidatum*" (white and translucent), the two main characteristics of porcelain are clearly indicated.

12. Steinbrück reports under the date March 28, 1709 (WA I A f2/169): "The inventor Herr Johann Friedrich Böttger has drawn up a most humble petition and handed it to His Royal Majesty, by which he offers to manage the making of the following: fine white porcelain together with the very finest glaze and all accessory painting, and it should be at least of the same quality as East Indian ware, if not superior to it."

13. Gröger, H.: *Tausend Jahre Meissen*, Meissen 1929, page 547 ff.

14. In the Steinbrück manufacturing calendar (WA I A f290) is found: "Regulations according to which Herr Johann Heinrich Blumenthaal had to look after the new corridor being constructed in the hall, and after the adaptation of the room of the forwarding department for the bookkeeper, and both the storage vaults as well as of the adjacent small room."

15. "Workers employed at the new manufactory in Meissen":

	Receive weekly	Shall receive weekly subject to further notice
Jo. George Schuberth	3	1.12
Davidt Köhler	3	1.12
Christoff Wirden	2.12	1.6

Paul Wildenstein	2	1.6
Samuel Stöltzel	2	1.6
Balthasar Gerbich	3	1.12
Hans George Bormann	2.12	1.6
Andreas Heinrich	1.6	1
Georg Kittel	3	1.12
Peter Geithner	3	1.12
Gottfried Lohse	3	1.12
Joh. Christ. Krumbholtz	2.12	1.6
Johann Donner	2.12	1.6
Christian Büscher	2	1.6
Johann Kittel	2	1.6
George Michel	1.12	1.6
Johann Meisel	1.12	1.6
2 apprentices at 6 gr.	12	12
Frantz Wander	3	1.22
Andreas Piltz	3	1.12
Jo. Chr. Leonhardt	3	1.12
Mstr. Christoff Rühle	4	2
Joh. Christ. Kratzenberg	3	2
Hennig Schmidt	1	1
2 men at 1 taler	2	1.12
The gardener Gebhardt	2	1
and his helper	12	12
The pipemaker Müller and	3	2
his 2 helpers at 1 taler	2	2
Extraordinary expenses	...	10.12

Total 50

Dresden, November 11, 1711

Johann Friedrich Böttger

Under WA I A f3/162 the following marks are found, used by Meissen workers and stamped on their products.

X Georg Kittel
✳ Peter Geithner
✳ Gottfried Lohse
✗ Johann Christoph Krumbholtz
✛ Johann Donner

✗ Johann Kittel
✗ Christoph Busch
♯ Johann Meisel
✳ George Michel
‖ Johann Michael Schumann

16. See Wildenstein's report, note 10.

17. Bartholmäi's instructions (WA I A f3/28) read: "... he must transpose everything that Böttger gives him into characters that nobody will be able to decipher ..." And in a petition (I A a23/293) Bartholmäi speaks of his collaboration as follows: "... in the first year, 1708, I acquired such skill in the red as well as in the white [porcelain] that the pieces made by myself could well be offered for sale, until the manufactory was finally removed to Meissen where it was carried on under my administration."

18. See Martin Mields in *250 Jahre Staatliche Porzellan-Manufaktur Meissen*, Meissen 1960 page 124.

19. In the Steinbrück annals (WA I A f3/145), a page from the Leipzig paper, May 14, 1710, appears, which describes the Meissen offering as follows:

"The new royal and electoral manufactory of Dresden has been opened here in the Blue Angel. The goods are of an extraordinary beauty, and the manufactory is heavily visited every day. The following types of vessels are offered. First, one finds tableware such as jugs, ·teacups, Turkish coffeepots, bottles, and other items suitable for use and for adorning the table. There are works made in both dark- and brilliant-red, artistically decorated with ornaments in the shape of latticework and leaves. Some, because of their extraordinary hardness, resemble jasper, so well '*goderoniret*,' or polished, are they. They are cut in angular shapes or in facets, and are of a wonderful luster and metal-like tone. Furthermore, there is a sort of red vessel that has been lacquered like the most beautiful pieces of Japanese work, and painted with gold, silver, and other colors that have been laid on in the fire in such a way that neither hot water nor anything else will make them run. Thirdly, there is tableware with a dark glaze, but into this glaze cuts have been made so that the original red color is still to be seen. The fourth type consists of red vessels with enameled relief flowerwork, partly trimmed with stones. Fifthly, there is the cheaper ware, which to some extent resembles East India terra sigillata, It differs, however, from that ware by its extraordinarily subtle form. It looks more like red wax than clay, and is also distinguished by its hardness and durability. These vessels can be made to resemble East India ware by additional cutting and polishing. Sixthly, there are for sale various kinds of blue and white pieces of the same type as Delft ware, sold for the price at which they are offered in Holland. Seventh, plates and centerpieces with relief festoons of leaves, covered with fine gold leaf gold on white glaze are offered. Finally, they are exhibiting some specimens of white porcelain produced in the manufactory at Dresden, glazed items as well as unglazed ones. These are very hard and translucent. They will not however be sold during this fair."

20. In Steinbrück's report (WA I A f2) the entry for July 5, 1710, says that the *Kaufdiener* Johann Wilhelm Stürzel traveled to Karlsbad on June 11 with goods worth 1,328 talers and to Berlin on July 5 with goods worth 6,150 talers. From Berlin to Hamburg a certain amount of goods was to be expedited.

21. In the preamble of the "impartial report" (Dresden State Archives, Loc. 41910, Fol. 14 ff.) one reads: "...Merchants who intend to establish new manufactories divide these into two classes. One kind imitates wares already manufactured in various localities and known in the marketplace. The other produces goods of recent invention, never seen before. In both cases, intelligent and experienced merchants must observe special rules before establishing a manufactory, and there are other factors to be considered."

22. Steinbrück writes (WA I A P2/344): "He [Böttger] declared that the red vessels, too, would in future be improved, since he had already conducted experiments that enabled, in a very simple way, the appearance of such vessels to be made much more distinguished by the addition of etching and other intricate work such as relief ornaments, as well as by silvering and gilding. But owing to limited time, no specimen could be shown."

 Concerning the etching of Böttger stoneware, Professor Beyersdörfer, an expert in the field of research on silicates, is of the following opinion: "It is possible that Böttger, when etching his stoneware, already followed the procedure invented by Heinrich Schwanckhardt (1670 Nuremberg). In this case, he must have used a paste of powdered fluorite and strong sulphuric acid."

23. Böttger reports in January, 1712 (WA I A P2/155): "Stoves, fireplaces, cabinets, table tops, columns and pillars, doorposts, small coffins, antique urns, slabs for covering floors, jewel-boxes, chimes, pastry boxes ('Handgranaten'), and chess sets" could be produced without difficulty.

24. According to a receipt (WA I A e7/Nr. 9 of the Miller receipts), Paul Hermann delivered three figurines that had to be reworked into Böttger ware by Bernhardt Miller before they could be exported.

25. Although Irminger was established and his requested salary of twenty talers per month was assured him in the autumn of 1712, it was only in 1716 that this sum was in fact paid promptly. (WA I A a/1/136 ff.)

26. On October 11, 1712, the painters Johann David Strohmann and Anselm Bader were "employed to paint porcelain vessels." (WA I A f2/387) Köhler was ordered to prepare the colors for the painters. Shortly thereafter Steinbrück noted in his journal for the last week in November that Bader "... has on the 29th of November on his own accord left his work in Meissen, where he had painted porcelain for several weeks, and he has not returned."

27. In a petition dated January 22, 1722 (WA I A a5/14 ff.), Funcke argued his high costs based on a complete inventory dating from May 13, 1713, to April 5, 1719.

28. David Köhler describes the various results of his experiments in underglazing as follows: "[there] is a good high blue, an even more beautiful blue, that looks quite black, is however black [sic], looks a little lighter, is beautiful and rich, is a beautiful, tender blue ..." (WA Pretiosum—the so-called Köhler book of experiments from January, 1720, to November, 1721).

29. Dresden State Archives, Loc. 1339, Vol. IV/321: "Specifications of the porcelain works which, in Poland, were most humbly presented to His Majesty on the occasion when the report of the 22nd of May was submitted:
 1 blue dish
 1 ditto plate
 2 ditto shaving basins
 1 ditto small bowl and cup enameled with gold. The compounder David Köhler at Meissen invented the above pieces and had them painted there.
 3 small blue and plain bowls
 1 ditto cup
 2 ditto chocolate mugs
 4 red enameled bowls
 1 ditto cup
 3 chocolate mugs

 The artisan, who has returned from Vienna, made all of these, and invented the colors used thereupon. The painting was done by the painter Herold, who came here with him."

30. "With a brush, he painted the yellow cup that was delivered yesterday by Steltzel [sic]. He required at least 3 hours for this work." (WA I A a4/22)

31. "... that the above painter has on command signed a good number of teapots and sugar bowls with the letters M. P. M. ..." (WA I A a5/215)

32. From the Marriage Register of the Jena parish office: "Johann Gregor Herold [sic], court painter at the Royal Polish and Electoral Saxon Porcelain Factory at Meissen, the youngest son by the second marriage of the late master Wilhelm Herold, citizen and head of the tailors' guild, and the maiden Rahel Eleonore Keyl, the legitimate and only daughter of the honorable Meissen councilor, Gottfried Keyl, have on the 6th of October, 1725, in Meissen been joined in marriage."

33. On March 9, 1739, Christian Friedrich Herold presented a report to the manufacturing commission (WA I A a25/54): "...how gilded relief work can be applied to porcelain, and how such relief work should be something new on porcelain, and magnificent in a unique way, so that he, therefore, would like to be considered the only master of it for the time being."

34. The letter of Adam Friedrich von Löwenfinck is presently in the Meissen Werkarchiv. (WA I A 2/24a/368-69) It was published for the first time by Dr. Kurt Röder. It appeared word for word, with a critical commentary by Otto Walcha, in K.F.S., No. 51, 1960, pp. 24–31.

35. Gröger, H.: "Die Arbeits- und Sozialverhältnisse der Staatlichen Porzellan-Manufaktur Meissen im 18. Jahrhundert." In: *Forschungen aus Mitteldeutschen Archiven*, Berlin 1953, page 171.

36. In report No. 17 for the year 1727, the following appears regarding Fritzsche's capabilities (WA I A a10/20a): "... he has, in 1727, embossed and made several animal and many other figures that had not been seen in the manufactory up to that time, and he has made them free-hand, without having any drawing or models." In addition, several months later it was reported that he "was rather skilled ... in invention ..." (WA I A a10/235)

37. How varied the tasks given to Johann Christoph Ludwig Lücke were is evidenced by the work list dating from the end of the year 1728. (WA III H 117/51) The following commands, among others, appear:

" 1. An ice bucket handle in the form of a Siren.
2. Knife and fork handle in the form of a head.
9. A Turkish bird-whistle in the form of a Janissary.
21. A cannon with carriage and wheels.
38. A handle shaped like the stem of a vine, for a chocolate cup."
The following statues are mentioned:
"25. A Pantaloon from the Italian opera.
26. A portrait of the king, *in voller Positur*, newly repaired.
41. The king *in voller Positur*, 16 inches high."
The statuette of Augustus the Strong that appears in the list does not originate from von Lücke. The form, having become dulled, had to be rebuilt.

38. Kirchner had previously stated his demands (WA I A a13/8): "... He wants to submit, en masse, all sorts of new ideas, but not to be bound by time deadlines, for set working hours and inspiration do not always coincide.
2. He wants to supervise the modelers, but to cast his own work, 'so that it is done artistically and the drawing is correct.'
3. He demands that the modelers be placed directly under him, for he wants nothing more to do with their 'malice.'
4. He wants to train the apprentices.
5. He promises to 'be so careful with the materials that nothing will be ruined or be used away from the premises.'
6. He wishes to recognize as his immediate superior only His Excellency the privy councillor. (By this he meant Johann Georg von Wichmannshausen, chairman of the manufactory commission.)"

39. The first inventory of the large shipments for the Dutch Palace shows the status of the project in November, 1731 (WA I Aa 15/522):

"List of the large vessels and other items of such kind manufactured according to the models and sketches presented by His Royal Majesty, and which for the most part are ready for firing:
1. Pieces that exist in clay and are yet to be molded, viz:
1 wild boar
1 elephant
1 rhinoceros
1 Apostle $3\frac{1}{2}$ ells high
His Royal Majesty on horseback
2. Pieces that have been formed:
3 statuettes of St. Nepomuk
4 Indian ravens, large
2 forest devils
90 ornamental pieces of various types
3 large dragons
4 large dishes
22 large vases
21 centerpieces shaped like birdcages
5 Sphinxes
3 statuettes of the Apostle Peter, $2\frac{1}{2}$ ells high
6 monkeys
2 Indian pheasants
4 Indian hawks
2 sea gulls
3 ospreys
2 birds
3 eagles
2 ospreys with carps
3 bald coots
2 large owls
White pieces, finished by final firing:
9 parrots
4 Sphinxes

1 bird

Pieces finished by final firing and enameled:

9 large monkeys of various types

3 ditto small monkeys

1 hawk or bird of prey

5 parrots

3 small owls

1 diving-bird

Meissen, the 13th of December, 1751."

40. According to the report of June 2, 1731 (WA V 2/11/82/, Kirchner incurred the following traveling expenses: "3 talers 8 groschen for 5 days, 16 groschen for the *Modellmeister* Kirchner, who was ordered to travel to Dresden on manufactory affairs."

41. The following is from an announcement of July, 1732 (WA I A b 4/153): "... In this month of July, the modelers Kirchner and Känntler once again fashioned the Apostles Peter and Paul in quite another manner, without many ornaments and extravagances. Time will tell whether these pieces will remain without flaws."

42. The report of March, 1732 (WA I A b4/108) relates: "In the month of March, the *Modellmeister* Kirchner has fashioned in clay and brought to full perfection a large figure of the Virgin with the infant Jesus in her lap, as well as other ornaments."

43. Early in 1737, the former *Modellmeister* Kirchner was awarded "30 talers which the sculptor Gottlieb Kirchner in Dresden requests for the modeling and casting of His Majesty's portrait made of clay."

44. Höroldt justified this procedure as follows (WA I A a14/21-40): "... by this means the young apprentices will be kept in better obedience. They must feel that they are bound apprentices to me, and must serve their regular six years' apprenticeship in order to be freed by myself. Then, as is the custom, they will be given their liberty with the gift of a sword."

45. The parish office at Fischbach informs us that Kaendler's birthdate can only be conjectured, not verified in the archives. In Seeligstadt, which is supposedly Kaendler's birthplace, and which falls under the religious jurisdiction of Fischbach, there exists no such personage.

46. Kaendler reports on this act in the "Grünes Gewölbe" in a complaint against Höroldt (WA I A e2/3): "... after I had been blessed with the opportunity for six years to make many ornaments in the so-called Grünes Gewölbe ..."

47. The exact wording of these directions is to be found in a supplement of May 19, 1731, to Vol. I A a15 of the Werkarchiv.

48. See: *The Crown of Poland: Saxony and Poland During the Northern War, 1700–1721*, Journals of the Historical Commission of Poland and the DDR, Volume 1. Berlin 1962.

49. The first well, which was intended only for the use of the manufactory, was "perfected as an essential installation. This well, which contains water more than 2 ells deep, was dug to a depth of 18 ells."

50. A report (WA I A a20/4) of 1734 announces: "... a glaze has been invented that enables painted blue vessels to be prepared in the kilns in such a way that a better quality results and the colors do not run. Therefore, the blue on these vessels is very beautiful and pleasing."

51. A work report of December, 1731 (WA I A b2/67) reads: "A table service is being worked on for the lord high chamberlain Count Friesen. The plates and all the other required pieces are 'scrafiret.' No painting shall be done upon them, but they shall remain pure white. Difficulties are encountered in the molding and in the *Scrafiren*." (By *Scrafiren* is meant the cutting of the ornamental motifs in the plaster forms.)

52. In a work report of December, 1737 (WA I A a24b/114), Kaendler vividly illustrates the concept of the Swan Service. "A model for a dessert service for ... Brühl is fashioned in clay. It consists of the following pieces, for which the idea is taken from sea shells and marine creatures. The main piece stands in the middle of the table. We see 4 Tritons riding on sea horses, supporting Neptune, who stands on shells into which you can put sweets. In addition, there is another work composed of shells on which there are female figures and dolphins, which support shells for sweets. There is also a Glaucos, who sits in a shell and supports on his head other shells for sweets. On each corner of the table we see a swimming swan, with the wings so formed that many sweets can be placed on them."

53. Kaendler describes the specimen plate of the so-called Great Service as follows (WA I A b9/265): "... made for the 'Grosses Service,' a soup plate in the form a shell, in which water is to be seen, embossed, on which two swans are swimming as well as two herons. There are reeds as well."

54. Kaendler's work report of April, 1737 (WA I A b9/52) refers as follows to the bust of Fröhlich: "I fashioned the face of the image of the so-called 'Joseph,' just the way he looks with

his hat the way he is accustomed to wearing it, with a big bunch of flowers and a very well made lace collar around his neck." This is, except for the missing bunch of flowers, which must have been modeled separately and added as decoration, the exact description of the bust of Fröhlich, which has repeatedly been ascribed to Kirchner.

55. Here are Kaendler's own words (WA Taxa Pretiosen 49/50): "A group showing the '*Teutsch* Frenchman' kneeling between two women who punish him for being an enemy of whalebone skirts. One of them makes use of a rolled-up whalebone skirt and flogs him with it, the other woman snatches the toupee from his head and flings it in his face." The *Teutsch* Frenchman was an anonymous contemporary man of letters who described in slang satirical poems the imbecilities of fashion and the affected social life of certain German-French circles.

56. Kaendler reported on the transformation of this group in his *Taxa* (WA Pretiosen 49/25): "A little group of three figures: a young man is sitting on the grass. A young woman joins him, bringing him a child in a baby's bed. She is accompanied by a lawyer with documents and letters." Another group treats the same theme. "A group consisting of a woman and a man in a dressing gown are sitting at '*à-Lombre-Tischgen*' and playing. Both are laughing. They can be combined with group described previously, as if they were laughing at the man to whom the baby had been brought." Two years later, on October 31, 1742, Kaendler wrote in his work report a "difficult group" of six persons, in which the fable of the foisting off of the child is completed.

57. Kaendler describes this group in detail in his *Taxa* (WA Pretiosen 49/28.9, 1745): "A group of three persons showing a man suffering from gout, who is sitting on a sofa and screaming in pain. Next to him is a woman who is putting cushions under his legs. By her a child is eating porridge from a pan."

58. From *Taxa* (WA 49, page 16): "A figure representing St. Hubertus, who is kneeling before a stag, between whose antlers is a crucifix which he is worshiping. A saddled horse is standing beside the figure and close to him there are two large trees with branches and leaves, indicating a forest."

59. The Werkarchiv reports on the making of the artificial teeth by Ehder as follows (WA I A b28/134): "Two rows of teeth to be placed in the mouth, with gums made from clay."

60. Peter Reinicke's work report of June, 1743, reads (WA I A b20): "Fashioned in clay for Count von Brühl: a pleasure house 12 inches high, 8 inches wide and 10 inches long. It is three stories high, with a broken-tile roof. In front and behind are pediments and balconies. There are windows on all sides ..."

61. In 1738, news of the changing Parisian styles was already being collected. In Vol. I A a24/d/194 of the Werkarchiv, issue No. XXII of the Utrecht newspaper appears because an unusual order is contained in it. "The Duke of Kingston has given an order from London to the famous goldsmith Melier to have two silver tureens made, each weighing 80 marcks. They are now almost ready, and surpass by far the best that has heretofore been made. The cover of one shows in a very lifelike manner the figure of a duck, a reddish seafish, a carp, and an artichoke. The other cover, or tureen lid, represents a partridge, crabs, a big Swedish turnip with its shrub, and a mushroom. The middle part of the tureen consists of shell work, and instead of a handle there is a savory and beneath it a celery root."

62. The complete title of the *Herbarium* of the Regensburg apothecary Johann Wilhelm Weinmann reads: "The Accurate Representation of Some Thousand Trees, Shrubs, Herbs, Flowers, Fruits and Mushrooms From All 4 Parts of the World. Published at Great Expense by the Famous Augsburg [sic] Artists Bartolomäo Seuter and Johann Elia Ridinger."

63. In 1740, Southern European shopkeepers complained about the alleged falling off the quality of the so-called Turks' heads: "The clear outlines ..., pure whiteness, slenderness, fragility, and translucent character of these vessels was popular with the Turks and Persians. The porcelain is now, however, tarnished and covered with black spots. It is so thick and heavy that one would hardly believe it to be genuine Saxon porcelain."

64. Inspector Auenmüller closes his observations on the disturbances caused by the war as follows (WA I A a32/123): "In spite of generally unstable conditions, the Royal Porcelain Manufactory has enjoyed considerable progress."

65. Peter Reinicke's collaboration on the busts of the king during the period of December, 1744 and January, 1745, is evidenced as follows: "(I) put the finishing touches on [corrigiret] the busts and embossed their faces ..."

66. The description of "Brühl's Cascade" appears in WA I A b23. "By the gracious verbal

orders of the cabinet minister, His Excellency Count Brühl, after a few days, I fashioned and completed the model of the Great Cascade, which is to be found in the garden at Ostra. The following figures are to be seen on it: Neptune, Amphitrite, a Triton, a Nymph, the child of a Triton, and the images of two old men by which the Tiber and the Nile are represented. There are also two sea horses, several shells, and ravines, all of which required considerable effort."

67. Meyer's memo to the manufacturing commission (WA I A b37/No. 41): "... that I need not be forced to work for sustenance only, when making my models, but may pursue my studies and training."

68. Kaendler's work report of September, 1731, reads (WA I A a22/265): "... Obeying the royal command, [I] stayed for three days in Dresden to fashion and present [a figure of] His Majesty on horseback."

69. Kaendler's memo of September 18, 1734 (WA I A 32/230-32) twice mentions that equestrian statues in porcelain of Augustus II and III could be erected ("His Majesty's likeness in porcelain with a life-sized jumping horse"). There are, in the report, technical suggestions as to how monumental figures may be, without the process being apparent to the observer, dismantled into several sections and reassembled by means of concealed structures. Kaendler also makes intelligent comments, which do not pertain to monumental pieces, regarding types of ornamental details and gilding.

70. Eberlein's work report of July, 1745 (WA I A b24) reads: "... during the rest of the time [I] assisted in making the statue of His Majesty on horseback."

71. Kaendler's petition of May 1, 1751, for the erection of a building to house the models is found in Vol. I A b/34/68 of the Werkarchiv. "By royal command His Royal Majesty in person on horseback shall be made in porcelain. But a special receptacle will be required wherein the model can be completed in its full-sized form. So that this great work, after the urgently sought approval of His Majesty, may be begun immediately during the good summer weather, using the small equestrian model that we have at hand. Meissen, May 1, 1751. Your most humble servant, Johann Joachim Kaendler."

72. In a memorandum written by Kaendler in connection with the preparation for work on the equestrian statue, a precise definition was given as to how the ideal horse should appear. This memorandum is now lost but was recorded by Sponsel (see Sponsel: *Kabinettstücke der Meissner Porzellanmanufaktur von Joh. Joach. Kaendler*, Leipzig 1900).

"1. Homogeneity in the form of body and limbs is necessary for beauty in a horse. 2. Delicate legs. 3. A nice head, with the forehead prettily elevated, small, short, thin and slender. 4. Three parts of a beautiful woman also belong to the perfect beauty of a horse: a nice chest, handsome posteriors, and mane and tail like her hair. 5. The nostrils of a horse must be wide and 'blowing' so that when it is excited, one can see the red that indicates a fiery temperament. 6. The back and chest must be almost equal in strength and breadth, which is said to be very rare. The back, especially, must be pleasingly round, and the hindquarters must not be bony. 7. Ears short and upright and well formed. 8. Wide, dark, and lively eyes. 9. A narrow jaw. 10. Thin lips. 11. A pretty, and not too narrow, mouth. 12. A gently bent neck, neither too thin nor too thick. 13. The neck better generously long than too short. 14. A thick, long tail. 15. A good strong chest in which you can see the muscles distinctly and which is not covered by superfluous flesh. 16. A strong back, unbent from the end of the neck to the beginning of the withers. 17. A well-filled small of the back with a flat groove divided into two parts. 18. A small, unprotruding belly. 19. Full and longish flanks. 20. Round and thick haunches. 21. Scrotum tightly tucked up."

73. In the middle of the Seven Years' War, in 1760, Kaendler demanded additional money for work that had already been done on the equestrian statue (Dresden State Archives, Loc. 1344, Vol. XVII/344–345): "In reference to the large royal porcelain statue that was started some years ago, under the aforementioned paragraph number 5 the petitioner has declared in the aforementioned statement under paragraph H that for the agreed work he had at first received only 3,836 rts. But after a reliable checking of the invoices it was found that he had demanded and received in cash 6,570 rts from 1752 to 1756 from the manufactory's pay offices at Dresden and Meissen for this art work ..." Kaendler demanded another 8,000 talers, although, "because of various troubles no work has been done on the statue for five years, and he has been persuaded for political reasons not to work, and the arcanists have not ceased to be plagued by undertainty and doubts."

447

74. From July, 1745, onward, Johann Martin Heinrici received a fixed salary (WA I A a32/132): "...to a painter who formerly received wages for piecework, because of his skill in making works with gold and silver applied, as well as with mother-of-pearl on porcelain."

75. The cost of living for the boarders was calculated by Christian Gottfried Hahnemann as follows (WA I A a39/63): "For food, first two and a half bushels of grain; secondly one cord wood, 9/4 ells long; thirdly in cash for food and linen 52 talers a year; and fourthly 2 talers for rent and 6 talers per year for a bed."

76. This is found among the reports of autumn, 1763 (WA I A a35/78–94): "A Short Historical Description of the Electoral Saxon Porcelain Manufactory of Meissen Anno 1709 Until 1763 Together with News of Its Commercial Activities and Its Sales."

77. A comprehensive report by Kaendler of the wishes of Frederick II is in the files of the Dresden State Archives pertaining to the manufactory (Loc. 1344/XVII/519 ff.). Among other things Frederick demanded "A service in the style of the newly designed dessert plate with flowers; a dark-blue-edged service painted with German birds; a silver service [silver plates from Paris had been shown as models] with yellow edges, painted with camels, monkeys, elephants, panthers, ostrichs, and parrots and other Indian animals; 10 Buddhas shaking their heads; a mantlepiece ornament of the four seasons: snuffboxes with portraits in the interior and Watteaus on the surface; a complete coffee service with sea-green glaze, the insides of the cups have a shell pattern and are also painted with flowers."

Precise specifications, even drawings made by the king for certain tableware, are preserved. "A table service of dishes and plates with antique hanging festoons which are joined to the heads of Cupids and which are made in bas-relief, for which His Majesty has himself made a drawing. The accompanying 'plat de ménage' shall have the form of an antique vase on which are found two genii. The tureens shall be made with feet, and not mounted on plates [Unter Schaalen]. The painting shall be of lovely flowers, such as roses, poppies, pinks, hyacinths, and tulips, and with beautiful auriculas ... His Royal Majesty graciously orders that more than two flowers never shall be painted on one plate or dish, and that the flowers shall be so well porportioned ... that the colors do not clash. It is also ordered that this service be called the Festoon Service. Furthermore, a large table service, for which His Majesty has provided a silver plate to be used as a model and which shall be called the Japanese Service [is ordered]. The plate shall present a somewhat antique and shell-like effect, as shall the entire service. The plat de ménage shall be made up of beautiful Japanese figures and shall harmonize with the rest of the service. As pertains to the painting, the edges of the service shall be painted in an attractive, mosaiced yellow. The inner edges of the plate shall be gently shaded in a pretty blue, so that the yellow contrasts with it. His Majesty orders that on each dish be painted, in tasteful proportions, an Indian animal or bird, for example a camel, an elephant, a panther, a baboon, an ostrich, or a parrot.

The tureens of the Festoon Service, by order of His Majesty, shall be decorated with designs of tuberoses, orange blossoms, anemones, and poppies. These flowers were drawn by His Majesty himself and presented to me by the valet de chambre Rudiger on November 13, 1762. For the Japanese Service, His Majesty has with his own hand written that Indian animals must be painted on the tureens."

78. Schlechte, H.: *Die Staatsreform in Kursachsen 1762 to 1763*, Berlin 1958, pp. 65, 66.

79. *Ibid.*, page 63.

80. Forberger, R.: *Die Manufaktur in Sachsen*, page 301.

81. In the manufactory report of April 15, 1763, we find (WA I A a35/6): "...in the morning, the members of the commission discussed ... with *Bergrat* Hörold various difficulties concerning the running of the manufactory."

82. This statement of expenses (WA I A a34/18) reads: "List of expenses from November, 1756, until March, 1763: 480 ts house rent from November, 1756, to October, 1758, twenty-four months per month 20 ts, 848 of such kind for 53 months, i. e., November, 1758, to and including March, 1763, per month 16 ts, 252 ts for firewood during 7 winters at 36 ts, totally amounting to 1,580 ts, from which must be deducted 51 ts 9 groschen for plaster casts, which *Kammerrat* Helbig paid for me, the total amounting to 70 ts 1 groschen. After deduction from the above mentioned 1,580 ts there remain 1,509 ts 25 groschen.

There remain, moreover:

104 bushels of oats per year, which runs to 624 bushels for 6 years

72 hundredweights of hay per year, which runs to 432 hundredweights for 6 years

4 *Schock* straw per year, which runs to 24 *Schock* for 6 years

NB: additional demand of 8,200 ts to be submitted to the royal mint.

Johann Gregorius Höroldt"

In his exile Höroldt received his full salary and most probably diplomatic missions were accorded to him as is revealed in a letter of November 9, 1762 (Dresden State Archives, Loc. 1344, Vol. XVII/518). Höroldt ordered in Meissen: "A small mantlepiece ornament, a teapot, a cream jug, five cups with white application, and saucers" in order that he might "best promote the interests of his most gracious king."

83. At a meeting of the manufactory commission on February 16, 1764, which took place in Höroldt's residence, he complained about "the laxity, the negligence, and the dishonesty of most of the officials, among whom he specially mentioned the court commissioner, Kaendler, who would give orders to the great prejudice of the manufactory and who would support the refractory workers in their troublemaking." (WA I A a39/68 ff.)

84. Apropos of his charges for his work on the equestrian statue, Kaendler speaks of this important technical innovation as follows: "...the invention of a new type of lid and bottom [to replace] those which previously had suffered serious damage in firing. [The new pieces] are now firm and durable. (Dresden State Archives, Loc. 1344, Vol. XVII/344–345)

85. The Amphitrite Group is described by Kaendler as follows (WA I A b48): "Made a drawing of a group intended to go to Russia, which is 1 ell wide and one ell high. It depicts the triumphant sea goddess Amphitrite in a shell carriage pulled across the sea by dolphins. Amphitrite is seated, crowned, in a heroic attitude. She holds a scepter in one hand and in the other a piece of sailcloth which floats above her. There are also other figures."

Kaendler modeled this group in December, 1772: "... It contains eleven figures and three animals—dolphins and a turtle. The pedestal consists of an antique, pleasingly curved *Zocce* with a delicate cornice decorated with antique ornaments and can be fitted together so that the water represents sea waves. On this sea there is found the main figure, Amphitrite, sitting on a shell carriage, a crown on her head and a scepter in her hand. A sail forms an arch above her ..."

In the course of this work he added the billowing drapery with "Three pretty, winged sea children who hover above the triumphant Amphitrite. Their 6 little hands hold flower festoons, a wreath, a palm branch and the Russian monarch's honored name, Catherine, as a sign of their homage."

86. In a memorandum concerning the fire of February 27, 1773 (WA I A a47), the rapidity and resoluteness shown by the workers of the town are emphasized.

87. In a report concerning the increase of salary of a worker with an income of 280 talers, the yearly expenses of a family of four are given (WA I A 41/42):

"house rent	24 talers
firewood	30 talers
for lighting at home and in the manufactory	18 talers
for maintaining a maid in board and wages	40 talers
for health insurance and for charity	12 talers
for the barber	1 taler
for the wigmaker	4 talers
for school fees, books and paper	10 talers
for offertory and New Year's gratuities	2 talers
food for husband, wife and two children estimated at 2 talers a week	104 talers
tea, sugar and tobacco 2 talers and 12 groschen a month	30 talers
writing fee for our work per annum	3 talers
	total 278 talers

88. The following is from the travel journal of Humitzsch and Elsasser, June 24, 1764 (WA I A a41/40 ff.): "After careful examination we found the Hoechst [sic] ware to be well constructed, but the colors are weak, with the exception of the black and the purple, both of which are very beautiful. They have a good sculptor, and a skilled flower painter. The selling prices are about the same as that of Meissen ware."

89. This interesting classification was made by Kaendler (WA Pretiosen 66): "Types of porcelain ware, how to classify them, and how to estimate them correctly: 1. figures 2. animals 3. birds 4. vases 5. centerpieces 6. tureens 7. circular tureens 8. oval bowls 9. circular dishes 10. preserve dishes and circular salad plates and bowls 11. plates 12. coffeepots 13. milk jugs 14. teapots 15. finger bowls 16.

large milk cups 17. sugar bowls 18. butter dishes 19. bouillon cups 20. sauce boats 21. soup pots 22. chocolate mugs 23. drinking mugs 24. table jugs 25. flowerpots 26. spoons 27. plats de ménage 28. vinegar- and oil- jars 29. salt cellars 30. plain ('glatt') salt cellars 31. watering cans 32. chamberpots 33. candlesticks 34. baskets 35. cosmetic boxes 36. snuff boxes 37. spirit bottles 38. clock cases 39. cane handles with faces 40. cane handles Considering the great variety of porcelain ware, many types will be found that cannot be immediately classified but which, however, must be dealt with. Such items could provisionally be put aside in a separate room and kept under lock and key by two persons, each of whom should, however, have a different key, so that the one couldn't enter without the other."

90. Schmidt, H.: "Die sächsischen Bauernunruhen des Jahres 1790." In: *Mitteilungen des Vereins für Geschichte der Stadt Meissen*, volume 7, Meissen 1909, page 325.
   P. Stulz, A. Opitz: *Volksbewegungen in Kursachsen zur Zeit der Französischen Revolution*, Berlin 1956.

91. A recapitulation of total expenditures for 1773 is most informative (WA V 2/41/218):
   "6,700 talers to the commissioners
   1,863 talers to the officials
   2,322 talers to the arcanists
   5,300 talers to the bookkeepers
   24,743 talers to the molders
   38,200 talers to the painters
   3,552 talers to the sagger-turners
   2,994 talers to the mass-workers
   5,880 talers to the firing hands
   753 talers to the glaziers
   2,294 talers to the general hands
   353 talers to the doorkeepers
   4,940 talers to the pensioners and to the sick
   3,909 talers for secret materials
   5,654 talers for the gilding
   1,780 talers for hay
   15,513 talers for firewood
   242 talers for moss
   1,635 talers for hardware and wooden articles
   124 talers for sand
   609 talers for fodder
   59 talers for writing materials
   113 talers for miscellaneous equipment
   3,481 talers for fittings and cases
   329 talers for 'brac'
   181 talers for general excise
   1,412 talers for general costs
   4,923 talers for damage caused by fire and for costs of reconstruction in accordance with a special invoice."

92. An inventory made in the reform period contains no fewer than 84 paintings, 2 pastels, and 8,773 graphic drawings, which were given to the manufactory by the king.
   Comprehensive folders were acquired in March, 1816.
   "Les Metamorphoses de Ovid à Paris par Chebeau—a book of drawings
   A portfolio with five sheets from the English book of drawings
   A copy of a fashion magazine
   A copper engraving of Kora's shell cabinet
   Preussler's book of drawings
   Merian's *Topographia Galliae*
   Johann Wilhelm Bauer: *Prospects of Italy, Friuli and Carinthia*, engraved by Melchior Küsel
   Titian's *Anatomy*
   Two parts of Rösel's *Amusements of the Insects*
   Eleazar Albini"

93. Busch, E.: Carl Hugo Tzschucke, Meissen Town Archives, manuscript MK 15.

94. Meissen Town Archives SO-Bgm 8

Plates

The following abbreviations have been used in the list below: PD – Porcelain collection (Porzellansammlung) in Dresden; BNM – Bayerisches Nationalmuseum, Munich; SM – Schauhalle (exhibition hall) Meissen. V & A – Victoria and Albert Museum, London.

451

Height 14 cm. PD

20 Head of Apollo in Böttger stoneware, c. 1714. Height 10 cm. In the style of Bernini. PD

21 Sugar bowl with lid in Böttger porcelain, c. 1713. Height 14 cm. PD

22 Reticulated goblet in Böttger porcelain, double walled, openwork on the outer wall, c. 1716. Height 17 cm. PD

23 Covered vase in Böttger porcelain with vineleaf decoration by Johann Jacob Irminger, after 1714. Height 27 cm. PD

24 Key-shaped vessel in Böttger porcelain with vineleaf motif by Johann Jacob Irminger, 1714. Height 39 cm. SM

25 Child's head in Böttger porcelain, c. 1715. Height 13.8 cm. PD

26 Pagoda in altarlike setting in Böttger porcelain, after 1715. Height 22 cm.: figure 10 cm. PD

27 Small cup in Böttger porcelain with gold luster decoration, c. 1718. Height 4.8 cm. PD

28 Beaker-shaped vase in Böttger porcelain, c. 1715. Height 19.5 cm. Blossom relief heightened with lacquer painting. PD

29 Two two-handled beakers in Böttger porcelain with gold chinoiserie decoration, c. 1720. Height 11.2 cm. PD

30 Hot water pot with gold decoration, c. 1725. Height 15 cm. Large pommel swords. PD

31 Bouillon cup with Augsburg gold chinoiserie decoration, c. 1722. Height 22 cm. PD

32 Teapot with lace decoration, c. 1720. Height 12.5 cm, PD

33 Four-sided tea caddy with indianische Blumen decoration, c. 1725. Height 12.5 cm. PD

34 Bowl with lid showing indianische Blumen decoration and phoenix, c. 1725. Height 19 cm. PD

35 Teapot with lambrequin decoration, c. 1725. Height 12.8 cm. PD

36 Teapot with fish and billows, c. 1725. Height 12.5 cm. Imitation of Chinese example. PD

37 Vase with colored ground, chinoiseries and indianische Blumen c. 1730. Height 45 cm. PD

38 Gourd-shaped bottle with indianische Blumen, c. 1732. Height 21.5 cm. Sword mark. PD

39 Pen drawings from Höroldt's sketchbook, 1725–27, from the so-called *Schultz-Codex* now in the collection of the Museum des Kunsthandwerks in Leipzig.

40 Vase with blue ground, chinoiseries and indianische Blumen by Johann Gregorius Höroldt, 1726. Height 39.5 cm. AR mark; signed "J. G. Höroldt fec. Meissen 17 Augusti 1726". PD

41 Mantelpiece clock, model by Johann Gottlieb Kirchner, decoration by Johann Gregorius Höroldt, 1728. Height 39.5 cm, not including the figure of a pagoda, now missing, which crowned the piece. Formerly in the Klemperer collection, now in the Schauhalle in Meissen.

42 Detail of the Höroldt painting on the clock by Kirchner, 1728.

43 Oval dish with red dragon from the Court Service, c. 1730. Height 14 cm. PD

44 Covered tureen with the *reicher alter Löwe* decoration, c. 1750. Height 24 cm. Sword mark. PD

45 Small lidded bowl with green ground and chinoiseries, c. 1730. Height 13 cm. Sword mark. PD

46 Goblet with chinoiseries, c. 1725. Height 15.5 cm. PD

47 Plate with Far Eastern decoration, painted by Johann Ehrenfried Stadler, c. 1725. Diameter 26 cm. PD

48 Lantern with painting by Johann Ehrenfried Stadler, c. 1725. Height 33 cm. Sword mark with Stadler's concealed signature. PD

49 Large covered vase with Indian branch motif, c. 1730. Height 32.5 cm. AR mark. PD

50 Octagonal two-handled cup with Kakiemon decoration, c. 1730. Height 7.5 cm. Sword mark. PD

51 Lidded jar with scale decoration, c. 1725. Height 13.5 cm. Sword mark. PD

52 Reserve of a yellow ground vase with motif of Fabeltiere, c. 1730. Height of reserve 7 cm. PD

53 Octagonal sake flask with indianische Blumen decoration, c. 1730. Height 16 cm. Sword mark. PD

54 Four-sided sake flask with chinoiserie decoration, c. 1728. Height 24 cm. PD

55 Globular vase with rich indianische Blumen decoration, c. 1730. Height 34 cm. Sword mark. PD

56 Plate with wheat-ear decoration and checkered ornament, c. 1728. Diameter 24 cm. Sword mark. HANS SYZ COLLECTION, WESTPORT USA (THE SMITHSONIAN INSTITUTION)

57 Plate with wheat-ear decoration and phoenix, c. 1728. Diameter 22 cm. Sword mark. PD

58 Leaf dish with checkered decoration, c. 1730. Length 37 cm. Width 23.5 cm. Sword mark. PD

59 Richly decorated bowl with harbor scenes, c. 1730. Diameter 32.3 cm. Large sword mark. BNM

60 Barrel-shaped coffee container supported by caryatids, richly decorated, c. 1728. Height 26 cm. BNM

61 Plate with chinoiserie decoration on a hunting theme, c. 1727. Diameter 29.7 cm. BNM

62 Reserve from a tureen with battle painting, c. 1740. Height of body of tureen 18.5 cm.

Sword mark. The painting in the manner of engravings by Georg Philipp Rugendas. BNM

63 Large tureen on stand with battle painting, *c.* 1740. Height 30.9 cm. Length 34.4 cm. Sword mark. BNM

64 Saucer with painting of a farm, *c.* 1723. Diameter 16.7 cm. Sword mark. BNM

65 Bouillon cup with landscape, *c.* 1723. Height 18 cm. BNM

66 Pot with I-shaped handle, landscape decoration, *c.* 1740. Height 30 cm. Sword mark. PD

67 Pot with spout in the form of a cavalier's head and landscape decoration around the body, *c.* 1740. Height 24 cm. Sword mark. PD

68 Lidded caddy with coastal landscape decoration, *c.* 1745. Height 12.5 cm. Sword mark. PD

69 Circular covered bowl with battle painting by Christian Friedrich Herold, *c.* 1740. Height 13 cm. Sword mark. From the service bearing the arms of the Duke of Ragusa. PD

70 Mounted jug with cover bearing a portrait and a view of Leipzig, *c.* 1730. Height 16.5 cm STÄDTISCHES MUSEUM, ASCHAFFENBURG

71 Reserve painting showing a hunting scene, *c.* 1740. Detail from a tureen. PD

72 Bowl on scroll feet adorned with putti, by Johann Friedrich Eberlein, *c.* 1740. Height 24 cm. Sword mark. PD

73 Pagoda after a Far Eastern example made *c.* 1720 by the molder George Fritzsche. Height 10.2 cm. PD

74 Grotesque vase modeled by Johann Gottlieb Kirchner after an engraving (Stella), 1728. Height 72 cm. PD

75 Elephant by Johann Gottlieb Kirchner, 1731. Height 61 cm. PD

76 Heron by Johann Joachim Kaendler, 1731. Height 74.5 cm. Sword mark. PD

77 Hen with chicks by Johann Joachim Kaendler, 1732. Height 34.5 cm PD

78 Vulture by Johann Joachim Kaendler, 1734. Height 80 cm. Sword mark. PD

79 Paduan cock by Johann Joachim Kaendler, 1732. Height 76 cm. Sword mark. PD

80 Pelican by Johann Joachim Kaendler, 1732. Height 75.5 cm. Sword mark. PD

81 Chamois buck by Johann Friedrich Eberlein, 1735. Height 52 cm. Sword mark, PD

82 Monkey taking snuff by Johann Joachim Kaendler, 1732. Height 47.7 cm. DR. ERNST SCHNEIDER COLLECTION, DÜSSELDORF

83 *Bolognese Hund* by Johann Joachim Kaendler, *c.* 1770. Height 32.5 cm. Sword mark. PD

84 *Mopshündin* (pug bitch) by Johann Joachim Kaendler, *c.* 1745. Height 15.3 cm. Sword mark. GERMANISCHES MUSEUM, NUREMBERG

85 Spouted vessel in the form of a monkey with young by Johann Joachim Kaendler, 1735. Height 17.5 cm. Sword mark. PD

86 Marmoset by Johann Joachim Kaendler, *c.* 1732. Height 23 cm. PD

87 Bust of Joseph Fröhlich, the court jester, by Johann Joachim Kaendler, 1737. Height 54 cm AR mark. PD

88 Bust of Schmiedel, the postmaster, by Johann Joachim Kaendler, 1739. Height 55 cm. PD

89 Bust of Chinese woman by Johann Joachim Kaendler, 1732. Height 60 cm. Modern casting. PD

90 Bust of a Chinese man by Johann Joachim Kaendler, 1732. Height 60 cm. Modern casting. PD

91 Candlestick from the Swan Service by Johann Friedrich Eberlein, 1739. Height 24.4 cm. Sword mark. After an engraving by Juste Aurèle Meissonier. PD

92 Tureen handle from the Swan Service by Johann Joachim Kaendler, 1738. PD

93 Sugar bowl from the Swan Service by Johann Joachim Kaendler, 1740. Height 22.5 cm. Sword mark. PD

94 Pot from the Swan Service by Johann Joachim Kaendler, 1737–41. Height 25.5 cm. PD

95 Candelabrum from the Swan Service by Johann Joachim Kaendler, 1737–41. Height 49 cm. Sword mark. PD

96 Large tureen from the Swan Service by Johann Joachim Kaendler, 1737–41. Height 54.5 cm. Sword mark. PD

97 Apfelsinenbecher (orange stand) from the Swan Service by Johann Friedrich Eberlein, 1738. Height 11.4 cm.

98 Finial from the large tureen of the Swan Service by Johann Joachim Kaendler, 1737–41.

99 "Element" vase by Johann Joachim Kaendler, 1741. Height 63.5 cm. Sword mark. PD

100 Vase with Japanese snowball tree decoration by Johann Joachim Kaendler, *c.* 1740. Height 48 cm. Sword mark. PD

101 River god from the table centerpiece for Count Brühl by Johann Joachim Kaendler, 1744. Height 26 cm. After the Mattielli fountain in Dresden-Friedrichstadt. V & A

102 River god from the table centerpiece for Count Brühl by Johann Joachim Kaendler (companion to 101).

103 The Apostle Matthew by Johann Joachim Kaendler, 1738. Height 44.6 cm. Sword mark. PD

104 Fröhlich, the court jester, by Johann Joachim Kaendler, 1737. Height 23.5 cm. Sword mark. PD

105 Fröhlich and Schmiedel, the two jesters of the Saxon court, by Johann Joachim Kaendler, 1741. Height 26 cm. PD

106 Woodchopper by Johann Joachim Kaendler, c. 1740. Height 17 cm. Sword mark. PD

107 Mining inspector by Johann Joachim Kaendler, c. 1750. Height 20.1 cm. Sword mark. PD

108 Potter by Johann Joachim Kaendler, c. 1750. Height 18.5 cm. PD

109 Spinstress by Johann Joachim Kaendler, c. 1750. Height 22 cm. Sword mark. PD

110 Carter by Johann Joachim Kaendler, c. 1745. Height 20.5 cm. Sword mark. PD

111 The Italian Comedy by Kaendler and others, c. 1745. Height 10–14.5 cm. DR. ERNST SCHNEIDER COLLECTION, DÜSSELDORF

112 Woman from Malabar, by Friedrich Elias Meyer, c. 1750. Height 32.5 cm. Sword mark. PD

113 Man from Malabar by Friedrich Elias Meyer, 1749. Height 32.5 cm. Sword mark. PD

114 Harlequin by Johann Joachim Kaendler, 1738. Height 16 cm. PD

115 Moor with white horse (detail)

116 Moor with white horse by Johann Joachim Kaendler, c. 1750. Height 41 cm. Sword mark. PD

117 Turkish woman holding a salt cellar by Johann Joachim Kaendler, 1748. Height 16.3 cm. Sword mark. PD

118 Turk holding a salt cellar by Johann Joachim Kaendler, 1748. Height 16.5 cm. Sword mark. PD

119 Monkey Band by Kaendler and Reinicke, 1747 and 1764. Height 12.2–18.4 cm. DR. ERNST SCHNEIDER COLLECTION, DÜSSELDORF

120 Bagpipe player by Friedrich Elias Meyer, 1750. Height 34 cm. Sword mark. PD

121 Court lady as a pilgrim by Johann Joachim Kaendler, 1741. Height 28.8 cm. Sword mark. PD

122 Persian by Johann Joachim Kaendler, c. 1748. Height 22 cm. Sword mark. PD

123 Hungarian hussar by Johann Joachim Kaendler, c. 1750. Height 21.8 cm. Sword mark. PD

124 Beltrame and Columbine by Johann Joachim Kaendler, c. 1740. Height 18.2 cm. Sword mark. PD

125 Shepherdess by Friedrich Elias Meyer, c. 1752. Height 23 cm. Sword mark. BNM

126 Tailor's wife riding on a goat by Johann Friedrich Eberlein, 1740. Height 18.5 cm. Sword mark. PD

127 Sea swallow by Johann Joachim Kaendler, c. 1750. Height 23 cm. Sword mark. PD

128 A hunting group by Johann Joachim Kaendler, c. 1758. Height 12.3 cm. Sword mark. PD

129 Aviary vase by Johann Joachim Kaendler, c. 1732. Height 51.5 cm. PD

130 Girl holding candelabra by Johann Joachim Kaendler, c. 1765. Height 29.5 cm. Sword mark. BNM

131 A two-branched candelabrum in the form of a group of fruit pickers by Johann Joachim Kaendler, 1748. Height 23.5 cm. Sword mark. PD

132 Parrot on a bronze candelabrum by Johann Joachim Kaendler, c. 1740. Height 29.7 cm. Sword mark. RESIDENZMUSEUM, MUNICH

133 Putto steering a carriage by Johann Joachim Kaendler, c. 1755. Height 27.5 cm. Mount and porcelain flowers made in Paris. BNM

134 Shepherd group playing instruments by Johann Joachim Kaendler, c. 1755. Height 25 cm. Sword mark. PD

135 Shepherd group beneath a tree by Johann Joachim Kaendler, c. 1750. Height 27.5 cm. Sword mark. PD

136 Cavalier writing a letter by Johann Joachim Kaendler. c. 1740. Height 13.6 cm. Sword mark. RESIDENZ, ANSBACH

137 A Painful Situation, group by Johann Joachim Kaendler, c. 1770. Height 12.5 cm. Sword mark. PD

138 The Old Woman in Love, group by Johann Joachim Kaendler, 1765. Height 12.5 cm. Sword mark. PD

139 Hairdressing Scene, group by Carl Schönheit, 1774. Height 18.5 cm. Sword mark. BNM

140 Child figures as members of the Italian Comedy by Johann Joachim Kaendler and others, c. 1760. Height 10.3–12.2 cm. Sword mark. PD

141 Fishwife by Johann Joachim Kaendler, c. 1755. Height 13.5 cm. Sword mark. PD

142 Clothier by Johann Joachim Kaendler, 1748. Height 18.7 cm. Sword mark. PD

143 Tea caddy with underglaze decoration, c. 1725. Height 12.5 cm. PD

144 Teapot, gold ground and underglaze decoration, c. 1725. Height 15 cm. Large swords in double ring. PD

145 Tankard, mounted, underglaze decoration, c. 1722. Height 22.5 cm. DR. M. COLLECTION, MUNICH

146 Mounted tankard with underglaze chinoiseries, c. 1725. Height 23.4 cm. PD

147 Mocha pot with underglaze decoration, c. 1728. Height 17.5 cm. DR. M. COLLECTION, MUNICH

148 Serving dish with *Zwiebelmuster* decoration, *c.* 1740. Length 45 cm. Width 35 cm. HANS SYZ COLLECTION, WESTPORT, USA (THE SMITHSONIAN INSTITUTION)

149 Eighteenth-century *Zwiebelmuster* plate. Diameter 22.5 cm. Sword mark. SM

150 Plate with underglaze bamboo pattern, *c.* 1740. Diameter 22 cm. Sword mark. SM

151 Underglaze chrysanthemum decoration, *c.* 1745. Diameter 23 cm. Sword mark. SM

152 Plate with *Gebrochener Stab* relief decoration and underglaze flowers, *c.* 1760. Diameter 22 cm. Sword mark. SM

153 Calyx-shaped vase with underglaze decoration, *c.* 1740. Height 34.5 cm. Sword mark. PD

154 Coffeepot with bird and fruit painting, *c.* 1765. Height 34 cm. Sword mark. PD

155 Tureen with shaded flower painting, *c.* 1745, Height 17.6 cm. Sword mark. PD

156 Four-sided cup with flower painting, *c.* 1745. Height 8.5 cm. Sword mark. PD

157 Pages from the Weinmann *Codex*, a many-volumed botanical work which appeared in Regensburg in 1735. (See note 62)

158 Tureen (*Neubrandenstein* type) with figure of maiden and bouquets of flowers, *c.* 1760. Height 32.5 cm. Sword mark. PD

159 Reserve from a tankard with flowers adapted from woodcuts (Holzschnitt Blumen) *c.* 1745. Height 21 cm. Sword mark. SM

160 Reserve from the same tankard as in plate 159

161 Tureen with branch handles and stylized flower decoration, *c.* 1760. Height 27 cm. Sword mark. PD

162 Coffeepot with stylized flower decoration, *c.* 1765. Height 24.5 cm. Sword mark. PD

163 Cup with stylized flower decoration, *c.* 1760. Height 6.2 cm. Sword mark. PD

164 Wine jug with relief flower ornament heightened in enamels, *c.* 1740. Painting of later date. Height 31.5 cm. Sword mark. PD

165 Covered vase with gold ground and rich flower decoration, *c.* 1750. Height 26.2 cm. Sword mark; painter's mark G. PRIVATE COLLECTION, MUNICH

166 Vase with gold lace and rich flower painting, *c.* 1745. Height 35.5 cm. Sword mark. PD

167 Needle cases with landscape and flower painting, *c.* 1740, possibly 1745. Lengths 7.5 cm. and 9 cm. PD

168 Cane handle with Watteau painting, *c.* 1740. Length 12.3 cm. PD

169 Cup and coffeepot with Watteau painting, *c.* 1745. Heights 23.5 cm. and 9 cm. Sword mark. PD

170 Tureen with raised decoration and diamond point etching, 1774. Canon von dem Busch, Hildesheim. Height 24.5 cm. Sword mark HANS SYZ COLLECTION, WESTPORT, USA (THE SMITHSONIAN INSTITUTION)

171 Mounted *tabatière* with battle painting in the manner of Christian Friedrich Herold, *c.* 1745. Length 8.5 cm. Width 6 cm. Height 4.5 cm. DR. ERNST SCHNEIDER COLLECTION, DÜSSELDORF

172 Portrait of Augustus III by Johann Martin Heinrici. 1753. Height 45.5 cm. Signed "Johann Martin Heinrici Pinxit 1753." Frame by Johann Joachim Kaendler. DR. ERNST SCHNEIDER COLLECTION, DÜSSELDORF

173 Lidded cup with scenes from Goethe's *Die Leiden des jungen Werthers* by Johann Georg Loehnig, *c.* 1780. Height with lid 10.2 cm. Sword mark with star. PD

174 Chocolate pot of the Marcolini period with alternating stripe decoration, *c.* 1780. Height 21 cm. Sword mark with star. PD

175 The Good Mother, group by Michel Victor Acier, 1774. Height 23.5 cm. Sword mark. PD

176 Children at the Cradle, group by Michel Victor Acier, *c.* 1775. Height 19 cm. Sword mark with star. PD

177 Portrait bust of Count Marcolini by Andreas Weger, 1809. Height 58.5 cm. Sword mark with star. SM

178 Amphora by Michel Victor Acier with sepia painting, 1780. Height 32.5 cm. Sword mark with star. PD

179 Plate from the Court Service with cornflower blue border, 1777. Diameter 24.5 cm. Sword mark with star. SM

180 Octagonal cup and saucer with flower and insect painting, *c.* 1770. Height 7.3 cm. Sword mark. PD

181 Detail of group by Michel Victor Acier, *c.* 1775. Sword mark with star. PD

182 Vestal virgin by Johann Daniel Schöne, 1801. Biscuit porcelain. Height 34 cm. Impressed sword mark with star. SM

183 Dice thrower, copy of a statue from later Classical times by Christian Gottfried Jüchtzer, 1798. Biscuit porcelain. Height 13.8 cm. Impressed sword mark with star. SM

184 Dying Gaul, copy in biscuit porcelain of a late Classical statue, by Johann Daniel Schöne, 1814. Height 14.5 cm. Impressed sword mark with star. SM

185 Miniature of Aristotle as Hermes by Christian Karl Schiebel, 1793. Height 16.5 cm. SM

186 Amphora with snake handle and gold ground, engraved, 1810. Height 27.4 cm. Sword

mark. BNM

187 Cup with relief portrait, interior gilt, *c.* 1820. Height 10.5 cm. Sword mark. SM

188 Allegorical plaque in the style of Wedgwood in white on blue biscuit ware, *c.* 1800. Height 9 cm. Impressed sword mark with star. SM

189 Dinner plate with vineleaf decoration, *c.* 1820. Diameter 23.5 cm. Sword mark. SM

190 Oval wicker basket, *c.* 1800. Height 7 cm. SM

191 Jug with swan handle and vineleaf decoration, *c.* 1825. Height 32.5 cm. Sword mark. SM

192 Cylindrical cups with portrait painting, 1807. Height 5.5 cm. Sword mark with star. The portraits are of the Duke of Trèves and his wife, Princess Kunigunde of Saxony. On the other cup: Princess Marie of Saxony. SM

193 Cylindrical cups with portrait painting, *c.* 1810. Height 5.5 cm. Sword mark with star. The persons represented are princesses of the Saxon court. SM

194 Plate from the Wellington Service, 1818. Diameter 19.2 cm. Sword mark. View of the Roman Catholic Hofkirche from Brühl's Terrace in Dresden. APSLEY HOUSE, LONDON

195 Portrait medallion by Georg Friedrich Kersting, *c.* 1825. Height 7.2 cm. SM

196 Plate with landscape from the Sächsische Schweiz, *c.* 1820. Diameter 19 cm. Sword mark. Felsentor near the Bastei bridge near Rathen, probably painted by Christian Gottlieb Hottewitzsch, who also worked on the Wellington Service. RUDOLPH JUST COLLECTION, PRAGUE

197 Ariadne by Heinrich von Dannecker, *c.* 1820. Biscuit porcelain. Height 26 cm. Impressed sword mark. SM

198 Statuette of Goethe by Christian Daniel Rauch, 1830. Height 18 cm. Impressed sword mark. SM

199 Wall plate with landscape and flower painting, *c.* 1860. Diameter 27 cm. SM

200 Cup with neo-Gothic decoration, *c.* 1855. Probably by Ernst August Leuteritz. Height 11.5 cm. Sword mark. PRIVATE COLLECTION, DRESDEN

201 Coffeepot in the style of Capo di Monte porcelain, *c.* 1872. Height 18.5 cm. Sword mark. SM

202 Ornamental vase with gold and platinum painting, *c.* 1875. Height 85 cm. Sword mark. SM

203 Lidded bowl with medallion in *pâte-sur-pâte* technique, 1870. Height 12.4 cm. Sword mark. SM

204 Plate with decoration by Richard Riemer-schmid, 1906. Diameter 19 cm. Sword mark. SM

205 *Jugendstil* plate with sweet-pea decoration, 1910. Diameter 17 cm. Sword mark. SM

206 Vase richly decorated with flower painting by Julius Eduard Braunsdorf, *c.* 1900. Height 52 cm. Sword mark. SM

207 Cup with *Jugendstil* decoration by Konrad Hentschel, 1906. Height 7.8 cm. Sword mark. PD

208 Wall plate with early *Jugendstil* ornamentation *c.* 1900. Diam. 27 cm. Sword mark. SM

209 Lady with bouquet by Theodor Eichler, 1904 Height 31 cm. Sword mark. SM

210 Toucan by Paul Walther, 1919. Height 49 cm. Sword mark. SM

211 Billy goat by Erich Hösel, 1907. Height 29.5cm. Sword mark. SM

212 Group of king penguins by Erich Hösel, 1913. Height 25 cm. Sword mark. SM

213 Seal in Böttger stoneware by August Gaul, 1922. Height 34 cm. SM

214 Mountain spirit by Ludwig Nick, 1928. Height 39 cm. Sword mark. SM

215 Foal by Willy Münch-Khe, 1937. Height 11.8 cm. Sword mark. SM

216 Powder container with putto by Paul Scheurich, 1937. Height 11.5 cm. Sword mark. SM

217 Container in the form of a Chinese man by Paul Scheurich, 1926. Height 12.5 cm. Sword mark. SM

218 Female flute player by Paul Scheurich, 1926. Height 20.8 cm. Sword mark. SM

219 Spanish woman by Paul Scheurich, 1930. Height 28.5 cm. Sword mark. SM

220 Venus by Paul Scheurich, 1921. Height 33.5 cm. Sword mark. SM

221 The Elopement by Paul Scheurich, 1933. Height 35 cm. Sword mark. SM

222 Europa and the Bull by Paul Scheurich, 1933. Height 64 cm. Sword mark. SM

223 Porcelain bell by Paul Börner, 1930. Height 59 cm. SM

224 Floor vase, design and decoration by Paul Börner. Height 40 cm. SM

225 Pot from a coffee service by Paul Börner, decoration by Arthur Findeisen, 1932. Height 34.5 cm. SM

226 Portrait plaque by Paul Börner, 1925. The person represented is Max Adolf Pfeiffer, director of the Meissen porcelain factory, 1918–1933. SM

227 Commemorative plaque by Paul Börner, 1930. Height 18 cm. SM

228 Commemorative plaque by Paul Börner, 1923. Height 21 cm SM

229 Underglaze vase by Otto Voigt, 1927. Height

457

Text illustrations

1682 Johann Friedrich Böttger born in Schleiz on February 4.

1700 The St. Andreas mine near Schneeberg yields kaolin (china clay).

1701 Böttger transferred from Wittenberg to Dresden.

1702 First meeting between Böttger and Tschirnhaus.

1705 Böttger in the Albrechtsburg at Meissen. Experiments to make porcelain or at least high-quality hard earthenware.

1706 Böttger in protective custody in the fortress of Königstein.

1707 Laboratory on the eastern bastion (Jungfernbastei) of Brühl's terrace in Dresden. Experiments with Tschirnhaus directed toward the invention of porcelain.

1708 On January 15, according to records kept by Böttger, came the first successful firing of white porcelain. Ehrenfried Walther von Tschirnhaus dies on October 11.

1709 On March 28, Böttger announces the invention of porcelain. A special commission— Zech, Löwendahl, Nehmitz, Holtzbrinck, and Pabst—investigates the report submitted on the invention.

1710 Veit Hans Schnorr, owner of the St. Andreas mine, delivers china clay for the first time. January 23: notification in four languages of the invention of European porcelain. First exhibition at the Leipzig Easter Fair. June 6: the manufactory is established in the Albrechtsburg under the directorship of Michael Nehmitz. December 29: Johann Friedrich Böttger recognized as administrator.

1711 Dr. Wilhelm Nehmitz, a chemist, and Dr. Jacob Bartholmäi, a physician, are separately instructed on secrets of porcelain making, i. e., each is granted partial knowledge of the arcanum. Johann Melchior Steinbrück made first inspector of the manufactory. Martin Schnell, court lacquerer, undertakes work for the manufactory. First mention of the sculptor Bernhardt Miller and the molder George Fritzsche.

1712 Johann Jacob Irminger, silversmith to the Dresden court, is engaged for design and the training of apprentices. The manufactory employs forty-three people.

1713 First sale of white porcelain at the Leipzig Easter Fair. Böttger constructs a new kiln for the Garbrand (full firing).

1714 Opening of the Dresden branch. Böttger's personal freedom restored.

1717 The presentation of the first examples of blue underglaze painting to the king on August 28.

1719 Samuel Stöltzel's flight to Vienna January 5. Böttger dies on March 13. First order for porcelain for the Dutch (Japanese) Palace.

1720 Stöltzel's return. He is accompanied by Johann Gregorius Höroldt. Introduction of Siebenlehn feldspar, vital for improved underglaze painting. The chief architect, Matthäus Daniel Pöppelmann, visits the manufactory.

1721 Unrest among throwers and molders because of outstanding wages. Stöltzel invents brown glazing.

1722 First consignment of porcelain with colored painted decoration to the Leipzig Fair.

1723 Grading of finished porcelain into Gut, Mittelgut, Brac, and Rommelhux (for destruction). Johann Melchior Steinbrück dies on March 1. David Köhler dies on April 30. Höroldt obtains the recipe for blue underglaze painting.

1724 Höroldt receives the title of court painter.

1725 The manufactory employs forty-one people (including ten journeymen and five apprentices) under Höroldt.

1727 First period of employment of the Dresden sculptor Johann Gottlieb Kirchner (dismissed April 24, 1728). Johann Christoph Ludwig Lücke, sculptor, also engaged (dismissed in spring, 1729). Large orders of porcelain modeled after designs by French artists placed by the Parisian dealer Rudolphe Le Maire. Strict embargo on kaolin.

1730 Kirchner reemployed, given the grade of master sculptor.

1731 Irregularities come to light. Hoym dismissed, Le Maire deported. Augustus the Strong takes over the directorship of the manufactory and establishes a commission (Wichmannshausen, Pflugk, and Fleuter). From June 1, Höroldt entrusted with the arcanum and made artistic director with the rank of court commissioner. Johann Joachim Kaendler employed as sculptor from June 15. Ninety-one employees in manufactory. Building extensions made by Simon, the county clerk. Sales office opened in Warsaw.

1733 Augustus the Strong dies on February 1. His son elected king of Poland on December 17 as Augustus III. Kaendler promoted to master sculptor.

1734 Athanas Manasses, the Turkish merchant, claims the sales monopoly for trade with Turkey. The woodcutters go on strike. Serious tensions between Höroldt and Kaendler. Timber escalator from the Elbe to the castle installed. Hähnel's *Ovaldrehscheibe*. Kaendler proposes two monumental statues of Augustus the Strong and Augustus III in white porcelain.

1735 Johann Friedrich Eberlein engaged as "*Adjuvante*" to Kaendler. Georg Michael Helbig's services engaged at the Dresden branch. Count Heinrich von Brühl, prime minister of Saxony, takes over the directorship with unlimited power to command and employ the manufactory for his personal needs.

1736 Flight of the painter Adam Friedrich von Löwenfinck to Bayreuth. Founding of the burial fund as first form of social security. Important commissions from Brühl. Kaendler's carillon (mechanism by Hähnel, master organ builder) is installed in the Japanese Palace.

1739 Johann Gottlieb Ehder engaged to work with Kaendler.

1740 Two hundred and eighteen employees. Kaendler instructs apprentices. Strict interdiction to sell unpainted porcelain.

1741 Johann Gottlieb Erbsmehl, landscape and figure painter, made supervisor of painting.

The manufactory receives a rich store of French copper engravings from the royal collection.

1743 Heinrich Jacob Fehling, Dresden court painter, engaged as drawing master to the apprentices. Peter Reinicke, the sculptor, hired.

1744 Extensive addition: two new kilns, the old Amtskornhaus made into a storage room, firepump room, stables near the guardhouse, large storage shelters near the Elbe.

1745 Johann Carl Schönheit enters the manufactory's service as apprentice embosser. Second Silesian War: the Albrechtsburg serves as a hospital from December 15, 1745, to January 18, 1746.

1747 The flower painter Gottfried Hahnemann is engaged. He proposes the reform of the drawing school and the founding of a boarding school for apprentices.

1748 Friedrich Elias Meyer, sculptor, is engaged. The records for the years 1748–1763 are missing, so no work reports available.

1749 Christian Heinrich Kaendler in charge of the molds.

1750 Kaendler takes the ornamental mirror to the Dauphine in Paris.

1751 Five hundred and seventy-one employees, 190 of them painters. Kaendler is authorized to make the large statue of the king.

1756 The Seven Years' War breaks out. The arcanists take flight. Höroldt sent to Frankfurt-am-Main.

1757 Frederick II of Prussia leases the manufactory to his military procurement agent, Schimmelmann, who in turn leases it to Helbig, the privy councillor. The Lücke brothers go to Frankenthal.

1761 Meyer is won over by Berlin.

1762 Carl Christoph Punkt engaged to work with Kaendler. Kaendler resists offers from Berlin.

1763 The Hubertusburg Peace. Deaths of Augustus III and Count Brühl. Höroldt's return. Introduction of female labor. Johann Georg Loehnig joins the manufactory.

1764 The Parisian sculptor Michel Victor Acier is engaged. Kaolin from Seilitz used for the first time. Hummitzsch and Elsasser go to Paris.

1765 The court painter Christian Wilhelm Ernst Dietrich is made artistic director and drawing master. The painter Otto undertakes his sales tour. The number of employees is at its height for the eighteenth century: 731, including 270 painters.

1766 Founding of a widows' and dependents'

fund for the members of the technical and artistic staff. Recipe for biscuit porcelain arrived at.

1769 Christian Gottfried Jüchtzer engaged as apprentice embosser.

1772 Commission for forty large mythological groups from Catherine II of Russia.

1773 Johann Elias Zeissig, known as Schenau, made reorganizer and head of the drawing school.

1774 Camillo Count Marcolini takes over the directorship on August 20.

1775 Höroldt dies on January 30, and Kaendler on May 18. Founding of the woodyard workers' burial fund.

1782 Wentzel, the mining official from Freiberg, improves blue ground color and underglaze blue.

1790 Dr. Poerner, arcanist and mining official, organizes at his own risk the three successful porcelain auctions of 1790, 1791, and 1792. The number of employees nevertheless drops to 524. The sculptor Johann Daniel Schöne engaged.

1804 Compulsory membership in the burial fund for all those employed at the manufactory for more than two years.

1806 Russia places an embargo on foreign porcelain.

1810 The manufactory is to be closed. A petition results in its remaining open. Centenary celebrations on June 6, the citizens of Meissen participating with enthusiasm.

1813 Town and castle occupied by the French, later by the Cossacks.

1814 Marcolini dies. The tax official von Oppel made director on March 17.

1817 Development of a new underglaze color.

1818 Georg Friedrich Kersting, a painter, made supervisor of painting.

1828 Ludwig Richter, a painter, engaged as drawing master.

1833 Mining official Heinrich Gottlob Kühn as manager. Introduction of circular furnace; invention of gold luster. The manufactory is placed within the jurisdiction of the Treasury.

1836 Ernst August Leuteritz, pupil of Rietschel, joins the manufactory.

1839 Introduction of coal-fired kilns.

1853 Installation of the first steam engine.

1862 Introduction of *pâte-sur-pâte* technique, a Sèvres invention.

1864 The new manufactory premises at Triebischtal, begun in 1861, completed. The changeover effected in the summer.

1867 Considerable increase in income.

1868 First consignments of feldspar from the North.

1870 Death of Director Kühn. He is succeeded by Moritz Oskar Raithel.

1872 The annual income tops the million mark.

1874 Julius Eduard Braunsdorf, the flower painter, joins the manufactory.

1895 Horst Carl Brunnemann is director.

1901 Paul Gesell is director.

1903 The sculptor Erich Hösel joins the manufactory as head of design.

1904 The sculptor Otto Jarl is engaged.

1906 The flower painter Arthur Findeisen engaged.

1910 Karl Ludwig Achtenhagen made supervisor of painting. Paul Börner joins the manufactory, later to become artistic director.

1912 Willy Münch-Khe, painter, graphic artist, and sculptor, joins the manufactory. The academic painter Hermann Limbach is employed. The academic sculptor Erich Oehme also engaged.

1913 Max Adolf Pfeiffer takes office as sales director, is made works director in 1918, and general director in 1926. Paul Scheurich works as free-lance sculptor. Rudi Lauschke, later to become head of painting, is engaged.

1916 Completion of the Schauhalle (exhibition hall) as an archive for models and museum for Meissen porcelein.

1918 Alexander Struck joins the manufactory.

1920 Contract with the sculptor Max Esser. Gerhard Schiffner employed.

1933 The National Socialist government of Saxony dismisses Max Adolf Pfeiffer. "*Betriebsführer*" with no special knowledge are in charge of the manufactory until the fall of the Hitler regime.

1939–1945 The manufactory is partly used for armaments until the end of the Second World War. Damage to buildings through war action. Total stoppage of work. May, 1945, total defeat of Nazis; work recommenced under direction of Herbert Neuhaus.

1950 Handing over of the manufactory, for a time a branch of a Soviet concern, as a nationalized industry of the Deutsche Demokratische Republik.

1951 Waldemar Wüstemann is director.

1958 Return of the stored porcelain to the manufactory.

1960 Celebration of the two hundred and fiftieth anniversary.

1966 Rudolf Richter becomes director.

1969 Professor Dr. Karl Petermann appointed director.

MUSEUMS WITH SIGNIFICANT
COLLECTIONS OF OLD
MEISSEN PORCELAIN

Amsterdam	Rijksmuseum
Arnstadt	Schloss- und Heimatmuseum
Berlin (DDR)	Kunstgewerbemuseum (Schloss Köpenick)
Berlin (West)	Kunstgewerbemuseum (Schloss Charlottenburg)
Bern	Bernisches Historisches Museum
Budapest	Iparmüvészeti Museum
Chicago	Art Institute of Chicago
Cologne	Kunstgewerbemuseum
Dresden	The Zwinger porcelain collection
Düsseldorf	Hetjensmuseum and the Schneider collection in the Jägerhof castle
Faenza	Museo Internazionale delle Ceramiche
Frankfurt (Main)	Museum für Kunsthandwerk
Gotha	Schlossmuseum
Hamburg	Museum für Kunst und Gewerbe
Leipzig	Museum des Kunsthandwerks
Leningrad	The Hermitage
London	Victoria and Albert Museum, The British Museum
Moscow	State Ceramic Museum, Kuskowo Palace
Munich	Bayerisches Nationalmuseum
New York	Metropolitan Museum of Art
Paris	Musée des Arts Décoratifs de l'Union Centrale des Arts Décoratifs
Potsdam	State castles and gardens
Prague	Umělecko Průmyslové Museum
Rastatt	Schloss Favorite
Schwerin	Staatliches Museum
Stockholm	National Museum and Royal Collection
Stuttgart	Württembergisches Landesmuseum
Vienna	Österreichisches Museum für angewandte Kunst
Warsaw	Muzeum Narodowe
Zürich	Schweizerisches Landesmuseum and porcelain collection in the Zunfthaus zur Meise

A CHRONOLOGICAL SURVEY OF FORMS AND DECORATIONS OF MEISSEN WARE

The choice of Meissen pieces in this survey was dictated by a desire to show the wealth of form and characteristic decoration in each period. At the same time the influence of other regions and periods is indicated. Pieces within each group are dated and, where possible, individual craftsmen are named.

The object of this selection of photographs, unlike that of the choice of plates, is to show typical products of the Meissen manufactory rather than unique pieces. It is not intended to provide an exhaustive catalogue of Meissen porcelain but rather to reveal the variety of Meissen products and the degree to which the oldest European porcelain manufactory influenced its successors in almost every aspect of ceramic art.

1

2

3

4

1 Teapot in red Böttger stoneware, smooth form modeled after Far Eastern example. The neck with wheel-polished concave circular faceting; finial and handle polished in facets. Height 14 cm. Produced from 1709.

2 Four-sided flask in red Böttger stoneware. During the Böttger period this type of slender-necked flask, four-sided, hexagonal, circular or elliptic, was frequently produced. The illustrated specimen is rather simple and without decoration except for the Attic plinth. Height 20 cm. Produced from 1709.

3 Free-turned goblet in red Böttger stoneware in the fashion of contemporary turned wood and ivory work. The hard-fired ware allowed the same precision of execution as these materials. Height 14 cm. c. 1715.

4 The same goblet as above but with both the interior and exterior surfaces entirely wheel-polished. The light-reflecting surfaces give the impression of semiprecious stone.

5 Box with lid in Böttger stoneware, polished, typically Baroque in its curved profile. The appearance of the piece is much enhanced by the light-reflecting quality of its surface. Height 11 cm. Produced from 1712.

6 Baluster-shaped vase in Böttger stoneware. Harmoniously molded, it shows hardly any distortions, proof of an already highly developed firing technique. Produced from 1712.

7 Tankard in Böttger stoneware, cut and wheel-polished in facets. Cutting and polishing of Böttger stoneware was executed in the Schleifmühle (royal grinding and polishing works) in the Weisseritztal. Produced from 1711.

8 Octagonal teapot in black-glazed Böttger stoneware. Whereas the main body of the vessel as well as the dragon spout are modeled after Far Eastern examples, the design of the handle is reminiscent of European silverware. The decoration in lacquer paint was executed in the workshop of Martin Schnell. Height 13 cm. Produced from 1712.

9 Black-glazed fluted vase in Böttger stoneware, part of a set of three or five. Decorated in Martin Schnell's workshop with delicate flower motifs in lacquer paint. Height 22 cm. Produced from 1715.

10 Black-glazed pilgrim's bottle in Böttger stoneware, richly decorated with raised ornaments: festoons, flower arrangements, lions' heads applied like door knockers, a border of foliage above the foot. The gilt edges were fired.

11 Circular flask in Böttger stoneware directly molded from a Chinese flask. The spout in the shape of a stylized animal's head was, like the flower decoration, modeled in its neck portion with a wooden tool. Height 19 cm. Produced from 1715.

12 Tea caddy in Böttger stoneware with raised foliage ornament after a Chinese model. The six sides exhibit a motif (birds in a tree) in a sequence of variations. The borders with zigzag pattern were freely modeled with a wooden tool. Height 12 cm. Known after 1715.

13 Vase in Böttger ware in imitation of an ancient goblet in precious metal. The lateral masks exhibit Medusa heads. The relief border of foliage above the fine Attic pedestal is left unpolished in order to contrast effectively with the polished surface of the vessel. Most probably designed by the court silversmith Johann Jacob Irminger. Height 23 cm. c. 1716.

14

15

16

17

14 Portrait medallion of King Frederick I of Prussia in Böttger stoneware, mounted. Such medallions, as well as commemorative coins, were molded from the same die as those made in precious metal. Diameter 10 cm.

15 Small head of Apollo in Böttger stoneware after a sculpture by Bernini. This sort of direct reproduction was justifiably regarded as a successful product of the manufactory. Height 10 cm. c. 1718.

16 Goblet with lid in Böttger porcelain. The sharp contours of this vessel and the elaborate leaf decoration, free of all Far Eastern influence, exhibit Johann Jacob Irminger's Classically inspired work. The goblet, which is 50 cm. high, was made by the thrower Kratzenberg, c. 1716.

17 Hexagonal tea caddy. This caddy, already known in Böttger stoneware, was worked in Böttger porcelain by Johann Jacob Irminger. The leaf decoration was meant to be painted in enamel colors. Height 11 cm. c. 1718.

18 Coffeepot in Böttger porcelain. Bold in design, of clear function, it demonstrated a distinctly ceramic concept. The beautifully quiet shape of the vessel offers plenty of scope for decoration. Height 27 cm. c. 1716.

19 Double-walled bowl in Böttger porcelain with the outer wall pierced in openwork of geometrical pattern. The molder Paul Wildenstein is repeatedly mentioned as the man who mastered this difficult technique. Height 10.5 cm. c. 1718.

20 Vase in Böttger porcelain with applied decoration of sprigs of flowers. Since Böttger had not yet developed a reliable palette of enamel colors, the vase had to be decorated with lacquer paint. Height 19.5 cm. c. 1717.

21 This small hot water pot in Böttger porcelain, which is not open at the top, is decorated with leaves in relief and gilded in the Augsburg fashion. A true copy of a Far Eastern pot. Height 15 cm. c. 1720.

22 In the early 1720s the Court Chancellory often requested imitations of Far Eastern table services. The teapot in the illustration is probably a part of one of these services. Its decoration could not, however, have been carried out before Höroldt had developed a rich palette of enamel colors. c. 1720.

23 Two of the many bell-shaped beakers with variously shaped handles produced throughout the Böttger period. They are decorated with chinoiseries which were, however, also executed after 1720 at Meissen by Höroldt in a masterly and witty fashion. Height 8.2 cm.

24 Small head of an infant in Böttger porcelain. Sparsely touched with enamel paint but enough to breathe life into the piece. Although the sculptor of this attractive small masterpiece is not definitely known, it may possibly be ascribed to a certain Bernhard Miller of Dresden, who was employed by Böttger as early as 1708. Height 13.8 cm. c. 1718.

25 This copy of a Chinese figure was undoubtedly made by George Fritzsche, a skilled modeler. The scattered flower decoration in the early enamel colors indicates a date around 1722.

18

19

467

20

21

22

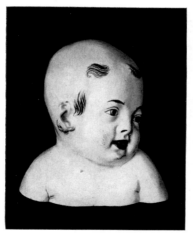

23

24

25

26

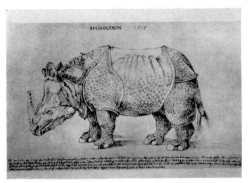

27

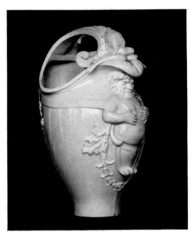

28

29

26 Cane handle in the shape of a man's head with jester's cap. Both the early mold number (269) and the fact that similar items were listed in his work report give reason to ascribe this piece to Johann Christian Ludwig Lücke, a sculptor who was employed at the manufactory for a short period during the year 1728. Length 9.5 cm.

27 A large statue of a rhinoceros was sculpted in 1752 by Johann Gottlieb Kirchner after this Dürer wood cut (based on the pen drawing of 1515).

28 Gigantic vase in the shape of a grotesque figure inspired by Stella's *Livre de Vases*. One of the four made by Johann Gottlieb Kirchner for the Dutch Palace. Height 72 cm. *c.* 1730.

29 Monumental sculpture of a bear made by Johann Gottlieb Kirchner in 1732. The treatment of the fur, however, shows Kaendler's touching up. Kirchner at this time was often prevented from working by illness. Height 60 cm.

30 Crowing Paduan cock. One of the most superb large birds created by Johann Joachim Kaendler for the Dutch Palace. Height 72 cm. Finished in August 1732.

31 Despite the death of Augustus the Strong (February, 1733) deliveries of monumental pieces for the Dutch Palace were continued until 1737. The sculptor Johann Friedrich Eberlein who joined the manufactory in 1734 was also engaged on these pieces. This he-goat was made during April and May, 1735.

32 Cockatoo made by Johann Joachim Kaendler in mid-September 1734. The foliage decoration on the otherwise white tree trunk is of great interest, for this kind of relief ornament was soon to appear on tableware.

33 In April, 1744, Johann Joachim Kaendler finished work on the group Papageien im Gezweig (Parrots in the Branches of a Tree). Height of group 37.5 cm. Mold number 644. The wide range of possibilities offered by this plastic material (the multitude of structural details, as well as the variety of possible decorations) are convincingly demonstrated in this example.

34 Jug in the form of three monkeys. This witty and inspired group was created by Johann Joachim Kaendler in July 1735. Although the custom of giving pouring vessels the shape of animals was already practiced centuries earlier, such an original specimen had rarely been seen before. Height 17 cm.

35 *Mops* (a fashionable kind of pug dog) modeled by Johann Joachim Kaendler in June 1741. Height 17 cm. Mold number 315. *Mops Hündgen* (*Hündgen* = little dog) are very frequently mentioned in private orders received by the master molder through Chladni. Among them were occasional requests for models after a particular living animal.

36 Cow made by Johann Friedrich Eberlein in April 1739. Height 6.5 cm. A fine example of the small animal figure (there are even smaller ones). Such figures were among the first of the collecting pieces later to become so profitable to the manufactory.

37 Precious works of eighteenth-century engravings were the main source from which animal sculptures were modeled. Rugendas' *Diversa Animalia Quadrupedia* figured prominently among them.

30

31

32

33

34

35

36

37

38

39

40

41

38 Doe Chased by Hounds, animal group modeled by Johann Joachim Kaendler in 1758. Height 18 cm. Groups of this nature were mainly produced by Kaendler and his team between the years 1748 and 1760. They were inspired by Johann Elias Ridinger's engravings.

39 Leopard, an animal sculpture by Johann Joachim Kaendler. Height 6.5 cm. c. 1740. Kaendler is known to have traveled to Dresden in order to study the living predators which were kept in the royal menagerie at the eastern end of the Jungfernbastei.

40 Monkey with Young on a Tree Trunk, animal group. Height 19 cm. Produced in March 1741. One of the many compositions of monkeys, which were popular pets at the time.

41 Small teapot lavishly decorated with painted sprays of leaves based on Far Eastern motifs with Islamic influence. c. 1724.

42 Hexagonal slender-necked vase with flower decoration in Japanese fashion. c. 1752.

43 So-called *Schlossvase* (palace vase). A vase with lid, richly decorated with *indianische Blumenmalerei* (Indian flowers) painted in enamel colors. Height 63 cm. c. 1735. This vase represents a climax of painted decoration in Meissen porcelain based on Far Eastern examples. It was made possible by the development of a wide palette of enamel colors as well as by the strict workshop discipline imposed by Höroldt.

44 One of Johann Gregorius Höroldt's chinoiseries on a yellow cup painted in 1725. Height of figure 3 cm. An exquisite example of Höroldt's inimitable brush technique devoid of any harshness of line.

45 Design for a chinoiserie by Höroldt, from his sketchbook now kept in the Museum für Kunsthandwerk in Leipzig. This master of the palette of enamel colors produced numerous copper engravings which were then printed on a press, especially installed for the purpose, in order to supply his workers with patterns. (See Plate 39).

46 Chinoiseries by Johann Christian Horn, one of Höroldt's pupils, differ essentially in character from those of his master as well as from those of his colleagues. In 1711, Horn is mentioned in the payroll of the faience factory (the so-called Steinbäckerei) and after 1721 as co-worker with Höroldt.

47 Chinese man mounted on fabulous animal. One of five such sample sheets in the works archives. Adam Friedrich von Löwenfinck developed a passion for these motifs.

48 Part of painted decoration freely adopted from a Chinese vase by Johann Ehrenfried Stadler (employed by Höroldt after 1723). His "handwriting" bears all the marks of an experienced faience painter: graphic elements and formal ornaments take precedence over the pictorial effect.

49 The Red Dragon motif surrounding two phoenix in the center was adopted from Japanese porcelain decoration of about 1700. In use from 1730. All ware decorated with it was strictly reserved for the electoral court until 1918, but from the middle of the nineteenth century onward the same pattern was produced for sale to the public in different colors (green, blue, purple, brown, black and also in polychrome).

50 How adaptable the *Hofdrachen* (court dragon) decoration was, is shown by this lidded dish made in the second half of the eighteenth century.

42

43

44

45

46

47

48

49

50

51

52

53

54

51 The *Reicher gelber Löwe* (rich yellow lion) decoration is here superimposed upon the so-called *Altbrandensteinmuster* (an applied decoration of basket-pattern and trellis-work). This lion motif was introduced in 1728. The small scattered decorative motifs of butterflies and single flowers were either placed arbitrarily by the enamel painter or were intended to conceal impurities in the porcelain surface ("iron spots").

52 Large tureen, the lid painted with the yellow lion motif and with the handle in the shape of a pine cone. This lion motif was painted in almost exact imitation of a Far Eastern example. It had been suggested by the Court Chancellery and was repeatedly ordered by the Royal Court Pantry until the end of the eighteenth century.

53 Plate with wavy-edged peripheral pattern, which is known as the *Neuer Ausschnitt* (new cut edge). The painting shows the *Fliegender Fuchs* (flying fox) pattern.

54 A rather rare decoration based on the Japanese is the *Vogel im Bambuszweig* (bird on a bamboo sprig). Its coloring in gray, black, overglaze blue and two different gildings must have added to the festive appearance of the table.

55 This decoration with *indianische Blumen* (Indian flowers) grouped in three bouquets is rather lavishly colored in scarlet, iron-red, bright-blue, blue-green and gold.

56 Plate with the *Gebrochener Stab* (broken rod) relief decoration which extends to the well. Superimposed on this plastic decoration is the *Ährenmuster* (spike pattern) painted in scarlet camaieu heightened with dotted gilding.

57 Based on Chinese originals, the so-called *Zwiebelmuster* (onion pattern) appeared for the first time in 1728. In this first version all the leaves, flowers and buds point inward. The motif in the center, also based on Chinese examples, shows chrysanthemum and bamboo in a superbly balanced arrangement.

58 A smooth-rimmed plate decorated with the *Zwiebelmuster* which achieved world-wide popularity. A successful underglaze blue could not be consistently obtained for serial production until 1739. After this a new version of this famous pattern, which, with slight variations, is still produced today, came to the fore. In this version, the individual patterns point alternately inward and outward, and the main motif covers the entire central area evenly. This decoration was mostly painted by apprentices who, for matters of comparison, had to mark each piece by adding their initials to the crossed swords.

59 Besides the *Zwiebelmuster* (see Nos. 57, 58), a considerable number of other Far Eastern floral patterns (*indianische Blumendekore*) were produced. One of the richest is undoubtedly the chrysanthemum design. It was painted from about 1749 onward.

60 This simple cup with the *Gebrochener Stab* decoration (see No. 56) is, without regard for its plastic ornamentation, painted with simple foliage.

61 Large bowl decorated with the so-called *Deutsche Blumen* (German flowers) in underglaze blue. *c.* 1745. The superb execution of this sort of decoration was only possible after the technique of underglaze painting had been developed to perfection.

55

56

57

58

59

60

61

62

65

64

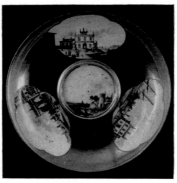

65

62 Cylindrical chocolate cup with twig handle, alternate bands in applied relief *(Dulong)*, and green monochrome Watteau painting. From a breakfast service ordered by the electoral court in 1745.

63 This green painting after Watteau, in which the camaieu (monochrome) painting of the Böttger period was revived, achieved great popularity. A large service painted with this decoration was ordered for the Royal Polish Court Pantry in 1745.

64 Engraving after a Watteau painting. Groups of individual figures from these engravings were copied on porcelain either in green camaieu or in polychrome painting. The porcelain craftsmen were particularly inspired by several hundred engravings after Watteau and Lancret which were ordered in 1741 by Count Hennicke, a high government official. Among the engravers of these works of art were lebas, Audran and Tardieu.

65 Gilded saucer. The center as well as these reserves are painted with coast and harbor scenes. The lack of any kind of formal ornament indicates the end of the eighteenth century.

66 Saucer with smooth rim and simple gilded zigzag border. The center is decorated with a panoramic coastal landscape showing fishing boats, groups of houses and distant mountains. *c.* 1750.

67 Saucer with smooth rim and rich gilded lace border, and an even more elaborate one around the center with a twelve-petaled rosette. The painted scenery with rocks, towers, shrubs and tall trees and groups of promenading and resting people is a superb example of sophisticated landscape painting of the second half of the eighteenth century.

68 Plate with border decorated with oblong panels in elaborate Rococo ornament. The harbor scenes seem to depict concrete motifs. In the center an arrangement of German flowers with the individual flowers painted in great detail.

69 In 1616 Claes Janss Visscher of Amsterdam published a volume of copper engravings by Petrus Schenk after van Goyen's landscapes. The Meissen manufactory based many paintings on porcelain on these engravings, and still does so today.

70 Plate with the so-called *Neuer Ausschnitt* (new cut edge) pattern. Plates with this pattern were at first (from 1745) decorated with the *Deutsche Blaue Blume* (blue German flower) in underglaze paint and soon afterward also with the *Bunte Deutsche Blume* (colored German flower) in enamel colors.

71 Between 1743 and 1746 Johann Joachim Kaendler created two cycles of monumental busts. Cardinal Albani in Rome had ordered sacred works of sculpture and the House of Habsburg requested a considerable number of busts of emperors. The bust of Maximilian I (mold number 12) was planned by Kaendler, molded by Peter Reinicke and received its final touching up again by Kaendler.

72 By request of the electoral court and inspired by Mattielli's work in Dresden, in the years 1738–42 Johann Joachim Kaendler modeled a large number of religious statuettes of which the Apostles and Evangelists are the best known.

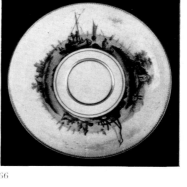
66

67

475

68

69

70

72

73

74

75

76

73 St. Mark the Evangelist. In November, 1737, Johann Joachim Kaendler was asked to execute twelve figures of Apostles for the Empress Amalie. In 1738, influenced by engravings of Bernini's figures of Apostles, this statuette of St. Mark was produced as one piece of the cycle. Height 45 cm.

74 The prolific number of architectural sculptures in the Dresden Zwinger (built from 1711–22), Balthasar Permoser's stone carvings and the work of his teacher, Benjamin Thomä, are influences clearly echoed in Kaendler's statuettes of The Four Seasons. They were made mainly around the year 1745.

75 This enchanting Bacchus group, created by Johann Friedrich Eberlein in 1745, was so popular that the molds became "worn out." In 1766, Kaendler's colleague Peter Reinicke was given the task of remodeling it.

76 Bacchanalian figures of all sorts, mostly adapted from existing sculpture in the electoral parks, dominated the production of figures in the Meissen factory for decades. The demands for these must have been particularly great around the year 1745 for they are repeatedly mentioned in the work reports by Kaendler, Eberlein and Reinicke.

77 Acis and Galatea, one of the most lovable groups taken from the inexhaustible store of ancient mythology. The illustrated version is the work of Johann Friedrich Eberlein; this can be deduced from the typically narrow faces of the figures. According to the work reports. Eberlein was engaged on this group in 1748.

78 By analogy with details from the Swan Service, it can be assumed that Johann Joachim Kaendler modeled the Glaucus group some time between 1741 and 1745.

79 Work on The Four Seasons, four groups each composed of two figures, was concluded by Johann Joachim Kaendler in 1755. The medallion was reserved for a portrait whereas the cartouches, surrounded by Rococo scrolls, had to take either a coat of arms or a miniature landscape after Watteau, as is the case with Winter, illustrated here. Mold number 2378.

80 One of Johann Joachim Kaendler's best-known pastoral groups. He started work on the model in November, 1764, finished it in December, and cut it up in preparation for the molds in February, 1765.

81 The Quack Doctor. In his work report of 1741 Johann Joachim Kaendler explains: "*Ein Zahnarzt mit einer grossen Peruque oder ein Markt Schreyer seine Medicamente anbiethend, hat neben sich einen Tisch stehen, darauff medicamente liegen und einen Affen, welcher Arzenay hält, wie auch einen Arlequin in lustiger Positur, in seinem Huth Kräuter habend.*" (A dentist with a large wig or a market crier offering his medicaments, has a table standing beside him upon which his medicaments lie and a monkey holding medicine, and also a Harlequin in an amusing posture with herbs in his hat.) A patient was added to this group at a later date.

82 The Fangstossgruppe (*Fangstoss* = coup de grâce). Around 1740 Johann Joachim Kaendler created a number of richly ornate lids *(Jagddeckel)* for hunting goblets which were very fashionable at the time. The most laborious *("der Mühsamste")* was the one ordered by Clemens Augustus, an archbishop-elector of Cologne. The one illustrated was made in 1739.

83 Jagdrast (The Hunt at Rest). This group was modeled by Johann Joachim Kaendler in 1743 and given the number 507.

77

78

79

80

81

82

83

84

85

86

87

84 Lady at her work table with cavalier. The model of this enchanting crinoline group (mold number 551) was, according to Kaendler's diary, finished in November, 1743. It was given the unusual description *Neues Frey Mäurer Grouppgen* (New Freemason Group). *c.* 1745.

85 Opernpaar (Couple at the Opera) – certainly not Louis XV and Mme de Pompadour. Figures and groups depicting scenes at the splendid opera performances at the court of Augustus III belong to the most varied and elaborate ever made. Mold numbers 543 and 547.

86 Group of Freemasons in front of a globe. In 1742 Johann Friedrich Eberlein created this group of two Freemasons, who, surrounded by the symbols of their society, pursue a cosmopolitan exchange of views. Mold number 376.

87 Child's Head. In 1760 Johann Joachim Kaendler was requested to produce a portrait figure of the daughter of the Dauphine, Maria Josepha of Saxony. In accordance with contemporary taste, he decorated the child's hood with naturalistically sculpted flowers. Mold number 2764.

88 Allegory of Abundance. This piece showing a wining and dining gourmet at a richly laden table is the work of the sculptor Friedrich Elias Meyer. Produced in 1750, it superbly reflects the spirit of the Rococo. Mold number 1447. Later a similar piece showing a female counterpart was made.

89 Most of the pieces of Johann Joachim Kaendler's popular Affenkapelle (Monkey Band) which are known today – twenty-two altogether – are actually specimens of a revised series by Kaendler and Reinicke made between 1765 and 1766. In comparison with the first design of 1747 these later figures were intended for more elaborate decoration.

90 Paris Street Musicians. This group immediately succeeded the figures of the street vendors (see No. 91). Apart from Kaendler, Reinicke and later Friedrich Elias Meyer tried their hands successfully at this series. Most of the figures were modeled after drawings by Bouchardon which had appeared in an engraved volume by Michel le Clerc around 1740.

91 Cris de Paris. In the summer of 1750 Johann Joachim Kaendler was sent to Paris to deliver a large mirror to the French court. Inspired by the turbulent street life of this populous capital, he conceived the idea of modeling traders, flower-sellers, itinerant craftsmen, fruit-sellers, etc.

92 After Count Brühl's death no less than sixty-seven little houses in porcelain were listed in an inventory of his estate. There were farmhouses, barns, a church, as well as various other buildings. They were made as table decorations, often illuminated by candles. The piece illustrated was made by Johann Gottlieb Ehder in 1743. Mold number 2230.

93 Saint Rosalie. In August, 1774, Johann Joachim Kaendler reports on a grotto group which had been ordered by an Italian customer. It had to figure Saint Rosalie "*wie solche in einer Höhle sterbend liegt*" (dying in a cave). The composition of this group is strikingly similar to Kaendler's monumental epitaph for Alexander von Miltitz. Height 27 cm. Mold number E 91.

479

88

89

90

91

92

93

94

95

96

97

94 The Labors of Hercules. A large group consisting of ten detachable parts, certainly a most wonderful piece of table decoration. This elaborate work was created by Johann Joachim Kaendler in 1744. With his profound knowledge of ancient mythology such a work was certainly to his taste. Height 65 cm. Mold number 201–210.

95 Pagoda. The fashion of Far Eastern objects had a late revival around 1760. Frederick II of Prussia requested no fewer than ten pagodas with nodding heads. One of these, modeled by Johann Joachim Kaendler, is illustrated here. Height 31 cm. Mold number 2884.

96 Sleigh group. In many a porcelain group one finds a humorous reflection of the attention paid not only by court circles but also by the public to the court jester Joseph Fröhlich as well as to his "opponent," the postmaster "Count" Schmiedel. This sleigh group depicts Fröhlich embracing a lady who is none other than Schmiedel in female dress. According to Kaendler's report in the *Taxa* it was made in 1741. Mold number 251.

97 Harlequin With a Wine Jug. One of the most beautiful of Kaendler's Italian Comedy figures. Mold number 3060. Most of these figures were made *c.* 1740.

98 Engraving after which the above figure was modeled. It comes from an Augsburg volume of engravings, dated 1700, which was sent, together with other volumes, to the manufactory at the request of Count Brühl's friend, Count Hennicke.

99 These figures from the Italian Comedy belong to a series which was not made until the 1770s. The Classical design of the pedestal and, even more, the lifeless gesticulations of the figures, give proof of this dating.

100 Within the cycle of the Italian Comedy, groups depicting pairs of characters from the Commedia dell'Arte were made after 1741. The one illustrated here shows the flattering Columbine with the vain Pantaloon. Mold number 289.

101 Besides the figures which were mentioned previously and which were mainly the work of Johann Joachim Kaendler, there are the so-called Gegner (opposing figures), mostly depicting a male and a female character dancing or courting. The themes were usually inspired by the numerous court festivities such as balls or masquerades. They were made in the years 1741 to 1745 and can be ascribed especially to Johann Friedrich Eberlein and Johann Gottlieb Ehder.

102 In the search for more and more themes for the production of these popular figure groups, a strong interest was taken in the so-called Exotics. As can be read in his reports, Johann Joachim Kaendler created various pairs of Gegner (see No. 101) as, for example, these Japanese figures.

103 These two figures belong to the so-called Schäferkapelle (Shepherd Band) modeled by Johann Joachim Kaendler and Peter Reinicke in the years 1760–3. Mold numbers 2828 and 2829. A few pieces had already been made by Friedrich Elias Meyer before 1761.

104 The elegance of movement in these figures of the Galante Kapelle (Orchestra of Gallants), represented here by the violinist and the cellist, suggests the hand of the sculptor Friedrich Elias Meyer toward the end of the 1750s.

98

99

100

101

102

105

104

105

106

107

108

105 Toward the 1750s, Johann Joachim Kaendler, in cooperation with Peter Reinicke, embarked upon the design of a cycle of great sociological interest, the groups of craftsmen. The examples illustrated, showing a butcher and a porcelain thrower, can, by their style, be attributed to Friedrich Elias Meyer. Butcher: height 20 cm. Mold number 1397. Thrower: height 18.2 cm. Mold number 1391.

106 Two of the large number of miners created by Kaendler, Reinicke and Meyer between 1741–55, these depict a miner and a mine inspector. Miner: height 21 cm. Mold number 1325. Mine inspector: height 20.5 cm. Mold number 1336.

107 On this colored engraving of a musician Johann Joachim Kaendler based his design for The Miners Band. The engraving was executed by Weigel after watercolors by Fehling, which were inspired by the great miners' parade staged for the occasion of the engagement of the electoral prince to Maria Josepha.

108 Large vase with elaborate applied figures symbolizing one of the elements: Water. It is one of the four so-called Elementvasen. Made by Kaendler in 1741. Height 64 cm.

109 Spice container, first made by Johann Joachim Kaendler in 1737 for the dining table of Count Brühl and, in a slightly varied form (new Marseilles pattern), repeated by Peter Reinicke for the Prussian court in 1745. Height 20.5 cm. Mold number 476.

110 Even more extravagant than the above piece is this mustard pot which Kaendler finished in October 1737. His report on this piece reads as follows: "*Solches ist in Gestalt einer Indianischen Henne wie eine Japanerin darauf reutet, welche zugleich eine Vase mit der einen Hand hält, woraus der Senf bequem herausgenommen werden kann.*" (This is in the shape of an Indian hen mounted by a Japanese woman holding in one hand a vase from which mustard can be taken easily.)

111 Salt cellar with candlestick upon a rocaille base. At the foot of the candlestick, between two wicker baskets filled with flowers, sits a female gardener. Between 1740 and 1745 a series of this nature was designed by Johann Joachim Kaendler after he had finished work on the Swan Service.

112 Girl holding candelabra, modeled by Johann Joachim Kaendler around 1755. A maiden in rustic dress is seated on the fork of a tree trunk holding tightly to the flower-decorated branches. Mold number 1130.

113 Mirror frame richly decorated with applied flowers. Around the year 1745, perhaps at the customer's request, Johann Joachim Kaendler cluttered pieces of this kind with naturalistic flower decoration to such an extent that the actual design almost disappeared beneath it. In 1750, accompanied by Georg Michel Helbig, Kaendler traveled to Paris to deliver a large *Trumeau* (an elaborate mirror, almost 3 m. high) to the French court.

114 Watch stand. This piece, consisting entirely of rocaille motifs with the rather insignificant head of Saturn, shows Johann Joachim Kaendler's departure from an architectural conception. According to work reports it was modeled in 1761. Height 27 cm. Mold number 2788.

115 Clock case with rich flower decoration and scroll feet. *c.*1755.

109

110

111

112

113

114

115

116

117

118

119

120

116 Gärtnerkinder (Child Gardeners). At the end of the 1750s, when the Rococo began to produce a conventional and formulated sweetness of interpretation, countless child figures and groups were made. The fashion reached its first climax in the so-called Dot Period (1764–74).

117 So-called Nationalitätenkinder (The Nationalities as Children). Illustrated here, Turkish male and female figures. Around and after 1760 many of the nationalities, shepherds, craftsmen, etc., were redesigned as children, in response to the new middle-class taste.

118 Among the cycles of child figures of the last decade of the eighteenth century, the so-called Comedy Children, diminutive representations of figures from the Italian Comedy, aroused particular interest.

119 Gärtnerkinder (Child Gardeners). The expressive gestures and features of the dancing gardener children, not found in many of the other child figures, indicate the cooperation of the sculptor Friedrich Elias Meyer, who probably made them around 1755.

120 Devisenkinder (child figures with explanatory mottoes). The designs for these well-loved 'amours avec devises' came from one of the manufactory's finest artists, Johannes Elias Zeissig, known as Schenau, who had been sent to Paris. They were carried out in porcelain by Jüchtzer, Schönheit, Acier and Matthäi.

121 Plate from the Sulkowsky Service showing Sulkowsky or ordinair Ozier pattern. This relief pattern, first designed for the Saxon Prime Minister Count Alexander Joseph von Sulkowsky in 1735, was the first of many fine Meissen tableware patterns which enjoyed popularity for many decades.

122 Ribbed pattern. This relief decoration rising from the edge of the hollow of the plate and becoming stronger toward the rim has been known as Gebrochener Stab (broken rod) since 1736.

123 Plate from the Swan Service. Work on the design of the Swan Service was started in 1735. The marked feature of this design is the entire covering of the vessels with relief decoration on the theme of water, with its flora, fauna and mythology.

124 Plate with the Altozier relief pattern. This dignified pattern, executed in the twelve sections of the border of the plate, is, as its name suggests, derived from basket weave.

125 Plate showing the Marseilles pattern. The name originates from a commission obtained via Paris. Produced from 1739.

126 Plate showing the Gotzkowsky relief which was in production from 1741 and was particularly suited to accommodate camaieu painting, especially the copper-green Watteau representations.

127 Plate with Altbrandenstein relief decoration. This was first carried out in the year 1738 for Friedrich August Brandenstein.

128 Plate with the Brühlsches Allerlei (Brühl's various) relief decoration. The wavy outline of this plate, produced from 1742, requires the free lively relief ornament of this pattern which here and there extends into the hollow.

129 Plate with Dulong decoration. This was first produced in 1743, commissioned by an Amsterdam merchant by the name of Dulong.

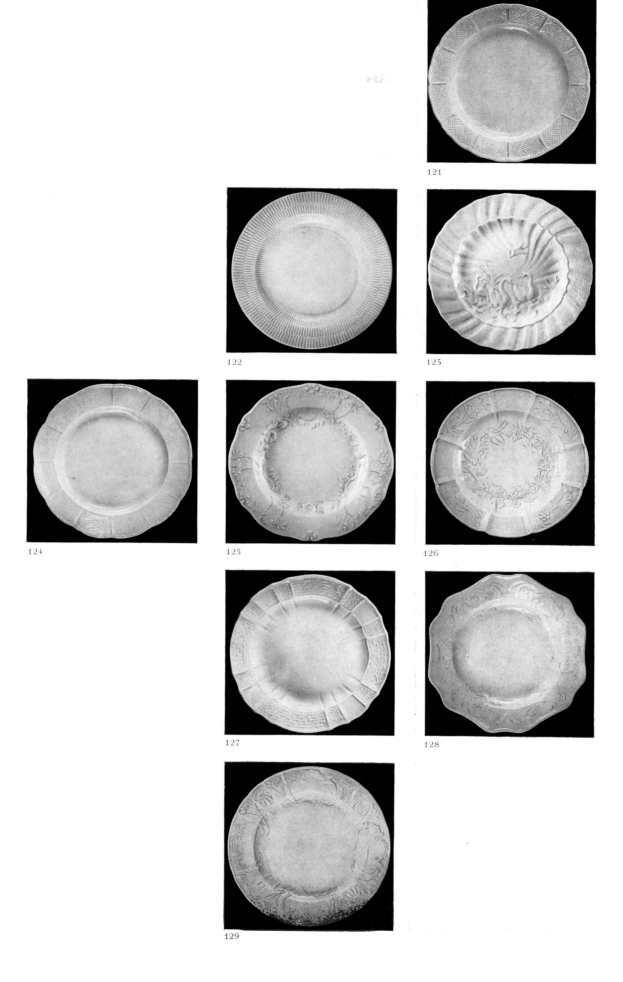

121

122

123

124

125

126

127

128

129

130

131

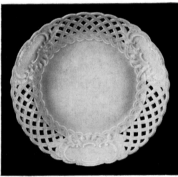

132

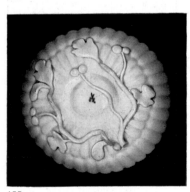

133

130 Plate with the *Neubrandenstein* pattern. In 1744 the radial devision of the *Altbrandenstein* pattern was substituted by a curved ribbing.

131 Plate in the *Gewundenes Muster*. The pattern consists of S-shaped grooves which gradually widen as they extend from the edge of the hollow to the rim of the plate.

132 Cake plate with openwork border punctuated by three shields. These shields and the hollow of the plate invite the most varied painted decoration. A very popular dessert plate design from 1760.

133 *Goderonnierte* saucer. The branch motif is skillfully developed to form three feet in the underside. Already employed in Böttger's day in imitation of Chinese ware, this technique, wholly suited to its material, was again frequently used with the growth of high relief decoration after 1738.

134 Tureen with *Neubrandenstein* sculpted ornament (see No. 130) and *Fliegender Hund* painted decoration. The basic shape of this vessel was standardized by Johann Joachim Kaendler around 1740. Characteristic are the forms of the handles on the side and the two entwined leaves on the cover.

135 Container from the *Schneeballblüten* (flowers of the snowball tree) design. The Schneeballblüten Service is already mentioned in 1739. The carefully formed tiny decorative elements unite to give an overall effect of serenity which is enhanced by the natural-looking rose forming the finial of the cover.

136 *Geflochtenes Körbchen* (small woven basket) already mentioned as a *Gothisches Dessin* (Gothic design) in 1772. The weave made great demands on the skill of the repairer and required careful firing.

137 Turkish mocha coffeepot in architectural baluster form with scrolled handles, animal spout with mask instead of plain opening. This is probably Johann Joachim Kaendler's first design, 1732, for a pot based on existing samples.

138 Coffeepot with I-shaped handle, a rosebud as finial and *Altozier* relief on the neck and lid. Designed by Johann Joachim Kaendler *c.* 1740.

139 Coffeepot designed by Johann Joachim Kaendler in 1742. The walls of the pot are smooth and bulging, suited for rich painted decoration. The handle, which is decorated in traditional style with a *Frauensbildgen* (female portrait), is known as an *Ohrenhenkel* (ear handle).

140 Two cups which, in their highly different designs, show the extremes of a considerable time span. The cup on the left shows an elegant beaker shape and an I-shaped handle. The cup on the right has the deep bowl and the angular handle of the Classical period. The development of vessels of various kinds shortly after the Böttger period brought forth forms peculiar to ceramic art, although there was some adoption of silverware designs. The cups of the Marcolini period, however, were inspired by architectural elements.

141 These two bucket-shaped cups with branch handles are given entirely different characters by means of their decoration. The left one is decorated with the *Marseilles* pattern, which, along with the waved rim, makes for a lighter appearance, whereas the right one seems more compact, almost architectural in appaearance, with its smooth surface and voluted feet.

154

155

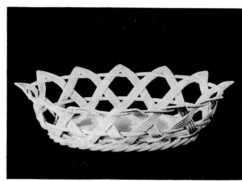

136

137

138

139

140

141

142

143

144

145

146

142 These two "*gemuschelten*" (shell-like) cups, designed by Johann Joachim Kaendler around 1740, are oval in cross-section. Far Eastern influence is still evident. The right-hand cup has a most practical handle, modeled by Kaendler around 1740.

143 These two cups, developed from the beaker shape, show *Altozier* borders, which neatly round off their parabolic outline.

144 Two cups with the so-called *Neuer Ausschnitt* (new cut edge).

145 In 1769 Johann Joachim Kaendler began to model a service ordered by the Duke of Anhalt-Dessau, the pieces of which were to be in the form of animals and fruits. An excellent example of this conception, artistically somewhat in the backwaters though it may be, is provided by this naturalistic tureen, not only in its shape but also in its ornament.

146 Cup and saucer entirely covered by a slightly raised foliage decoration. Around 1750, from motifs which hovered between Rococo-like abstraction and the tendency to naturalize, Johann Joachim Kaendler developed a relief decoration which covered the whole surface of the vessel, rather in the manner of the Swan Service.

147 Classical cup with lion feet and scroll handle. The cup's severe yet elaborate design enjoyed increasing popularity from 1790 on account of its suitability for decoration. The illustrated example is decorated with Watteau scenes and scattered flowers.

148 Title page from the series of copper engravings by Daniel Chodowiecki illustrating Goethe's *Die Leiden des jungen Werthers*. At the end of the eighteenth century and the beginning of the nineteenth these engravings were often copied for the decoration of Classical tableware.

149 Cup in the antique style with pedestal. The trapezoidal reserve on the ultramarine background is boldly painted with garden flowers. *c.* 1820.

150 Colored copper engraving from *Plantes de la France*, a collection of engravings showing various types of roses, published in 1829 by Jaume Saint-Hilaire in Paris.

151 The life-style of the Biedermeier period is reflected by this cylindrical teapot with its elegant, almost puritanical form painted with a rose, rosebuds and leaves.

152 Biedermeier cup with a copy of a painting from the Dresden Gallery (Inv. No. 387) "Potiphar's Wife", painted by the Italian artist Carlo Cignani around 1650. This is one of the many paintings which were copied on porcelain at the end of the eighteenth and throughout the nineteenth century.

153 From 1780 the Wedgwood style was adopted in Meissen, encouraged by Marcolini's commissions. The mode is illustrated by this teapot. Classical elements are evident in the acanthus motifs around the base of the spout and on the handle.

154 Similar influences were at work when this round teapot was designed. Here, the plastic decorative elements strike a sentimental symbolic note.

155 The cream jug matching 153 shows the minimum of decoration on its noble harmonious form. Like almost all successful pieces in the Classical style, this smooth jug achieves its effect without any painted decoration.

147

148

149

150

151

152

153

154

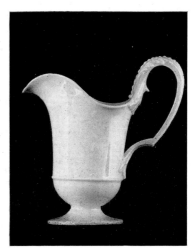

155

156

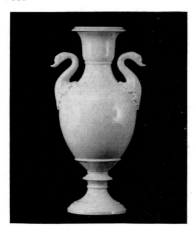

157

158

159

156 Chocolate pot, conical, Classical shape, widening upward with trapezoidal handle, indented lid and plantlike knob.

157 Amphora-like vase with Attic base and swan-neck handles. It widens beakerlike to the opening, so that the entire silhouette is harmoniously rounded off.

158 Classical display vase with a portrait of Cimon. *c.* 1770. The unharmonious juxtaposition of antique formal elements and sentimental motifs reflects the clash of aesthetic aims and literary allusions.

159 Design for an urnlike showpiece with fluted sides, acanthus wreath and pine cone finial. From a French book of ornaments for the use of craftsmen published at the end of the eighteenth century.

160 Large tureen in the form of a Classical crater with Attic base. Row of knobs at rim. Handles in the form of rams' heads with laurel wreaths. *c.* 1785.

161 Countless putti groups were made by Michel Victor Acier and Johannes Carl Schönheit after designs sent from Paris by Schenau (Zeissig) in the 1770s. An example of these is this group showing Meleager and Atalanta (1774). Greek mythological themes were sweetened to suit late Rococo taste.

162 Die zerbrochenen Eier (The Broken Eggs). A group very typical of the sentimental allusions of the time, modeled by Michel Victor Acier in 1777. Mold number 65.

163 Zeus and Neptune. Two of the busts in biscuit porcelain very popular at the time as made by Jüchtzer and Schönheit after examples from the royal collection of casts in Dresden.

164 In accordance with artistic taste based on literary themes, at the end of the eighteenth century almost all the well-known figures from intellectual life were modeled in small, Classical-style busts. These two show Dürer and Goethe. They are 12.5 cm. high and were modeled by Johann Daniel Schöne. *c.* 1810.

165 In 1779 Michel Victor Acier made a 21-cm.-high porcelain reproduction of the Gellert memorial designed in Classical-style by the Leipzig painter Oeser. In March, 1775, shortly before his death, Johann Joachim Kaendler had modeled a small Gellert monument conceived as an obelisk ornamented with figures and medallions.

166 The memorial for Christian Fürchtegott Gellert designed by Oeser, one of Goethe's teachers, was drawn by Chodowiecki and engraved in copper by Geyser.

167 Goblet in the Wedgwood style with raised biscuit porcelain decoration on a blue ground showing battle scenes from Classical times. The foot and the bowl-like base of the body of the vessel are glazed, as are the interior walls. *c.* 1780.

168 Pipe bowl in the form of a bust of Napoleon. This was made by Johann Daniel Schöne, employed at the Meissen manufactory from 1783.

169 This court service with blue border was made for the elector Frederick Augustus III around 1775. Like many pieces from the Neoclassical period it shows raised and colored decorative elements in clumsy and harsh juxtaposition. Its best feature is the rich and finely executed fruit, flower and bird (*Federvieh*) painting.

160

161

162

163

164

165

166

167

168

169

170

171

172

173

170 Cake dish with cut out *(ausgeschnitten)* border, which is ornamented at three points by flower sprays also in openwork but raised and painted. The hollow of the plate is decorated with a mixture of naturalistically painted flowers and fruits.

171 Plate, smooth with the so-called *Neuer Ausschnitt* (see N. 70), from a service with a harmonious decoration of songbirds, butterflies and insects.

172 Swan-handle pot of the Biedermeier period painted with the chromium-oxide green underglaze vineleaf motif which from 1817 achieved a similar popularity to that of the blue *Zwiebelmuster* (see Nos. 57, 58).

173 Vase in the form of a Communion chalice, modeled in 1849 by the head of design at the time, Ernst August Leuteritz. Mold number I 86. The attempt to transpose all historical styles into the medium of porcelain resulted in the use of the vegetable forms of the late Gothic period, as seen in this piece.

174 Design for a cup with "Gothic" ornament by Ernst August Leuteritz, dating from 1848.

175 Small rounded amphora on square plinth with lateral flower garlands, designed by Ernst August Leuteritz, Mold number B 178. Made from 1855.

176 The form of the vase in the previous illustration already shows the rise of the so-called second Rococo period in the applied arts. This tendency is evident in this head of a child, modeled by Leuteritz in 1850.

177 A strange hybrid was produced in the form of this coffeepot with the raised decoration around it in the style of Capo di Monte pieces. This *Neuheit* (novelty), launched on the market in 1865, was a great commercial success, particularly as an export to England.

178 Wall plaque with a representation of Psyche in the so-called *pâte-sur-pâte* technique. The technique of applying several layers of slip was derived from ancient Chinese works and was taken up in Sèvres by Heintze. Its artistic application was principally carried out by Julius Hentschel and Theodor Grust from 1880 onward.

179 Large wall plaque with *Scharffeuermalerei* by Georg Voigt. As a result of this technique, mastered in 1880, amazing three-dimensional effects could be achieved, which entirely suited the contemporary desire to produce a realistic effect in decoration.

180 Plate with blackish-brown, gold-edged border, framing a rich flower and fruit painting of excellent quality. *c.* 1880.

181 Wall plaque with a view of Dresden before the Second World War. The so-called *Städteteller* (town plates, i. e. with views of towns) had become popular collecting pieces from 1910. This specimen was designed by the head of painting, Hermann Limbach, in 1935.

182 Plate from the service designed in the *Jugendstil* by the interior decorator Riemerschmid in 1905. Underglaze painting.

183 Smooth-rimmed plate with stylized flower decoration.

184 Plate from a service designed by Paul Börner. The elegance and harmony of line and the simple relief decoration make for a timeless appeal not subject to the dictates of fashion.

174

175

176

177

178

179

180

181

182

183

184

185

186

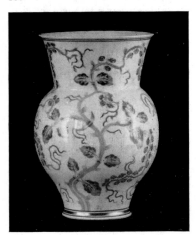

187

188

185 One of the popular Christmas plates in blue underglaze painting. This specimen was designed by Paul Börner in 1927. The design was scratched out with a hard dry brush in the sprayed ground color.

186 Large decorative wall plaque with cobalt blue underglaze painting, showing stylized plants and birds. By William Baring, 1910.

187 During the artistic directorskip of Paul Börner, monumental sculpture began to regain its former importance at the Meissen manufactory. In 1930 a series of large vases with imaginatively stylized plants and foliage decoration was made.

188 Porcelain bell with raised decoration after a design by Paul Börner. Height 60 cm. The first carillon made by the Meissen manufactory was the one for the Japanese Palace in 1736, and a second was constructed in 1741 for Count Brühl. Both were the work of Johann Joachim Kaendler. In 1929, when the town of Meissen celebrated its thousandth anniversary, Paul Börner created a modern carillon for the Frauenkirche.

189 Fruit dish from the splendid Reineke Fuchs (Reynard the Fox) Service by Max Esser, 1922. The idea of beautifying pieces of dinner services with sculptured ornament, so wonderfully carried out by Johann Joachim Kaendler in his Swan Service, was revived and given new emphasis by Esser at the end of the *Jugendstil* period.

190 This small figure of a wild boar, interpreted convincingly by Max Esser in spite of his adherence to a style, is part of the Reineke Fuchs Service (see No. 189).

191 The *Jugendstil* movement gave a decisive impulse to art, particularly to the applied arts, as is proved by these small porcelain figures from a chess game by Max Esser, which was produced in 1923 and entitled Meeresfauna (Sea Fauna).

192 Porcelain wall decorations (an aspect of porcelain design which saw such original creations in the eighteenth century) were made by Esser and the sculptor Paul Walther in the form of animal heads and similar items. This delightful small rhesus monkey is the work of Paul Walther and dates from 1927.

193 Animal sculpture enjoyed a considerable revival at Meissen shortly before the First World War. Among the many specialists in this field, the sculptor Paul Walther was particularly prolific. This piece, the Heulender Schakal (Howling Jackal), was made in 1914. Mold number E 205.

194 An elaborate animal group modeled in 1908 by the sculptor Otto Pilz. Mold number I 155.

195 Erich Hösel, the manufactory's artistic director, made various journeys to the Near East and America, sparking off the new versions of the exotic figures so popular in the eighteenth century. Height 21 cm. Mold number V 121.

196 Child figures were interpreted realistically during the *Jugendstil* period as is shown by this small figure of a child at play, modeled by Konrad Hentschel in 1905. Height 17 cm. Mold number W 120.

197 The small figures made in Meissen during the short *Jugendstil* period include a number of excellent works complete in themselves and suited to their medium. One such work is the Couple Dancing the Tango by the sculptor König, 1912. Mold number D 213.

189

190

191

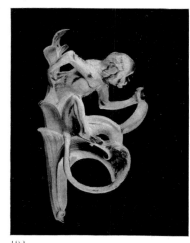

192

195

194

195

196

197

198

199

200

201

198 The sculptor Tuaillon, who became known for his equestrian statues, made this, entitled Herkules, den erymanthischen Eber bändigend (Hercules Capturing the Boar of Erymanthus) in 1923. Height 39 cm. Mold number J 203.

199 An echo of expressive Baroque movement is found in the figure sculptures by Paul Börner. The bagpipe player (mold number A 1103) and the tambourine player (mold number A 1105) shown here belong to the cycle known as the Sizilianische Hirtenkapelle (Sicilian Shepherd Band) made in 1925.

200 Modern Amoretten (Amor und Psyche) designed by Paul Börner in 1927 translate traditional motifs into the language of our times.

201 The sculptor Alexander Struck designed a number of groups on folklore themes. Among them is this peasant couple at the harvest dance, made in 1954. Mold number R 276.

202 In this Madonna group the beauty of the Meissen material is complemented by the nobility of line attained with the fall of the drapery. It is clear that this group had to remain undecorated if it was to retain its artistic effectiveness. Made by Ludwig Nick in 1928.

203 In 1929 Paul Scheurich made a dwarflike cavalier (height 18.5 cm., mold number A 1218) and in 1931 a picturesque crinoline lady (height 20 cm., mold number A 1232) after the well-known Callot prints.

204 The Zwergen-Kabinett (Cabinet of Dwarfs) after Callot was the inspiration for Paul Scheurich's grotesque dance figures.

205 Plaque dedicated to admirers of the manufactory designed in 1931 by Paul Scheurich showing a witty representation of two jesters fencing.

206 The engraving shown here is from Jacques Callot's work *Capricci di varie figure* which appeared in 1617 in Nancy and was often used as a source of ideas in the applied arts. Scheurich took this engraving and based his relief plaque on it.

207 Another approach to the design of commemorative plaques is shown in this one by Richard Langer dating from 1928.

208 Recently single decorative wall plaques have regained favor. The one shown here, designed by Heinz Werner in 1958, combines etching on plaster of Paris with an interesting colored decoration on a gold ground.

209 Since the eighteenth century, witty interpretations of everyday situations in a material ideal for this purpose have become traditional. This statuette of a young girl making up her face, made in 1966 by Peter Strang, carries on this tradition in the idiom of our times.

210 One of the delightful group of long-legged birds by the sculptor Elfriede Reichel-Drechsler demonstrates what can be achieved in the way of realistic effect by means of advanced firing techniques. Height 28.5 cm. Mold number H 216.

211 The yellow ground so popular in the eighteenth century was used in a coffee service designed by Ludwig Zepner in 1964. Heinz Werner filled the reserves with illustrations from the Münchhausen stories.

202

203

204

205

206

207

208

209

210

211

212

213

214

215

216

212 This modern functionally designed coffee service by Ludwig Zepner is decorated with traditional (Braunsdorf) underglaze painting by Heinz Werner and purplish-red flowers in fired overglaze painting achieving a powerful rich effect.

213 A modern vase designed by Ludwig Zepner in 1966, with its contrasting effect obtained by means of the crystal-like decoration on the walls and the calm lines of the neck and mouth.

214 This delicate uncluttered mocha service was designed by Horst Michel in 1959. Its quiet surfaces offer scope for either modern or traditional decoration.

215 The fluid lines of this vessel designed by Grosser make it a fitting recipient for Heinz Werner's flower painting.

216 A Thousand and One Nights. Dinner service of modern design by Zepner, Werner and Strang, made in 1966–1967. It is oriental in inspiration, with its cool, calm outline and restrained relief decoration showing a different motif on each piece.

1 The Augustus Rex monogram was used at a very early date as a sign of the king's ownership, probably before the adoption of the sword mark. From February 1, 1733, to October 5, 1733, the son of Augustus the Strong had the FA (Frederick Augustus) mark applied to his porcelain since he had not yet been crowned king of Poland. On April 8, 1734, the Court Chancellory gave orders for the AR monogram: "*auf keinerley Arth und Weise, als vor die allerhöchste königl. Mayestät nachzumachen*" (under no circumstances to be reproduced except with the consent of His Majesty).

2 The AR mark for porcelain to be delivered to the king appears in many variations. The one illustrated is on a cup decorated with Höroldt chinoiseries dating from 1725.

3 The so-called caduceus, which seldom appears as a Meissen mark, is sometimes found in connection with the AR monogram. It was definitely not intended—as is often stated—for deliveries to south European countries. It is also improbable that it was confused with the Staff of Mercury at the time, but is rather to be regarded as an allusion to the fact that the reinvention of porcelain was the work of a pharmacist.

4 K.P.M. (Königliche Porzellan Manufactur), K.P.F. (Königliche Porzellan Fabrique) and M.P.F. (Meissner Porzellan Fabrique): these marks often appear on their own, but also often with the electoral swords underneath, in the latter case not before the middle of the year 1722. On April 7, 1723, there was an announcement in the *Leipziger Postzeitung* to the effect that sugar bowls and teapots were being marked in this fashion. The same annoucement was made in Prague on August 7, 1723.

5 K.P.M. (Königliche Porzellan Manufactur) with the electoral swords, part of the electoral arms, as seen on a teapot dating from 1725. The swords of the early period are, without exception, straight swords with pommels but with greatly differing hilts.

6 The swords with pommels and S-shaped hilts, rather large and in a double circle (after the Far Eastern manner) occur in the period 1725 to 1732.

7 A similar form of the pommeled swords which again appear within a double circle. The unsureness of the line perhaps indicates that the mark was made by the youngest and most inexperienced apprentices.

8 From 1756 onward, a dot was placed between the swords' hilts, at first only occasionally, then regularly. The blades are now given for a while a saber-like curve. This mark was used until the beginning of Marcolini's directorship (1774).

9 The "dot" swords, primitively executed in this example, from a vessel with underglaze painting. The letter O could refer to the painting apprentice Otto.

10 The apprentices' efforts in underglaze painting were checked by means of their adding the first letter of their surname to the sword mark.

11 The mark of a painter in blue underglaze in the "dot" period, referring to an apprentice whose surname began with an L.

12 The star below the swords indicates the period of Camillo Marcolini's office (1774–1814).

13 The occurrence of various dots under the Marcolini star represents personal marks made by craftsmen for the purpose of quality control.

14 From the Marcolini period biscuit porcelain was marked either additionally or, in most cases, exclusively with impressed swords sometimes surrounded by a triangle.

15 An indication of the place for which items were commissioned is provided by the overglaze and fired letters K.H.C. (Königliche Hof Conditorey = Royal Court Pantry) and C.H.C.

(Churfürstliche Hof Conditorey = Electoral Court Pantry).

16 A mark for the Polish residence was also used: K.C.P.C. (Königliche Churfürstliche Polnische Conditorey = Royal Electoral Polish Pantry).

17 Some time after 1814, a I was placed under the swords, now that the Marcolini star was not employed.

18 After 1820 the I below the swords was followed for an uncertain number of years by a II. In the nineteenth century, incidentally, until about 1860, the pommeled swords were used again.

19 Throughout the nineteenth century and in the first quarter of the twentieth, the swords had a saber-like curve and crossed high up on the blade. Up to the 1860s the pommels are often emphasized.

20 During the directorship of Max Adolf Pfeiffer, between the years 1924 and 1933, a dot was placed between the tips of the elegant pommel-less swords.

21 In 1947 a curved line, tips pointing upward, was placed beneath the swords.

22 The present-day mark is not applied particularly unobtrusively, but elegantly. The swords cross roughly in the middle of the blade. The hilt of one sword runs almost parallel to the blade of the other.

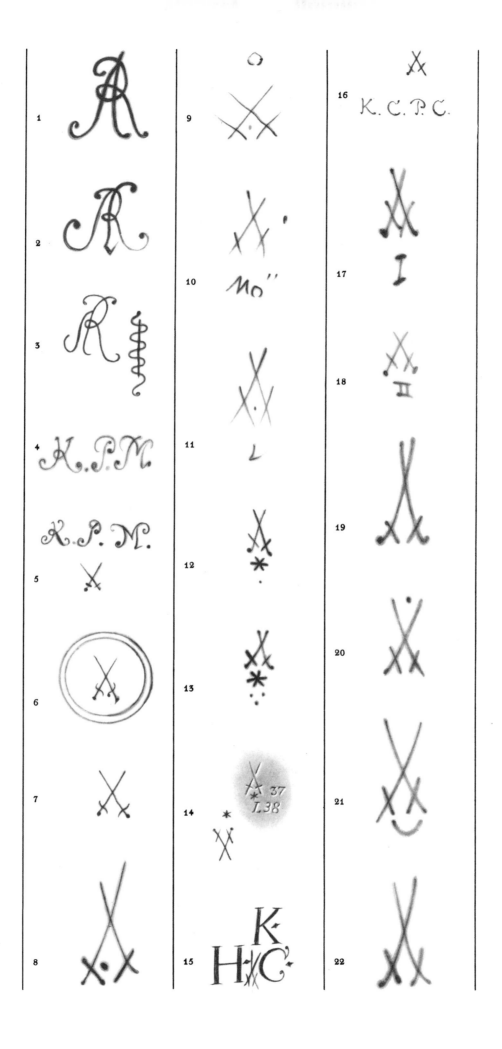

502

Amphora (Greek) Ancient vessel for storage of wine or oil, with oval body and two handles connecting the mouth with the shoulders; the body is widest in the upper third.

Arcanum (Arabic) A closely guarded secret. In the eighteenth century, workmen with a knowledge of the process of porcelain making and pottery were called arcanists.

Biscuit A porcelain body that has been fired once (i.e. an article without the glaze).

Bossierer (German) A embosser.

Böttger porcelain A hard-paste porcelain consisting of kaolin, alabaster, or lime and quartz.

Böttger stoneware A high-temperature-fired, red, hard stoneware invented by Johann Friedrich Böttger (1682–1719). Its body consists of red bolar earth and clay.

Camaieu (French) A method of painting in different tones of the same color.

Celadon Chinese porcelain with characteristic gray-green glaze. The first specimen reached Europe in the fifteenth century or perhaps even earlier.

China clay see Kaolin.

China stone A fusible stone of granitic origin but in a less advanced stage of decomposition than kaolin (which see). In the production of hard-paste porcelain it fuses with the kaolin at a temperature between 1300 °C and 1400 °C. Fused with lime or other fluxes it is also the base of the glaze. Also known under its Chinese name *Petuntse*.

Crater (Greek) Ancient vase of varying shape with wide mouth and handle.

Crazing Very fine cracking of the glaze.

Crystalline glaze A glaze containing crystals of various kinds which were formed while the glaze cooled. Other glazes are amorphous.

Deferrization De-ironing, the elimination of all ferrugineous matter from the raw material used in compounding the paste.

Deutsche Blumen Style of decoration on porcelain taken from botanical illustrations of the eighteenth century.

"Dot period" (1764–74) Known in German as the *Punktzeit (Punkt =* dot, *Zeit =* time) and in French as *Saxe au point*. It takes its name from the dot placed between the pommels of the sword mark at this time, and is in no way con-

nected with the rather unimportant Carl Christoph Punkt, as is often erroneously recorded in literature.

Embosser The worker in a porcelain factory who assembles the individual parts of a porcelain figure or ornaments the figure.

Enamel color A (usually) lead-based pigment with a melting temperature lower than that of the glaze. It is usually applied to the surface of the article by means of an oily medium.

Faience Tin-glazed earthenware.

Feldspar A mineral composed of alumina, silica and sodium or potassium. A very important flux. In the production of Meissen porcelain it was used instead of lime after 1721. Mined near Siebenlehn in Saxony, it was also known there as Flemming's stone.

Filter press A device for the removal of surplus water from the paste.

Flux A substance which lowers the vitrification temperature of the porcelain body, glaze, or enamel colors. In its early years the Meissen factory used the so-called Nordhausen Alabaster, a substance of high lime content, which was later substitued by feldspar (which see).

Frit A flux consisting of a half-fused siliceous material, not soluble in water; used in the preparation of glaze and soft-paste porcelain *(frit-porcelain)*.

Garbrand (German) Also known as *Glattbrand* or *Gutbrand* (it means full-firing or smooth-firing). The final firing of the porcelain body at temperatures up to 1450 °C after the glaze has been applied by dipping. In the course of this firing the article shrinks to 6/7 of its original size.

Gilding' The process of fixing gold (or a substitute) on the surface of an article. Unfired gilding used gold leaf on a lacquer base but this was impermanent. Honey-gilding was practiced by using ground gold leaf or precipitated gold powder in honey, and then firing it. This process was replaced in the late eighteenth century by mercury-gilding, an amalgam of gold and mercury being painted on and the latter then driven off by heating. In the nineteenth century these methods were replaced by the use of the cheaper "liquid gold," giving a liquid film. (Text kindly supplied by R. J. Charleston.)

Grand feu colors Also known as *Scharffeurmalereifarben*; *grand feu* (French: great fire). All sorts of pigments suited to withstand the firing temperature of the glaze. In hard-paste porcelain underglaze, copper-red and cobalt-blue are usually used.

Hard-paste porcelain see China stone.

Indianische Blumen Also known as *fleurs des*

Indes (French: Indian flowers). Flower decoration of Far Eastern character, usually based on Kakiemon (which see).

Kakiemon Name of a Japanese porcelain factory. Its products, especially those of the second period (1680–1770), were much liked in Europe because of their brilliant enamel decoration. In 1730, Augustus the Strong ordered the Meissen manufactory to imitate these decorations.

Kaolin (Chinese) A refractory white clay formed by the decomposition of granitic rock.

Lambrequin (French) Formal ornament in the shape of a pendant.

Lithophanies Transparencies made of porcelain, molded in intaglio. In transmitted light they appear as pictures in grisaille. First produced in Meissen in 1828.

Mark see Taler.

Mufflekiln Kiln for low-temperature firing (usually between 700° and 900 °C) of vitreous enamel colors into the glaze. The articles are fired inside an interior chamber (the muffle) thus not coming into contact with the fire. For the earliest mufflekilns, wood was used as fuel, later charcoal took its place until the electrically fired kiln came to the fore.

On-glaze decoration see Over-glaze decoration.

Over-glaze decoration Painted decoration on already glazed and fired porcelain. The colors, which are usually composed of various metal oxides, are mixed with a flux and applied to the glaze by means of an oily medium. It is then fired into the glaze by firing at *c.* 800 °C in a so-called enamel kiln. Also known as on-glaze decoration.

Petuntse (Chinese) see China stone.

Porcelain see Hard-paste porcelain; Böttger porcelain; Kaolin; China stone; China clay.

Quartz Crystallized silica (SiO_2). See also Böttger porcelain.

Reichsmark see Taler.

Reichstaler see Taler.

Sagger Box made of fire clay *(chamotte)* in which the ware is fired in order to keep it out of contact of both the fire and the fumes.

Schwarzlot (German) A method of decoration mostly applied to glass: copper oxide, mixed with black enamel pigment, is painted on to the surface of the article and the design then scratched out.

Smear glaze A glaze applied to the sagger in which the ware is fired. In the course of the firing process it is transmitted to the article by volatilization.

Taler Also known as Reichstaler; also spelled Thaler. The currency of the German *Länder*. Its English equivalent around 1750 was *c.* three shillings and sixpence. After 1750, the South German *Länder*, Austria, and Poland used the so-called Konventions-Taler as opposed to the Prussian Taler. After the founding of the Second German Empire the Mark was established by law (Dec. 4, 1871); 1 Taler was the equivalent of 3 Marks. After the inflation (1923) it became known as the Rentenmark, and from 1924 the Reichsmark. The Prussian Taler however remained legal tender until 1907.

Thrower see Throwing.

Throwing Shaping an article (usually a vessel) on the potter's wheel.

Verglühbrand (German) Glost Kiln. A first, light firing of the porcelain body to *c.* 900° C. After this the still absorbent material is glazed.

BIBLIOGRAPHY

The following titles are listed according to publication date, and do not constitute an exhaustive selection.

A   Local history

Iccander (Johann Christian Crell): Das wegen seines Altertums, Ruhms und lustigen angenehmen Gegend in gantz Europa bekannte Königliche Meissen in Sachsen. Dresden 1730

C. Gretschel and Fr. Bülau: Geschichte des Sächsischen Volkes und Staates. Vols. 2 and 3, Leipzig 1863

K. Sturmhoefel: Illustrierte Geschichte der Sächsischen Lande und ihrer Herrscher. Vol 2: 2, 3, Leipzig 1908

P. Reinhardt: Die Sächsischen Unruhen der Jahre 1830 bis 1831 und Sachsens Übergang zum Verfassungsstaat. Halle 1916

H. Gröger: Tausend Jahre Meissen. Meissen 1929

R. Kötschke and H. Kretzschmar: Sächsische Geschichte. Vol. 2, Dresden 1935

P. Stulz and A. Opitz: Volksbewegungen in Kursachsen zur Zeit der Französischen Revolution. Berlin 1956.

R. Forberger: Die Manufaktur in Sachsen vom Ende des 16. bis zum Anfang des 19. Jahrhunderts. Berlin 1958.

H. Schlechte: Die Staatsreform in Kursachsen 1762–1763. Berlin 1958

J. Mrusek: Meissen. Dresden 1959

Autorenkollektiv: Deutsche Geschichte. Vols. 1–3, Berlin 1967 and 1968

B   On porcelain in general

Johann Georg Theodor Graesse: Beschreibender Catalog der K. Porzellan- und Gefäß-Sammlung zu Dresden. Dresden 1873

F. Jaennecke: Grundriss der Keramik. Stuttgart 1879

Georg Lehnert: Das Porzellan. Bielefeld and Leipzig 1902

R. L. Hobson: Porcelain. London 1906

Adolf Brüning: Porzellan. In: Handbücher der Kgl. Museen zu Berlin, Berlin 1907

Ch. de Grollier: Manuel de l'Amateur de Porcelaines. Paris 1914

Otto von Falke: Deutsche Porzellanfiguren. Berlin 1919

Max Sauerlandt: Deutsche Porzellanfiguren des 18. Jahrhunderts. Cologne 1923

Otto Pelka: Keramik der Neuzeit. Leipzig 1924

Gustav E. Pazaurek: Deutsche Fayence- und Porzellan-Hausmaler. Leipzig 1925

Robert Schmidt: Das Porzellan als Kunstwerk und Kulturspiegel. Munich 1925

Friedrich H. Hofmann: Das Porzellan der europäischen Manufakturen im 18. Jahrhundert. Eine Kunst- und Kulturgeschichte. Berlin 1932

William B. Honey: German Porcelain. London 1947

Arno Schönberger: Deutsches Porzellan. Munich 1949

William B. Honey: European Ceramic Art from the end of the Middle Ages to about 1815. A. Dictionary . . . London 1952

George W. Ware: Deutsches und österreichisches Porzellan. Frankfurt 1952

Graesse und Jaennecke: Führer für Sammler von Porzellan. Brunswick 1953

Ludwig Dankert: Handbuch des europäischen Porzellans. Munich 1954

Ludwig Schnorr von Carolsfeld: Porzellan der europäischen Fabriken des 18. Jahrhunderts. Fünfte, von E. Köllmann neu bearbeitete Auflage, Brunswick 1956

Annelore Leistikow-Duchardt: Die Entwicklung eines neuen Stils im Porzellan. Heidelberg 1957 (Dissertation)

George Savage: 18th-Century German Porcelain. London 1958

Siegfried Ducret: Deutsches Porzellan und deutsche Fayencen. Baden-Baden 1962

Ruth Berges: From Gold to Porcelain. New York and London 1963

Otto Walcha: Porzellan. Leipzig and Heidelberg 1963

Rollo Charles: Continental Porcelain of the eighteenth Century. London 1964

R. Weiss: Das Ullstein-Porzellanbuch. Berlin 1964

C   Meissen porcelain: general

M. Chr. Beatus Kenzelmann: Historische Nachrichten über die Königliche Porzellan-Manufaktur zu Meissen und deren Stifter Joh. Friedr. Frh. von Böttger, Meissen 1810. Abdruck in den Mitteilungsblättern der Keramikfreunde der Schweiz, Nr. 29, Zürich 1954

Victor Böhmert: Urkundliche Geschichte und Statistik der Meissner Porzellanmanufaktur von 1710–1880 mit besonderer Rücksicht auf die Betriebs-, Lohn- und Kassenverhältnisse. In: Zeitschrift des Kgl. sächs. statist. Bureaus, Vol. 26, Dresden 1880

Karl Berling: Das Meissner Porzellan und seine Geschichte. Leipzig 1900

Willy Doenges: Meissner Porzellan. Berlin 1907 and Dresden 1921

Egon Mew: Dresden China. New York 1909

Karl Berling: Festschrift zur 200 jährigen Jubelfeier der ältesten europäischen Porzellanmanufaktur Meissen 1910. Leipzig 1911

Ernst Lange: Die Königl. Porzellan-Manufaktur und deren "Verwandte". Geschichtlicher Überblick mit Berücksichtigung der örtlichen Beziehungen. Meissen 1911

Otto Pelka: Alt-Meissen. Leipzig 1923

Ernst Zimmermann: Meissner Porzellan. Leipzig 1926

Fritz Fichtner: Meissner Porzellan. Leipzig 1936

Siegfried Ducret: Meissner Porzellan. Berne 1952

William B. Honey: Dresden China. London 1954

250 Jahre Staatliche Porzellan-Manufaktur Meissen. Meissen 1960

Erich Köllmann: Meissner Porzellan. Brunswick 1965

D   Meissen porcelain: special areas

Die denkwürdigste Lebensbeschreibung des weltberühmten Herrn Ehrenfried Walther von Tschirnhaus ... ingleichen Nachrichten von seinen Schriften und seltenen Erfindungen. In: Das Sächsische Curiositäten-Cabinet, Drittes Repositorium, Dresden 1732

Nachricht von Herrn Johann Joachim Kändlers Leben und Arbeiten. In: Neue Bibliothek der schönen Wissenschaften und der freyen Künste, Vol. XVIII: 2, Leipzig 1776

Carl August Engelhardt: Johann Friedrich Böttger, Erfinder des Sächsischen Porzellans. Biographie aus authentischen Quellen. Hrsg. von August Moritz Engelhardt. Leipzig 1837

Arthur Pabst: Das gräflich Brühlsche Schwanenservice. In: Kunstgewerbeblatt, Vol. 1, Leipzig 1885

Woldemar von Seidlitz: Die Meissner Porzellanmanufaktur unter Böttger. In: Neues Archiv für sächsische Geschichte und Altertumskunde, Vol. 9, Dresden 1888

Woldemar von Seidlitz: Die frühesten Nachahmungen des Meissner Porzellans. Die Fabriken in Plaue, Wien und Venedig. In: Neues Archiv für sächsische Geschichte und Altertumskunde, Vol. 10, Dresden 1889

W. Loose: Lebensläufe Meissner Künstler. In: Mitteilungen des Vereins für Geschichte der Stadt Meissen, Vol. 2, Meissen 1891, page 200 ff.

F. Wolf: Das Meissner Ultramarin. In: Mitteilungen des Vereins für Geschichte der Stadt Meissen, Vol. 2, Meissen 1891, page 560 ff.

Jean Louis Sponsel: Kabinettstücke der Meissner Porzellanmanufaktur von Johann Joachim Kaendler. Leipzig 1900

Ernst Zimmermann: Die Erfindung und Frühzeit des Meissner Porzellans. Ein Beitrag zur Geschichte der deutschen Keramik. Berlin 1908

Ernst Zimmermann: Johann Friedrich Böttger, der Erfinder des Meissner Porzellans, nach der Schilderung eines Zeitgenossen (Steinbrück 1717). In: Neues Archiv für sächsische Geschichte und Altertumskunde, Vol. 33, Dresden 1912

Karl Berling und A. v. Kaull: Die Meissner Porzellangruppen der Kaiserin Katharina II. in Oranienbaum. Dresden 1914

Max Adolf Pfeiffer: Steinbrücks Geschichtskalender von 1712. In: Staatliche Porzellan-Manufaktur Meissen. Bericht über das Jahr 1919. Leipzig 1920

Otto Horn: Die Münzen und Medaillen aus der Staatlichen Porzellan-Manufaktur zu Meissen. Leipzig 1923

Gustav E. Pazaurek: Meissner Porzellanmalerei des 18. Jahrhunderts. Stuttgart 1929

Ernst Zimmermann: Kirchner, der Vorläufer Kändlers an der Meissner Manufaktur. Berlin 1929

Johannes Michael: Die kaufmännische Leitung der Porzellan-Manufaktur Meissen zur Zeit Augusts des Starken. Berlin 1934

Helmuth Gröger: Die Arbeits- und Sozialverhältnisse der Staatlichen Porzellan-Manufaktur im 18. Jahrhundert. In: Forschungen aus mitteldeutschen Archiven. Zum 60. Geburtstag von Hellmut Kretzschmar. Berlin 1953

Arno Schönberger: Meissner Porzellan mit Höroldt-Malerei. Darmstadt 1953

Ingelore Handt: Johann Joachim Kaendler. Dresden 1954 (Das Kleine Kunstheft, Nr. 7)

Helmuth Gröger: Johann Joachim Kaendler. Der Meister des Porzellans. Dresden and Hanau 1956

Ingelore Handt — Hilde Rakebrand: Meissner Porzellan des 18. Jahrhunderts, 1710–1750. Dresden 1956

Hilde Rakebrand: Meissner Tafelgeschirr des 18. Jahrhunderts. Darmstadt 1958

Carl Albiker: Die Meissener Porzellantiere im 18. Jahrhundert. 2nd edition, Berlin 1959

R. Forberger: Tschirnhaus und das Sächsische Manufakturwesen. In: E. W. von Tschirnhaus und die Frühaufklärung in Mittel- und Osteuropa, herausgegeben von E. Winter, Berlin 1960

Martin Mields: Aus der Jugendzeit des europäischen Porzellans. In: Sprechsaal für Keramik, Glas, Email, Vol. 93, Coburg 1960

Otto Walcha: Quellen zur Manufakturgeschichte Meissens. In: Keramikfreunde der Schweiz. Neujahrsgabe 1960. Zürich 1960

250 Jahre Meissner Porzellan (Sammlung Schneider, Düsseldorf). In: Keramikfreunde der Schweiz, Nr. 50 (Jubiläumsheft), Zürich 1960

Otto Walcha: Rivalen. Die Lebenschronik des Bergknappen und Arkanisten Samuel Stötzel. Berlin 1963

Günter Reinheckel: Plastische Dekorationsformen

im Meissner Porzellan des 18. Jahrhunderts. Halle 1965 (Dissertation)

Martin Mields und Rudi Lauschke: Praxis der Porzellanmalerei, Leipzig and Munich 1965

I. Menzhausen: Die künstlerische Gestaltung des Böttgersteinzeugs. In: Böttgersteinzeug, Böttgerporzellan aus der Dresdner Porzellansammlung, hrsg. Staatliche Kunstsammlungen Dresden, Dresden 1969

M. Mields: Die Erfindung des europäischen Porzellans, Dresden 1969

Siegfried Ducret: Meissner Porzellan bemalt in Augsburg 1718–1750. Brunswick 1972 (2 Vol.)

B. Böhm: Heute vor 27 Jahren. In: Manufakturecho, Betriebszeitung des VEB Staatl. Porzellan-Manufaktur Meissen, 15th year, 1972 Vols. 10 and 11

E   Articles in professional journals

Otto Bank: Über die Kgl. Sächs. Porzellanmanufaktur in Meissen. Ein ästhetischer Beitrag zu den Kunstgesetzen der Keramik. In: Dresdner Journal, Feuilleton, Dresden 1885

C. v. d. Busch: Die Radierungen des Kanonikus Busch auf Alt-Meissener Porzellan. In: Monatsberichte über Kunstwissenschaft und Kunsthandel, 3rd year, Munich 1903

Adolf Brüning: Schau-Essen und Porzellanplastik. In: Kunst und Kunsthandwerk, Vol. 7, Vienna 1904

Ernst Zimmermann: Die Inkunabeln des Meissner Porzellans. In: Jahrbuch der Kgl. Preußischen Kunstsammlungen, Vol. 25, Berlin 1904

Julius Ludwig Ferdinand Heintze: Zur Geschichte der Erfindung des Porzellans. In: Zeitschrift für angewandte Chemie, Vol. 20, Berlin 1907

Ernst Zimmermann: Wer war der Erfinder des Meissner Porzellans? In: Neues Archiv für sächsische Geschichte und Altertumskunde, Vol. 28, Dresden 1907

Richard Graul: Gellertdenkmäler in Meissner Porzellannachbildungen. In: Leipziger Kalender. Illustriertes Jahrbuch und Chronik, Vol. 6, Leipzig 1909

Ernst Zimmermann: Frühe Watteauszenen auf Meissner Porzellan. In: Der Cicerone. Vol. 1, Leipzig 1909

Ernst Zimmermann: Von Friedrich dem Grossen neu in Auftrag gegebene Meissner Porzellane. In: Der Cicerone Vol. 2, Leipzig 1910

Karl Berling: Eine bisher unbekannte Meissner Kaendler-Gruppe. In: Kunst und Kunsthandwerk, Vol. 13, Vienna 1910

Ernst Zimmermann: Die Anfänge der Blaumalerei im Meissener Porzellan. In: Mitteilungen aus den sächsischen Kunstsammlungen, Vol. 2, Leipzig 1911

Ernst Zimmermann: Die Chinoiserien Herolds. In: Mitteilungen aus den sächsischen Kunstsammlungen, Vol. 3, Dresden-Berlin 1912

Karl Berling: Altarschmuck aus Meissner Porzellan, ein Geschenk an die verwitwete Kaiserin Amalie. In: Kunst und Kunsthandwerk, Vol. 16, Vienna 1913

Ernst Zimmermann: Die Statuetten König Augusts III. in Meissner Porzellan. In: Mitteilungen aus den sächsischen Kunstsammlungen, Vol. 4, Dresden 1913

Ernst Zimmermann: Der Tafelaufsatz aus dem Service des Generalfeldmarschalls Grafen von Münnich. In: Mitteilungen aus den sächsischen Kunstsammlungen, Vol. 5, Dresden 1914

Georg Wilhelm Schulz: Neues über die Vorbilder der Chinesereien des Meissner Porzellans. In: Mitteilungen des Städtischen Kunstgewerbemuseums zu Leipzig, Nr. 11/12, Leipzig 1922

Ludwig Schnorr von Carolsfeld: Kupferstichvorbilder für Meissener Groteskgefässe. In: Jahrbuch für Kunstsammler, Vol. 3, Frankfurt 1923

Max Adolf Pfeiffer: Ein Beitrag zur Quellengeschichte des Meissner Porzellans. In: Werden und Wirken, Leipzig 1924

Georg Wilhelm Schulz: Augsburger Chinesereien und ihre Verwendung in der Keramik. In: Das Schwäbische Museum, 26th year, Augsburg 1926

Max Adolf Pfeiffer: Ein Beitrag zur Geschichte der Erfindung des europäischen Porzellans. In: Keramische Rundschau, Vol. 35, Oranienburg-Bernau 1927

William Funk: Böttgers Erfindung und ihre Bedeutung für die Stadt Meissen. In: Keramos, Vol. 8:11, Bamberg 1929

The Earl of Ilchester: A notable service of Meissen porcelain. In: The Burlington Magazine, Vol. 55, London 1929

Otto von Falke: Ein Meissener Porzellanpokal der Königin Sophie Dorothee von Preussen. In: Pantheon, Vol. 8, 1931

William B. Honey: A Porcelain Tankard painted by C. W. F. Dietrich. In: The Burlington Magazine, Vol. 59, London 1931

Otto von Falke: Meissener Barockvasen: In: Pantheon, Vol. 9, Munich 1932

Fritz Fichtner: Die Alt-Meissner Reifrockgruppen. In: Dresdner Anzeiger, Nr. 290, Dresden 1932

Fritz Fichtner: Phantastische Pläne Augusts des Starken und ihr Schicksal. In: Sprechsaal, 69th year, Coburg 1936

William B. Honey: Zwei deutsche Porzellanprobleme. I. Augsburger Goldchinesen und Watteaubilder auf frühem Meissner Porzellan. In: Pantheon, Vol. 22, Munich 1938

Fritz Fichtner: Meissner Porzellan für Polen und Russland. In: Berichte der Deutschen Keramischen Gesellschaft, Vol. 21, Berlin 1940

Siegfried Ducret: Unbekanntes Porzellan (Huldigungsgruppe auf August III.). In: Pantheon, Vol. 32, Munich 1944

Siegfried Ducret: Die Chinoiserievorbilder Joh. Gregor Höroldts. In: Pro Arte, Nr. 35, Geneva 1945

Siegfried Ducret: Architectures en porcelaine de Saxe. In: Pro Arte, Nr. 56, Geneva 1946

Siegfried Ducret: Johann Martin Heinrici, Miniaturist in Meissen (1711–1786). In: Faenza. Bolletino del Museo Internazionale delle Ceramiche in Faenza, Vol. 37, Faenza 1951

Siegfried Ducret: Deutsche Holzschnittblumen von Johann Gottlieb Klinger. In: Weltkunst, Vol. 21, Nr. 8, Munich 1951

Siegfried Ducret: Chinoiserien in Gold. In Faenza. Bolletino del Museo Internazionale delle Ceramiche in Faenza, Vol. 39, Faenza 1953

Martin Mields: Johann Friedrich Böttger, der Erfinder des europäischen Hartporzellans. In: Glas-Email-Keramo-Technik, June 1957

Hans Schulze-Manitius: Johann Friedrich Böttger, der Schleizer Scharlatan und Gründer der deutschen Porzellanindustrie. In: Silikat-Technik, Vol. 8, Berlin 1957

Erich Köllmann: Bergbau und Porzellan. In: Der Bergbau in der Kunst, Essen 1958

Fritz Fichtner: Das Porzellangeheimnis. 200 Jahre vergeblichen Bemühen. In: Sprechsaal für Keramik, Vol. 92, Coburg 1959

Otto Walcha: Holländische Mitarbeiter der Meissner Manufaktur während der Böttgerzeit. In: Vrienden van de nederlandse ceramiek, medelingenblad, Amsterdam 1959

Hans Syz: Distinctive Features of Löwenfinck's paintings. In: Antiques, New York, June 1960

A. L. Den Blaauwen: Meissen en het Journal van Lazare Duvaux. In: Bulletin van het Rijksmuseum, Vol. 9, Amsterdam 1961

Otto Walcha: Tradition und Fortschritt in der Meissner Gefässgestaltung. In: Jahrbuch des Instituts für Angewandte Kunst, Berlin 1961

Carl Christian Dautermann: Colossal for the Medium: Meissen porcelain Sculptures. In: The Metropolitan Museum of Art Bulletin, New York 1963

Martin Mields: Die Entwicklung der Aufglasurpalette des europäischen Hartporzellans bis 1731 mit besonderer Berücksichtigung der Arbeiten von Johann Gregorius Höroldt. In: Keramische Zeitschrift, Vol. 15, Freiburg 1963

Siegfried Ducret: Kändlers Vorbild zum Schwanenservice. In: Weltkunst, Vol. 33, Munich 1963

Günter Reinheckel: Friedrich Elias Meyer, ein Porzellanplastiker des 18. Jahrhunderts. In: Silikattechnik, Vol. 14, Berlin 1963

Ingelore Menzhausen: Eine Meissner Porzellangruppe von 1775: "Die glücklichen Eltern". In: Dresdner Kunstblätter, Part 7, Dresden 1963

Siegfried Ducret: Tschirnhaus oder Böttger? In Weltkunst, Vol. 34, Munich 1964

J. Fontein — A. L. Den Blaauwen: "Picturae Sinicae ac Surratenae" van Petrus Schenk sc. In Bulletin van het Rijksmuseum, Vol. 12, Amsterdam 1964

Martin Mields: Gedanken zur Porzellanerfindung in Europa. In: Sprechsaal für Keramik — Glas—Email — Silikate, 98th year, Coburg 1965

Numerous articles on individual works, as well as on the artists and various disputed questions pertaining to Meissen porcelain, may be found in the publications of the Keramikfreunde der Schweiz (KFS) (Swiss Friends of Ceramics) and in the magazine Keramos (KE), published in Düsseldorf. The most significant contributions are as follows:

Hanns E. Backer: Ein Meissner Wappenservice von Bonaventura Gottlieb Häuer (KFS 13–14/49). Eigenhändige Arbeiten von J. G. Hörold (KFS 39/57). Komödienfiguren in der Sammlung Dr. Ernst Schneider (KFS 50/60)

A. L. Den Blaauwen: Keramik mit Chinoiserien nach Stichen von Petrus Schenk jun. (KE 31/66)

Siegfried Ducret: Joseph Hackl, Hausmaler in der Seuterschen Werkstatt in Augsburg (KFS 11/48). Zum 250. Geburtstag Johann Joachim Kaendler (KFS 36/56). Die Arbeitsmethoden Johann Gregor Hörolds (KFS 39/57). Frühmeissner Dekors (KFS 50/60). Die Wahrheit um Adam Friedrich von Löwenfinck (KE 15/62). Die Vorbilder zu einigen Chinoiserien von Peter Schenk (KE 31/66)

Yvonne Hackenbroch: Meissen Porcelain Sculpture from Kirchner to Kaendler (KFS 50/60)

Rudolf Just: Unbemalte Augustus-Rex-Vasen (KFS 48/59). Meissner Prunkvasen der Frühzeit (KFS 50/60)

Adalbert Klein: Über die Erfindung des Hartporzellans (KFS 50/60)

Ernst Kramer: Ein Porträt Johann Friedrich Böttgers (KE 30/65)

Ingelore Menzhausen-Handt: Christian Friedrich Herold (KFS 50/60). Das Glockenspiel aus Porzellan (KE 22/63). Böttgersteinzeug mit Emailmalerei und Edelsteinen (KE 24/64). Eine neue kryptische Signatur von Höroldt (KFS 67/95)

Günter Reinheckel: Nachrichten über eingeschickte Vorbilder und Modelle aus den Akten

F   Catalogues
(With two exceptions, the catalogues of the Meissen manufactory are not included)

Christian Scherer: Die Porzellansammlung des Schlosses Wilhelmsthal bei Kassel. In: Zeitschrift des Vereins für hessische Geschichte und Landeskunde, N. F. Vol. 17, Kassel 1892

Friedrich Schlie: Altmeissen in Schwerin. Erste und zweite Ausstellung altsächsischer Porzellane im Grossherzoglichen Museum. Schwerin 1893

Justus Brinckmann: Guidebook: the Hamburgische Museum für Kunst und Gewerbe. Hamburg 1894

Maurice Demaison: La Porcelaine de Saxe. Collection Chappy. In: Les Arts, Vol. 11, Paris 1903

Europäisches Porzellan des 18. Jahrhunderts. Exhibition catalogue of the Berliner Kunstgewerbemuseum. Berlin 1904

Ernst Zimmermann: Das Porzellanzimmer im Königl. Schloss zu Dresden. In: Dresdner Jahrbuch 1905. Vol. 1, Dresden 1905

Adolf Brüning: Handbücher der Kgl. Museen zu Berlin, Kunstgewerbemuseum: Porzellan. Berlin 1907

Friedrich H. Hofmann: Das europäische Porzellan des Bayerischen Nationalmuseums. Catalogue of the Bayer. Nationalmuseum, Vol. 10, Munich 1908

Catalogue of the well-known collection of Old Dresden Porcelain. Auction catalogue. Christie's, London 1908

H. Carl Krüger: Sammlung des Freiherrn Adalbert von Lanna, Prag. Auction catalogue. Lepke Nr. 1605, Part II, Berlin 1911

S. *Troinitzky:* Galerie de porcelaine à l'Ermitage Impérial. In: Starye gody (Old Times), St. Petersburg 1911

Friedrich H. Hofmann: Guidebook. The Porzellan-Kabinett der Königl. Residenz in München 1912

Karl Berling: Meissner Porzellan in der Ermitage zu St. Petersburg. In: Kunst und Kunsthandwerk, Vol. 17, Vienna 1914

Rudolf Sillib: Schloss Favorite. Heidelberg 1914

Robert Schmidt: Sammlung Kommerzienrat Jacques Mühsam, Berlin. Auction catalogue. Glückselig, Vienna 1925

Ludwig Schnorr von Carolsfeld: Sammlung Darmstaedter, Berlin. Europäisches Porzellan des 18. Jahrhunderts. Auction catalogue. Lepke Nr. 1933, Berlin 1925

Ludwig Schnorr von Carolsfeld: Sammlung Margarete und Franz Oppenheimer. Berlin 1927

Ludwig Schnorr von Carolsfeld: Porzellansammlung Gustav von Klemperer. Dresden 1928

Staatliche Porzellan-Manufaktur Meissen, Figuren und Gruppen aus den Jahren 1919–1928 Vols. 1 and 2, Meissen n. d. (1928)

Carl Hernmarck: Porslins-Fabriken i Meissen och dess Produkter i Nationalmuseum, Stockholm 1930

Fritz Fichtner: Von der kurfürstlichen Kunstkammer zur Porzellangalerie Zwinger. In: Berichte der Deutschen Keramischen Gesellschaft. Vol. 21, Berlin 1939

Heribert Seitz: Catalogue of the Collection of European Porcelain of the Hallwyl Museum of Stockholm. Stockholm 1941

C. Louise Avery: Masterpieces of European Porcelain. A special exhibition. The Metropolitan Museum of Art New York 1949

Mr. and Mrs. Kramarsky: Masterpieces of European Porcelain. New York 1949

M. A. Palmer: Meissen Porcelain in the Cecil Higgins Museum, Bedford. In: Apollo, Vol. 51, London 1950

George W. Ware: German and Austrian Porcelain. Katalog Weinberg, Frankfurt 1951

Exhibition catalogue "Porcelaines de Saxe". Musée National de Céramique, Sèvres 1952

Fritz Fichtner: Das Schloss Favorite bei Rastatt. Einer der letzten noch erhaltenen Porzellanbestände des Barock. In: Sprechsaal für Keramik, Glas, Email, 86th year, Coburg 1953

Robert Schmidt: Frühwerke europäischer Porzellanmanufakturen: Sammlung Otto Blohm. Munich 1953

Hans Weinberg: Coronation Exhibition 1953. London 1953

Ingelore Handt: Staatliche Kunstsammlungen Dresden. Porzellansammlung im Zwinger. Dresden 1954

Yvonne Hackenbroch: Meissen and other Continental Porcelain, Faience and Enamel in the Irwin Untermyer Collection. London 1956

Europäisches Rokoko: Kunst und Kultur des 18. Jahrhunderts. Exhibition catalogue, Munich 1958

Roselt: Katalog des Schlossmuseums Arnstadt. 1958

Catalogue of the Hetjensmuseum Düsseldorf. 1958

The Blohm Collection. Auction catalogue. Sotheby, London 1960 (Part I) and 1961 (Part II)

A. L. Den Blaauwen: Saksisch Porselein 1710–1740. Rijksmuseum, Amsterdam 1962

Hilde Rakebrand: Staatliche Kunstsammlungen Dresden. Porzellansammlung im Zwinger. Dresden 1962

Franz Adrian Dreier — Peter Wilhelm Meister: Figürliche Keramik aus zwei Jahrtausenden. Frankfurt am Main (Museum für Kunsthandwerk) 1963

The René Fribourg Collection, European Porcelain. Auction catalogue. Sotheby, London 1963

Catalogue of Fine Continental Porcelain. Auction catalogue. Sotheby, London 1964

European Porcelain Figures of the Eighteenth Century. Museum of Art, Rhode Island School of Design, Providence 1965

Ingelore Menzhausen — Friedrich Reichel: Staatliche Kunstsammlungen Dresden: Porzellansammlung im Zwinger. Guidebook. Dresden 1965

Ernst Schneider: La Collection de Porcelaine du "Schloss Jägerhof" à Düsseldorf: In: La Revue Française, Paris 1965

Hans Christoph von Tavel: Deutsches Porzellan des 18. Jahrhunderts. Exhibition catalogue. Schloss Jegenstorf, Bern 1965

Robert L. Wyss: Porzellan. Meisterwerke aus der Sammlung Kocher. Deutsches Porzellan des 18. Jahrhunderts im Bernischen Historischen Museum. Bern 1965.

The Constance I. and Ralph H. Wark Collection of Meissen Porcelains. Cummer Gallery of Art, Jacksonville, Florida, 1965

Catalogue of Fine Meissen Porcelain. Auction catalogue. Sotheby, London 1966

Rainer Rückert: Meissner Porzellan 1710–1810. Exhibition in the Bayerischen Nationalmuseum München, Munich 1966

Neues Schaffen 1949–1969 des VEB Staatliche Porzellan-Manufaktur Meissen DDR. Meissen 1969

Staatliche Kunstsammlungen Dresden. Böttgersteinzeug, Böttgerporzellan aus der Dresdner Porzellansammlung. Dresden 1969

Stodel, Embden: Meissen and Science, Exhibition, London 1971

514

CREDITS

The black-and-white photographs, except for those listed below, and also those on page 56 and Plate 115 are by Ulrich Frewel, Potsdam. The color photographs are by Klaus G. Beyer, Weimar. Other photographs are printed with permission: Bayerisches Nationalmuseum, Munich: Plates 8, 59–65, 70, 82, 84, 125, 130, 132, 133, 136, 139, 145, 147, 165, 186; Foto-Brüggemann, Leipzig: page 125, Plate 8; Deutsche Fotothek, Dresden: pages 18, 81; Foto-Grahl, Meissen: Plates 249, 250; Carlfred Halbach, Ratingen: Plates 111, 119, 171, 172; Museum des Kunsthandwerks, Leipzig: Plate 39; Schlossmuseum, Gotha: Plate 17; Silvia Seidel, Dresden: Plate 251; The Smithsonian Institution: Plates 56, 148, 170; Victoria and Albert Museum, London: Plates 101, 102; Werk-Foto VEB Staatliche Porzellan-Manufaktur, Meissen: pages 17, 20, 21, 24, 29, 32, 37, 44, 56, 59, 69, 91, 96, 114, 117, 157, 184, 185